EUROPEAN SOCIETY IN UPHEAVAL

EUROPEAN SOCIETY IN UPHEAVAL

SOCIAL HISTORY SINCE 1800

PETER N. STEARNS

The University of Chicago

The Macmillan Company   Collier-Macmillan Limited

London

Fifth Printing, 1969

Library of Congress catalog card number: 67–13147

The Macmillan Company
Collier-Macmillan Canada, Ltd., Toronto, Ontario

Printed in the United States of America

To my wife, Nancy

ACKNOWLEDGMENTS

I wish to acknowledge the assistance I have received in the preparation of this essay. I am grateful to Professor Emile Karofiol for reading the manuscript and for his suggestions. Mrs. Mary Fisch and Miss Carol Widrig provided invaluable secretarial service. My wife assisted in the preparation of the manuscript and gave much-needed advice and encouragement. Most of all, I wish to thank my students at the University of Chicago. Their interest in social history, their suggestions and questions, and their researches have encouraged and shaped the book in innumerable ways.

P. N. S.

INTRODUCTION

The basic fact of European history since 1800 has been an unprecedented social upheaval. The continent was not socially static before this time. Beginning in the eighteenth century, however, demographic, economic, and political forces arose that were truly revolutionary in their intensity. The population of the continent began to expand rapidly and, in addition, became exceptionally mobile. Much of Europe was increasingly urbanized, a process that altered both city and countryside. The economy of Europe was transformed. Production expanded greatly, and new methods of marketing and transport arose. The base of the economy shifted from agriculture to industry. Finally, governments gradually adopted important new methods and policies, often spurred by the rise of new groups to political consciousness. The result was a type of government that increasingly sought change in many areas—in basic aspects of agriculture, in the organization of cities, in industry and technology, as well as in more conventional political matters. Government supported the more fundamental forces of demographic and economic expansion. The face of European society was accordingly transformed.

The transformations wrought by the broad process of industrialization seem, on balance, to have been beneficial. Preindustrial society was not completely dismal or static; and certainly modern social change brought great stress and hardship. Yet a progressive tone can be discerned in the rising standards of living and the new levels of education. In fact, industrialization brought a concept of progress to most people for the first time.

Social upheaval naturally left its mark on every aspect of modern European history. It is this whole process of change that concerns the social historian. A broad social history attempts to convey what most people were doing most of the time. This involves attention to such traditional topics as political and intellectual history, but not to these alone. Even groups that were consciously involved with politics and formal ideas had other concerns, such as family life, recreation, and economic activity. Their whole style of life must be described. And social history has a democratic bias; it deals with groups that emerge only rarely in standard political and intellectual histories precisely because they lacked formal consciousness of such matters.

Obviously, this range of interest is so broad that methods of summarization must be found. Two primary principles can be employed here. A system of periodization must be introduced within which social behavior and the main lines of change can be treated in common terms. Year-by-year detail is avoided; seldom is adequate information available for this. Beyond this, the burden of treating all members of society is reduced by dividing society into roughly coherent groups. In 1800, Europe was divided into a number of social groupings; by the twentieth century the groupings had changed in nature, but society remained far from homogeneous. To understand the effects of a phenomenon such as the industrial revolution or to describe religion or family life in the nineteenth century, one must begin first by distinguishing the major social classes of the period.

The term *social class* is used in this essay to define very broad groupings. Some sociologists prefer the word *stratum* to *class,* reserving the latter term for a group that is conscious of its cohesion. In the European context at least, class seems a more appropriate term. It designates a very large number of people who share a range of economic interests and, often, a sense of place in society. Members of a class did not necessarily know that they belonged to it. Peasants, for example, seldom had any clear sense of the peasantry in general, although they could usually recognize a nonpeasant as a stranger. And certainly most classes had no organizational unity. Even working-class unions, late in the nineteenth century, embraced only a minority of the class they purported to represent. Members of the major classes, however, shared many attitudes and forms of behavior; and the members of a class usually recognized a certain separation from other groups. The artisan class shared a tradition from its guild past, a roughly comparable standard of living, a sense of threat posed by the industrial revolution, a widespread interest in education, and often some susceptibility to violent protest. Artisans possessed, then, a distinctive if very general combination of attitudes and patterns of behavior. This shared behavior makes a class such as the artisans a vital unit of analysis in modern social history. Through a description of social classes and their evolution much of modern European society can be described.

A European social class was bound together by four fundamental factors: sense of status, income, type of work, and tradition. These factors were often related. Their balance varied from class to class, and the combination tended to change with time.

Sense of status is the broadest and most common feature but the hardest to define. For preindustrial society particularly, it could include a distinctive legal position. A class often emphasized its status by a distinctive pattern of consumption. The class as a status group provided the framework for most marriages; that is, members of a class recognized other members as the only appropriate marriage partners. This sort of criterion offers the best view of actual status relationships. But full information on marriage and even consumption patterns has seldom been explored, though it often exists.

Type of work can supplement descriptions of status. Differences in occupations, not always reflected in income, provided the basis for many distinctive contacts and values. The lower middle class often earned less than workers, yet they maintained a sense of separate status based on type of work. Tremendous variations in income and position within the aristocracy should not obscure a shared feeling of the importance of landed income and government service as against commercial ventures.

Tradition played a great role, particularly for older groups such as the aristocracy and artisans. Again, it helped mold a distinctive set of values.

Income was of great importance in defining classes, particularly in the industrial period. By that time, and to some extent even before, members of most social classes earned or possessed within a common range. From this and other shared features flowed comparable educational experiences, comparable patterns of family life, comparable political outlook—in sum, a distinctive manner of living.

Obviously, a reliance on the social class as the primary analytical unit involves certain difficulties. Many movements and institutions transcended class lines. Artisans and the middle classes shared a fervor for education and for political reform in the early nineteenth century in western Europe. Later in the century nationalism was shared by members of many classes, although it affected the middle classes most strongly. Institutions such as church or state had interests of their own that cannot be fully described in terms of a broad class; but in no case did they blur class lines completely. Institutions and their bureaucracies, while admittedly distinctive, usually conformed to the interests of one class or a coalition of classes. Their actions might influence other classes, but the effects varied with the class. Widespread social movements such as nationalism differed in nature and extent from class to class. Recognition of common influences does not destroy the value of class analysis.

The social classes cannot be regarded as rigid units. In modern Europe changes in the position and behavior of major classes often seemed to overwhelm elements of continuity, although important traditions usually persisted.

Even within a single period, class behavior does not describe the behavior of all individuals in a class. Some members of a class in fact might devote much of their life to avoiding class behavior, to aping some other group. The social historian cannot describe individual deviations. He attempts to develop a sense of the norms of behavior and outlook. But his class analysis must be made sufficiently supple to deal with major subgroups within a class. None of the classes used in this essay can be accepted without question as logical groupings. All possessed internal subgroups, often in considerable opposition to each other. These groups were themselves defined by income, tradition, type of work, political power. Fully as much attention must be given to them as to the broad class. Theoretically, subgroups could be further refined into smaller coherent units; in a broad essay this will not be possible. But major distinctions must be traced within a class. Usually, there is much room for further study to determine the most relevant units of social analysis in modern European history.

Finally, attention to class and even to subgroup must not obscure mobility. Much of modern European social history consists of movements from one class to another. The social historian cannot trace individual cases, but he must describe the larger movements. Even in this effort a class analysis is valid. Workers of peasant origin retained clear traces of their original class that often distinguished them from other workers. Workers of middle-class origin in contemporary Europe remain more conservative than their fellows. Managers of worker origin reflect their roots in unusual radicalism, although they are more conservative than workers. Here, at least in political matters, is a distinctive subgroup based on mobility. And for many individuals mobility itself is rooted in the existence of recognizable classes and a desire to advance within a class system.

The reliance on social class as the fundamental analytical unit assumes a certain cohesion in social structure across the boundaries of nation and region. It assumes that in a study of European society it is more realistic to link Russian and English workers than to link Russian workers with the Russian middle class. This does not deny the importance of national conditions and problems. On the most superficial level revolutions took place in some countries and not in others during our period; in cases of concomitant revolutions the results and methods differed widely from case to case. Regional distinctions must be used, therefore, to explain many important events and trends.

A detailed social history would have to take a multitude of geographical factors into account. Major regional differences existed within a given country. Peasants in the poor, mountainous areas of the Auvergne differed greatly from other French peasants. Industrialists in Mulhouse resembled their Swiss brethren, with whom they shared a Calvinist religion and many family ties, far more than their colleagues in the rest of France. Obviously, a great many similar distinctions could be made; equally obviously, there will seldom be space to make them. Even national distinctions will be introduced only when they reflect clear divergence of patterns within a given class.

Above the national level, however, certain large regional variations will be consistently noted. There the major distinction lay between eastern and much of southern Europe on the one hand, and western Europe on the other. Basic differences in patterns of land tenure formed a major element of this distinction. The result was a profound division in the outlook of both nobles and peasants even within some individual countries, notably Germany and Italy. Similarly, western Europe was distinguished by the possession of a well-established middle class before the industrial revolution. No generalization about the middle class can neglect a distinction of this sort. Even here, however, certain common elements existed. Despite huge differences in land tenure patterns, peasants underwent the pressures of population growth and industrialization. Their basic responses were similar, although the manner of expression differed according to regional situations. A study of European society is possible precisely because of the common social forces operating in the last century and a half. In fact, only a firm recognition of the continental scope of social change can permit a proper assessment of the very real regional and national differences that did exist.

The social forces operating on European society did not, however, function at precisely the same time over the continent as a whole. The population expansion that began in England in the mid-eighteenth century did not significantly affect Italy until a century later. Industrialization was introduced in Great Britain in the late eighteenth century, but spread only gradually to the east and south. Hence Russia began to industrialize in the 1890s, and some of the Balkan countries as well as the southern regions of Spain and Italy were scarcely engaged in the process even by 1914. Changes in governmental structure showed a similar tendency to spread from west to east. By 1914 most of the major regions of Europe had been touched by demographic, economic, and governmental changes. But the most western regions had been involved for over a century and had passed from the stage of hesitant and confused beginnings to advanced, if often still confused, development. In no sense, then, can the social historian discuss the whole of Europe in the same terms for any given decade. Differences in stages of development must be kept constantly in mind.

The result is a rather complex chronology. The first section of this book deals with European society around 1780, before industrialization. Regional distinctions must be made, even for this date, but the most important point is that preindustrial structures continued without basic alteration until the last half of the nineteenth century in east and south. Similarly, the demographic, industrial, and political forces of change, outlined in the second section, involve some common European patterns. The rate and impact of change varied with the date and with previous social structure. Once more, however, the key fact is that a roughly common process began at widely different times. The late eighteenth century saw political, industrial, and demographic revolutions launched in western Europe. These had some social impact even on the east, but there the full process of change began only a century later.

The third section of the book deals roughly with the period 1800–1870. It focuses on the first generations to live under the impact of industrialization and therefore deals primarily with western Europe. Certain analogies can be drawn with eastern Europe at the end of the century. For the peasantry particularly a discussion of the period 1789–1848 in the west can apply to the period 1850–1914 in the east and south; in both cases the peasantry faced transformations of demographic and legal structure.

In the west by about 1870 society had entered a second stage of adaptation to industrialization. The industrial economy itself altered. The character of the middle class changed; the class seemed to split to some extent. Workers were increasingly conscious of their position and power. The peasantry faced no challenges so great as in the earlier period, but this class too was altered. In general, the end of the century saw a maturation of industry and industrial society. But in eastern Europe industrialization was just beginning. The industrial process resembled the earlier western developments in part, but it also borrowed many of the advanced forms of the contemporary west. Although eastern European society was basically in a first industrial stage, there was some correspondence to western developments in the same period.

The First World War and the Russian revolution brought further social change to all regions. The rise both of communism and fascism reflected these changes, but we will not study the social policies of the totalitarian regimes. Even so, there is ample reason to deal with the interwar period as a separate unit. However, it can be suggested that social structures had evolved rather than basically altered; that is, eastern and southern Europe remained in a first industrial phase, although it was more clearly developed, while the mature industrial society of the west was shaken but not yet surpassed.

The impact of economic depression and the Second World War opened a more basic change in European society than the First World War had done. In eastern Europe a mature industrial society at last developed, and the social old regime was uprooted, with partly familiar social effects. In western Europe a third stage of industrial society was arising. These trends can only be suggested, not clearly defined, because this new period has not ended, so its full character cannot yet be known. Nevertheless, an outline of the new social climate is possible, and with this the book will end.

The sources for the social history of modern Europe are scattered and often inadequate. Despite its importance, social history is a comparatively new branch of historical study. Relatively little attention has been given to the lower classes of society except in periods when they spring into political importance, as in a revolution. And even the governing classes have seldom been studied in their nonpolitical and nonintellectual activities, that is, in their family life, their standard of living, or even in their economic functions. Important work has been done on most of these subjects, and fortunately the pace of study is increasing. There remain, however, many unexplored facets of modern social history and many others that have been studied in only one country or even one region. Artisans, for example, have been briefly studied in Germany and in England, but even there interest has centered on their ability to organize protest movements; in France, where artisans were an even more important part of the social structure, they have not been studied ,directly at all. Similar gaps exist with regard to all the major social classes. A broad essay on the social history of the period must be partly tentative. Generalizations are often based on rather limited examples. The only excuse for this is the need to provide even a brief overall picture of European society under industrialization and the encouragement that such an introduction should give to the many further studies needed.

Because of the general character of our study, it has seemed pointless to burden it with footnotes. However, a basic bibliography provides an indication of the leading secondary sources of information and offers some guidelines for further reading in the major aspects of modern European social history.

CONTENTS

[xv]

4

THE RISE OF THE MASSES

7

CONCLUSION

European Society in Upheaval

1

EUROPE BEFORE
THE INDUSTRIAL
REVOLUTION

Industrialization was based on various changes in the complex society of the eighteenth century. Quite commonly, for example, a major increase in population preceded the industrial revolution by several decades—by fifty years in England, seventy in Prussia, and over a hundred in Russia. Other important social changes also characterized the preindustrial* period in many countries. The introduction of domestic manufacturing followed close on the heels of population growth; only by this means were the added numbers supported in the countryside. In France and England during the eighteenth century, in Germany during the early nineteenth, and

* The term *preindustrial* is used, for convenience, to describe a situation prior to the industrial revolution. In no sense is the term intended to denote an absence of industry and manufacturing. What was absent was a system of factory and power-driven production.

in Russia even later, domestic industry spread to an unprecedented degree. In the west, particularly, the preindustrial period was marked by a growth in commerce and so in wealth, especially among the middle classes. Colonial and other trade steadily increased the riches and power of merchant groups in Britain and France throughout the eighteenth century. In France, especially, the political frustrations of the class increased as well, with explosive results at the end of the century. Particularly in the western countries the two centuries before industrialization had seen a steady growth in the importance and size of cities, which presaged the greater urban movement of the nineteenth century.

There were, nevertheless, important elements of continuity in preindustrial society. The aristocracy held the leading position in society, government, and the established churches. Its grip, though increasingly challenged, was nowhere effectively broken until after 1789. Everywhere the peasantry was by far the most populous class, and although often threatened by the rise in population, it had almost nowhere abandoned the traditional methods of agriculture or the traditional structures of village and family. Changes in these methods and structures had to begin before industrialization could gather momentum, but custom dominated the major features of peasant life in most places well into the nineteenth century. In the west, where cities were important, there were more definite signs of innovation. But even the middle classes were preponderantly traditionalist in their economic purposes and methods. The cities were filled with artisan groups who clung to the customary guild structures as long as they could.

When the combination of demographic, economic, and political change swept over Europe in the nineteenth century, it encountered a largely traditional social structure. Shaken by developments presaging the full tide of change in the west in the eighteenth century and elsewhere during the nineteenth, society had a preindustrial structure that provided the first reaction to social and economic upheaval.

AGRICULTURAL SOCIETY

The basis of European society in 1800 was agricultural. Everywhere the leading social class, the aristocracy, depended ultimately on agriculture for its economic support. And everywhere the most numerous class were the peasants and associated rural artisans who lived in small towns, villages, and sometimes on isolated farms. In 1800, 95 per cent of the Russian population and 80 per cent of the French population was rural. Even in 1850 France was still 75 per cent rural, Germany 65 per cent, and Austria 82 per cent. And as late as 1900 Russia was 88 per cent rural, Greece 85 per cent, and France still over 50 per cent.* Throughout the century, then, though in declining proportions, agriculture and activities directly related to agriculture remained the source of support for the majority of people throughout most of Europe. Focus on the industrialization and urbanization of Europe leads naturally to a tendency to neglect the continued importance of rural life. Obviously, however, attention must be given to this life in any period. The agricultural basis of society must be understood particularly when considering society before the industrial revolution, before there was any massive inducement to leave the countryside for the city.

Agricultural Methods

In 1800 agriculture was almost everywhere designed primarily to feed the owners and workers of the land on which production took place. Certainly there were outside markets for agricultural production. Cities depended on the possibility of buying food. Even areas in eastern Europe, notably Poland and the Ukraine, exported grain to the more urban west. Obviously, producers near cities had frequent market contacts. Regions with specialties such as wine growing had some local exchanges at least and often sold more widely. Areas on navigable rivers were naturally more exposed to market opportunities than other regions. Finally, some exchanges were necessary even for agricultural communities themselves. Salt and metals had to be brought in. Wealthy peasants in parts of Austria and Germany bought meat imported from Hungary.

Nevertheless, even in comparatively wealthy and urbanized countries most peasants were concerned primarily with production for their own needs. Even many large estates produced for only a local market, and almost all estates filled most of the consumption

---

* The term *rural* is not totally accurate here, because in most countries it includes all residents of agglomerations with less than 3,000 inhabitants. Although the bulk of this category was indeed rural, a minority were small town artisans and bourgeois dependent on rural society only indirectly.

needs of the local labor force. In general, only industrialization created a sufficiently massive market to induce peasants and land-owners to concentrate on production for distant sales rather than for local consumption. In eastern, and to a lesser extent southern, Europe the rise of cities in the west after 1800 did create a potential market for export even before industrialization occurred locally; and agricultural methods were accordingly altered early in the century. But almost everywhere in 1800 agriculture was still intended above all for local consumption.

This fact explains a number of the key features of preindustrial agriculture. Agriculture was not, in 1800 and even after, designed primarily to maximize production. In a predominantly nonmarket situation maximization simply made no sense. The local market was finite, traditionally at least. The number of people to feed in a village or on an estate could not expand rapidly. Undue attention to production would be a waste of time because there would be no way to dispose of a major increase. Efforts had to concentrate primarily on assuring existing standards for the existing population. Agriculture was designed, particularly for the peasants but also to a degree for the aristocracy, to maintain traditional (and often rather low) levels of consumption and to support the structure of rural society more generally. Notions of expansion and progress came hard to the rural producer.

The character of preindustrial agriculture showed most clearly in the methods employed, which were largely traditional and severely limited the productive capacity of agriculture. Even after major improvements in method were developed, beginning in Eng-land in the eighteenth century, they were extremely slow to spread, for producers could see no need for them. Farm machinery was nonexistent. Only a few simple tools aided the various processes of planting and harvesting. The wooden plow was often pushed by hand, and women and children distributed the seed. Harvesting was done by hand with at most a sickle for cutting; peasants thrashed their grain by flailing it or walking on it.

With such simple methods, the amount of land that any one family could cultivate was obviously very small, and production was low. In a good year the methods did allow production somewhat beyond the needs of the producers themselves. It was on this margin that aristocrats lived and preindustrial cities survived. But the margin was small indeed, and it was curtailed by the traditional practice of leaving much of the land fallow each year. This was the only way known to replenish the fertility of the soil. In most areas one third of the cultivated land was left fallow annually; in some parts of southern Europe half the land was set aside. By 1800 alternative methods of restoring nitrogen to the soil by planting clover or turnips had been developed, but such methods were used by only a few large estates in England and northern France. Similarly, new systems of drainage that allowed the utilization of fields previously too wet for cultivation and improved the yield in existing plots were confined initially to the British Isles.

Finally, most villages possessed, usually as commons land, substantial tracts regarded as unsuitable for cultivation; at most they were devoted to occasional forestry and scrubby pasture land. Large sections of most countries, particularly on the continent, had never been opened to agriculture at all. Only developments in the nineteenth century would show that cultivation of many of these areas was possible. In the meantime, agriculture before industrialization was characterized not only by simplicity of tools and methods, but also by a real limitation of the amount of land that was used at any one time.

Preindustrial agriculture was also dominated by the need to produce almost all the foods needed locally. Only a few products were brought in from the outside. Most villages were isolated from major markets. Only rutted wagon tracks connected them even to other villages in the neighborhood. Outside merchandise was a rarity and was usually either brought by itinerant peddlers or available on regular but infrequent market days in the area. Actual shops were unknown in most villages. Most goods needed for day to day consumption had to be locally produced. Even individual families typically attempted substantial self-sufficiency in what they themselves produced.

Primary attention had to be given to a starchy staple. By 1800 in many areas of northern Europe this staple was the potato, the cheapest of all starches to raise. Often one of the cheaper grains, such as rye or oats, was relied upon for bread. And in a few favored regions, such as parts of northwestern France, wheat was fairly well developed. In addition to the staples, however, a variety of other products were necessary. At least a few animals were kept for fiber, hides, and milk as well as for meat. Many regions raised a few grapes for wine; in other areas grains were used for beer and liquors. And of course each area sought its fuel in woods nearby. Most families made their own clothes and built or maintained their own housing. Some important activities required a degree of specialization. Shepherds, millers, and sometimes a variety of artisans took charge of work no one family could do for itself, but they too engaged in more general farming of their own. Such specialization remained almost entirely local. Only for a very few products or services did a village or estate have to look beyond its borders.

This was another important deterrent to maximization of agricultural production. Regions failed to specialize fully in the products for which their soil and climate were best suited. Some regions had to attempt production, such as wine growing or meat raising, for which they were ill adapted. Small estates and villages with highly diversified agriculture were inefficient and uneconomical in all their products, resulting in poor quality and high costs even in the villages themselves. And the tendency to self-sufficiency severely limited the consumption standards of most localities. Products that could not be raised in the area, such as coffee and tea, were generally unknown. Areas ill suited to production of a major staple were doomed to poverty regardless of their potential for more specialized production; and if a vital crop failed in any year, local famine might well result. The agricultural family lived largely on its own efforts and those of its immediate neighbors. Preindustrial agriculture both recognized and perpetuated this fact.

Land Tenure

The methods and conditions of preindustrial agriculture were expressed in one of the most basic features of rural life, the patterns and uses of land tenure. Correspondingly, a change in land tenure patterns was one of the prerequisites for any major alteration of agricultural methods. Hence Great Britain, the one area of Europe in which a rapid rise in agricultural productivity was taking place during the eighteenth century, was also the scene of tremendous changes in landholding. On the continent substantial changes were also taking place, but usually they confirmed and extended earlier methods. Systems of rural tenure and labor still conformed to the character of preindustrial agriculture.

There were, of course, a variety of systems of tenure. In certain areas, such as parts of central France, land was worked on the basis of individual farms and might even be enclosed by fences; the plots were relatively small and the methods and the tenure itself highly traditional. In general, however, two primary systems of tenure existed in Europe. Both systems could be found in most regions. Both had some support in tradition; even in the most recent cases, such as Russia, several centuries of development had led to the patterns existing in 1800. The two systems were, however, vastly different; so were the resulting positions of peasantry and aristocracy. Furthermore, each system was dominant in different parts of Europe, and in the decades around 1800 each tended to increase at the expense of the other in its areas of dominance.

Roughly speaking, northwestern Europe was an area of smallholding. Most peasant plots were still part of a large estate, and some dues and services were owed to the lord. However, the obligations were relatively slight, and peasants could usually buy, sell, and leave the land without difficulty. There were some large holdings as well that depended on peasant labor, but they were not typical. From the Elbe River in the east to the Atlantic in the west, from Tuscany and northern Spain to Scandinavia, most rural residents based their life on small plots of land operated as part of a village structure.

In eastern Germany and beyond and in southern Italy and southern Spain large estates dominated. The major exceptions to this were the areas of modern Serbia and Bulgaria, where most peasants were free from noble control of any sort. But around 1800, in eastern Prussia, for example, about 62 per cent of the land was held directly in large units. The rest of the arable land was operated in a village system, over which landlords usually had feudal rights. Even on the large estates villages often administered the land; this was generally the case in Russia. But ultimate control rested with the landlord, and in many cases he administered the estate directly. Certainly the social and economic character of these regions was determined by the preponderance of large estates.

The older of the two systems was that of village smallholding. Many villages and their basic tenure patterns dated from early medieval times. The system was highly traditional and in many ways was a typical expression of peasant agriculture and social structure. The system therefore had some importance even outside its stronghold in western Europe. In England, where a rather new system of agricultural labor was taking shape in the eighteenth century, village tenure had flourished earlier and still hung on in some cases. In eastern Europe, where the system was overlaid by the dominant large estates, smallholding had existed earlier and persisted in a minority of cases. In Russia, when the emancipation of the peasants cut down the large estates in 1861, village smallholding was resumed under government encouragement. And in France, western Germany, northern Italy, and elsewhere in the northwest the system was clearly dominant by 1800. Large holdings existed and were important in certain fertile regions such as Normandy, but the revolution of 1789 removed the last restrictions on peasant ownership of most of the land. In western Germany, to be sure, many peasants remained under some feudal obligations well into the nineteenth century, but they were imposed over a smallholding system.

The average holding in the regions of peasant tenure was tiny indeed. The typical smallholding was only nine acres in France in the midnineteenth century. In Russia, where the climate was far less favorable, the average peasant holding after emancipation was about twenty acres. Holdings of this average size were usually manageable by a single peasant family, with some extra help at harvest time. And they were sufficient to support a family, except in regions of low fertility or in years of bad harvests. However, peasant tenures were by no means uniform. Inequalities varied from region to region and tended to increase with time; during the eighteenth century some French peasants managed to accumulate substantial farms and were bitterly resented by their poorer brethren. Similar discrepancies, though less pronounced, existed in 1800 in Germany and elsewhere. Rarely, however, were there large numbers of actual landless; inequalities did not yet go this far.

In 1800 the most important smallholding regions, such as northern France and western Germany, were characterized not only by small average plots but also by division of holdings into separate strips and by a substantial portion of land held in common. Each village was surrounded by several basic fields, usually three in the areas where one third of the land, that is, one of the basic fields, was left fallow each year. The individual family possessed one or more small strips of land in each of the fields. Furthermore, another part of the land around the village was owned by no individual but by the village as a whole. In 1800, one sixteenth of all the land in France was thus devoted to village commons. Both the commons and the division of land into individual plots clearly expressed the purposes of village agriculture.

Village agriculture involved a substantial element of cooperation and, relatedly, one of minimal protection for all members of the village. The commons were used for cooperative grazing and, where forested, provided wood for the whole village. The village itself determined the use and organization of the common land. The commons also served to protect the poorer members of the village. Often peasants without land could eke out a living by gathering wood, tending flocks, and even cultivating part of the commons. Division of individual plots into strips protected each owner by giving him holdings in different places. If disaster overtook one section, no one family would bear the entire burden. If one section was more fertile than the others, all landowners would share in its fertility. In a few areas this general concern for sharing was extended to periodic redistribution of the land according to need. In Russia after the emancipation a minority of villages redistributed land as often as every ten years according to family size; there was in these cases no real private ownership at all. This was, of course, an exceptional development; most village tenure, as we have seen, involved substantial inequality. But universally there remained the desire to offer some collective control and protection.

Division of land into separate strips reflected another type of protection as well. The peasant family sought to protect its various members. In many cases it left land to all the sons; each son would take a section of each strip, so that the good and the bad land would be equally divided. This resulted in the welter of tiny, divided strips in most villages.

Finally, division into strips required cooperation. The plots were too small to farm individually, and they could not be fenced in. The village collectively decided times of planting and harvesting. The village, and village tradition, determined what land would be left fallow. Animals in collective flocks were allowed to graze in all the fields after harvest. The organization of village agriculture required joint effort at many stages.

Village agriculture was not easily adapted to change. Its collective framework allowed little room for individual daring. The small size of most plots offered scant margin for risk or capital for unusual investment. But there was some collective security for all members of the system. In preindustrial agriculture this had to be the primary goal of small producers.

The other major system of tenure presented many contrasts to the village structure. Most obviously, landholdings in eastern and southern Europe were typically quite large. Junker estates in east Prussia, for example, averaged three hundred acres, and some ranged as high as two thousand. Again, there was great variety and inequality, but the scale was quite different. The estates were capable of significant production, and this production was above all designed to benefit the owner. The estates usually produced most of what their laborers required for consumption. But production did not end there; estate agriculture made sense only if a significant surplus was available for the profit of the owner. Estates therefore tended to expand in importance in the areas they dominated as market possibilities increased. In the early nineteenth century German and Russian landlords eagerly took advantage of the markets created by a rising population and by the urbanization of western Europe and extended the estate system. Many small peasant holdings were purchased. Other peasants, still legally serfs, were forced to include their land in the lord's domain. Well into the nineteenth century the estate system showed a dynamism that was less evident in the smallholding system.

The methods used on the estates were not greatly different from those used in village agriculture. To be sure, more complex equipment could be used on these large holdings, and some was introduced. There was experimentation with new specialized crops, such as sugar beets in eastern Germany. Some Junkers even built their own refineries and distilleries to capitalize on their substantial production. But on the whole it was not new equipment or products that gave vitality to the estates of eastern and southern Europe; rather, it was a system of servile labor.

Serfdom was virtually unrelieved in the areas of large estates until 1848 at the earliest. Efforts at reform, as in Prussia during the

Napoleonic period, came to little. In fact, many estate owners sought to increase the severity of the impositions on their peasants to provide additional income. Except in Prussia after 1807, landlords continued to control the movements of their labor force; peasants could not leave the estate without permission. Heavy quotas of work service were required, often backed by floggings and other punishments. The resulting cheap labor was the basis of landlord profits. Aspects of the system continued in most areas, except Russia, even after serfdom was abolished. Although increasingly pressed, the large-estate system usually endured unless forcibly abolished by political means.

Both village agriculture and the estate system were changing in the preindustrial period. Many smallholding areas saw some concentration of plots in the hands of more prosperous peasants. In Denmark there was even some enclosure of peasant plots. The large-estate system tended to spread in eastern Europe and around 1800 its impositions on the peasantry became more onerous.

Finally, two other changes in tenure were developing in the eighteenth century in western Europe. In several areas, such as France and southern Italy, there was increasing purchase of estates by prosperous members of the middle class. This was a trend that developed in eastern Europe later on. Middle-class owners usually purchased existing estates, although they often nibbled at peasant holdings too. More important, they definitely tried to make the system more efficient and profitable. This involved some changes in methods and more rigorous treatment of peasant labor.

In England a distinctive system of large estates was arising in the eighteenth century. The enclosure movement, at its height in the sixty years after 1760, involved the withdrawal of massive tracts of land from village tenure. Landlords, predominantly aristocratic, not only withdrew their own lands from peasant farming, but also bought up much of the land of poorer peasants. Government acts, burdening many peasants with obligations to fence in their own land, literally forced many small owners to sell. By the early nineteenth century over 67 per cent of British farm land was included in large estates. This was another, massive case of response to the new possibilities of market agriculture arising at the end of the eighteenth century.

The British landlords, unlike their east European brethren, were not content with merely expanding their holdings; they fenced in their land, thus separating it from any remnants of village agriculture. They installed tenant overseers, often drawn from the more ambitious ranks of the local farming population, and paid them well to organize the estates on a basis of rational exploitation. Fallow fields were replaced by fields planted in nitrogen-rich turnips or clover. Drainage was installed. Cattle raising was extended and the stock much improved. Agriculture was geared to produce effectively for the market and to earn the highest cash return possible. Workers were ill paid, to be sure, but the system did not depend on serf-type labor; in fact, with improved methods the productivity of labor was greatly increased.

In 1800, nowhere on the continent were such radical changes being made. In France some aristocrats, returning after the revolution, withdrew their land from peasant cultivation and installed new methods, but peasant tenure remained typical. Even more members of the middle class, often taking advantage of land sales during the revolution, installed themselves as farmers and applied commercial principles to their agriculture. The movement was far more hesitant and less general than in England, but the possibilities of efficient market agriculture were being explored. Even in Russia small groups of landlords studied possible improvements. The rural economy was beginning to change.

THE RURAL CLASSES: THE ARISTOCRACY

The aristocracy was based primarily on preindustrial agriculture. It was capable of seeking agricultural change but seldom of basic innovation. Many of the common features of the class and its evolution in the nineteenth century were rooted in its agricultural traditions. In northern Italy, where aristocrats were traditionally urban, the class was less distinctive than it was in the rest of Europe, where there was a landed base.

The class as a whole, however, was defined primarily by a common and intense sense of status. In places like East Prussia the aristocracy was the only group allowed to own land until 1808; there the class and land ownership were long virtually synonymous. In most areas the aristocracy carefully protected its landed base by practicing strict primogeniture or entail in inheritance. But there were great varieties in the extent of landholding among aristocrats, and not all members of the class were economically dependent on landholding. In Russia, where estates were split in inheritance, 84 per cent of the aristocracy had almost no land by 1820. In most countries noble younger sons, cut off from inheritance by primogeniture, maintained a position in the aristocracy by some other means. In many areas a service aristocracy had been created since 1600 to fill positions in state bureaucracy. This group often had some land—in Russia the service aristocracy gained increasing land by state gifts in the eighteenth century—but often not enough for full support. Ties to the land were important for the class as a whole, especially for its leading members, but they did not constitute the only criterion of membership in the class.

The aristocracy was rooted in a sense of separate and superior status passed on by birth and recognized by law. In the blood, in the mere fact of birth within the class, lay the essence of aristocracy. Many aristocratic families were still of relatively recent vintage by 1800; many governments elevated bureaucrats or wealthy businessmen to the nobility late in the nineteenth century. But new members of the class quickly tried to establish antecedents that would give them a literal birthright to the aristocracy and at least instilled in their children a sense of a birthright that was firmly founded. One of the great strengths of the class was its ability to persuade new entrants and even nonmembers of the importance of gentle birth.

The aristocracy naturally viewed society as a whole in terms of inherited status; where a man was born, there he was to remain. And the aristocracy took pains to enforce its sense of inherited distinctions in society. Intermarriage with other classes was rare in 1800, particularly in eastern Europe. Peasants were required to show great respect; in the Baltic regions they addressed their lord as "Father." In the hierarchical society of the aristocracy inheritance was the key to the kingdom.

Ancestry alone did not, of course, complete the definition of the aristocrat. It was assumed that birth transmitted certain unique virtues. The qualities regarded as aristocratic varied with the region and type of aristocracy, but there were certain common features. The aristocrat was expected to maintain a particular sense of honor. In Prussia aristocratic honor was given legal recognition, and an aristocrat's word was accepted in court without affidavit. In most places sense of honor was expressed in dueling. Aristocratic honor abhorred commercialism and usually commerce itself. Slavery to the earning of money and the petty, dishonorable haggling that this entailed were to be shunned.

The aristocrat cultivated physical bravery; everywhere military service and leadership were typical expressions of the aristocratic code. The aristocracy also clung to a belief in *noblesse oblige,* in a superior aristocratic ability to care for the lower orders of society. This led them to expect, and in 1800 usually to obtain, the leading places in government. It could also lead them, even in areas of great aristocratic exploitation of labor, to claim and even to implement paternal feelings for the poor. In Russia, for example, the nineteenth century saw many efforts by aristocrats to improve the health and education of their peasants.

Finally, the aristocracy felt itself to be the bearer of a distinct and superior code of manners and culture. It was a leisured class, devoted to activities inaccessible to the crowd. It strove to maintain a peculiar style of life. This effort took the form of dandyism for the British court aristocracy, of widespread gambling, which provided excitement and showed scorn for money, of the adoption of French language and culture by many Russian nobles, of distinctive homes and clothing in many areas, and of the perpetuation of exclusive hunting rights almost everywhere. In the concepts of distinctive honor, manners, bravery, and public service the aristocracy saw the fulfillment of its superior status.

Structure of the Aristocracy

The special position of the aristocracy rested on several factors. The class was a small one. In Hungary one eighth of the population claimed aristocratic status; one quarter of ethnic Poles were aristocrats. But these were exceptional cases. Generally, reliance on inherited status and the relatively expensive style of life severely limited entry. In 1789 there were only 400,000 French aristocrats, a substantial number but less than 2 per cent of the population. A little later only 1 per cent of the Russian population was aristocratic.

The aristocracy was divided into distinct subgroups. Small aristocrats were numerically the largest portion of the class. Such were most Prussian Junkers and the English and Russian gentry. Some of these people were absolutely impoverished. In France there were aristocratic beggars and gamekeepers. In Poland and Hungary there was a particularly large element with only a tiny plot of land; the Polish *golota,* or barefoot nobility, comprised the bulk of the class.

Actual gentry were above this level. Some had government or army jobs. Many lived on the land but depended on some administrative income as well. Others ran their small estates alone. In any case, the gentry had substantial political and economic power although usually only within the locality. They named judges and parish church officials. In eastern and southern Europe they made local laws and provided rudimentary police services. They received dues and work services from the peasantry on their estates. In western Europe, where servile obligations were relatively low, they used tenants, sharecroppers, or paid labor to work their estates. In any case, revenues were usually sufficient for a distinctive style of life.

The gentry lived simply but well. Their manor houses were plain but solid. They hunted, held lavish feasts and dances, and often gambled. They married in their own group, although sometimes a match with a merchant's daughter was sought for economic reasons. This was not a cultured group, although some in government service obtained extensive education. But there was no question of the firm position of the gentry. Even the magnates were scorned as urbanized and vain.

At the top of the aristocracy was a handful of magnates of great wealth and sophistication. In Hungary, around 1800, out of a total of 75,000 aristocratic families, there were at most two hundred magnate families. This was an elite group. It had few contacts with lower levels of nobility. Intermarriage between magnates and lesser aristocrats was unlikely. Both groups had more contacts with local middle class elements of roughly comparable wealth than they had with each other. Despite shared legal status and many common values, the differences within the aristocracy could seem overwhelming.

The magnates were distinguished, basically, by the greater economic power behind them. They were the possessors of the most extensive estates in both eastern and western Europe and, correspondingly, of the most imposing family backgrounds and titles. Almost never did the leading aristocrats bother with the detailed administration of their estates; that was left to paid overseers. Increasingly the magnates lived in the towns. The income from their estates freed them to devote much time to leading positions in the state, the army, and the church. They traveled extensively; the continental tour was an accepted part of the education of leading young aristocrats in Russia and England alike. Great attention was given to polished manners and dress and to the patronage of the arts. Far from these aristocrats were the violence, vulgarity, and simplicity of the lesser nobles. Their education was extensive; Baltic aristocrats, for example, had tutors for their primary schooling, and then went on to private secondary schools and often to a university. In general, education was designed to provide grace and polish. Training in the classics and attention to sports were designed to produce general ability and distinction. Well rounded and cosmopolitan, the upper aristocrat could recognize his peers in any country. And in almost every country the group remained in control of the major institutions of society well into the nineteenth century.

Aristocratic Power

The aristocracy both large and small rested not only on distinctive status and economic power, but also on diverse political privileges. The local political power of landowners, particularly in the east and south, was one aspect of this. But other functions were fulfilled both by the landowners themselves and by the younger sons and brothers who had to be given positions of suitable prestige without breaking up the family estate by divided inheritance. As in all realms, the aristocracy tried to exclude most outsiders from its own special preserves. Through its economic power, through actual law, and through the social cohesion of the class the aristocracy managed to dominate many institutions. These institutions in turn gave the class power, important income, and a sense of fulfilling the special duties and characteristics of the aristocracy.

The aristocrats filled the upper ranks of the army in most countries. The upstart armies of Napoleon, themselves led by newly made aristocrats, were defeated by forces led by the dukes and princes of Europe. Aristocrats felt, in fact, that their peculiar sense of honor and bravery qualified them and them alone for military leadership.

Similarly, aristocrats felt a particular responsibility to the church.

Here the obligation to care for the lower orders of society could be expressed. Here younger sons, trained already in at least the rudiments of the classics, could find a suitable income and social position. It was relatively easy for aristocratic churchmen to arrange for their peers to fill the leading posts in the established churches. Furthermore, religion was an important part of aristocratic life. Some aristocrats, especially in the west, had dabbled with irreligion in the eighteenth century, but the combined attacks on religion and aristocracy during the French revolution brought even this minority back to the churches. Thus, in the late eighteenth century the upper echelons of the Catholic, Lutheran, and Anglican Churches were dominated by the aristocracy. In 1789, all French bishops were aristocrats. And everywhere the aristocratic dominance of the established churches was a major factor in promoting social and political conservatism within the churches. For as the aristocracy served the church, so it expected service in return.

The most important institution in which the aristocracy took a leading and traditional role was, of course, the state. There was some ambiguity here. There were traditions of state service for both old landed families and more recent bureaucratic nobles. But there was also hostility to the growing central power of most monarchies, which cut into local privileges. And in western Europe the hostility of the French revolution toward both monarchy and aristocracy added further confusion.

The basic political tradition of the aristocracy was one of weak central government supplemented by the local political power of the aristocrats themselves. Since 1600 particularly, the central state had developed greatly, from France to Russia, and had deprived nobles of full power over law courts, taxation, and the like. It was always tempting to defy the central state and seek a return to localism. Through the *parlements* many French nobles had fought the state during the eighteenth century; their resistance, expressed in the Assembly of Notables of 1787, set the stage for the revolution. Even later the localist tradition was maintained by men like de Tocqueville.

However, it was in eastern Europe that the localist impulse remained strongest. Most regions still had diets, controlled by the aristocracy, with substantial powers over taxation and regional administration. In Russia, by the 1760s the government had greatly increased local aristocratic power, particularly legal power over serfs. But this only whetted the appetites of many gentry to cut down the central autocracy still further. In Poland and Hungary the size of the nobility and the fact that central government was foreign led to even more active resistance well into the nineteenth century.

In the west the rise of middle-class social and economic competition tended to draw aristocrats closer to their monarch for mutual protection. The French revolution completed this development, and by 1800 most western aristocrats had stopped attempting resistance to monarchy. In 1815, when the monarchy was restored in France, aristocrats not only filled the major positions in government but also tried to recover monarchical powers that the king himself realized had to be abandoned. In eastern Europe, where revolution seemed a remote threat, some localist agitation continued. But even there most nobles were loyal to the monarch, and many served the state directly.

Hence, not only the leading statesmen but even middle-range civil servants were preponderantly drawn from the aristocracy in the 1800s. The noble Talleyrands, Metternichs, and Hardenbergs at the center of political leadership were backed by countless aristocratic diplomats and civil servants. Here again, aristocrats could find social prestige and income; the small landowner could often triple his revenues by a local administrative job. In many cases well-paying sinecures, such as the office of the Lord Warden of the Cinque Ports in Britain, were available for some aristocrats. More important were the numerous active administrative posts that aristocrats filled. Before 1789 and after 1815, many of the principal regional agents of the French government were aristocrats. The Prussian civil service was dominated by the aristocracy, although middle-class bureaucrats had some role.

Aristocrats also controlled most of the legislative organs that existed in 1800. Houses of Peers in Britain and, after 1815, in France were exclusively aristocratic and exercised real influence over legislation. In some of the German states and elsewhere legislatures met as estates still, in the old regime tradition, with aristocrats representing one of the three or four estates and as such effectively controlling the whole body. Finally, aristocrats exercised great power even in somewhat more broadly based assemblies. Restrictive suffrage in

France after 1815 allowed the class to send many of its number to the Chamber of Deputies. Similarly, more than half the members of the British House of Commons before 1832 were nominated by the aristocracy. Through the variety of positions they held in the early nineteenth century aristocrats took the lead in advising and administering the various activities of the major governments.

Aristocratic Resurgence

Not content with maintaining traditional distinctiveness, in many areas the aristocracy was trying to increase its power toward the end of the eighteenth century. The effort was significant at the time, and in eastern Europe it continued well into the nineteenth century.

There were several bases for aristocratic activism. In some areas the strength of central governments was waning. Particularly in France and Russia this opened possibilities for definite gains. Even in Prussia the state was increasingly sympathetic. More generally, there were new economic pressures and opportunities. Prices were rising, and to maintain an expensive style of life nobles had to increase their resources. Some early urbanization in the west opened new agricultural markets. Finally, there was some sense of a need to modify middle-class competition by increasing economic and political power. This was particularly true in the west, but even in Russia the rise of a small entrepreneurial class in the eighteenth century spurred the aristocracy to protests and to some competitive activity.

The political efforts of the aristocracy against central government have already been outlined. In the west they ceased with the French revolution; from that time on the aristocracy was on the political defensive. A similar change occurred in the east only after the 1860s. In the meantime, Russian nobles had gained new local powers prior to 1800; Prussian Junkers won some new privileges and lost others; and Hungarian nobles made a major political breakthrough as late as the 1860s.

The new economic activities of the aristocracy took two forms. There was an effort to increase the traditional burdens on the peasantry; here was an obvious means of counteracting price rises. French nobles often tried to raise feudal dues during the eighteenth century. The *obruk,* or feudal tax, was increased in Russia after 1760.

A minority of nobles also engaged in new economic practices. The innovations of British landlords were part of this effort. East European aristocrats tried to increase exportable production. During the Napoleonic continental system, when western agriculture was disrupted, this effort grew. Some estates also introduced manufacturing, particularly by peasants in the home. A minority of Russian aristocrats developed such systems extensively and even encouraged their peasants to act as merchants. Most nobles remained bound by economic routine and a distaste for commercialism; but there were enough exceptions to provide some new vitality.

Finally, nobles in many areas tried to improve their social position. Russian aristocrats induced the state to reduce the privileges of middle-class entrepreneurs. In France accessions to the aristocracy from below, previously common, were virtually eliminated after 1750. Even British nobles tried to draw away from the middle class. By the end of the century London musical activities, for example, were increasingly an aristocratic preserve, whereas previously they had been open to the middle class as well.

In various ways, then, the aristocracy was becoming more active during the eighteenth century. The movement was general. Nevertheless, there was a growing gap between western nobles and those of the east and south. The eastern aristocracy faced no real challenges in 1800. Western nobles were on the defensive politically and to an extent economically. The class maintained important strength, but its relative power was declining, and to perpetuate it, many aristocrats had to engage in increasingly novel practices. In the east absolute gains were achieved well into the nineteenth century.

East and West

Feudalism was dead in western Europe. It had long been less vital in the west than in the east, and the French revolution had completed its destruction not only in France but also in the adjacent parts of Italy and Germany and in the Low Countries. The aristocratic economy could no longer be based on the receipt of feudal dues and services. Increasingly aristocrats lived largely on ordinary rents from their land. And with the notable exception of England they controlled less land than was the case in the east and south. Those aristocrats who retained land therefore had to modernize their methods. They had to find and encourage tenants who would innovate. They depended on wage labor instead of work service. All this could be done successfully, as in England, but it required new thinking.

At the same time many western aristocrats lost all ties with the land. Some depended on careers in government for their whole livelihood. Some entered commerce and industry. Nobles in France and England directed several mining ventures, for example. Again, novelty was essential. In eastern Europe manufacturing was often newly installed or extended; but there it was part of the estate system and commonly used servile labor. In the west a more complete economic reorientation was needed.

Political changes reinforced these developments. In the west the aristocracy could no longer rely on exclusive privilege to bolster its position. The abolition of feudalism meant the abolition of many, though not all, local political powers. In the central governments, leading positions were open to the middle class as well as to the nobility. In politics, as in the economy, the western aristocracy was forced to develop new flexibility and even new values and was thrown into increasing contact with the rising middle class.

In the east and south a feudal economy and legal privileges remained the basis for the aristocracy. To be sure, certain changes were apparent even here. In East Prussia it was legal, after 1807, for peasants to leave the land; and soon thereafter the government allowed them to redeem their land from feudal dues. These changes were important, but they caused no fundamental alteration of aristocratic structure or attitudes. The Junkers managed to have the new local administrative districts coincide with the boundaries of their own estates, so they lost no local political power. They improved their economic position by expanding their estates, but, unlike the English case, this involved no extensive changes in agricultural methods and economic attitudes. Similarly, the legal ability of peasants to escape feudalism in practice simply solidified the Junkers' control. Peasants might avoid their feudal dues only by turning one third of their land over to their lord. Few of them could afford to do this, and most peasants remained serfs until the 1850s; and those few who did redeem their land contributed to the expansion of Junker estates. In other parts of eastern Europe and in the south changes in the feudal structure were even less important, and obligations could often be increased. Four years before the French revolution Russian aristocrats gained the power to buy and sell serfs and to inflict any punishment on them except the death penalty. Nowhere was the gap between the two regions more obvious.

The divergence was clear. Aristocrats in the west were required to adapt to new political and economic systems several decades before their eastern counterparts. Yet they had less landed and political power to begin with. East and west were marked off increasingly not only by the date of new pressures on the aristocracy, but also by the different potential for resistance.

THE PEASANTRY

Almost everywhere peasant society in 1800 was highly traditional and closed to most outside contacts. Peasant agriculture expressed this self-sufficiency and traditionalism, and the same features characterized most other aspects of life. The units of peasant society were local; there was tremendous diversity of custom even in a given country. Yet similarities in basic values allow much common treatment of the whole class. At the same time major regional variations must be described, particularly in the economic and political framework in which peasants lived. In the west, important distinctions, coinciding largely with variations in land tenure, must be drawn within the class. Finally, description of peasant traditionalism must not becloud important changes taking place during the period. Some peasants sought change; many more found it imposed on them. Movements within peasant society prepared for further change, even industrialization itself, in the following century; for, given the numerical mass of the peasantry, no social upheaval could occur without some basis in this class.

Peasant Tradition

The foundation of peasant society was family and village. Everywhere these structures, or the recent memory of them, persisted. They long antedated any feudal impositions. In the west, where aristocratic power was limited, their expression was clearer and less qualified. But even in the east and south these basic institutions coexisted with feudal obligations; and they were to outlive feudalism in the nineteenth century. In 1800 they constituted the essence of peasant life.

Family and village were not formal structures alone but were expressions of the crucial values of the peasantry. Perpetuation of the family through marriage and children was one of the main goals of peasant life. The family was, typically, patriarchally controlled. Women were allowed only indirect voice in family affairs, although older women often played a great role. The head of the family determined economic policy and assigned tasks in the fields and in any other forms of production. Work was done in family groups. While the man pushed the plow, wife and children planted. Peasant weavers used wife or children to prepare their warp. Economic rewards were also distributed by the family. For example, if a younger son did some work as a home weaver, he was expected to turn his pay over to the head of the family for allocation. In return, the family tried to protect all its members. It supported, as well as it could, its aged and ill. It was an extensive unit; not only parents and children but also grandchildren, brothers, and sisters were expected to assist each other and were commonly subject to some guidance by the head of the family. This extended family was a social as well as an economic grouping. Marriages were arranged by heads of families. Holidays were celebrated by family gatherings and feasts. Knowledge was transmitted within the family from parents and grandparents to children.

Above the family stood the village, a collection of several extended families who were themselves often closely related. Varying in population, but nowhere composed of more than a few hundred people, villages served a large number of functions. They were, of course, residential groupings. Only in a few regions did peasants live on isolated farms. Their houses clustered in a village, and their fields spread around it. The village was an economic unit producing most of the goods the peasants required. The village itself directly organized much economic activity. Many villages, as in Britain before 1750, appointed shepherds and cowherds, decided what crops to plant, and governed the use of the commons. Villages also often settled land disputes among their members. After 1861 the Russian central government even used villages as units of government responsible for approving sales of land. Although this is an extreme case, clearly the village served in many ways as an important governing unit.

Further, villages usually had a definite governing structure. In some cases villages actually met to make major decisions; in Britain before 1750 a three-quarters majority was required to determine what crops should be planted. Russian villages in the late nineteenth century had village assemblies composed of all heads of families, which in turn elected elders as officers. Elsewhere leadership was sometimes less formal, composed of older males, often those with relatively large plots of land. In any case, the village was capable of exercising definite direction over its members and at the same time operated on the basis of some consensus.

The communal tone of village life extended to recreation. Festivals, religious celebrations, and even marriage involved the whole village. Typically, although specific customs varied, village participation in weddings extended to a celebration around the house of a newly wed couple in some form of charivari.

Few peasants had much experience beyond the village. There were traders and fairs, which provided entertainment and news as well as goods, but both were infrequent. Further, the peasant distrusted towns and wandering traders as much as he enjoyed them. Both represented forces outside the village and so could not be fully understood. Similarly, in 1800, agents of the central government reached the peasants only infrequently in the form of tax collectors, recruiters, and rural police. They were known and often disliked, but they were not a regular part of peasant horizons. Even the church affected the peasant primarily by reinforcing localism. The church was a village church, the priest usually a peasant from the region and possessed of little education.

In this situation a peasant's first loyalty was inevitably given to his immediate area. Even dialects and costumes were fairly local, although both extended well beyond a single village. Peasants had little interest in national politics. Their political focus was on the village and local aristocracy; in larger terms they were apolitical. Well into the nineteenth century peasants had no demonstrable interest in matters such as civil liberties or governmental structure. There was, generally, a traditional loyalty to the king as protector of his people. Even when peasants rose in protest, as in France in 1789 and in Russia as late as 1905, they would commonly express their affection for the king and blame his advisers for any wrongs. Such risings were over economic grievances rather than political ones, and when land reforms were granted, as in France by 1793, the peasants lost interest in further revolution. Political revolts by urban elements were commonly ignored by the peasants, as in the French revolution of 1830 or the Neapolitan rising of 1820. In these and other cases the issues involved were irrelevant to the peasantry. Similarly, peasants had little active concern for other areas and peoples. There might be some traditional hostility to invaders; Balkan peasants, for example, often disciplined their children by threatening to call in a Turk. From Alsace east the Jew was known and disliked as an outsider and a moneylender. But aside from a few highly traditional general views, the peasant found his standards and goals within his immediate surroundings.

Peasant localism strengthened, and was strengthened by, a pervasive traditionalism. The decisions made by village or family about economic or social matters were based primarily on local custom. The peasant's reliance on custom was quite natural. It expressed his isolation from other groups and regions and his need to rely on oral sources of knowledge. Peasants were predominantly illiterate. In 1800 only 11 per cent of the peasants of one Irish county could read at all; in France during the Restoration, less than 30 per cent could read. In such circumstances knowledge came not from schools or books but from what older people in the family and village taught. One of the bases, in fact, for the importance of elders in peasant life was their ability to obtain more folk wisdom and experience by their very age. Peasant knowledge was thus primarily a matter of traditional beliefs and practices orally transmitted. Aspects of the tradition were ancient indeed. Certain pagan rites and superstitions persisted everywhere. Old medical lore was carried on. Invasions, plagues, and revolts from previous centuries might be remembered as yesterday because they were carried on as part of a living tradition.

Ceremonies of marriage and burial involved an elaborate ritual, varying of course from region to region, but always grounded in tradition. In parts of Ireland in 1830 a bride was supposed to flee with the best man on a horse; the groom would ride after and seize his prize. Elaborate precautions were taken against the presence of witches, who might produce a childless marriage by their spells.

Ceremonies existed to cure barrenness and disease. Pregnant women sometimes took mud from long ditches called "Priests' Beds" to avoid a painful labor. Various omens were taken to indicate good or bad luck in ventures such as marriage. Many ritualistic precautions were developed to protect new-born infants against bad fortune and evil spirits; often they intermingled Christian and pagan practices. No general statement can cover the huge variety of peasant rituals; but these rituals entered deeply into the life of the class.

Another vital feature of peasant tradition was an ambiguous view of social hierarchy. There were strains of egalitarianism which could crop up against rich peasants. More commonly, in time of bad harvest or other hardship peasants might rise against the outside rich, the landlords and merchants. In all this there was at least a sense of natural justice, an idea that customary economic levels and practices should be maintained without change. Grievances would then be expressed in action against the presumed agents of change. Peasants were not always ready to protest unusual hardship. There was a great deal of traditional resignation, and much bitter poverty was normal. Risings were difficult to organize for a localized, illiterate group. Nevertheless, risings did occur in the eighteenth century and continued through much of the nineteenth. They ranged from attacks on food merchants during famines to larger campaigns against the property and records of landlords. The former were most common in France until 1789, for conditions were good for many peasant owners. Pugachev's great rebellion of 1773–1775 in Russia was an extreme case of a larger rising.

On the other hand, unless impelled by unusual distress, peasants were content to regard local nobles and notables as natural leaders in the world outside the village. Many serfs recognized that it would be inappropriate for their masters to do certain kinds of work. Several times in the nineteenth century Polish peasants were mobilized by their lords against Russian rule; Spanish priests played a somewhat similar role in resistance to French invasion after 1808. In two years of crisis, 1848 and 1871, French peasants given the vote elected local notables to represent them in the National Assembly. It is clear from these instances and others that peasants viewed society primarily in traditional and hierarchical terms. The hierarchy was vital for providing some intermediary between the village and larger society, of which the peasant was barely conscious.

Peasant Stability

Peasant social structures and traditions were designed above all to provide stability. Minimal material protection was assured everyone. A few villages tried to enforce economic equality. Egalitarian villages existed in the Pyrenees, while others were developed in Russia at least after 1861. More commonly, gradations in land ownership were accepted. Intermarriage took place between families of comparable landed standing. Wealthier peasants usually guided village government. As we shall see, the extremes of peasant hierarchy could be significant. But there were some limits. Most important, everyone was supposed to have some land of his own. The village could protect a few landless with jobs in shepherding and space on common lands, but most members of the village had at least a garden plot. In regions where there was little fertile land, as in mountainous areas, village links were relatively loose. Peasants had to wander as agricultural or military laborers; they could not retain a purely village focus. The village system depended on some material stability; this in turn depended on land.

Nowhere was the stress on stability clearer than in peasant marriage patterns. Marriage was contracted by mature members of a family, not left to adolescent whim. It was designed to benefit all parties. The husband contributed his land, the wife a dowry to help establish the family on sound footing. Furthermore, peasants, particularly men, delayed marriage until relatively late in their lives. In many areas the average male did not marry until he was twenty-six, the average woman not until twenty-two. This delay allowed the man's parents to benefit from his mature labor for several years and allowed the man sufficient time to earn or inherit land of his own. The establishment of all families on a secure economic footing was thus encouraged. On a larger scale, the late marriage age served as a prudential restraint on the number of children in the subsequent family by restricting the childbearing years within a marriage. Families and the whole village were thereby less exposed to the danger of having more children than the available land could support. In some individual cases unwanted babies were left to die of exposure. On the other hand, when war or plague reduced village populations, marriages could take place at an earlier age and more children would be born. Again, what was sought was a stable relationship between the people and the land within the village. Individual families attempted, by controlling their birth rate, to stabilize the size of their holdings and their resulting social position not only for themselves but also for their progeny.

Peasants in some areas had more to safeguard than those in others. Regions of individual holdings, most notably France, saw greater efforts to impose restraints on births than did areas of large estates, where peasants had far less to protect. Landless peasants, or peasants who relied more on domestic manufacturing than on land, could marry earlier than their landed fellows. In the former case there was no land to protect; in the latter resources existed that freed the peasant from dependence on a rather static amount of land. On the whole, however, peasants did have a holding and tried to protect it against undue demands. It gave them economic livelihood and a clear place in village society.

Tradition and a secure communal society represented the framework of peasant life within which the peasant sought his material and emotional satisfactions. Material levels were low, although they varied greatly with the fertility of the region and the landed possessions of the individual peasant. Even in a rich agricultural country like France many peasants lived badly. Housing was often mean and small, with earthen floors, inadequate light and air, and crude construction from clay or logs. Animals frequently shared the small space. Diseases such as tuberculosis were widespread. Clothing was crude, of rough wool or linen, and it lacked variety. Many peasants went barefoot, or at most had a pair of wooden shoes. Food was typically simple. For some peasants meat and drink, aside from water, were rarities, and the basic fare was a coarse black bread or the potato. Many peasants in fact starved; in Ireland it was estimated that a quarter of the population starved to some extent every year. Conditions of work were generally hard. Hours were long in the growing season, and the work for the whole family was manual and strenuous. In the winter more repose might be possible; many poor peasants almost hibernated to avoid irreparable drain on their energies. In other cases domestic manufacturing, such as weaving, might fill the winter months with long and arduous labor.

For peasants with adequate land conditions were, of course, considerably better. Work was still hard, for few peasants could afford outside help except perhaps at harvest time. Housing, clothes, and food were simple. But houses were more solidly built, clothing a bit more varied; many peasants possessed an elaborate costume for celebrations. Food, especially, was more abundant. The wealthier peasants ate meat and milk products at least once a week, had wine or beer to drink, and used a higher quality starch as a staple. Bad harvests might still bring real deprivation, but in normal times some modest comfort was possible.

Even the poorest peasants found comfort in a number of emotional and recreational outlets. The limitations of peasant horizons and the rigor of material existence had some compensation in religious and other celebrations. Peasants in most areas, particularly in the Catholic and Orthodox countries, took fairly frequent holidays. Local saints' days, general religious holidays, traditional festivals such as May Day, as well as events like weddings and funerals, provided many occasions for celebration. Relatively rich foods were served. Drink was abundant and often potent especially in the northern countries, where fermented grains were produced. Dancing and a variety of games completed the entertainment.

Religion was another regular part of peasant life. Only a very few areas, particularly in France, are known to have been de-Christianized by 1800. Christian doctrine gave hope for a brighter future to people for whom life was in many ways bleak. It could help explain tragedies such as the frequent deaths of infants or a failure of crops. Traditional rituals offered diversion and solace. On occasion peasants were capable of intense religious emotionalism. In the 1820s, for example, the French Church held a number of meetings throughout the countryside; the vigorous exhortations met with truly fervent response. For some peasants at some times religion could provide exaltation. For most it provided regular comfort and ceremony.

The material and psychological pressures of village life required other outlets for a few peasants. Rates of insanity may have been high in some cases, but precise statistics are not known. More definitely, violence was relatively frequent. Rates of murder and other crimes against persons were regularly higher in the countryside than in the city. Property, protected by village traditions, was less subject to attack except in outright riots. But in regions of increasing poverty, such as England during the enclosure movement, acts of banditry increased. Only a minority of peasants were involved in activities of this sort, but the activities could express some of the real constraints in peasant life. For peasant society was in many ways inflexible. Its localism and communality could protect but could also stultify. Its social relationships could prove too rigid, if not for most peasants at least for a minority. Most important, its traditionalism could prove inadequate to cope with outside forces.

East and West

Two important qualifications must be made to the real, if quite general, framework of peasant life. First, there were major regional differences. Second, there were increasing pressures on peasant traditions, varying in part by region.

Western peasants differed from eastern and southern ones in several major respects at the end of the century. Their material standards were higher. They had fewer feudal dues and work obligations and none at all in most cases after about 1793. Some worked as tenants or sharecroppers, but most had at least a small plot. The peasant could buy and sell land; he could leave the land.

In contrast, eastern peasants were not only poorer but also far less free. In Russia they could not sell their land and could not leave it without the lord's permission. Courts of law and local administration were dominated by nobles even where feudalism was modified during the Napoleonic period, as in East Prussia and Spain. But overriding all else were the economic impositions of feudalism. Work service in Russia could take the whole labor of the peasant. More commonly, even in Russia, where most peasants worked on state rather than noble land, work service took several days out of the year. Yearly payments were owed in money and in kind. In southern Italy and Spain, where sharecropping was spreading, this could involve surrender of half the annual crop. Dues were also levied for the obligatory use of the lord's grain mill and other services. These various fees could again consume half the peasant's own production. Finally, in the few cases in which feudalism was formally abolished in the east around 1800, semiservile conditions remained. After 1807 peasants could technically free themselves in

East Prussia; but those who did gain freedom often had so little land left after giving up a third of it in compensation, that they had to work as estate laborers at miserable wages. Landlords in Estonia similarly freed their serfs without land between 1816 and 1819. Again an impoverished labor force was the result.

The hardship of peasant life in the east and the often increasing feudal demands resulted in a number of major riots around 1800. There were several hundred small risings in Russia in the 1790s. A rising tide of agitation began in southern Italy after 1810. But in no case did protest prove successful in the large-estate areas; the forces of repression were too strong. Only in Serbia did an essentially peasant rising succeed, in 1804–1806, under the leadership of the merchant Kara George. But there peasants were smallholders by tradition and were protesting efforts to introduce feudal obligations for the first time.

Western peasants, in contrast, were able to rise successfully against their lighter obligations in several cases, notably France in 1789. Their greater wealth made their pressure more substantial. Aristocratic opposition was less firm. Also, the peasants themselves were more enlightened. There was a minority of literate peasants. More peasants produced something for the market and had greater contacts with the outside world. This fact produced its own discontents, but it stimulated further change. Western peasants remained tradition-bound in 1800. But their horizons were less limited and their economic and political freedom far greater than those of their eastern counterparts.

At the same time, partly because of their greater freedom, there were distinctions within the western peasantry that did not exist in the east. In most villages there was a definite gap between peasants with twenty-five to fifty acres and those with less than five. The latter served as labor for the rich peasants and were often brutally exploited. Wealthy peasants had more contacts with outside markets; some, as in Bavaria, even left the village for some formal education. The substantial peasants intermarried among themselves or with rural or even urban artisans. Here was significant stratification. Seldom had it entirely broken peasant tradition or village structure, but everywhere in the west it was increasing. During the nineteenth century it was to divide the peasantry clearly.

Pressures for Change

Peasant life was faced with a number of novel pressures in the eighteenth century, even before the French revolution. New aristocratic demands, particularly in the east, altered conditions. In the west and even in southern Italy members of the middle class gained increasing control over aspects of peasant economy. This came through direct land purchases and attempts to improve the profitability of new estates. It also came through efforts of millers and other merchants to control peasant production and of manufacturers to use peasant domestic labor. Some peasants could profit by contacts with middle-class economy, but there was great resentment at presumed exploitation as well. During the French revolution many peasants were to express their distrust of mercantile methods. Finally and most generally, the beginnings of population growth already put great strain on village systems. In most cases the full effect of these pressures came only in the nineteenth century, but certain lines of change were already clear.

In Britain the enclosure movement was destroying many village systems of agriculture. A few peasants were able to become tenants and managers on the newly expanded estates and so advanced into a sort of rural middle class. But far more lost their small holdings and commons through enclosure. At the same time massive population growth was creating many peasants born without land in the first place. Landless peasants generally sought work on estates as paid labor. Their standards of living fell drastically, for the need for labor did not keep pace with supply. Far less meat and cheese was consumed, for example, as more and more peasants dropped to near subsistence levels. Many, in fact, depended on poor relief for survival.

Nowhere on the continent were changes so great in 1800. Population growth was significant, but had not yet reached crisis proportions. But in western Europe, particularly France, there was an excess population that could not be incorporated in village systems. Begging increased. Domestic manufacturing spread widely in the countryside among landless or near landless peasants. Even within the villages some peasants tried to take advantage of new market opportunities by buying out poorer peasants and even by dividing commons land. There was a beginning of adaptation to market production, but innovation remained halting.

In eastern Europe changes were perhaps less important. The aristocracy did increase its hold over the peasantry in several areas. There was a growth of domestic manufacturing, although not to the levels of the west. By 1820 there were several hundred thousand home producers in Russia, mainly in textiles. And there were many efforts to improve peasant productivity in agriculture. All of this altered conditions notably; often peasant discontent increased. But the more radical challenge to rural traditions was still to come.

THE CITIES

Urban society was more recent in origin than rural, but it too had a long history in Europe. The cities themselves were old. Their systems of government as well as many of their physical facilities had been established centuries before. The two principal urban classes, the bourgeoisie and the artisans, had both originated in the middle ages. Both classes had been renewed and added to since that time, but many of the institutions and values of the classes were extremely traditional. However, the cities were not closed to innovation. Social structures could not be totally rigid; the very physical proximity of a large number of people of varying positions caused a certain tension. The cities themselves were expanding in the century and a half before 1800, although at a relatively slow rate. The wealth of cities was also increasing, for cities were based primarily on trade, and western Europe expanded its trade radically in the seventeenth and eighteenth centuries. The concentration of intellectuals in some of the larger cities created another sort of ferment in the same period. Finally, the leading urban class was usually mobile in the preindustrial period. The middle class in western Europe was based on wealth, primarily nonlanded wealth. Though by no means totally venturesome, the class as a whole did tend to try to expand its wealth to improve its social as well as its economic position. As its wealth grew, the middle class tended to press for equivalent changes in its social and political structure. Despite important traditional features, then, the cities were sources of considerable dynamism in the preindustrial period. From the cities, in fact, issued many of the innovations that created a radically new social and economic climate by about 1800.

The urban map of Europe at the end of the eighteenth century was rather complex. Cities scarcely existed in eastern and southeastern Europe. There were a few centers, sometimes rather new, such as St. Petersburg. Some commercial activity took place in these cities, but the level was low. The few major cities of eastern Europe existed primarily as political and administrative centers. Cities that lacked these functions were of little importance; Athens, for example, had dwindled to a population of only a few thousand under Turkish rule. Correspondingly, the urban classes of eastern Europe were both tiny and weak. Commercial middle classes and artisans scarcely existed; much of the scanty trade that did go on was in the hands of foreigners. There was a bureaucratic middle class in Russia, but it was tiny and lacked independence. In terms of social structure cities were unimportant in these areas. Along with the distinctive features of rural classes, the effective absence of cities was one of the basic elements of eastern European society.

In western Europe important cities did exist. Urban population in Scandinavia and Spain, at the extremities, was less than 10 per cent of the whole, but significant commercial and artisan classes were present. In France, the Low Countries, and Britain about 20 per cent of the population lived in cities. It was in those areas that cities had been expanding in size and wealth. Even in western Europe, however, most individual cities were small. There were a few giant centers; Paris had a population of 700,000 in 1814—one sixth of the urban population in the country as a whole. The rest was scattered in smaller cities. Only Lyons had more than 100,000 inhabitants. A few other centers approached this figure, but far more had populations of only 5,000 or 10,000. The largest cotton manufacturing city in France, Rouen, had fewer than 80,000 residents in 1815; vital regional commercial and administrative centers such as Toulouse had fewer than 50,000. In France and elsewhere the average city was modest in size, and such cities were widely scattered over the country as a whole.

The physical organization of the city reflected its size. Cities were compact. Traditions of crowding together for defense and ease of building remained. Many cities still tried to live within defensive walls, even as they expanded. Paris undertook a new wall early in the nineteenth century. Streets were small and narrow. Houses were also narrow and were often attached in rows. Crowding pushed members of different social classes into close proximity. Many houses were divided into apartments, with wealthy burghers occupying the lower floors and poorer artisans the upper. A large city such as London did have residential areas more clearly separated by wealth and profession, but even there important residential mixing occurred.

City governments generally undertook only limited functions before the industrial revolution. Many were still controlled by aristocrats and churchmen. In England regulation of hygiene and trade scarcely existed. Police forces were rudimentary, fire prevention and transportation left entirely to private hands. On the continent, however, central governments took an increasing role in city life in the eighteenth century. They undertook some housing regulation and fire prevention. More streets were paved, more sewers covered. Police forces spread even to small towns.

Even on the continent the dangers and difficulties of urban life were numerous. Crime and violence were common. Disease was widespread and epidemics frequent. In fact, almost every city before 1800 experienced more deaths than births in a given year; population was maintained or increased only by immigration from the outside.

The economies of most cities were as simple as their physical facilities. Local trade and artisan manufacturing were the economic bases of the typical urban center. Small shops sold foods, clothing, tools, and various luxury items to residents of the city and surrounding region. Products were commonly manufactured and sold in the same shop. Even so, few people were employed in a given shop because the operation was on a very small scale. Only a few enterprises reached out for more than local sales. Major cities like Paris produced some luxury goods for sale all over the world. Some other centers had a specialized production destined for wide sale. Lyons exported much of its silk production; on a more modest basis, Thiers sent cutlery all over France. Even in these cities the units of production involved only a few workers. But above these units, large merchants exercised important control, bringing in raw materials and arranging for the sale of the products.

Increasingly, cities became centers of a widespread system of rural textile manufacturing as well. Large merchants again brought in raw materials, but in these cases sent them out to peasant homes all over the surrounding region. Mulhouse entrepreneurs in the eighteenth century spread spinning and weaving into the valleys of the Vosges mountains; Paris merchants used workers as far away as Picardy. Foremen served as middlemen, allocating raw materials and collecting cloth. Only a few finishing operations took place in the city; but the city was the economic center of the industry, and to the city flowed the profits. Only in a minority of cities did merchants engage in extensive putting-out production; only the most dynamic centers manufactured more than could be sold close to home. Most entrepreneurs and workers alike were involved in small operations in which neither complex tools nor complex business organizations were needed. For every far-flung export concern there were hundreds of tiny shops relying on the manual skills of one or two workers and the simplest of business and accounting procedures.

Urban Society: The "Dangerous Class"

At the bottom of the urban social and economic scale a class of occasional, largely unskilled labor existed in every city. The group was largest in big cities, ranging up to 20 per cent of the population. In areas of western Europe where population pressure drove increasing numbers into cities, the group was growing rapidly. Yet it is a hard group to describe. Though vital to urban economy, it was not a stable part of it. It had no defined place in city social structure.

The unskilled workers did digging and hauling in construction work and carried goods within the city. Both forms of work were ill paid; neither offered secure employment. Construction work was seasonal, and the amount of it varied from year to year. Transportation labor was usually hired on a day-to-day basis and depended on the needs of the moment. Frequent unemployment as well as bad pay led to low material standards. Clothing was often ragged, food poor, housing crowded and mean. Workers in this group often depended on charity. Many drifted from city to city or back and forth from the countryside as need and opportunity arose. Most of the less skilled stone masons in Paris came, often seasonally, from the Limousin area; in fact, the process of rough-walling was known as *limousinage*. Peasants from the infertile region of Auvergne also came regularly into Paris seeking work.

The transience of some elements of the unskilled laboring population, combined with often intense poverty, hampered the development of firm social structures within the class. Family life was sometimes limited. Transients usually could not bring their families with them to the city; hence many informal unions were contracted. Poverty forced children to earn their own living outside the home at an early age.

On a broader scale, the group lacked lasting structures common to unskilled labor as a whole. These workers were too poor to afford funds for any endeavor or to take time off from seeking a living to participate in organizational activity. They had no clear notion of the possibility of improving their lot. They had no social standing in the city and certainly no political rights. Some of the transients, of course, did not regard the city as their real home. More generally, what little extra time and resource the laborers might have were devoted to personal pleasures, such as drinking, rather than to any large effort. Hence, although this group was the most deprived element of urban life, it was normally incapable of collective protest. Misery and discontent were expressed in personal ways designed to aid in the difficult task of surviving. Begging and sometimes stealing were the recourse of the most destitute, and both were common in the cities of the time. Occasionally unskilled labor might join in a riot. But seldom did they start one and never could they sustain one. Such activities required resources, organization, and a sense of purpose in society—none of which the laborers possessed. The group remained isolated and disorganized in the city, vital to the city's economic life but largely ignored by other urban elements.

Servants

Few middle-class or aristocratic households in the cities lacked at least one servant, so the servant class made up as much as 20 per cent of the urban population. In Elbeuf approximately 250 members of the middle class employed 194 servants in 1785. Generally, servants were housed and boarded by their masters. The conditions provided were often meager, and few servants received much income beyond their board and room and some handed-down clothes. Many servants did have a certain security of position, however, including care during old age. And with their basic needs provided for, some were able to save. Many servants also participated in social activities, such as church attendance, organized by the household.

Among the more affluent and secure members of the group attachment to a substantial family undoubtedly created a feeling of personal importance. Leading servants could express their position in distinctive costumes. Habits of the upper classes, such as the ability to read, could be imitated. At certain levels, then, a sense of secure status combined with dependence on the upper classes and physical separation into individual households to produce a feeling of distinction from other groups in the city. The more menial servants, often women, might live in conditions resembling those of unskilled labor; certainly they could have no clear sense of special status. However, the peculiar conditions and attitudes of the servants in general did set them apart in important ways from other elements of the urban masses.

Artisans

The largest class in the city was the artisan class. A distinctive economic position and distinctive social organizations and attitudes defined the class. On the basis of their activities and attitudes, as well as their numbers, artisans played a far more articulate and important role in city life than did servants or laborers

The foundation of the artisan's position was the possession of a definite and traditional economic skill. Artisans made lace and embroidered cloth. They wove and finished cloth, particularly expensive cloth like silk with luxurious patterns. They worked as tailors, printers, bakers, and butchers. They were the leading construction workers in the city, carpenters, painters, roofers, and masons. They made furniture; they made tools and other metal objects. In other words, they were the basic labor force for the urban economy, manufacturing most of the products required locally and some important items for more distant markets as well. Their methods of work were largely traditional. They worked with simple tools, lacking elaborate mechanical contrivances. They worked at home or in small shops, usually with no more than five other craftsmen. There was little division of labor in the artisan's work. A few young workers, particularly apprentices, often served relatively menial functions. They carried raw materials and finished products, swept the shop, and assisted in some of the more difficult procedures of the artisan himself. Aside from this, the artisan typically carried his operation through by himself, from preparing the materials for production to taking care of the tools. The complexity of the operation and the simplicity of the equipment meant that real skill was required. Artisans invariably underwent an important period of training, usually in a formal apprenticeship program. Even relatively simple jobs, such as lace making, required at least a year of apprenticeship, and more complex trades involved up to seven years of training.

Artisanal work was, of course, conducted in the countryside as well as in the city. Many peasant villages had long supported at least part-time artisans. Large estates in eastern Europe generally depended on some specialists. And the spread of rural manufacturing in both the west and the east created hundreds of thousands of rural manufacturing workers who, like artisans, labored in their homes with simple equipment and skill sufficient to require some training.

Rural artisans were not exactly peasants, although they often did some agricultural work. They often earned more. They were more often literate. Their consumption habits were frequently more urban than rural. And yet they cannot be fully assimilated to the urban artisanal class; they were rather a subgroup of the peasantry. And it was only in the west that there was a substantial and well-established urban artisan group.

Urban artisans differed from rural ones in several respects, and those differences were to be magnified by the early results of industrialization. Rural manufacturers were concentrated in the textile industry. Their level of skill was lower than that of most urban artisans, and their apprenticeship was correspondingly shorter and less formal. Due to the spread of domestic production in the seventeenth and particularly the eighteenth centuries, they were, for the most part, newer to their trade than were the families of urban artisans. Their rural residence made contacts among them difficult, whereas urban artisans lived and worked in close proximity in a given city. Relatedly, rural manufacturers were usually more dependent on a large urban merchant than were most urban artisans. Some rural producers did buy their raw materials themselves and took their own products to market. Many, however, depended on a merchant for supply and sales and were to an important degree simply employes; and the number of these workers increased steadily with time. The type and conditions of work for such home workers were set by the merchant. Urban artisans of some types, particularly those in the textile industry, were faced with similar pressures, but for the most part they still had little direct contact with capitalist merchants. Finally, the leading categories of urban artisans possessed an economic, social, and political structure—the guild—which almost no rural manufacturing workers could match. Further distinctions in behavior and position flowed from this fact, for the guild was at the center of the life of urban artisans.

Artisan guilds existed in most cities before 1789, especially on the continent. Outside of the British Isles guilds retained the legal power to deny a worker the right to practice his trade unless he belonged to the guild. Through this device guilds typically tried to limit the number of workers in a given trade in a city; the guild existed not to maximize production, but to protect the standard of living and the economic opportunity of its members. By limiting the number of workers it tried to assure employment for all. It also tried to limit production so that artisans would receive suitable pay and prices for their work and products. Guilds therefore maintained strict controls over the methods used in work and generally prevented any major innovation in technique. By this means production could be controlled and prices and wages maintained. Further, the value of traditional skills would be upheld. Opportunities for the ambitious and clever might be limited as a result, but such opportunities were irrelevant to the guild's primary goal of protecting the welfare of all its members.

Moreover, important mobility was provided within the structure of many guilds. Artisans were divided into three major categories: apprentices, journeymen, and masters. Artisan tradition, and to some extent continuing practice, held that each artisan should have an opportunity to pass through all three stages during his productive life. The period of apprenticeship was, of course, vital to the artisan's position. Beginning usually in the early teens, the apprenticeship provided training for the job. A fee commonly had to be paid for the privilege of entering apprenticeship, and a stiff contract bound the apprentice to his tasks. On the other hand, tradition and guild supervision attempted to insure fair treatment of the apprentice. The master was required to feed and house the apprentice and train him to the level necessary for full participation in artisan production.

After apprenticeship the artisan typically became a journeyman, working for wages, often supplemented by food and housing provided by the master. Following some years as a journeyman, in which hopefully some savings could be accumulated, opportunity might arise to become a master. This involved ownership of a shop and equipment and often employment of other journeymen. It did not mean that the master became separated from his work, for masters worked beside their employes in most cases. Under guild rules and protection the artisan was provided with a social and economic ladder he could climb as he gained skill and capital.

Guilds offered, then, some economic security and protection of skills. They helped limit the gap between master and journeyman. In addition, they provided some political experience, as guild appointments were made by vote of all the masters. In some cases artisan guilds had a voice in city governments. Certainly the general recognition of guilds by city and even national governments gave the artisan significant contact with politics more generally. Guilds often provided travel experience for the young artisan. Journeymen in many trades often traveled throughout a country for a few years. They obtained social contacts and employment information in each city from the guild in their craft.

Guilds expressed and provided many of the values maintained by artisans well into the industrial period. However, the picture should not be overdrawn. In the first place, not all urban artisans were involved in guilds. Certain populous trades, such as lace making, were never organized in guilds; this was particularly true of work in which women were primarily involved. Even in the masculine crafts certain cities never developed a full range of guilds. On the whole, however, the major artisan professions had a guild tradition and important guild structures still.

More important for these professions were certain changes in the position of guilds, changes that were increasing by the late eighteenth century. In many professions, particularly in England but also elsewhere in western Europe, guilds were breaking down in the eighteenth century. They were no longer able to limit the number of entrants sufficiently to protect artisans against excessive competition. Relatedly, many professions were now too complex and crowded to allow most journeymen to rise to the position of master. In printing, for example, there were far more journeymen than masters by the late eighteenth century. The capital required to buy printing equipment was too great for most journeymen to amass. In printing and some other trades there was a clear separation between master and journeymen due to the master's relative wealth and the journeyman's inability to rise. Often, in fact, journeymen had founded their own organizations to protect their interests as best they could, ignoring the guild, which either declined or became the creatures of the masters alone.

In certain textile operations even more radical changes were occurring. Large merchants were assuming basic control of such industries. Seldom did they modify artisan methods too severely, although technical changes were often introduced. Rarely did they even expand the units of production beyond recognition, but they usually increased the size of shops. The big merchants did, however, remove basic control of conditions from the guilds and the artisans in the cases in which they assumed control. They set the prices at which the artisans would work, and they determined the quality and design of the product. In the Lyons silk industry, for example, large merchants purchased silk thread. They turned this thread over to small shops at an assigned piece rate for a given quantity of cloth. The weaving was actually done by a master weaver who owned his looms and who in turn usually employed one or two journeymen. In this case a capitalist system of trade was imposed over an artisan structure. Many artisan values became irrelevant or unrealizable in the process.

By the end of the eighteenth century, then, many artisans were facing increasing change in the economy and urban society. Not all of these changes were novel; even in the Middle Ages gaps had arisen between masters and journeymen. But certain pressures, such as those from capitalist merchants, were relatively new, and the magnitude of change was unprecedented. Despite the forces of change, however, vital elements of artisan tradition remained valid. Guild structures themselves remained widespread, particularly in areas such as Germany, where new forms of manufacturing were largely unknown. Even in areas where guilds were weakened or even destroyed many artisan economic traditions remained intact. Methods and equipment were not significantly changed for most urban artisans. Only a very few groups, such as cloth printers, were affected by major technical changes, and even those groups continued to be able to apply high levels of skill to their work. Units of production remained small, and contact between journeymen and masters usually remained cordial. Even where artisan production was overlaid by a capitalist element, as in the Lyons silk industry, journeymen still ate and slept in the houses of their immediate employers. In most industries producing largely for local sale, such as construction or baking, control by large merchants was almost nonexistent, and small masters and their journeymen predominated.

Finally, among artisans generally, even where subject to considerable change, many of the values associated with guild tradition remained important. Artisans remained interested in organization among themselves along craft lines. Hence, when guilds were ineffective, masters and journeymen alike frequently founded organizations to defend their economic position. Beyond this, artisans retained an interest in skill as a basis for economic and social well-being. They preserved at least elements of their tradition of limiting the labor force in their craft in the interests of economic security. They continued to feel that they should be treated with respect and even friendliness by their masters and that their masters should regard themselves as coworkers, not just as employers. Artisans in the leading trades valued their own traditions highly and felt that a distinctive social status was, or should be, attached to their position. In the decades that followed 1800 artisans were by no means able to defend all their values in practice. Time and time again, however, the values would be expressed.

Artisan Life

The artisan of 1800 spent most of his waking hours at his job. In years or seasons of peak activity many artisans worked at least twelve hours a day. The job and attitudes relating to the job naturally dominated the artisan's life. Some urban artisans, in fact, had little time or resources to devote to nonproductive activities. Single women doing embroidery in their room, for example, received such low pay that even subsistence was difficult. Only long hours of labor could produce a bare livelihood. Some male artisans in occupations involving little skill, heavy competition, or weak demand also suffered from long hours and low earnings. Journeymen in an overcrowded trade faced frequent periods of unemployment alternating with periods of excessively long hours. In construction work winters of little activity alternated with summers of great pressure even for highly skilled workers.

All artisans, finally, were subject to economic slumps when their services were in little demand and their incomes correspondingly low. Agricultural failures, particularly, could produce disastrous conditions in the towns. Lack of food caused high prices; since the bulk of the artisan's income was spent on food, a rise in food prices affected him severely. With higher food prices all elements of the population curtailed their expenditures on manufactured goods; this in turn meant fewer jobs and lower pay for many artisans. Slumps of this kind were not unusual, and most artisans encountered several in their lifetime. They could survive by restricting their purchases to the barest minimum, by not paying their rent, by pawning some of their furniture or even tools, and by seeking charity. But certainly they could never feel totally secure in their economic position.

Standards of living varied, then, both with the conditions of the year or season and with the position of the artisan's own trade. Some artisans lived and worked in the same room. Their food was poor, and what little they could afford beyond a basic starch was often low in quality or even spoiled. Clothing was also frequently shabby. The position and trade of many artisans could often be determined by their costumes. Peculiarities of health and appearance also distinguished many crafts. Weavers were particularly subject to chest diseases because they pushed their looms with their chests. Chemicals affected the lungs and blood of many painters. The lot of large numbers of artisans was by no means easy.

On the other hand, many masters and even journeymen enjoyed some real comfort in normal times, when their services and products were in steady demand. Many artisans earned enough to vary their diets with meats and vegetables. Many possessed several changes of clothing, usually in a style typical of the artisan class of the region. Many master artisans owned their own homes or rented substantial apartments; their journeymen were accordingly given space and furnishings beyond the bare minimum. Finally, many artisans were able to save. Artisan tradition assumed an ability to save for the purchase of tools and a master's shop. For most artisans savings were irregular and small, and for some they were impossible. But artisans usually sought and often obtained some margin above their subsistence needs that could be used for their advancement.

Apart from wandering journeymen, most artisans attempted to found families and integrate them into their economic lives. Wives were usually expected to work, if possible as assistants in the tasks of the journeymen or the business of the master. Marriages were often contracted with an eye to establishing the artisan with a dowry or a useful connection with a master. Children, too, were customarily brought up to respect the artisan life and to prepare for entrance into their father's trade. Considerable attention was therefore given to their training and education, and the artisan tried to build up sufficient capital to establish his sons as apprentices and to provide his daughters with suitable mates in their own class.

The majority of the urban artisans were literate. Many went to school for at least a few years before entering apprenticeship. Apprenticeship itself typically included some practical arithmetic for measurement and accounting. Guilds and other artisan clubs, particularly in the larger cities, often provided reading matter and opportunities for conversation about the issues of the day. Other entertainments, such as dances and plays, were available to many artisans in the cities. Depending greatly on the position and means of the artisan, numerous possibilities existed for recreation and even learning beyond the craft itself.

Many artisans had definite political interest and knowledge. In the smaller towns politics were usually confined to local issues of guild and urban government. In larger centers, and particularly in capital cities in which craft workers were generally numerous, many artisans had sufficient education and traditional interest to concern themselves with regional and national matters as well. Artisan groups were accustomed to appeal to urban and national governments for protection of the guilds and for assistance in times of hardship. As long as governments seemed to support their position, there was little active political discontent among the artisans. Artisans were seldom concerned with political matters that did not directly affect their position. Loyalty to traditional institutions and rulers was often quite high.

However, artisans were capable of expressing active discontent, particularly in periods of economic collapse. Artisan strikes were not uncommon during the eighteenth century. More common, however, was urban rioting, in which artisans usually took the leading role. Grievances over rising food prices motivated much of the rioting; artisans were more likely to feel abused as consumers than as workers. A general dislike of the wealthy was also involved, and attacks on rich homes were a normal part of riots. Political issues often played a role, particularly when middle-class or even aristocratic agitators helped stir artisan groups. Before the end of the century, however, artisans followed no distinct political line in their protests. They rioted as often for conservative as for radical causes. Only after about 1780 did artisans begin to develop a consistent interest in the rights of man and other radical political ideas, and then only in places like France and Holland. A willingness to riot was clear before this time; a sense of traditional economic justice already existed. But a definite political stance came only in the subsequent period.

In retrospect, artisan life around 1780 seems largely dominated by tradition. Methods of work, social institutions, even political interests were backed by solid custom. This was a group with clear and respectable status. The class was growing in the cities but not yet radically. However, changes were already taking place. Guild structures were declining, west of Germany at least. There was competition in some fields from rural producers, in a few others from machines. The price rise of the eighteenth century had hurt some groups. And some artisans, a politically alert minority, were learning of new political ideas in reading clubs and political associations. By the 1780s a few artisans in France, Britain, and Holland were involved in republican groups. All of this foreshadowed the emergence of artisans as the most revolutionary class in western Europe after 1789.

The Middle Class

The middle class was the least coherent social grouping in Europe both before and after the industrial revolution. Its limits can be fairly clearly defined, particularly in the preindustrial period. Members of the class were wealthier than artisans, but not so rich as aristocratic magnates and much of the gentry, and they lacked noble titles. But within this broad range there was substantial diversity. Even in this brief introduction to preindustrial classes unusual attention must be given to subgroups. Finally, there is the familiar distinctiveness of western Europe to establish. And major currents of change, particularly in the west, must be evoked.

The middle class possessed and managed the bulk of the commercial wealth of the cities. On this basis the class developed a relatively high standard of living and sought social status and political power in the city and the country as a whole. For money was a fundamental index of worth in the eyes of the class. Relatedly, the class respected work; the ideal was a man who actively earned financial success. Those who did not earn were distrusted; one of the most common complaints about the aristocracy was that the class seemed more interested in spending than in amassing wealth. To be sure, elements in the middle class sought other forms of status. There was respect for family ancestry. Many cities were governed by a traditional element of the middle class that was fully as proud of its heritage as of its wealth. And there were constant efforts to imitate the aristocracy by polishing manners and education, entering government service, or buying land. But even these often depended on previous financial success.

In its reliance on wealth, the middle class was open to new membership and improvements in status by the acquisition of new wealth. Established members of the class often frowned on novel economic practices; but they too tried to expand their wealth in the eighteenth century. And even in eastern Europe a number of newcomers tried to rise by entering commerce.

Class Structure

The major distinctions within the middle class naturally rested on differences in wealth; from such differences stemmed important variations in educational level, style of life, and political interest. The class was a large one in the cities, representing up to 20 per cent of the urban population or about 4 or 5 per cent of the total population of western Europe. The class shared certain values, including an esteem for wealth. It had even some sense of the existence of a separate middle class. But within this framework significant social and economic gradations did exist.

The lower levels of the middle class are hard to define in the preindustrial period. Most shopkeepers, for example, were artisan masters. Only in big cities were there a truly independent shopkeeping element. In many small towns artisans had higher status than the few retail shopkeepers. Foremen in the domestic putting-out system, the employes of large merchants who supplied and directed home workers, were also akin to artisans in many ways. They often earned only a little more; they had to know the skills of the craft they directed. Many of these foremen, whose number expanded rapidly as domestic industry grew, were of artisan origins. Finally, many artisan masters, owners of equipment and shops, were frequently entering lower-middle-class status. Masters who increasingly directed their workers as employers and who expanded the size of their operations were on the threshhold at least of entry into the middle class. So there was an embryonic lower middle class in existence, separated from most artisans by earnings, property, and nonmanual labor. The group was clearly growing, but in this period it was still small and indistinct.

Far clearer, though defined more by type of work than by income, was the professional element of the middle class. This was a rapidly growing group. Rising commerce created new needs for doctors and lawyers. Even more, the expanding bureaucracies of most governments provided many new professional jobs. Most notably in Prussia professional bureaucrats easily constituted half of the whole middle class; so this group was not confined to the west. New universities in Prussia and elsewhere increased opportunities for entry into the professions. Almost everywhere this was a major social force.

Certain types of professional work bore high social prestige. Some bureaucratic positions carried an aristocratic title. And professional incomes were often high. Town officials often had great prestige and regular contacts with the aristocracy. This was the case with notaries in France and Italy or university-trained lawyers in Germany and England.

Other professional positions were less secure and prestigious. Lawyers without university training and many doctors might barely eke out a living on the lowest middle-class level. Many bureaucrats had considerable security of employment but not necessarily a high income. Journalists and writers also ranged from precarious subsistence to notable wealth. Some members of the professional group possessed inherited wealth, but many others depended on what they could earn. For the professional element as a whole was characterized by reliance on training and mental ability rather than ownership of commercial property. Despite great variety in position and income, this fact distinguished the group as a whole within the middle class.

The professional group was the only segment of the middle class that regularly received at least secondary education. This was also the only segment that maintained consistently high interest in intellectual and political affairs. A variety of organizations in many cities provided opportunities to discuss political and philosophical problems in western Europe, and lawyers and doctors as well as writers participated extensively in them. It was among these groups that the ideas of the Enlightenment spread during the eighteenth century and that ideas of reform in religious and political matters were current. The secure position and wealth of many professional elements inclined some to conservatism. Nevertheless, professional people were more open to radical ideas than were other elements of the middle classes. They were more attracted by intellectual issues because of their greater education and the association of their work with political and scientific matters.

The large merchant and manufacturer represented the final important segment of the middle class. In any city a significant number of merchants owned enterprises far beyond the level of the little shop. They were the men who ran wholesale operations in food or who controlled some branch of exports or imports, the owners of colonial trading companies, and the directors of domestic manufacturing systems. In most of these businesses it was possible to earn considerably more than a mere shopkeeper did. The wealthiest elements controlled large commercial empires, combining interests in trade, manufacturing, landholding, and banking activities. Standards of living were accordingly high. A large number of servants, extensive purchases of books and artistic objects, possession of a coach and horses, rich dress, and imposing houses set many members of this group apart from their more modest colleagues.

Gradations in wealth were steady, from shopkeeper to merchant prince. There were many newcomers to mercantile activity in the century as commerce rapidly expanded. These people usually began on a small scale. And many had to limit their consumption expenses to buy supplies and equipment. Relatedly, many new merchants were set apart socially by the very recency of their arrival. Older merchants and professionals shunned the newcomers and tried to exclude them from political influence in the city. France and Italy

saw many conflicts over city government between old and new
business groups during the eighteenth century. In many cases the
older group shared ties with the aristocracy, as well as a belief in
the value of distinguished ancestry. Cities such as Orleans were
governed by an old upper-middle class and the aristocracy. In Britain
older merchants joined aristocrats in participation in national politics
to the exclusion of both less wealthy and less traditional middle-
class groups.

Social and political status, education and type of work, as well
as wealth marked the distinctive elements of the middle class. An
upper group had a sense of traditional caste and, locally at least,
maintained some aristocratic characteristics, which could include
possession of landed estates. The professional element had distinctive interests based on education and type of work. Other business elements were graded by amount of wealth.

In the middle class generally, then, there was tremendous variation in length of establishment and sense of status. Housing ranged
from a small apartment to an elegant mansion. Political rights and
interests varied: the traditional upper group had at least local
political voice; the professional group was expanding its political interest; many businessmen had concern for government only insofar
as it affected their economic operations. Variations of this sort were
great in 1789 and would increase subsequently.

Middle-Class Values

Common elements of middle-class attitudes can be described
only with constant recollection of the many internal variations; but
common elements did exist. The class valued material well-being. A
small, upper segment achieved real luxury. More commonly, patterns of consumption retained some simplicity. Few in the class
had huge wealth; until well after industrialization began almost no
merchant could rival the upper aristocracy in spending, so of necessity tastes remained fairly simple in the eighteenth century. Comfort and respectability were sought in clothes and housing. The class
did not deny itself material pleasures.

At the same time there was need to moderate expenses; the class
depended on the accumulation of some capital. Funds were needed
to maintain and perhaps expand a business; they were also essential
to provide dowries and education for children in order to perpetuate

the family standing. Material success was not viewed in terms of comfort alone, but as the establishment of some productive property. This was a possessing class. Only in the professional group did this criterion not entirely fit—a vital distinction for some individual professionals—but even here it was generally applicable.

The ethic of the middle class, which was taught to children, suited the economic goals of the class. Hard work was stressed; and most merchants and professionals did work long hours and trained their wives and children to do the same. Saving was praised. Education, particularly practical training, was valued. Perhaps most basically, family virtues were emphasized. Middle-class life commonly centered around the family and the assurance of its proper status. The family was under firm patriarchal control. Women assumed an inferior position in the home and certainly in any larger society. Children were firmly disciplined. Most of the leisure time of the middle class was spent at home with the family, and in a real sense the economic goals of the class were devoted to the family as well. For it was assumed that children should be supplied with the means to maintain the family's economic and social level; and this was no small task. It involved provision of some education, at least for sons. Marriages were arranged with families of comparable standing. Sons were endowed with a business or a profession, daughters with large enough dowries to encourage suitable marriages. Quite naturally, then, the middle-class ethic stressed family loyalty and discipline.

Beyond work and the family there were some other middle-class interests at the end of the eighteenth century. Religion played an important role for most. Many members of the class were fervently pious; some felt that their economic activities and successes were dedicated to the greater glory of God. Others took a more relaxed view, seeing religious practice as socially pleasant and morally useful. Some members of the class, particularly in France, were receptive to attacks on church corruption and religious superstition. Few actually renounced religious practice, but many sought religious reform that would give greater stress to earthly morality and greater recognition to the social and political position of the middle class.

Finally, the middle class had some political consciousness. This should not be exaggerated. The political sense was usually local above all, for city governments touched the class most closely. For obvious reasons the most general political interests of the class were economic. There was widespread concern for sound economic practice within the government, including defense of property and the honoring of debts owed to commercial groups. The middle class usually sought government economic encouragement in the form of favorable tariff policies, improvements in transportation, removal of traditional restrictions on the free movement of techniques, goods, and labor. As long as governments maintained a suitable economic climate, the middle class was usually content with relatively little direct voice. In eastern Europe the class was too tiny to hope for more. Businessmen in Russia, Prussia, and elsewhere depended on the existing governments for whatever economic gains they might make. Furthermore, a small but important element of the class had or hoped for jobs in expanding government bureaucracies. On the continent government jobs were sought by the middle class as prestigious and potentially lucrative. Nowhere did the class control the highest levels of bureaucracy. But in many areas, notably in Germany, positions of second rank were open to the middle class and were highly valued.

In western Europe, however, the middle class had a mounting belief in its right to regular political participation. This was seen as the only means of assuring proper economic regulations; even businessmen could become restive on this basis. In some places, notably in France, the valued opportunity for government jobs seemed increasingly closed to new men. But beyond all this the western middle class had a certain sense of mission. As wealth and numbers rose in the eighteenth century, the class saw itself as the principal bearer of social virtues. The hard work, thrift, and sober respectability of the class were contrasted with the idle parisitism of the aristocracy. Enlightenment ideas of freedom and equality of opportunity against inherited privilege gained increasing currency.

Various segments of the middle class experienced a new dynamism during the eighteenth century, partly because new men were pushing into the class. There was a new interest in personal and political advancement. New forms of trading and manufacturing were developed. Artisans and even peasants in western Europe were increasingly touched by middle-class economic activities. The wealth of the class grew, and so did its confidence in its own abilities and values.

STATUS SOCIETY

Despite the changes in both rural and urban life toward the end of the eighteenth century, European society was still composed of groups with relatively fixed status. Status society was clearer in eastern than in western Europe, because of the absence of major cities and the firm legal and economic structure of feudalism. But even in western cities a customary framework existed for most social groups and activities. The economic innovations of the middle class had not yet overturned traditional systems of production. New forms of political consciousness had not yet penetrated the whole class. Even in France elements of the middle class were drawn into the revolution of 1789 only by the extraordinary weakness of the government and the clear political lead provided by dissident aristocrats. And before 1789, at least on the Continent, it was nowhere clear that the traditional hierarchy of society was faced with major challenge.

Most basically, this meant that the average individual could expect his social station, economic methods, and general values to be roughly the same as his parents'. Mobility from one class to another did occur on almost all levels, but most people were not involved. More important, there was no challenge yet to the general class structure.

The major social classes possessed fairly definite personal institutions with clear and accepted functions. Family life, though differently based from class to class, was firm. Organizations such as the village or the guild organized larger groups.

Finally, the classes themselves were recognizable and traditional. There was an amorphous lower group in the cities. Changes in balance among classes were occurring in western Europe. But there was no major disruption yet. Most people knew the group to which they belonged and had some sense of where this group fit in relation to other relevant segments of society. Many of the main lines of status were recognized in law. Artisans and some bourgeois as well as aristocrats had certain privileges that could not be touched by other groups. In parts of Germany even substantial peasants had rights not granted to the near landless.

Few groups professed active interest in changing the boundary lines. Even the middle class had profoundly traditionalist elements who had a fixed position and wished only to maintain it. Most discontent could be alleviated by imitation of or even entry into another class. Middle-class aspirations were still commonly fulfilled by purchases of land or efforts to intermarry with the aristocracy. Even in this way the recognition of a clear basic social structure was expressed.

In 1800 it was easy to tell a man's status by the clothes he wore. Aristocrats dressed more luxuriously and gaudily than the middle class. Merchants wore knee breeches, artisans long trousers. Artisans of a particular craft dressed distinctively. Peasant homespun, in turn, contrasted with artisan dress. Again, the boundaries of status were fairly clear and traditional.

All of this was going to change. Boundaries would be directly challenged. Balance among traditional classes would change, and totally new groups would arise. Some institutions, such as guilds, would almost disappear. Others, such as villages and families, would weaken and find new demands put upon them. Perhaps most basically, the idea of inherited, legal status would largely disappear. Social classes, including traditional upper groups, would persist, but even they could not rely primarily on birth and law. Wealth, and to a lesser degree political power, were to be the new criteria of social standing. These criteria could never be as clear and fixed as the older idea of status had been.

In western Europe the social upheaval was already brewing in the eighteenth century. Most groups were touched by major, if preliminary, change. But the process was only beginning. Classes and their values were preindustrial still. The character of the nineteenth century was determined not only by tremendous forces of change but also by the elaborate and traditional social structure that these forces encountered.

2
THE FORCES OF CHANGE

A variety of new forces were operating on European society, particularly in the west, by the end of the eighteenth century. In a real sense these forces were to bring about a revolution in social structure. Three related movements were of fundamental importance. All became particularly intense after the middle of the century and all continued and even increased in the nineteenth century, when they began to affect society most profoundly.

THE STATE

The first of these changes was political; it involved a new relationship of government to society. For over a century governments in most European nations had been extending the scope of their operations. They tried to increase their contact with distant sections of their country, curtailing the regional power of aristocrats. Bureaucracies were expanded, and middle-class elements were brought into some of them. Most important, the government began to deal with activities that had previously been left to the control of local and private groups. Many states codified laws on a national basis, establishing clear and presumably rational standards to replace local traditional rules. Governments felt active concern for the economic health of the nation. At the end of the seventeenth century, governments from France to Russia tried to introduce new industries and techniques. Several governments, such as the Prussian, encouraged better agricultural methods; they sponsored drainage projects and supported new products such as the potato. To promote commerce, several states provided clearer standards in currency and in weights and measures; Britain even established a semiofficial national bank. Efforts were made to cut down local tolls and other barriers to a national market. Roads and canals were extended. There were even direct attempts to encourage population growth.

In none of this, however, was there any intention of altering basic class structure. There was some talk of governmental responsibility for the well-being of all subjects. Some rulers increasingly saw their interests as separate from those of the aristocracy and other traditional bodies, such as the national churches; hence non-aristocratic bureaucracies and religious tolerance grew. But above all continental governments wished to develop their economic and military power. This required reforms in military techniques and recruitment. It required an improved economy, particularly in the manufacturing sector. It required greater governmental efficiency in many respects. But this was not a revolutionary purpose. Governments avoided challenging major privileges, especially those of the aristocracy, because such challenges would distract from the cohesion of the state. In eastern Europe nobles were able to increase their power. Governmental action did spur some economic and administrative change, but for an attack on class structure some new impulse was necessary.

This impulse came from the French revolution. From the beginning the revolution was a social one. It involved replacing the old governmental structure and the old ruling class. The revolution pursued many of the interests of other governments in military power and economic improvement; in fact, the revolution occurred partly because the French state had lagged in these matters in the eighteenth century. But in all such issues the revolution brought basic structural reforms.

The government was in the hands of the middle class. By the autumn of 1789 the legal and economic bases of the aristocracy had been attacked. Feudal rights and privileges were destroyed; government service was theoretically open to anyone with the necessary ability. The church was stripped of lands and privileges; religious tolerance was extended. Peasants were relieved of feudal dues. In matters of law and taxation they dealt with government agents instead of local notables. Guilds were abolished, and all combinations of workingmen forbidden. It was now legal for anyone to set up economic operations and to use any methods he desired. In sum, the revolution altered the structure and personnel of government and drew new groups into political consciousness. It attacked the legal basis of the old regime by replacing hereditary and group privilege with equality under the law. It promoted a capitalistic market economy not only in manufacturing but also to a degree in the countryside. Thus, the revolution provided the political basis for the social development of the nineteenth century.

The revolution was not confined to France. Its principles had wide appeal to various groups, and the appeal was to increase in the next generation. In 1793–1794 merchants and artisans agitated in Holland for a revolutionary change, and there was stirring elsewhere in western Europe. In the east, where there was no significant urban element, the revolution had repercussions among other groups. Some peasants in Bohemia, Hungary, and even Russia learned vaguely of the revolution. Some aristocrats in Russia and Poland, chafing under autocracy, were attracted by ideas of the rights of man. Quite generally and for very diverse groups the revolution promoted an idea of change and showed the path that change should take. Invocation of revolutionary principles was basic to most political agitation in the next century.

Furthermore, French armies directly carried the gains of the revolution to many areas adjacent to France. Guilds and feudal privileges were abolished in the Low Countries, western Germany, and northern Italy. Equality under the law was proclaimed, law codes rationalized, the church weakened.

Beyond these areas, monarchist statesmen were impressed by the revolutionary ferment and tried to prevent comparable disorder at home by timely reforms. Even after this the memory of revolution lingered, leading conservative statesmen to sprinkle their repressive measures with some reforms. More important, the military and political efficiency of the revolution appealed to rulers in their own terms. Efforts to rationalize bureaucracy were undertaken in Prussia and Russia; new interest arose in improvements in commerce and agriculture. Not all these changes were effective; some were revoked after the revolution. But a door had been opened to change in every corner of the continent.

POPULATION GROWTH

Europe's population grew tremendously after 1750. Although the movement was related to certain political measures, it affected all classes, particularly those remote from political concern. In the eighteenth century a number of major countries saw their population expand by 50 to 100 per cent, with the greatest growth coming after 1750. The Hapsburg Empire grew from twenty to twenty-seven million; Spain rose from five to ten million and Prussia from three to six million. France increased from twenty to twenty-nine million, Britain from nine to sixteen million. Growth continued throughout the nineteenth century. A few countries, such as Spain, stagnated, but others, such as Italy and the Balkans, only began their major growth after 1870. In Europe as a whole population rose from 188,000,000 in 1800 to 401,000,000 in 1900. This was an increase of truly impressive proportions. Its significance may be measured by comparing the rate of expansion with the 3 per cent increase in Europe's population during the entire century between 1650 and 1750. Clearly, a demographic revolution occurred after 1750.

The expansion of population was European in scope. Certain regions—even whole countries—experienced an unusually rapid rise. Britain and Germany approximately tripled their populations during the nineteenth century after a notable increase in the eighteenth. France barely doubled her population between 1700 and 1900. Obviously, differences in degree must be noted. Distinctions in date are equally important. The demographic boom in western and central Europe was most intense between 1750 and 1850; French population began to rise even in 1680. The factors promoting this boom touched eastern and southern Europe but only in a limited way. There the period after 1850 saw the most significant increase, and the spread of western techniques of midwifery and vaccination played a leading role. By 1900 virtually every area of Europe had contributed to the tremendous surge of population; but each major region was at a different stage of demographic change.

The unprecedented increase in population was the most important feature of demographic change, but it was not the only one. Between 1800 and 1930, Europe sent forty million people to the two Americas, Asiatic Russia, and other areas. Emigration was one of the clearest expressions of the upheaval that increasing population brought to European society. In the first generations of population rise economic opportunities failed to keep pace with the population. Emigration was most intense when population grew most rapidly and tended to decline once industrialization developed sufficiently to absorb most of the increase. Britain and Ireland supplied most of the emigrants in the first part of the century, reflecting the intensity of population pressure in the two islands. The agricultural crisis of midcentury convinced many German peasants that the land could no longer support them, and a wave of German emigration ensued. Eastern and southern Europe provided most emigrants at the end of the century. From 1800 to 1914, seventeen million people emigrated from Britain and Ireland, four million from Austria-Hungary, two and a half million from Russia, and ten million from Italy. Only a few countries, such as France, largely escaped the movement.

Though only a minority of Europeans actually emigrated, the movement affected a far larger number. The wave of emigration greatly increased Europe's influence in the world. It brought new economic opportunities and new knowledge to many Europeans. Equally important, it disrupted many families, many villages, and exposed countless people to contact with new ideas about the possibility of mobility and change. Information and myth about the possibility of emigrating and the nature of life in new lands had significant effects on many villages and towns. They represented one aspect of the change in outlook that population growth brought to European society.

The populations of Europe not only grew in the nineteenth century, but also changed in physical character. Health improved. In 1800 the life expectancy of a Frenchman at birth was twenty-eight years; by 1900 it was almost fifty. Physical size increased. In western Europe the average man was about five feet tall in 1800. A century later average height had increased by six inches, and weight was accordingly greater. Physical deformity became less common as diet improved and many forms of manual labor were lightened by the introduction of machines.

Causes of Population Growth: Stage I

Before 1750, and even later in certain areas, Europe was characterized by high birth rates roughly balanced by high death rates. Mortality was particularly great among children. In some areas almost 50 per cent died before reaching two years of age. If a person survived his infancy, his life expectancy was more than forty years. In England between 1700 and 1750 approximately 32.8 people were born annually for each 1,000 inhabitants, while 31.5 people died. Similarly in Lombardy in the late eighteenth century, 39 people were born and 37 people died for each 1,000 inhabitants. Clearly, major alteration had to occur either in birth or mortality rate before the expansion of population could begin. In fact, both rates changed: families began to have more children and a lower percentage of the population died each year. Much is still unknown about the precise developments in population rates in the eighteenth and nineteenth centuries, but certain general features seem clear. During the period 1750–1800, for example, the population of England grew at a rate of over 1 per cent a year. Approximately 80 per cent of this can be accounted for by a decline in mortality; by 1800 only 27.1 per 1,000 died each year. But there was also a startling rise in the numbers of children born annually.

Several basic factors contributed to a decline in mortality rates in the eighteenth century. In central Europe and in France deaths in wars declined. Epidemic diseases became less common. Plagues still occurred; in the 1830s cholera killed a large number of people in western Europe. But the historic pattern of periodic decimation by epidemics, like the fatal wave of influenza in western Europe in the 1720s, was really broken. Better methods of hygiene, particularly in the cities, accounted for some of this decline. English cities kept

streets cleaner in the late eighteenth century and paid more attention to sewage disposal. More generally important, however, was the
improvement of border controls against entry of diseased persons
and animals. Particularly, the growing efficiency of the Hapsburg
government helped block the traditional route of plagues from the
Middle East into Europe, and even outside Europe epidemics declined temporarily in the eighteenth century.

Growth in population also depended on expansion of food supply.
Better diets improved health, and increased food production curtailed
famine, another traditional killer in Europe. The introduction of the
potato was one of the most important changes in the agriculture of
western and central Europe. The spread of corn in southern and eastern Europe had somewhat similar effects. The potato offered more
caloric value per unit of land and labor than any other starch. Many
of the regions that began their population growth in the eighteenth
century had introduced the potato in the same period. The potato
allowed people to survive, even if in great poverty. In Ireland particularly it encouraged a population growth that could not be
supported in any other way; the Irish population has never regained
the size it achieved before the potato blight of the mid-1840s. Elsewhere the potato was only one of several basic factors in population
growth; in some areas, such as Spain, population growth occurred
even without extensive cultivation of the potato.

Food supply was also increased after 1750 by the cultivation of
new lands. In western Europe, particularly in England, better
methods of drainage allowed new lands to be opened up. Increasingly, cultivation of nitrogen-fixing plants replaced traditional systems of fallow, greatly expanding the amount of land cultivated in
each year. In eastern Europe the governments of Prussia, Russia,
and the Hapsburg lands fostered colonization of wilderness regions.
The Russians expanded cultivation in the rich lands to the south
and west and in the nineteenth century began an important movement eastward. New areas of Hungary were opened up to agriculture. There again the resulting increase in agricultural production
assured food to an expanding population.

The opening up of new land also provided a positive inducement
to have more children. Peasants typically delayed their marriage
until land was available for the new household. With the new land

many peasants married in their teens and had more children as a result.

In western and central Europe other factors promoted earlier marriage and larger families. The spread of domestic manufacturing in the eighteenth century gave hundreds of thousands of peasant families in England, France, Prussia, and Austria a chance to earn money away from the land and to marry early. Young people with a cash income could set up a family in an appropriate style. The marriage age was distinctly lower among peasants doing some manufacturing work than among those still completely dependent on the land. In England especially, the displacement of peasants from land ownership by the enclosure movement also helped to reduce restraints on marriage age and childbirth. Finally, in some sections of central Europe, easing of marriage laws helped raise the birth rate. Various new opportunities and pressures combined to induce a rising birth rate in many regions at the same time that mortality was declining.

Causes of Population Growth: Stage II

By the nineteenth century the causes of population rise were changing. In eastern and southern Europe the familiar combination of high birth rate and reduced mortality was just beginning to take effect. There, in addition to agricultural changes, definite improvements in medicine and hygiene aided the process. In western Europe population growth continued, but it changed in nature, particularly after 1850, and it definitely declined in rate.

New reductions in mortality provided the main continuing impetus to population expansion. Various improvements in procedures at birth, in urban hygiene, and in diet greatly increased life expectancy. Particularly, by 1900 death at infancy had been reduced to about 10 per cent in the west. The discoveries of Pasteur and others after the 1860s resulted in many improvements in medicine and hygiene. On the other hand, birth rates were declining drastically. Populations still grew as a result of earlier expansion; that is, the absolute number of children born was increasing because there were more people of childbearing age. But the size of families was definitely shrinking. The decline in death rate was increasingly counterbalanced by the reduction of the number of children per capita. A new stage had been reached in the population structure.

France was the first country to reach this new stage. A number of the social classes in France developed various reasons for reducing their family size. The middle class, always the first to limit the number of children, tried to protect its material well-being and its ability to establish what children it did have in proper style. Artisans and later the factory workers followed suit. They too wished to devote more of their earnings to personal enjoyment rather than supporting a large family. The peasantry, finally, while it reduced its birth rate less than the urban classes, undertook a reduction at an unusually early date. Proud of their individual land holdings, forced by French law to give all children an equal share in inheritance, peasants tried to protect the integrity of the family plot by restricting the number of children. By 1820, then, the major period of French population growth was over. From 1815 to 1911 France expanded only from twenty-nine to thirty-nine million. This was a significant growth and had important social consequences. But it left France not only relatively but even absolutely behind a number of European countries in demographic strength.

The French pattern of a declining growth rate gradually emerged in other countries. By 1840 the British birth rate began to fall rapidly. Germany's followed within two decades. Italy and Russia entered this stage around 1900, and areas such as Bohemia experienced a reduced birth rate only after 1910. Everywhere the birth rate was first reduced by the middle classes, then by other urban elements, and finally, and always to a lesser degree, by the peasantry. In all cases population continued to increase sharply in the thirty years following the beginning of birth-rate reduction. After this period growth slowed notably and was produced almost exclusively by a declining mortality rate. By 1900, then, western Europe had completed its major expansion. France, in fact, was even receiving immigrants from places like Italy. Eastern and southern Europe maintained a greater demographic dynamism, but they too were to follow the western pattern in the next century.

General Effects of Population Growth

Population increase was an inherently dynamic factor. New numbers required new agricultural and industrial procedures for their support. Rising population meant rising competition for position in society; it became harder to defend exclusive privilege.

Various traditional institutions were pressed. Armies had to deal with new numbers if they were to maintain their accustomed percentage (about 1 per cent in 1800) of the nation under arms. Universities, though still drawing primarily from the upper classes, grew from a comfortable few hundred students to an impersonal several thousand. Rising population, in the early stages, increased the percentage of young people in society. Young people were capable of great vigor but also of unusual turbulence. The youthfulness of the population was an important backdrop to the agitation in western Europe at midcentury and in eastern and southern Europe later on.

The changing patterns of population growth put great pressure on family structure. At first the principal alterations resulted simply from the need to provide for the larger numbers of children who survived infancy. For most peasant and worker families this meant finding work for children at an early age. Increasing numbers of children had to work outside the home as agricultural laborers or, commonly, as manufacturing workers. Many peasant families lacked sufficient land for their sons. Many artisans could not find suitable jobs for theirs, particularly because artisan masters increasingly reserved their shops for their own offspring. Large families posed problems for middle-class families too. Fathers had to provide education for numerous children. They had to supply dowries for daughters, suitable positions for sons. Provision for a large family at a suitable economic and social level was an important motivation for many developments in business and industry. Companies were expanded to take care of many sons or brothers; new methods were sought to make support of the family more certain. Population expansion put economic pressure on every family. Some of the methods developed to meet this pressure weakened the unity of the family. The pressure itself could create major discontent when a family was unable to provide for itself as it was accustomed to do.

Changes in population age structure affected family life. Improvements in diet and reduction of disease increased longevity and thereby increased the likelihood that both marriage partners would live through twenty or thirty years of marriage. In 1800 it was far less likely that a man who lived sixty years would have only one wife than it was in 1900. Death dissolved marriages later and less frequently. Increased longevity also posed problems, for families and for society as a whole, of support for the increasing numbers of older people. Particularly in the later nineteenth century, as a higher standard of living and improved medicine allowed more and more people to live beyond sixty years of age, the elderly represented a growing segment of society. Attention had to be given to their economic and social role.

Finally, after the first stage of population growth was ended, the decline in birth rate reflected new patterns. The desire to protect the material well-being of the family and to provide a suitable economic and social future was gradually translated into restriction on the number of children a family had. This naturally posed the problem of how to effect this restriction. Contraceptive devices were known early in the nineteenth century, but do not seem to have been widely used until later. Abortion was practiced by some, and increasing numbers of children were abandoned. In some cases marriage age rose and marriage rates declined. Factory workers, for example, frequently delayed marriage until their late twenties. Rates of illegitimate birth tended to expand at the same time. Finally, many couples practiced rigorous restraint of sexual impulses as a means of restricting family size. This brought certain tensions of its own, but it was effective. Middle-class families practiced restraint most commonly and urged similar self-discipline on the more procreative lower classes. For some the unwillingness of lower classes to restrain themselves was a sign of their barbarism. Gradually, however, the lower classes extended their interest in limiting their families through restraint and increasingly through the use of contraceptive devices.

The tradition of large families was strong. Rural areas, particularly religious areas, all maintained higher birth rates than the average. Limitation of birth rates was part of a general movement of throwing off tradition. In the French mining town of Montceau, for example, the birth rate dropped over 30 per cent in the same decade, the 1890s, that religious practice declined and unionization and strikes increased. Quite suddenly, workers realized their interest in material improvement and tried to implement it in a variety of ways. New methods of family planning resulted from an increasing desire for economic well-being and the fact that more children survived.

As families limited their size, with increasing assurance that their children would live to maturity, a new attitude toward children naturally developed. This attitude was encouraged, in the upper classes at first, by doctrines of loving and caring for children preached by intellectuals like Rousseau. Sentimentality about children and interest in their education and well-being rose throughout the century and affected all classes. Upper-class philanthropists urged attentiveness to the children on the presumably brutal lower classes. Laws were passed to protect children in factories and later in homes. Increasingly, children were treated as independent beings, to be handled with concern as well as with authority.

On individuals as well as whole societies, then, population trends exercised a powerful effect in the nineteenth century. Demographic expansion created pressure on the land supply, on family structure, and on existing military, educational, and governmental facilities. Most important, it contributed to the third basic innovation in European society at the end of the eighteenth century, the industrial revolution. Without population growth the industrial revolution would have been unnecessary; without a radically new industrial structure population growth could not have been sustained. The two forces were intertwined in their occurrence and effects. Population growth came first and for a few decades exercised independent pressure in most areas. It was fed at first by an expansion of domestic manufacturing. But the industrial revolution followed almost everywhere and modified and supplemented the pressure of population expansion. In the long run, in fact, the industrial revolution was to prove the most basic and enduring social force in modern Europe. It resulted in a fundamental restructuring of European society.

THE INDUSTRIAL REVOLUTION

Technology

The industrial revolution was, in essence, a radically new technology and organization of the manufacturing process. The exact nature of the technology and organization depended on the date and conditions of industrialization in any area. Nevertheless, certain common features underlay the whole movement.

The basis of the industrial revolution was the application of mechanical power to manufacturing. At first this power often came from water wheels, but the invention of the steam engine about 1770 allowed far more massive mechanical power to be developed. By providing powerful pumps the steam engine allowed deeper mine shafts to be sunk, greatly increasing the amount of coal available for mining. In metallurgy steam engines were soon applied to power the bellows for blast furnaces and to operate automatic hammers and rollers for metals. Productivity in metallurgy was also greatly expanded by the substitution of coal and coke for charcoal in smelting and refining. The new fuels were cheaper than charcoal and could fire larger furnaces and ovens. Through a combination of these technical improvements the output of iron could be vastly increased. Furthermore, the spreading use of steam helped create a growing need for coal and iron to build and power the new machines. Rapid growth of production in both industries, based on important new techniques, was a fundamental feature of every industrial revolution.

Steam engines were applied to many other industries as well. Grain mills and sugar refineries used a large number, though more traditional methods survived for a long time. Far more important, and more extensive, was the mechanization of textiles. Unlike mining and metallurgy, textile production was well developed before the industrial revolution; need for textile goods was basic to life. Far more workers and entrepreneurs were involved in the industry and a far more valuable total product was created than in the heavy industries. Therefore, although technical changes in mining and metallurgy were vital and the output in these industries increased far more rapidly than in textiles, the mechanization of the textile industry was the change that affected the most people and the greatest product in the early industrial revolution.

The initial inventions in the industrial revolution were developed largely within the textile industry. Well before a practicable steam engine was produced, British inventors had devised major changes in both spinning and weaving. At first these improvements were designed to increase productivity in domestic industry with no change in the source of power. The flying shuttle, invented in 1733, raised the productivity of manual weaving about 50 per cent by having the shuttle, which carries threads across the loom, return automatically instead of requiring another weaver to push it. The spinning jenny, developed a few decades later, wound fibers around a spindle automatically, permitting a single spinner for the first time to operate several spindles. In other words, inventions in textiles decreased the need for direct manual operation in certain key stages of production. They were therefore adaptable to mechanical power. First in spinning, then in weaving, water and gradually steam power were introduced to provide the motive force for production. By the 1780s the basic processes existed in England for a technical revolution in the textile industry, although the development of power looms was not yet complete. Along with new methods in mining and metallurgy, they ushered in the first stage of the industrial revolution in Europe.

Certain inventions, notably the steam engine, were basic to the industrial revolution, but the movement involved steady and dramatic change in techniques even after it was well begun. Improvements were made in existing machines; the number of spindles on spinning machines greatly increased in the early nineteenth century; weavers were given two, then four, then six or eight power looms to operate as the century continued. Furthermore, other industries were gradually brought into the movement. The invention of the sewing machine in the 1840s allowed the gradual mechanization of tailoring and shoemaking. Most important, the invention of the Bessemer converter in 1856 and later the discovery of the open-hearth process revolutionized the metallurgical industry, at a time when demand for metal products was increasing drastically with the development of railroads. These new processes expanded the size of smelting furnaces; they eliminated the need for many workers to stir out impurities in iron by hand; and they allowed the addition of carbon to iron to make steel. The result was a superior metal product and a great increase in productivity per worker. By the midnineteenth century, then, major technical changes had been developed for all stages of the textile, mining, and metallurgical industries. Using more automatic methods and new sources of power, these changes vastly increased the amount any individual worker could produce. The technical basis for the industrial revolution had been established.

Industrial Structure

The industrial revolution involved not only technical change but also a new organization of industry. This organization followed from the new techniques but had advantages and consequences of its own. Basically, the process consisted of concentrating the ingredients of production in larger, more compact units.

First, the workers themselves were concentrated in a factory. Utilization of water or steam power required that workers be gathered around the wheel or engine. Instead of being scattered in small shops or their own homes manufacturing workers were assembled under direct central control. Greater supervision of workers was possible under this system. Division of labor could be substantially increased, raising productivity by having each worker specialize in one small part of the productive process. The factory system, in other words, had advantages even aside from the utilization of mechanical power. Early factories were generally rather small, often using only about twenty workers. As the size of engines and machines increased, and as better methods of supervision were developed, factories steadily grew.

The factory system concentrated capital as well as workers into units of unprecedented size. The new machines were expensive. Factory buildings themselves cost money. Never before had manufacturing required the assembly of capital on such a large scale. In domestic production workers themselves had usually bought the equipment and the housing; the manufacturer needed only operating capital to buy raw materials and pay initial wages. With new machines and plants far greater investment was necessary. In metallurgy and mining, where machines were particularly expensive, most new firms were launched only through the participation of a number of wealthy men in some form of expanded partnership. In the textile industry an individual family could often set up a small unit with its own funds, supplemented by some borrowing and perhaps a temporary partnership. Subsequent expansion was usually financed by the profits of the firm itself, and the textile industry has retained a system of family ownership to the present day.

Even within the textile industry, however, the average size of capital in an individual firm expanded steadily. It was discovered quite early that big machines were more efficient than small; a twenty-horsepower engine, for example, did not consume twice as much fuel as one of ten horsepower. Furthermore, a large firm had certain other advantages over a small enterprise. It had greater control over its supplies and might in fact produce its own raw materials. There was an increasing tendency for cloth producers to add a spinning plant or for metallurgists to acquire a mine. Large size permitted greater control of markets. A large firm could afford a better marketing organization and was in a better position to dictate terms to its buyers than was a small enterprise. It could expand to include the production of its own finished products; metallurgical companies often added not only mines but also the production of machines to their operation, a process of vertical integration in both directions. In a variety of ways, then, expansion of a firm's operations provided greater security and greater opportunity for profit.

In the early stages of the industrial revolution the number of firms in an industry proliferated. After the first generation, however, the number began to decline. Only the most powerful, generally the largest, firms survived. The process of concentration of resources and power occurred on an absolute basis. The requirements of size were so great in certain cases, such as in heavy industry, that new forms of organization were developed. The rise of the corporation, beginning in England before 1850, was due to the need to assemble capital on a larger scale than ever before. This was simply a further step in the concentrated organization of labor and resources that was part of the industrial revolution itself.

Patterns of Industrialization

The revolution in techniques and in industrial organization was a process of fundamental economic change. Changes in technique required an adaptation of workers to new and more rapid methods. They required adjustment by consumers to more uniform and abundant products. Changes in organization required that workers labor in new places and be subject to new control. They brought new power to owners, but they also brought a need for novel methods in finance, marketing, and accounting. These changes and their many results were not easy. Many established workers and entrepreneurs resisted such novelty, preferring to rely on more traditional techniques. It took time to assemble the capital necessary to buy machines and construct an industrial firm. Again, many resisted the innovations because they lacked the funds to adapt. In no sense, then, was the industrial revolution a sudden occurrence.

Traditional mining and metallurgical firms, employing only a few workers and using simple tools, persisted for several decades after technical change began. In France the use of coal and coke in metallurgy was introduced by several firms around 1820, and these firms generally prospered. But by 1848 half the iron produced in France was still smelted and refined by charcoal.

In the textile industry the pace of change was similarly slow. Cotton spinning was usually the first industry to be affected by mechanical production. Cotton was an easy fiber to handle on machines, and cotton production was relatively new, so there were fewer established producers to resist change. Within a decade after industrialization began in an area, cotton spinning was done entirely by mechanical means. Wool spinning generally followed, but linen spinning lagged, because difficulty with the fiber and a sense of routine in the industry prevented rapid modernization. Weaving always took longer to change, although it too followed the pattern of cotton first, then wool, then linen and silk. Power looms were less productive than mechanical spindles, so manual methods could compete for a longer time. It took fifty years or more for hand weaving to admit defeat in an industrial country.

Finally, many industries were not initially affected by new methods at all; food processing, the building trades, tailoring, and the like were nowhere significantly altered until after 1850. These were the industries most solidly organized in a precapitalist artisan structure.

The progress of the industrial revolution within an industrializing country was gradual and uneven. Given the fundamental nature of the change, the movement was extraordinarily rapid; the word *revolution* is not inappropriate. In every case, however, the revolution was slowed by lack of capital, lack of knowledge, and positive resistance to change.

The difficulties of the industrial revolution were reflected in the variety of regional patterns of industrialization. A number of factors might cause certain areas to enter the path of industrialization unusually early and to develop with extraordinary rapidity. Other areas even in the same country lagged in both time and rate of development if they lacked one or more of the vital ingredients. Southern France continued to employ traditional procedures of textile production long after the north had industrialized; as a result, industry gradually declined in the south in the nineteenth century. Everywhere, the industrial revolution heightened the regional concentration of industry. The vital importance of coal to industrialization, in combination with the bulk and cost of coal transport, brought to coal-rich regions most of the new industry in the nineteenth century. Consequently, the center of early industry developed along the massive belt of coal extending from northern England through Belgium and northern France to the Ruhr. Areas of more traditional industry, such as southern England, declined not only relatively but absolutely in this period. Clearly, the path of modern industry did not respect national boundaries.

It is convenient, however, to note certain general national differences in patterns of industrialization. And some of the factors involved in the movement did operate largely along national lines, most notably legal structure, transportation policy, and the size of the principal market unit.

Britain, of course, was the leader. The initial inventions took place in England and Scotland and by 1780 were being widely introduced. By 1850 most of the major manufacturing industries had been transformed. Great changes were still to come, but the pioneering period was over. Britain possessed enough trained workers, managers, and investment capital to insure the continuation of the industrial movement in every branch of production.

By 1850 several other countries were involved in earlier stages of industrialization. Belgium and France both began to introduce significant mechanization about 1820, but Belgium proceeded at a much more rapid rate. France, in fact, was not to achieve the full transformation of her major industries until about 1914, and even then an unusually large number of artisans and small shops persisted. Germany began to industrialize in the 1840s and reached substantial industrial maturity about 1900. Sweden entered the industrial revolution about 1850, Italy and Austria about 1870, and Russia clearly in the 1890s; all were to reach industrial maturity in the twentieth century, with the Italian process requiring the longest time. By 1900, then, most of Europe was caught up in some phase of the industrial revolution; only the Balkans were relatively untouched. The stage of development differed widely, however, from one area to another. The western countries were relatively mature industrial powers, with France lagging somewhat. The east and south were only beginning to industrialize. These significant differences in the spread of the movement must constantly be recalled in assessing the social structure of any country at a given time. They must also be kept in mind in considering the causes of this complex movement.

Causes of Industrialization

A number of general factors entered into the industrial revolution in every area. Certain factors were necessary to stimulate the movement; others were needed for the stimulus to be successfully answered. Britain, obviously, possessed the needed combination at the earliest date. The same general features were found, however, in the other industrializing areas later. A country deficient in any major factor either delayed its industrialization until a supplement was found or proceeded at a much slower rate. The industrial revolution involved features of government, population, class structure, past wealth, and physical geography. The combination was complex; only such complexity could account for the fundamental economic change.

The key factor in causing the industrial revolution in any area was the creation of a new level of need for manufactured goods. The movement was not created in advance of such need. Even the major inventions resulted from a preestablished need for new techniques. Hence an expansion of domestic production usually preceded the adoption of mechanical methods and encouraged the development of new productive devices.

New need, or market, for manufactured goods arose from a number of sources. Population growth was essential. In every major case population growth antedated industrialization by several decades, providing a major new market stimulus. Countries where population growth was relatively small, such as France, saw their industrial possibilities correspondingly limited.

Rising export possibilities also added to available markets. In western Europe and particularly Britain expanding colonial trade in the eighteenth century was an important stimulus to manufacturing. Eastern Europe, deprived of colonial markets, found other opportunities after the midnineteenth century, particularly in the possibility of exporting to the industrial west. The rising wealth of industrial countries, therefore, not only encouraged their own industries but also those of other areas.

Market potential was also aided by the progressive elimination of customs barriers. In Germany formation of the Zollverein in the 1820s was an important step toward industrialization.

Improving transportation, finally, encouraged the growth of national and international markets. Britain, with a large fleet and an exceptionally extensive network of navigable rivers, had far better transportation facilities than the continental countries in the eighteenth century. Improvements in roads and canals in western Europe in the same period provided general, though more limited, transportation possibilities. Outside western Europe the industrial revolution did not occur until after a railroad network was established. In France and particularly in England transportation and market possibilities were sufficient to allow initial industrialization before the railroad. In Britain the railroad was actually a result of the need for improved transport resulting from significant industrialization. In Germany, however, the beginning of a railroad network in the 1840s coincided with the first stage of industrialization; in Russia and elsewhere, railroad building preceded industrialization by as much as twenty years. The railroad greatly added to the accessible market in every country. It also created a new demand for coal and iron to build and operate the railroad itself. Industrialization after the railroad, then, was encouraged by a tremendous increase in available markets even aside from population growth.

Differences in market potential help explain the various dates of industrialization. Britain had a high rate of population growth, favorable transportation, lack of internal trade barriers, rising wealth, and expanding foreign trade. She also benefited from exhaustion of wood supply in certain regions, creating an early market for coal production.

On the continent as a whole creation of comparable new markets depended on certain other developments including the railroad and the possibilities of exports to industrial Britain. Governments also took a greater role in providing markets. Following Britain's industrial rise there was a general desire to imitate her technical power. Continental states frequently tried to encourage national market possibilities by protective tariffs. They took a major role in building railroads, which in Britain was left largely to private hands. Even in France the pace of industrialization was not rapid until after 1850, when the government of Napoleon III increased transportation facilities and provided direct markets for metals and coal by building railroads and port facilities. Finally, most of the continent benefited after 1850 from expansion of market possibilities through the increase of precious metals available in Europe. This increase tended to drive up prices and so encouraged production to take advantage of these prices. In a variety of ways, and at significantly different times, the need for new levels of manufacturing spread throughout Europe.

To supply new industrial markets, mineral and fiber resources were necessary. Britain had an exceptionally favorable supply of cotton from colonial sources. Germany, without such sources, was never able to develop her textile industry to a comparable level. However, the industrial revolution depended primarily on access to coal and iron. Britain had substantial deposits of each; further, they were close together or connected by rivers and sea. Belgium had excellent coal and fair iron resources. Germany had even better coal resources than Britain and substantial iron deposits; but she lacked a network of navigable rivers to connect the two. Russia was in a similar position. In both countries the resources became effective only when a railroad system allowed their combination. In France and Italy lack of iron and particularly coal limited industrial development throughout the century; these nations matured industrially only in the present century, when petroleum fuels released industry from dependence on coal. France had only about 6 per cent of the coal resources of Europe outside of Russia compared to Germany's 47 per cent. On the basis of resources alone she could industrialize only partially in the nineteenth century. Usable resources, then, proved to be a major factor in the date and extent of industrialization.

The industrial revolution depended also on available labor. Despite the productivity of the new machines, vast numbers of new workers had to be recruited for the factories, particularly in heavy industry. Population growth provided new labor, but workers could be freed for industry only as a result of improvements in agricultural productivity. Better fertilizers, better tools, and more efficient crops such as the potato were essential. New systems of tenure, which provided larger and more compact plots of land, also increased agricultural productivity.

In all these developments Britain had a clear lead in the eighteenth century. Her agriculture was the most productive in Europe. The enclosure movement provided more efficient units of land and actually forced many peasants off traditional holdings. Elsewhere in western Europe agricultural methods improved more slowly. Land holdings remained smaller and more divided. A labor force was freed only gradually; and in France its size was limited by the slowness of population growth. But in time better methods and changes in tenure improved productivity and drove some peasants off the land entirely.

Even where excess labor existed in agriculture, it was often unavailable for industry. Only when the abolition of feudalism freed the peasant from obligations to remain on the land could a substantial industrial labor force be drawn away from agriculture. Population growth, agricultural change, and legal reforms eventually developed the labor force everywhere; but again, the dates and rates of development varied.

The industrial revolution required capital. Britain and western Europe possessed substantial holdings of commercial capital resulting from internal and colonial trade. Agricultural capital proved loath to invest in industry. The wealth of the middle classes was crucial to industrialization in Britain and western Europe. These countries, and especially Britain, benefited from an early banking system as well. Banks, while not leading investors in early industry, did provide some capital and facilitated the movement of credit generally.

In central and eastern Europe industrialization was delayed by the lack of commercial capital; this led to reliance on western capital and distinctive governmental role in industry.

Foreign investment, from Britain and other industrial nations, was essential in all later industrial revolutions. Half the investment in Russian industry before the First World War was foreign; and a substantial part of Germany's capital came from abroad. In addition, governments vigorously aided capital formation. They encouraged the development of investment banks; even the French government was active in that field after 1850. And they provided capital directly, notably in the building of railroads. Through their powers of taxation and borrowing, they helped compensate for the lack of capital in private hands. Industrialization in capital-poor countries involved greater governmental control and a larger reliance on corporate structure and banking.

The availability of capital, labor, and resources largely determined the ability of an area to respond to expanding market opportunities. One final, less tangible, ingredient was necessary. An area could industrialize only if it possessed individuals willing to take the risks of engaging their work and funds in unfamiliar and risky ventures. Competition was rugged in the early industrial period; failures were frequent. Only relatively hardy souls were willing to engage in this process.

It is difficult to determine the source of an entrepreneurial spirit. In many cases minority Protestant groups took a lead. Dissenters in England, blocked from access to government posts and social prestige, tried to compensate by building industrial empires. Calvinists in Alsace similarly took a disproportionate role in French industrialization, as did Dutch Protestants in Belgium. On the other hand, certain Catholic groups, such as those in northern France, developed a fully entrepreneurial spirit. They too were willing to work hard and to save; they too spoke of glorifying God with economic success. But, of course, industrial dynamism cannot be explained by religious factors alone.

The pioneers of industry came largely from middle-class backgrounds. They had the commercial spirit and interest in material success of the middle class generally. Areas that lacked a middle class therefore lagged in industrialization at first. But as time passed, entrepreneurial spirit counted for less. Industrialization became increasingly a matter of copying Britain and other leaders rather than of developing really new processes. Foreign entrepreneurs, particularly British, emigrated to backward areas in large numbers to build up industry. And again, the government played an increasing role in encouraging industrial innovation by subsidies, protection, and actual development and ownership. Industrialization remained a difficult and risky process, but it was no longer a venture into the unknown.

The industrial revolution involved new opportunities and new as well as old potential. Differences in the way various factors were supplied created important differences in the process itself. Particularly after 1850 increased reliance on heavy industry and the greater role of government marked off later industrializers from the pioneer areas. The ability to imitate earlier movements allowed many regions to speed up the process. Advanced techniques such as the railroad were introduced from the first. Elaborate forms such as the corporation were used, making capital formation less difficult. For all this, however, the industrial revolution brought no less fundamental changes to the economy. The precise form of the movement differed importantly, but the basic fact of a revolution in technique and organization was common to all industrializing nations. For the first time in human history, more people lived from industrial than from agricultural work. For the first time, once industrialization was well advanced, more lived in large cities than in the countryside.

Immediate Effects of Industrialization

The introduction of machines and factories brought a number of economic consequences. New techniques often increased the productivity of an individual worker ten or fifteen times. In some industries, such as coal and iron, many new workers were added to the manufacturing force. Particularly in heavy industry, then, production rose greatly from the first. In 1800 Britain produced twenty-six pounds of iron per person; in 1880 she produced 260. Her gross production rose twenty-seven times between 1800 and 1860. Germany's per capita output of iron rose from 41 pounds in the 1860s to 170 in 1890. Coal production rose even more strikingly. Even France increased her output from 1 million to 13 million tons between 1840 and 1870. Prussia's coal production rose from 1.5 million tons in 1825 to 20.5 million in 1865. Output in certain other industries rose comparably. The machine-building industry grew from almost nothing to a position of major importance in the early stages of industrialization. Sugar refining in France increased 900 per cent during the July Monarchy alone. Even textiles, which had been widely manufactured by older methods, expanded greatly. During the July Monarchy French production of cotton and wool cloth doubled. In every branch of industry touched by the new methods a sharp rise in production was one of the major results of the industrial revolution.

The rise in production was accompanied by a change in the balance among industries. Industry as a whole, of course, became the major producer of wealth in society by the third or fourth decade of the industrial revolution; agricultural production also expanded in value, but it could not keep pace. Within manufacturing certain traditional products declined due to failure to adapt. The linen industry, hit by the competition of cheaper machine-made cotton cloth, faded in importance. Lace making and a few other artisan activities lagged for similar reasons. The importance of the textile industry as a whole steadily declined in the face of rising heavy industry, but textiles remained dominant until after 1850. A steel industry arose almost from nothing. The chemical industry, at first confined to the production of dyes, expanded and later in the century developed into an industrial leader.

Increasing production drove prices down fairly steadily. On the whole, rising productivity allowed industrialists to meet the need to lower their prices without diminishing their own profits. In individual cases, however, falling prices put real pressure on companies. Particularly before 1850, when business activity was not accompanied by a sufficient increase in the supply of money, the downward trend of prices was severe indeed. Between 1830 and 1848 prices of cotton goods in France fell 66 per cent, of wool goods 31 per cent. After 1850 prices of manufactured goods still declined, but at a much slower rate due to the increased availability of precious metals. Nevertheless, the general tendency was clear, and price drops in turn opened new markets for a variety of goods previously too expensive for ordinary use. Significant changes in consumption patterns resulted. One observer in France hailed 1830 as a revolutionary year not because of the political upheaval, but because at about that time ordinary urban workers found they could afford stylish cotton clothing. In France and elsewhere in the west around the same period forks became a common utensil in the average home. Increasing availability of goods, through falling prices, was a necessary result of the industrial revolution.

Cheapness alone, however, did not insure sales. New marketing techniques were also necessary. National and even international trade rose greatly, displacing earlier local patterns. The international trade of every industrial country expanded rapidly. In 1820, two million tons of goods entered British ports; by 1870 British ports handled fifteen million tons. Every industrial country quickly became involved in literally a worldwide network of imports and exports. Major companies set up factories in leading cities all over the world. Within an individual country the effects of expanded production on market structure were even more revolutionary. New facilities for mass marketing everywhere followed industrialization. Firms sent out trading agents, and contacts were set up in centers all over the country. In rural areas small shops gradually replaced itinerant peddlers; there was too much to sell to rely on occasional opportunities. Similarly, local fairs declined in favor of permanent wholesale and retail outlets. In larger cities, the department store developed as one symptom of the greater need to sell. Beginning in Paris in the 1830s, the store specializing in masses of products spread all over urban Europe during the nineteenth century.

New transportation facilities, essential for the expanding markets, everywhere accompanied industrialization. At first the main emphasis was on increasing numbers of ships, improving paved roads, and building canals. Then in the early nineteenth century in Britain the omnipresent power of steam was applied to transportation as well as to manufacturing itself. The steam locomotive, invented in the 1820s, was first economically applied in a line between Liverpool and Manchester in 1830. In the 1830s local lines were built in Britain, Belgium, Austria, and between Paris and Versailles. During the next decade Britain and various German states began to build a more general system. France planned such a system, but completed it only in the 1850s and 1860s. By the 1870s the major countries of western Europe had a substantial network of trunk lines. Local lines had been established in Austria and Italy, and plans existed even in more distant regions. Along with the telegraph, which spread during the 1830s, the railroad provided more rapid communication of news as well as transportation of goods and people. It cut into local isolation and allowed more effective contact between central governments and outlying regions. Most important of all, it represented a major development in the quest of industry for more widespread and substantial markets.

Improvements in shipping increased trade and communication among nations and continents during the nineteenth century. Before 1850 both iron and steam had been applied to shipping. Both improved the speed of shipping and increased the capacity of each ship. After 1870 ships were sufficiently large and rapid to allow intercontinental competition even in agricultural goods.

But the economic interest of the age lay in production, not marketing. Leading economists stressed the virtue of increasing production; an extreme liberal, J. B. Say, even asserted that sales would take care of themselves. Industrialists themselves devoted most of their attention to problems of investment and technology. The industrial revolution was first and foremost a change in the technique and organization of manufacturing goods. It was stimulated by new market opportunities. But, once started, the process could outstrip the growth of the markets.

It was natural that the disposal of products caused the greatest economic difficulties of the early industrial revolution. In this period Europe was still a poor society. The resources of the masses were barely if at all above subsistence level. Their numbers were increasing, and their ability to consume rose gradually as prices fell. However, no change in consumption power occurred in the nineteenth century to correspond with the real revolution in ability to produce. Many of the economic difficulties of the century, and even beyond, were based on this disparity.

The disparity between what society could produce and what it could consume gave rise to fierce competition for the available markets. Many innovations in technique resulted from the competition for lower costs and greater production. Many bitter individual failures resulted also, particularly during the early decades, when many new firms were established. An atmosphere of conflict permeated the early industrial revolution. Even successful entrepreneurs felt hemmed in by the forces of competition. As transportation improved, the sense of competition from distant areas grew. Particularly on the continent, where British rivalry was keenly felt, a desire for tariff protection resulted. Everywhere competition encouraged pressure on working conditions because of the need to reduce prices and seek sales that would keep pace with production.

The most agonizing symptom of disparity between production and consumption was the frequency of industrial crises in the nineteenth century. In the first half of the century such crises generally occurred as a result of bad harvests, which decreased the income of peasants and raised food prices generally, leaving everyone less able to buy manufactured goods. Production declined, prices of industrial products fell, and employment, profits, and wages dropped. Later in the century crises more frequently resulted from financial difficulties. The capital needs of new industry created an increasing dependence on banks and the exchange of industrial stocks. It was not uncommon for banks and stock issues to be overextended, in terms of the real productive power of the investments that secured them. Speculative countries such as the United States were particularly prone to overextensions of this sort. The growing international economic links easily translated financial crises in one area to the whole industrial world. Such crises made sales more uncertain and dried up funds for further investment and purchases on a long term. The result again was declining production, wages, employment, and profits.

Crises in industry were never totally disastrous. Most people managed to survive, and some even profited. Difficulties in sales induced many entrepreneurs to undertake major technical improvements in the hope of cutting costs; such improvements set the stage for the next expansion of production and of consumption.

During a crisis itself, however, there was real misery. And crisis years were frequent. Major slumps occurred in the late 1820s, in 1837, in 1846–1847, in 1857, and in the middle of the 1870s, 1880s, and 1890s. Other declines occurred in certain localities and industries even more frequently. Crisis seemed to be a part of industrial life. It created a sense of insecurity among manufacturers and workers alike.

On the whole, however, industrialization steadily created new wealth through its expansion of production. This new wealth was by no means uniformly spread, but it came to benefit most elements of the population. Within a few generations it reduced the numbers living on the borderline of subsistence from a majority to a minority in the industrial areas. At the same time the industrial revolution changed the residence of the average person in Europe. It changed the type of work he did; it changed his pace of work. Along with population expansion and a new legal structure, it freed or forced the population of Europe from traditional ways of action. None of this was accomplished without difficulty and hardship; none of it occurred overnight. The novelty of industrial development dominated many aspects of society during the nineteenth century. Established social classes had to contend with this, and so of course did the new groups that the industrial revolution created. In combination with basic movements in law and population, on which it depended, industrialization caused a real social upheaval in Europe. The movement was fraught with difficulty and opportunity. It has not ended to this day.

3
THE IMPACT OF
INDUSTRIALIZATION

In the first decades of industrialization most people remained outside the factory system, even outside the burgeoning cities. Only after 1850 in England and after 1870 in Belgium and Germany did factory production dominate other forms. This initial period saw decisive social changes. Early industry created new economic groups, although they remained rather small; and it put pressure on many traditional producers. Population pressure and legal changes were at their height during this period, and both extended the possibilities for a commercial economy. These developments rather than factory industry itself dominated western Europe (except England) up to 1850; industrialization emerged from this situation. A similar extension of commerce, including trade to the industrial west, preceded early industrialization in eastern Europe later in the century.

The focus for the first fifty years of industrialization in any area must be on a broad range of economic changes, including the rise of a factory system. These changes dislocated many established groups and values; there were even direct efforts to resist them. Few groups recognized that they were benefiting from the industrial revolution. Even in the middle class, the clearest initial beneficiary, many suffered. The first impact of industrialization must be assessed primarily in terms of disturbance.

THE AGRICULTURAL CLASSES

Market Agriculture

During the nineteenth century a system of market agriculture replaced the previous system of local subsistence production. Peasants and landlords alike began to depend increasingly on sales to distant markets. Production increased to take advantage of new opportunities for sales. The growing trend toward market agriculture was spurred by the population expansion and particularly by the rise of cities as part of industrialization, both of which extended the potential market. Changes in transportation also furthered the process. The railroad and rapid and capacious shipping both allowed more substantial shipments of food to population centers. New manufactured goods were brought to rural areas, attracting many producers to the sort of production that would allow them to buy outside products. Changes in law also encouraged market agriculture. Abolition of feudal dues meant that landlords increasingly depended on commercial profits from their land rather than on traditional revenues. Peasants were released from the protection of their former lord. No longer were the charity and other services of the lord readily available. Again, the only major recourse was to produce increasingly for the market. In many countries, peasants were also subject to new taxes by governments once they were considered free agents; their needs for cash rose. German and Russian peasants also required some cash, for a certain period, to pay the redemption fees demanded for the abolition of feudal obligations. Both opportunity and necessity existed for the development of market agriculture.

Substantial profits could be made on the market. Demand for

agricultural goods rose steadily and prices remained favorable until the 1870s; producers in a country like England, where methods were relatively advanced, knew a golden period of earnings. However, market agriculture involved certain pressures and even risks that were new to most peasants and landlords. Production for the market meant subjection to the whims of demands. The railroad brought the products of one region into competition with those of another. Despite rising consumption, competition increased steadily during the nineteenth century, to the detriment of less efficient producers. The expansion of the market invited greater production. Some of this could be supplied by opening new land to cultivation, but ultimately more efficient methods were required. And improvements in methods in one area tended, through the pressure of competition, to produce improvements elsewhere.

Ironically, and sometimes tragically, the economic traditionalism of the agricultural classes was peculiarly ill-suited to such radical novelty. Changes did occur; European agriculture vastly increased its production and efficiency. By 1830 England, for example, produced two to three times as much grain as it had in the eighteenth century. Huge cities could, therefore, grow, and famine became a thing of the past after 1850 in all but a few eastern regions. Such immense development put real pressure on the customs and structures of agricultural existence and even on the economic well-being of many producers. Much of the life of the agricultural classes during the nineteenth century was determined by the clash between new economic forces and a highly traditional way of life.

Methods and Products

Market agriculture required major changes in agricultural methods, equipment, and products to meet the need for greater efficiency. Existing land had to be used more fully. Better drainage methods spread, allowing use of marshy land. The planting of nitrogen-fixing clover or turnips increasingly permitted the suppression of fallow land on the continent, as it had in Britain in the previous century. Common lands were gradually divided and cultivated at great cost to peasant traditions and to the livelihood of many poor peasants. Finally, animal and chemical fertilizers were developed early in the nineteenth century, and their use slowly spread, greatly increasing the yield of the land.

Changes in agricultural equipment also increased productivity and decreased labor costs. Such a simple improvement as the use of the scythe instead of the sickle raised the productivity of harvest workers by up to 50 per cent. More massive productive equipment became available also, but it spread slowly. Heavier, larger plows were manufactured. Threshing and reaping machines were invented. In agriculture, as in industry, it became increasingly possible to substitute machines for human power and labor.

Finally, market agriculture required specialization in a cash crop; general production of many crops could not be efficient. Europe became increasingly divided into grain-growing, wine-growing, and stock-raising areas. Such areas were dependent on the market for the purchase of foods that they did not raise. Although this specialization greatly improved productivity, it had certain dangers. Failure of one crop could wipe out one's whole livelihood; for example, great misery resulted from the destruction of French vines by phylloxera in the 1860s. Constant attention was necessary to keep a specialty crop up to rising standards of quality. Particularly in stock breeding, improvements in the product were fairly steady in the nineteenth century. Changes in consumption patterns could threaten the profitability of a specialty crop. Sheep-growing areas were hit by the rise of cotton fiber and the declining popularity of mutton. Growing wealth in western Europe caused a general movement away from the cheaper grains, such as rye, and toward wheat by the midnineteenth century. Again, substantial adjustment had to be made by producers.

More productive methods, better equipment, and new crops created great possibilities for agricultural development during the century. They were encouraged by government information programs and by many agricultural societies, which tried to introduce and expand a variety of new techniques. Nevertheless, in many cases development was very slow. By 1870 only one third of even the large farms in northern France had threshing machines, and only after 1890 did such equipment become really common. Not until about 1880 did use of mineral fertilizer expand significantly in France. In all these cases it had required decades of spreading information plus a new rise in competition to produce major change in equipment. Similarly, many of the necessary changes in crop specialization occurred only slowly if at all.

Ignorance and traditionalism accounted for much of the lag between what was possible and what was done. The illiteracy of many peasants and the aristocratic hostility to commercial activity favored the status quo in most areas. Furthermore, major improvements in equipment or the quality of the crop required capital. Peasants and small landlords alike had little monetary capital; what they owned was the land itself. Credit facilities were not extensive in rural areas. In the early part of the nineteenth century loans could only be obtained at rates of interest up to 60 per cent. Later government and cooperative funds were established to ease the situation, but credit remained tight. Finally, many peasants' plots were too small to apply machines successfully. Even simple improvements, such as the suppression of fallow, proved impossible for many farmers. They did spread, causing a great increase in production, but they ruined many peasants and aristocrats in the process.

Despite the transformation of agriculture and the huge increase in production, the agrarian classes were unable to maintain their traditional importance in society as a whole. Their production sank steadily as a percentage of total national product, and agriculture employed a declining share of the total labor force. Most of the population increase in western and central Europe went into the cities. The agricultural classes grew only slightly in the century as a whole, and in a few areas, such as France and Britain, they began to decline in absolute numbers after 1870 as improved methods and increased competition curtailed the need for labor. By 1900 only 10 per cent of the population of Britain depended on agricultural work. Along with the great change within agriculture, the altered position of agricultural producers in society contributed to the major changes in rural life during the nineteenth century.

THE ARISTOCRACY

Economic Base

The decline in the relative importance of agriculture hurt aristocrats severely, particularly in the west. Control of much of the land no longer assured them economic supremacy. Their average earnings were rapidly challenged by the owners of industry. In 1800 the British aristocracy controlled almost 20 per cent of the annual production of the nation; by 1850 it commanded less than 10 per cent. It became increasingly difficult to maintain a style of life distinguished by luxury. Some aristocrats attached themselves to the rising fortunes of industry despite the general prejudice against commercial activity. Few of them actually managed enterprises, but a number invested and served on boards of directors. However, aristocrats never rivaled the middle class for control of industry. Their economic base remained the land, and the importance of the land was declining.

Changes within agriculture challenged aristocrats more generally. The demands of market agriculture for commercial ability and technical innovation touched even eastern Europe during the early nineteenth century. There were definite attempts to adapt to market opportunities. Junkers and Hungarian nobles increased their landed holdings at the expense of the peasants. Production for export did rise. Some eastern landlords introduced crop rotation and even machinery quite early. By the 1840s Baltic aristocrats began converting to stock raising in the interests of improving their markets. And generally, the use of wage laborers spread. However, only a few individuals modernized their agriculture substantially. There was relatively little general change in method; in Hungary, many nobles depended primarily on extending servile work obligations for their commercial product. Nowhere was there so fundamental a conversion to market agriculture as was occurring in Britain.

Yet a conversion was increasingly necessary. Not only did market pressures rise, but the aristocracy also lost its feudal rights over the peasantry. In western Europe by 1800, in central Europe by 1850, and in Russia after 1861 feudal dues were abolished. In Prussia one third of the peasantry had redeemed their obligations even before midcentury. Aristocrats who had depended on dues rather than domain, as had the majority in the west, lost much of their traditional income by this change. Even where there was a domain, adaptation was essential.

Many landlords retained considerable power over peasant labor. Russian nobles received redemption payments in return for the abolition of feudal dues. Elsewhere some peasants continued to pay rents. In southern Italy and southern Spain many peasants were so poor in land and capital that they became sharecroppers for the lords. In none of the large domain areas except Russia did the abolition of feudalism break up the big estates, and even in Russia the lords kept much of the best land. The Rumanian abolition of serfdom in 1864 actually destroyed peasant smallholding and divided almost all the land into large estates for the first time. There and elsewhere freed but landless peasants were available for cheap labor.

However, the traditional sources of income were irrevocably lost. Peasant labor had to be paid in cash, even if wages were low. In the south sharecropping meant little if the sharecropper's product was not profitable. In other words, the abolition of feudalism inevitably forced the landed aristocracy to participate in market agriculture.

Most landed aristocrats were unable to respond to the new conditions of agriculture. They failed to introduce new equipment, and they failed to develop new crops. Many went heavily into debt to compensate for the inadequacy of their income from the land. Many became impoverished or eked out only a meager living on the basis of sharecropping or tenant returns. Many lost their land.

Even in the early nineteenth century, when market conditions were excellent, many aristocrats had to sell out to more dynamic landlords from the middle class. They lacked the capital and technical knowledge to keep going. In Prussia a third of the Junker estates were bought by members of the middle class between 1815 and 1848 alone. By 1885 about 87 per cent of the east Prussian estates had changed hands. Except to a limited extent in Russia, estates were seldom broken up; the peasantry did not gain in the large estate regions. But increasingly many estates were administered by the middle class on a commercial basis. Only in a few regions, such as England, where aristocrats converted to radically new methods, or the Baltic provinces of Russia, where new methods were combined with semifeudal control over peasant labor, did the aristocrats avoid major competition from new landlords.

Social Status

Aristocrats faced a crisis of legal and social status. Their sense of superior status had depended on high incomes and consumption power, both of which were now under attack; it had also depended on real legal privilege. The abolition of feudalism and the establishment of theoretical equality under the law destroyed such diverse privileges as exclusive hunting rights, the right to try certain crimes in manorial courts, and the right to have one's word accepted in other courts without challenge. Some privileges remained. Systems of voting based on ownership of property, particularly landed property, gave aristocrats disproportionate voting power in many countries. France retained such a system until 1848, Prussia until 1918. On the whole, however, the legal status of aristocrats was little different from that of other citizens by 1815 in western Europe and by midcentury elsewhere. This fact, along with growing economic pressure, made it increasingly difficult for aristocrats to maintain their traditional feeling of hereditary superiority.

Two general lines of action could preserve some sense of special status. The social exclusivism of the class could be asserted against the rise of the middle class; and special political powers could be maintained, which could provide income as well as status.

Everywhere in the early and midnineteenth century aristocrats tried to protect their distinctiveness in new ways. They formed exclusive social clubs, in which they could conduct distinctive activities such as gambling. Intermarriage with the middle class may have declined, as in Germany; it was certainly disapproved. Rigid social barriers were maintained against contact with nonaristocrats in hunting groups and at dances. Until 1918 Prussian nobles used a rope to separate themselves from the middle class at any dance. After 1815 Parisian nobles began to build a purely aristocratic suburb, the Saint Germain quarter. Aristocratic schools often sought to exclude the nonaristocrats, and continued to stress subjects such as classics and sports, which were suitable for refinement and leisure rather than for economic utility. German universities maintained an aristocratic code of honor in their dueling societies. Wealthy urban nobles perpetuated and even increased when possible their association with cultural activities. In a variety of ways, then, large and small aristocrats continued to seek a distinctive pattern of life and society.

In addition to its stress on style of life, the aristocracy tried to maintain its special political importance. The class continued to believe in its peculiar fitness to rule. Political activities allowed aristocrats to exercise their traditional concern for the well-being of society. They brought dignified jobs and income, including loans and subsidies to large estates. Junkers could push for free trade to help their exports; French nobles sought and obtained agricultural protection. Political power could be used to defend traditional aristocratic values such as religion and military prowess.

Finally, through politics some of the more objectionable features of the middle class could be attacked. In the early nineteenth century many aristocratic politicians in Britain and France encouraged the passage of legislation limiting the rights of employers over workers by defining conditions of child labor and hours of work. In France Villeneuve-Bargemont led attacks on the abuses of the new factories; in Britain the Earl of Shaftesbury promoted the Ten-Hour Law of 1847; in Germany aristocratic parties supported restoration of guilds after 1848 and later backed the first social insurance laws in the 1880s. Only a minority of aristocrats took an interest in these efforts, and a fear of the unruliness of the masses increased in the class as time passed. However, aristocratic paternalism and hostility to the middle class expressed through the use of political power, provided one of the foundations for more vigorous state regulation of industry in the nineteenth century. Here, as in many other ways, the aristocracy tried to use its political power to support traditional position and values.

The aristocracy retained a number of types of political power in the nineteenth century. It continued to dominate the military and generally tried to limit the opportunities for nonaristocrats to enter the ranks of officers. Control of some of the leading positions in the state churches gave aristocrats another important form of institutional power. Aristocrats generally defended the established church with great vigor during the nineteenth century as one means of protecting tradition and stability in society. During the French Restoration aristocratic politicians passed a law decreeing the death penalty for sacrilege in the Catholic Church to defend religion against hostile attack. The British House of Lords long resisted measures passed by the Commons to allow Jews to become members of Parliament or to permit nonconformists to enter the universities. The aristocracy tried to retain a leading role in military and religious institutions and vigorously defended the institutions themselves.

It was in government, however, that the main aristocratic power lay; even church and army were increasingly defended by political means. Nobles retained considerable local authority. In Russia and Prussia the local administrators established after the abolition of feudalism were usually aristocrats. In Spain landlords continued into the twentieth century to nominate local officials. Their nominees controlled much of the local police and were therefore able to intimidate the peasantry; they could also defend the aristocrats' interest against the central government. In France and Britain many regional administrators were aristocrats, and many more were subject to aristocratic influence. Despite changes of regime in France, for example, the regional prefects changed little in social type between 1815 and 1850; they were not exclusively aristocratic, but the aristocracy played a considerable role.

The aristocrats had legislative power in government also. Their local popularity and prestige encouraged their election even in countries where universal suffrage was established. In 1905 one twelfth of the British House of Commons was aristocratic; this was a notable decline from the figure of one sixth in 1860, before the establishment of universal suffrage, but it was a significant figure, nevertheless. In France aristocrats played major roles in parliaments in such crisis years as 1848 and 1871 because of their local prestige among new peasant voters. Furthermore, many legislative bodies preserved an even greater role for aristocrats until 1914. The British House of Lords retained a full legislative veto until 1911. Suffrage limitations in Italy and systems of class voting in Prussia and Austria, by which every class got the same number of votes regardless of its size, returned large numbers of nobles to legislatures in these countries until the late nineteenth century and even later.

It was in central administration, however, that the real political power of aristocrats lay. Even after democratic parliamentary regimes were established in Britain and France, administrators tended to be appointed by cooption rather than by determination of the populace or legislature. Aristocratic exclusivism and the prestige of the class even in the eyes of middle-class representatives tended to reserve the principal roles for aristocrats. In eastern Europe, where the power of parliaments and democratic bodies was small, aristocrats played a fuller role in administration. There the principal ministers as well as the leading diplomats and civil servants were aristocrats. In France the aristocracy saw its hold on the ministries weakened after 1830 and largely destroyed with the establishment of the Third Republic in 1875. In England nobles shared the ministries with commoners throughout the century. Even in France and England, however, many of the chief administrative bodies beneath ministerial rank, such as the diplomatic corps, remained largely in the hands of the aristocracy.

Aristocratic dependence on administrative positions made the class an increasingly conservative force. There were three notable exceptions to this. In Poland and Hungary resentment against foreign rule and the deteriorating economic position of the gentry caused a rise of rebellious nationalism after 1815. There the lesser aristocrats had little political power to defend, so it was understandable that Polish risings in 1830 and 1863 would be led by nobles. The liberal, nationalist Hungarian revolution of 1848 was primarily a rebellion of the gentry. Only after 1867, when the Hungarian aristocracy won great national and local political power, did the switch to conservatism come. In Russia some members of the gentry, particularly educated bureaucrats and military men, had grievances against the autocracy; a few of them led the abortive December rising of 1825. By the 1830s liberal gentry were forming the first elements of the discontented intelligentsia, but this radicalism was not characteristic of aristocrats generally, even in Russia. And by the 1860s in Russia, even the minority was being weaned away from opposition to the tsar. The factors in this process were familiar ones. Economic difficulties increased with the abolition of feudalism; the gentry depended on state help. Local political power grew; the gentry filled most of the positions on the *zemstvos,* the new regional assemblies.

Generally, aristocrats provided the principal support for formal conservative groups during most of the nineteenth century. In France many nobles defended the Bourbon, or legitimist, tradition of monarchy into the 1870s and later despite three intervening regimes. In Prussia the aristocrats also gathered increasingly around the king. Politically as well as religiously, the class defended traditional institutions and through them their own customary leadership.

By 1870 the position of the aristocracy had been altered substantially. Land remained a source of power but an increasingly shaky one. Social distinction remained also, but it had to be defended with new and formal devices. Titles were generally recognized, usually supported by the government. Only in Norway had aristocracy been fully abolished. In politics the nobility retained great power and used it consciously to defend the whole range of aristocratic interests.

If one notes the important legal and economic decline of the class, one must also note aristocratic resiliency. Even in the economic sphere all was not lost. Certainly in politics and administration the nobility remained the dominant element except in some parts of western Europe. The class felt increasingly beleaguered. Its actions were often belligerently defensive. But many traditional values persisted. The class remained a distinctive and important social element.

THE PEASANTRY

Changes in the situation of the peasantry during the nineteenth century in some ways mirrored those within the aristocracy. Both classes were traditional and tradition-minded. Both were faced with major economic and legal change. Both defended many of their customs against change and with some success. Aristocrats and peasants both remained more religious and more politically conservative than did urban classes during the same period. Both were opposed to certain values of the triumphant middle classes and to the rise of the urban masses.

Unlike the aristocracy, however, the peasants were not a traditionally privileged class. They suffered less from legal changes than did the aristocracy. Less conscious of social status, they were able to adapt more fully to the needs of market agriculture. Poor, even destitute, they were capable on occasion of turning violently against existing society, against the aristocracy itself, in a way aristocrats could not because of their continuing stake in the existing order. Peasant life altered fully as much as did that of the aristocracy, but the alterations inevitably took vastly different forms.

Despite many changes, certain aspects of peasant traditionalism persisted. Local festivals continued to constitute one of the major forms of peasant recreation. Even in England peasant songs and folklore were virtually unaltered into the 1840s. Distrust of distant regions, including the city, was still common. A great attachment to the land remained. Peasants gave up or left their land reluctantly, usually under the pressure of considerable misery. If they could, they commonly tried to counter economic novelty by confirming their hold on the land and even acquiring more.

Traditions of village and family unity loosened during the century, but both remained a vital focus for peasant life. Many villages maintained some supervision over local agriculture and law. Village courts in Russia continued even at the end of the nineteenth century to rule on land and inheritance disputes on the basis of quite local customs. Peasant families maintained tighter links than did families in other classes, and peasants typically had more children per family than other classes did. Religious practice remained important for most peasants, although there were de-Christianized rural areas in France. Church attendance and festivals remained major events in village life; many peasants devoted a substantial part of their income to support of the church. Material acquisition remained a less important goal for the peasant than for the urban classes. An interest in material gains developed, but most peasants seemed content with a lower standard of living than that prevailing in the cities. Traditional recreation, the land, the family, and the church provided satisfactions that supplemented the material standard of living.

Economic Pressure

Major alterations in peasant existence were brought about by massive pressures that the peasant could neither resist nor fully understand. Population growth was the most general and fundamental problem. Decline of domestic manufacturing increased the economic pressure. New legal systems encouraged the growth of a landless element. Finally, market agriculture itself brought great difficulties.

In the eighteenth century in western Europe and in the nineteenth in other regions the land available per person began to contract. The number of peasants in European Russia doubled by the end of the nineteenth century with no notable expansion of the land under cultivation. Real land hunger developed in such circumstances, violating village and family traditions of a stable relationship to the land. The number of actual landless peasants rose greatly. Common lands were no longer capable of supporting the local poor. Misery, even destitution, increased. Many peasants depended on wage labor for the first time, and as population increased even agricultural wages tumbled due to an excess of labor supply. To be sure, new land was opened up, even in western Europe. Better drainage and gradual suppression of fallow land increased the demand for agricultural work—but this demand did not keep pace with the rise in rural population in the same period. By 1780 many British peasants depended on charity for survival; others wandered in search of work in different areas and even in the cities. The local economic stability of peasant life had been destroyed.

Almost everywhere, in the early stages of the population boom, domestic manufacturing provided considerable relief from the pressure on the land for a while. Rising population created both markets and labor for rural production of textiles and other goods that could be made in the home without elaborate equipment. Hundreds of thousands of peasants were engaged in manufacturing work in Britain and France in the late eighteenth century, in Germany in the early nineteenth, and in Russia in the late nineteenth century. In many cases domestic workers helped with harvest labor and even cultivated a small garden plot; the ties with the village economy were not broken.

But domestic manufacturing weakened many peasant customs. Independent cash incomes could split the family, particularly beyond the basic unit of husband and wife. Children could leave home earlier, marry earlier, and in general break their attachment both to the land and to patriarchal control. In Switzerland and elsewhere, home industry often spread most rapidly in poor areas where family and village ties had always been less strong. Domestic workers, with wages better than those of agricultural labor during the initial spread of manufacturing, also exhibited unusual interest in improving their levels of consumption. In Switzerland domestic workers discarded customary dress and diet and adopted urban clothing styles and such commodities as coffee, tea, and candy. The character of whole villages was changed by the prevalence of manufacturing and the desire of the workers to distinguish themselves from ordinary peasants.

On the whole, however, the novel effects of manufacturing work were limited. Workers remained attached to land and village. The principal dislocation came not with the introduction of domestic work but with its decline. As industry was mechanized, the conditions of rural manufacturing deteriorated. The mechanization of spinning displaced hundreds of thousands of female spinners, but at the same time it encouraged home weaving for a time because of the availability of cheaper thread. In France between 1810 and 1825, for example, rural weavers earned up to ten times more than the average agricultural worker. However, such good years did not last; the mechanization of weaving and imports from other industrial countries caused rapidly falling wages and increasing periods of unemployment. Within twenty years—in the 1840s in France, in the

1850s in Germany—the number of rural weavers began to fall rapidly; in the interim, conditions of rising misery had prevailed. The decline of domestic industry as a recourse for excess rural population naturally increased the pressure on the land and on average incomes in peasant communities. In combination with population rise, the collapse of rural industry usually caused the peak period of peasant discontent.

At about the same time a number of other changes affected the peasantry. Many of the crucial alterations in peasant tenure and legal status were introduced during the period of major population pressure. Peasants themselves often encouraged such changes, notably the abolition of feudalism, through riots and attacks on local landlords. More commonly, legal changes were introduced from above and simply heightened the difficulties of the peasants. Legal freedom for the peasant to sell his land instead of remaining attached to it often resulted in pressure from landlords or rich peasants to sell out completely. In Britain governmental requirements that land be enclosed in some areas forced many peasants who could not afford fences to sell. The Prussian reforms of feudalism decreased the land available in a period of population pressure. By 1849 there were two million landless in Prussia; in 1770 there had been almost none. In southern Spain and southern Italy peasants were freed from feudal dues, but were given no significant share of the large estates. Many sold what little land they had in an effort to obtain temporary relief; in Spain after 1855, as in Prussia after 1807, legal freedom to leave the land resulted in significant dispossession. In 1894, as a result of similar pressure, 3,275,000 Italian peasants, particularly in the south, possessed less than two and a half acres.

Landless peasants depended for their livelihood on wage labor, mainly on the big estates. Furthermore, the large estates in every area were increasingly coming under the control of members of the middle class; even in Russia, by 1900 one seventh of the big holdings were owned by the middle class. Generally, middle-class landlords treated agricultural labor far more harshly and charged their tenants higher rents than aristocrats had done. Particularly in the large-estate regions, then, peasants were subject to loss of land and new systems of rent and work after the abolition of feudalism. Standards of living in such areas were invariably far lower than in smallholding sections. But even in the west the gap between landed peasants and their landless employes grew steadily.

In Russia peasants fared a bit better. Their emancipation in 1861 included provision of considerable land; the average peasant held over twenty acres, although not always fertile ones. On the other hand, peasants were subjected to a number of postfeudal restrictions. They could not leave their village without village permission. In some villages land was to be redistributed every ten years; these repartitional villages allowed no permanent ownership. Most important, peasants were obligated to pay redemption to the state for their emancipation; these payments were sometimes higher than the rental value of the land. There, as in most areas of large estates, legal freedom involved new obligations, which pressed the peasant severely.

Once the peasants were legally free, governments often imposed burdens of their own, regardless of the degree to which peasants were economically independent. Taxes frequently rose. After 1861 the Russian government collected both taxes and redemption payments from peasants. Southern Italian peasants were taxed according to the standards of northern Italy after unification, although they continued to owe massive sharecroppers' dues to the landlords; landlords were, in fact, empowered to collect taxes as well as their own fees. Cases of this sort were exceptional in Europe as a whole and reflected the trap of southern peasants between a continuation of semifeudal large estates and the requirements of market agriculture. However, the increase of governmental exactions on landed property affected peasants generally during the nineteenth century.

All the new pressure on the peasants increased the need to produce for the market. Ability to buy and sell land placed the land itself increasingly in a commercial system. New taxes and redemption payments augmented the need for cash. Population pressure heightened the need to produce for sales because the available land was so often insufficient to support an owner without the greater efficiency of specialization. Improved transportation and even the competition of products from other agricultural areas attracted peasants to new possibilities for sales and purchases. Cheaper manufactured goods made many home products seem less desirable and even inefficient, again tempting the peasant to greater dependence on buying and selling. In sum, a variety of pressures and possibilities drew peasants into market agriculture even as their life became more difficult in many respects. Through improvements in methods and crops the peasant might actually hope to compensate for some of the hostile features of his new environment. In practice, however, adaptation to market agriculture could only come slowly and was not sufficient to bring real relief for several decades save for a small minority of wealthy peasants.

The barriers to major improvements in productivity included dependence on oral tradition, lack of education, and lack of capital and credit facilities. The village tendency to rely on collective decisions deterred innovation. It was impossible to introduce a new crop or tool on one's own land without affecting others.

The various pressures on the peasantry, particularly intimidating because they acted in combination, usually resulted in a period of declining material standards. British peasants consumed less meat and dairy products in the late eighteenth century than they had before. The income of the average Italian peasant declined between 1861 and 1895. Russian peasants at about the same time possessed fewer animals than they had before. Everywhere, years of bad harvest still brought actual famine to some sections of the peasantry. Peasants suffered, then, not only from the psychological impact of novelty on their highly traditional life but also from increasing material hardship.

Peasant Rebellion

In every major area peasants reacted to their difficulties by vigorous and rising protest. Protest was not unceasing, and many peasants remained apathetic and resigned. However, the periods in which population pressure was at its height, in which new legal structures were beginning to reach the peasantry, and in which new systems of marketing and industry were beginning to affect all forms of peasant production were also periods of major peasant agitation. In western Europe in the late eighteenth and early nineteenth centuries and in eastern and southern Europe in the late nineteenth century peasants rose in similar fashion for similar goals. These movements had a great effect on society as a whole, particularly when they coincided with urban revolutions. They often won major changes in peasant conditions. Certainly they were a sign of the crisis that the peasantry was undergoing.

Peasant discontent was usually translated into rising rates of crime, particularly crime against property. An increase in crime was often the first symptom of protest because it was the simplest way to respond to material hardship. Peasant crime in Ireland increased fivefold in the late nineteenth century alone. Poaching and thefts from the fields were the responses of many English peasants to the hardships of the late eighteenth century. Crime rose in Spain and Italy around the midnineteenth century, and in some cases organized bandits operated with the support of whole villages. Much peasant crime represented not only an effort at material gain but also an expression of resentment against landlords for depriving the peasants of needed space. In Russia 144 landlords and 29 stewards were killed between 1835 and 1854. Peasants felt that the land was theirs if they worked it. They could not consistently assert this claim, but when they did their action could be violent.

A rising tide of riots focused on the apparent causes of misery. Merchants were often attacked during periods of high prices as a result of the increasing dependence of peasants on outside purchases. In 1795 British peasant women rioted in a number of market towns. In the years of poor harvests in France, such as 1828 and 1847, peasants often attacked shops and grain convoys. Grain dealers were attacked in Italy in 1898, again a symbol of resentment against the condition of market agriculture.

In periods of agitation peasants often refused to pay taxes or redemption payments, as in Russia in the late nineteenth century. Rioters sometimes attacked tax offices; more than resentment was involved in such attacks; peasants often burned records in the hope of eliminating the hated assessments. Domestic workers frequently attacked factories and machines. Luddism, though not confined to peasant manufacturers, was often an important concomitant of more general peasant discontent.

The most bitter and extensive riots, sometimes a part of major revolution, were directed against the landlords. When it was most purposeful, peasant agitation tried to destroy feudal obligations and remnants of such obligations and to acquire more land. Such agitation was usually precipitated by a year or two of bad harvests and resulting misery, but it sought more than temporary material relief. In response to population pressure the peasants sought more land and outright control of the land they already had.

Peasant risings against landlords employed many methods. Refusal to pay rents was a common preliminary to an actual rising. Angry and violent attacks on the house and more rarely, the person of the landlord were part of many riots. Rioters usually stole from the lord's property. Peasants on large estates often went on strike. Two features of the major risings were most indicative of the basic purpose. The records of the landlord were pillaged and burned to destroy feudal and sharecropping obligations where these still applied; or government offices collecting redemption payments were similarly treated. Peasants wanted to remove the burdens placed upon them by the lords and felt that no compensation for this removal was justified. Furthermore, peasants often took over part of the lord's land and cultivated it. Here was a naked expression of the land hunger of the peasantry during its time of crisis.

Peasant risings were largely apolitical. They might coincide with political revolution, as in France in 1789, Germany and Austria in 1848, and Russia in 1905, but the peasants had little concern for political goals. Most commonly, they expressed their loyalty to their traditional monarchy, blaming bad advisers for any mistakes the government had made. If they obtained their demands concerning feudal payments, they were content; hence after 1793 the French peasantry largely lost interest in the revolution. In the Russian Revolution of 1905 there was a Peasant Congress, which formulated political demands, but it was in no way representative of the bulk of the peasants who had risen.

Most of the peasant risings lacked any clear doctrine. Russian peasants actually resisted the efforts of university students to spread agrarian socialism during the later nineteenth century. There are, however, two cases in which an ideological element was present. Why this developed in Sicily and southern Spain and in no other major area cannot be fully explained. Some suggestions can be offered, but a fascinating problem remains.

Sicilian peasants accepted the leadership of urban socialists during the Fasci revolt of the 1890s, and they expressed demands for equality of bread and work and even the realization of a new fraternal order in the countryside. Peasants found in socialist doctrines a way to express their old ideals of sharing and equality. In Andalusia in the same period peasants found a doctrine, brought in by foreign and urban agitators, that expressed many of their own hopes. Andalusian peasants were massively converted to at least some of the slogans of anarchism. They tried to free themselves from the encroachments of the central government by eliminating government in favor of purely village rule. They wished to divide all the land equally. By these means misery would be destroyed and a perfect social order established. Both southern Spain and Sicily were areas in which peasant misery and lack of land were particularly acute; both were areas of traditional resentment of the government and high religious fervor. Even in these cases, although doctrine was brought in by outside agitators, the basic purposes of the peasants were expressed. More generally, doctrine was neither needed nor available, and peasants sought their own goals in their own way.

The organization of peasant risings was vague and informal. Risings usually spread from one locality to another by contagion rather than by advance planning. Leadership even among Spanish anarchists was local, since the movement was hostile to organization. There were no special funds to support peasant agitation, and it was difficult to sustain the agitation for more than a few months. Rebellions might recur, as they did in Spain about once every ten years after 1870, but they usually burned themselves out fairly quickly. Direction of peasant risings commonly came from people with some resources and standing in the community. Landed peasants and sometimes rural artisans had a greater sense of direction than did the purely landless. The landless might riot out of misery, attacking merchants or even landlords, but their riots were brief expressions of anger. Landed peasants had some stake in the village, which they saw increasingly threatened by population pressure, taxation, and other exactions. Hence in the major risings it was not the most miserable who took the lead. Peasant rioters in Russia in 1905 came predominantly from the middle group of landowners, neither rich in land nor without land altogether. Spanish anarchists found some support among the landless, but the leadership again came from landed and rural artisan elements. In its organization as well as its main purposes peasant agitation drew from the traditional importance of the land and local structures.

Regional patterns and dates of protest varied greatly. British peasants rioted frequently up to about 1850. They used some distinctive methods, notably burning of buildings. They might attack merchants, as in 1795, or new taxes and tolls, as in the 1843 Rebecca riots in western Wales. Most important, they often turned against machinery. The 1830 riots in Kent and elsewhere were directed against threshing equipment in the name of just wages. Some rural domestic workers attacked the source of their competition, the new machines and factories. In this Luddite agitation, beginning in 1811 and cropping up occasionally later, small groups of weavers and others destroyed many machines in northern England by well-coordinated night attacks. The Luddites developed a doctrine based on the presumed virtues of manual methods.

In France a major rising occurred in 1789. Peasants attacked the records and the estates of the nobility in many sections. Although feudal dues were abolished in the autumn of 1789, agitation continued until redemption payments were eliminated in 1793. Then the peasantry remained largely quiescent. There were important, though brief, local riots in famine years until the middle of the nineteenth century. Domestic workers, pressed by increasing factory competition, occasionally struck and rioted locally. In a few of the poorer regions, such as the mountainous Auvergne, peasants rioted during the ferment of 1848. But the peasantry as a whole ignored and even opposed agitation in most cases, and the major revolutions of 1830 and 1848 had few repercussions in the countryside.

German peasants rioted occasionally in the early nineteenth century; banditry also increased. In 1848 peasants in many sections of Germany and Austria followed the lead of revolution in the cities and attacked their feudal lords. After two years of bad harvests peasants in several areas, especially in the southwestern part of Germany, attacked, pillaged, and burned many castles and record repositories. In eastern Germany there was less revolutionary activity, but peasants were restless and some urged a redistribution of property.

Southern and eastern Europe witnessed some major peasant riots in the early part of the nineteenth century, but there agitation increased after 1870. Because of deteriorating conditions in agriculture generally and the poverty and pressure on the land in these areas of big estates, the period of agitation was often more extended than it had been in western Europe. In Andalusia anarchism spread after 1870. There were a number of major strikes by workers on the latifundias; anarchists even seized land and tried to set up an idealized village government and economy. The Sicilian revolt of the Fasci in 1893 followed three years of declining wheat production and wine prices and a concomitant rise in unemployment. Peasants tried to seize the land, claiming it was theirs by a tradition of possession akin to the possession of common land. Rioting broke out again in 1898 in Sicily and central Italy against grain dealers and bakers; many town halls containing tax records were attacked.

Riots were frequent in the Balkans in this same period. Rumanian peasants rose several times in their hunger for land; a major outburst in 1907 resulted in thousands of deaths. Bosnian peasants rebelled against their Moslem landlords in 1875; they were spurred by a crop failure and by their resentment at having to surrender up to half their crop to the lords. There was one distinctive element in some of the Balkan agitation. Nationalist doctrines attracted increasing numbers of peasants as a means of expressing the common grievances. Nationalist agitators found considerable support among the peasantry in Bosnia, Serbia, and Macedonia. Peasant nationalism was directed particularly against the Moslems because they were landlords and unbelievers; but it could be turned against other outsiders, such as the Austrians. The assassin of Franz Ferdinand showed how peasant hardship could take a nationalist form: "I have seen our people going steadily downhill. I am a peasant's son and know what is happening in the villages . . . All this had its influence on me and also the fact of knowing that he [the archduke] was a German, an enemy of the Slavs." Peasant nationalism was a significant feature of Balkan history at the end of the nineteenth century; it also gave an unusual and vaguely political turn to peasant discontent.

Russian peasants engaged in some riots in every year of the century; between 1826 and 1849 there were about sixty local outbreaks a year. After 1856 petitions to the government or to landowners for freedom from servile obligations increased, spurred by the discontent of soldiers returning to the villages from the Crimean wars. News that the government was going to emancipate the peasantry and then dissatisfaction with redemption payments and lack of land caused a rise in the numbers of riots. In the first months of 1861 alone there were 1,340 outbreaks. This number was unusual, but in succeeding decades a great deal of agitation occurred, particularly in years of bad harvests and famine, such as the 1870s. In Russia as elsewhere, a combination of population pressure and dissatisfaction with legal changes created a high pitch of discontent.

The culmination came in 1905, when peasants rose in many areas, spurred by bad harvests and the failures of the war with Japan. They pillaged forests and estates, refused to pay rents, and burned records in the familiar pattern. Peasants in the repartitional communes, who lacked firm, individual ownership of land, were most active in the rising, which extended over a two year period. After 1906 the pace of rioting declined quite notably until war and revolution brought renewed agitation to the countryside.

At some point in the nineteenth century, peasants in most areas tried to protest their changing situation. They tried to defend and increase their traditional attachment to the land by attacking outside ownership and obligations. Their level of discontent was high, just as the pressures upon them were considerable. Large numbers were roused from customary resignation into an active defense of their dearest traditions. The period of protest, whenever it occurred, marked a major turning point in the lives of the peasants.

Adaptation to the Market

The period of protest in almost all cases reached an end during the nineteenth century. Only in a few areas, such as Andalusia, did conditions remain so stagnant that the protest period extended well into the twentieth century. In France the major risings were over by 1793, and most of the minor ones in France and Britain ended by 1850. German and Austrian peasants were largely quiescent after 1848, and Russian peasants were relatively calm between 1907 and the March revolution. The situation of the peasantry and the attitudes of peasants themselves had changed. In particular, peasants with middling or large holdings found that they could adapt to the new conditions of agriculture.

A number of factors combined to relieve the pressures on the peasants. The full abolition of feudal dues and redemption payments was crucial in satisfying the peasantry in France after 1793; in parts of western Germany, northern Italy, and the Low Countries soon thereafter; in Austria and Germany by the 1850s; and in Russia after 1906. This abolition often resulted directly from peasant risings. It helped placate peasants particularly where individual holdings predominated, as in western Europe and in Russia. But even in east Prussia a minority of peasants had satisfactory holdings. Peasants who owned land now owned it free and clear, although in Germany some rental fees were still paid.

At the same time the rise of new factories provided an outlet for most of the excess rural population. Certain areas, such as Brittany, remained poor and overcrowded because they were too far from industrial centers; it was still difficult to travel very far. On the whole, however, industrial growth absorbed those who could not find a place on the land, sometimes with the help of emigration. In Germany, for example, the expansion of cities accounted for almost the entire increase of the total population after 1840. This alleviated discontent even in the eastern areas of large estates. Cessation of major population pressure and elimination of remnants of feudalism without redemption changed the conditions of the peasantry considerably. Only in parts of southern and eastern Europe (aside from Russia) were peasants still bound by traditional structures by 1914. Subservience to the exactions of landlords remained there even though formal feudalism had been abolished. And population pressure was unrelieved by industrialization. So massive discontent did persist in these regions.

In most of Europe the alleviation of population pressure and, usually, elimination of obligations to landlords created a new environment for peasant agriculture. Peasants began to alter their own patterns of tenure and of production. Particularly in the areas of predominantly small holdings, including Russia after the emancipation, these changes were of major significance. Peasants began, hesitatingly, to adopt new methods. They suppressed systems of fallow and introduced new crops. Some specialized in truck or dairy farming. There was a general effort to improve yield and take advantage of market possibilities. This effort was aided by the development of better agricultural credit by government and cooperative banks.

Alterations in landholding patterns were an essential part of this adaptation. Usually encouraged by governments, common lands were gradually divided and put into private hands. This increased the amount of cultivable land and released the commons from the conservative control of the village. Individuals could now introduce improvements such as better drainage and fertilization on the former commons. The scattered strips typical of peasant tenure in many areas were gradually consolidated, although the process was never complete. Again, consolidation allowed an individual to initiate improvements without coordinating them with his neighbors' activities in adjacent plots. It often created units of sufficient size to make some grazing possible and to allow the use of machines in cultivation.

Finally, a large minority of peasants bought more land. Here was an intensely felt goal, for which peasants often went into debt. After 1861 Russian peasants purchased from noble estates. Elsewhere substantial peasants bought from the near landless. Tiny tenures declined in most cases. More and more owners employed hired help. Landless laborers increased in number; in Germany by the end of the century they outnumbered landed peasants by one third. Yet even for the landless conditions improved as wages rose due to the stabilization of the rural labor force. There was greater inequality now but less hardship. There remained a possibility of resentment by poor peasant of rich. This developed particularly in Russia after 1906. Aside from that there was no major trouble. Landed peasants were content. The landless were less hard pressed. Though still quite poor, they usually found protest activity impossible.

What was occurring, clearly, was a real restructuring of the peasant economy away from tradition and village controls. Villages remained important social units, but they no longer made economic decisions. In Russia there was even a small movement toward setting up isolated farmhouses on the newly consolidated lands after 1906, but this was not typical. A gradual but definite increase in economic individualism was the main peasant response to market agriculture. Nowhere was the desire of peasants for innovation more apparent than in Russia after 1906. Between 1861 and 1906 peasants had been held to the patterns of village agriculture not only by traditionalism, but also by law. Villages were collectively responsible for redemption payments; they determined whether or not a peasant could leave the village; in some cases they periodically reallocated the land. Commons were retained, and holdings were generally divided into strips. After 1906 the government, under the leadership of Stolypin, tried to alleviate peasant discontent by releasing peasants from the hold of the village. Peasants could, on petition, abolish common land and repartitional communes and could consolidate strips. Taking advantage of these possibilities, most peasants withdrew their land from repartitional communes; almost half applied for some consolidation of strips. In a very short time the new economic interests of the peasantry became clear.

Peasant Life

As part of their adaptation to the market peasants tried to improve their standards of living. The desire for individual proprietorship was not only an economic one; clearly peasants felt that land owner- ship gave them social status and security as well. But there was a growing interest in improvement of living standards, even on the part of landless peasants. And as peasants made a gradual transition to market agriculture, standards of living definitely rose. Diet im- proved. Better transportation and higher levels of production elimi- nated famines even in years of poor harvests. In western Europe 1846–1847 represented the last case of real starvation in the country- side. In addition, levels of meat consumption, use of white bread, and purchases of fruits and vegetables gradually increased. New commodities such as coffee and sugar spread widely. Clothing be- came at once more stylish and more varied due to purchases of factory products. In most respects peasant material standards lagged consistently behind urban levels, but improvement did come.

As their interest in material well-being and individual property grew, the peasants' family structure began to alter. Increasingly, peasants limited their birth rate. Soon after their control of the land was confirmed in France, for example, peasants began to restrict the number of children per family. In Germany and Britain, where peasant ownership was less certain, restraint in birth occurred only later in the century. Birth rate among peasants in Russia began to decline only at the very end of the nineteenth century. Dates varied, but in every case peasants ultimately tried to protect their land and their material standards from the burden of too many children.

Family structure changed in other respects. Paternal control was weakened because children could seek work in the cities or as agricultural labor. By 1906 children in Russia were free to leave the family without paternal consent after their maturity, and they increasingly freed themselves from their fathers' decisions about their work or the disposition of their earnings. The ties among more distant members of a family loosened as individualism increased.

Less responsibility was felt for grandparents or uncles and aunts. The trends toward change in family structure were only gradual. Marriages were still arranged in many cases; ties within the family were still keenly felt. But changes had occurred, particularly within the extended family, and they were increasing with time.

Industrialization and the spread of market agriculture also affected the relationship of the peasant to his broader society. Growing contact with merchants and shopkeepers expanded his horizons. Although most transactions still took place in the village, many peasants traveled to larger towns at least occasionally in the course of their business. Improvements in transportation aided this process. Poorer peasants often had to travel to seek employment in harvest work. Their attachment to a single village declined, and their movements could inform other peasants as well. As many poor peasants obtained factory employment, their new experiences and attitudes often affected those who had remained in the village. It was quite common for new factory workers to return to the village for harvest work or even on weekends if they lived close enough. The type of work, levels of pay, and knowledge of city life that former peasants obtained could easily affect the values and expectations of villagers who heard about their activities. A gradual spread of government education systems and of military service provided even more general exposure to the world beyond the village.

By the late nineteenth century peasant life had changed in many respects. In western Europe the varied and grave pressures on agricultural life had taken the peasant through a period of major ferment. In the east and south agitation was at a peak. Everywhere traditional influences remained, now supplemented by a growing interest in individual landed property. At the same time new material concerns and changes in family patterns linked the peasant to more general social trends. Old superstitions declined under the pressure of change, as in Ireland after the famine of the 1840s. Still, peasant society remained separate in many ways. Within the framework of outside forces such as government and industry peasants themselves had guided the process of change. Where they could not shape their lot in accordance with acceptable values, as in southern Europe, they remained rebellious. Elsewhere they had abandoned rebellion precisely because they had formed a satisfactory society.

URBAN SOCIETY

Growth of Cities

Urbanization was a natural result of population growth and industrialization. Expanding population and rising agricultural productivity released hundreds of thousands of people who were not needed and could not be supported in the countryside. Improved food production, along with better transportation, made it easier to supply urban populations.

The most rapid rates of urban growth occurred in the new factory centers, for mechanized industry required a large pool of labor. Many of these cities were essentially new, for factory location was increasingly determined by access to coal, and many of the coal-rich areas had been only sparsely urbanized before. And the peak period of urban expansion corresponded to the rise of substantial factory industry.

Other types of cities grew in the nineteenth century, without necessarily developing an elaborate factory system. Cities with port facilities were encouraged by the industrial revolution, because the expansion of trading and exports increased the need for commercial outlets. The growth of cities such as London, Liverpool, and Marseilles was based more on rising trade than on industry directly. The increasing need for centralized banking facilities to amass and administer the huge capital both required and produced by industry stimulated the growth of Paris and London. The gradual extension of government activities and personnel attracted many to the capital cities. The urbanization of some whole countries, such as Holland, was based primarily on the commercial, banking, and governmental functions of cities. Expansion of trade in agricultural goods and imported industrial products provided a basis for the growth of cities such as Budapest in areas which the factory system had scarcely touched. In general, however, urbanization developed as a direct result of the various functions that industry brought to the cities.

The dependence of city growth on industry also determined the peculiar pattern of urbanization in the nineteenth century. Cities did not grow uniformly. Many older centers declined or stagnated. Improved transportation and marketing reduced the need for purely local trading and manufacturing cities. Even artisan production tended to move from local towns to a small number of cities, such as Paris. The railroad itself operated most efficiently between large centers. Lines could not be built everywhere at first; cities not located on a trunk line were usually doomed to decay. Even when lines were built, it was uneconomical for trains to stop and start too often. Railroad transport tended to encourage the growth of major centers, rather than towns generally. Similarly, the need for a pool of labor and massive capital and commercial facilities dictated the expansion of cities best located with regard to resources and transportation. Urbanization involved, then, the concentrated growth of some new industrial cities and of major centers generally. Many older towns, such as Norwich in Britain and Vézélay in France, actually declined as part of the urban movement.

Favored cities expanded rapidly. In Britain, the first country to experience major urban expansion just as it was the first to industrialize, some of the new manufacturing cities grew as much as 40 per cent in a single decade; many northern cities, such as Leeds, Birmingham, and Sheffield, did so between 1821 and 1831. Between 1801 and 1851 Birmingham grew from 73,000 to 250,000, while Liverpool expanded from 77,000 to 400,000. Manchester rose from 25,000 to 367,232 between 1772 and 1851. London also continued to grow but at a slower rate. French urbanization was naturally both later and slower than British, as French industry and population expanded less rapidly. Between 1830 and 1851 four fifths of France's population rise went into the cities; between 1851 and 1871, eleven twelfths did so. Some industrial centers grew with great rapidity but never to the size of the British giants. Saint-Étienne rose from 16,000 to 56,000 between 1820 and 1850 and Roubaix from 8,000 to 34,000. The great growth of Paris overshadowed the provincial centers during most of the century, making French urban development far less balanced than was the case in other countries.

In Germany urbanization had clearly begun by the 1860s. In that decade city growth absorbed the whole German population gain. Berlin and the industrial centers in Saxony and the Ruhr grew most rapidly. In 1870 there were eight cities in Germany with populations of more than 100,000; in 1900 there were forty-one, and five were over the half million mark. Scandinavia and the Low Countries entered their period of urban growth around midcentury also, and eastern Europe soon followed. Austria's city population rose from 18 per cent to 32 per cent of the total between 1850 and 1890. During the last three decades of the century Warsaw grew by half a million, and the industrial city of Lodz rose from 31,000 to 310,000. Russian cities grew rapidly, with Moscow rising by 400,000.

In 1800 Europe had twenty-two cities with a population over 100,000; in 1895 she had 120, and their inhabitants represented 10 per cent of the European population as a whole. Several areas, in fact, were over half urban. Britain passed this point in 1850, and by 1900 over four fifths of her people lived in cities. Germany was over half urban by 1900, France by 1930; and the trend spread widely.

City growth slowed down in most countries after the first decades of industrialization. In Britain, for example, the most intensive period of urbanization occurred between 1841 and 1851; and in Austria, it took place between 1880 and 1890. After several decades of extraordinary development cities generally settled down to a more modest though still substantial increase. By that time the nature of the cities and their place in society had been radically altered. New urban areas had risen, and more massive agglomerations than had ever before been known.

City Population

The initial decades of urban expansion depended largely on immigration from the countryside. The cities themselves had only scanty margins of births over deaths in this period; they were not capable of significant natural increase. In some of the fastest-growing centers two thirds of the residents had been there less than fifteen years. Many rural residents were attracted to the cities by the opportunities and excitement of urban life, but more were forced to come. Population pressure, loss of land, and more productive agriculture made many peasants unnecessary in the countryside, and factory competition displaced domestic manufacturers. After a period of declining wages and lengthening periods of unemployment, huge numbers of rural people sought refuge in the cities. Often they went first as transients, hoping to return to their village after a period of factory work. Gradually, their contacts with the countryside declined, and they became fully urban.

Some of the cities' new residents had traveled long distances from their homes in towns and villages. Large cities such as Berlin and

Paris drew from all over the country. Barcelona attracted thousands of southern Spanish peasants. A substantial number of foreigners came into many cities. Irish peasants sought work in the new British centers, and Belgians and Germans helped build up towns like Roubaix and Mulhouse; Poles later came into the Ruhr. But many of the smaller industrial cities relied primarily on their own regions for their expansion. Even in these cases, however, the move to the city meant a real break from the past. Adjustment to urban life was not easy. The city had material problems and opportunities very different from those of the countryside. The crowding, the pace, the very novelty of the cities created their own pressures. Nineteenth-century urbanization involved an internal migration of major proportions. It also involved adjustment to a radically new setting and way of life by hundreds of thousands of people.

The city population was young. The bulk of the immigrants from the countryside were between twenty and forty years old, the age at which one had the vigor and courage to tear up ties with the village or town. The youth of the urban population in turn contributed to the dynamism of the cities. The immigrants were at the most economically productive age, and this helped build the prosperity of the new cities. The energy of the young newcomers might also contribute to rising urban agitation.

Urban conditions and growth set the city population apart from the rural in other ways. Family life changed because of the strangeness and new opportunities of the city. The urban divorce rate was three or four times higher than the rural; the birth rate was lower, and the percentage of marriages within a given age group was also lower. There were twice as many illegitimate births as there were in the countryside. Rates of suicide, insanity, and crimes against property were notably higher.

There were even physical differences between urban and rural populations. Urban residents were physically larger, on the average. They were less afflicted with congenital idiocy, because there was greater crossbreeding in the cities. The percentage of women was higher in the city due to a higher male death rate and the fact that the ratio of males to females at birth was lower than in rural communities. In vigor, in composition, and in many basic habits the people of the new cities were different from the people of the villages. There were many vital distinctions in class and behavior within the city, but urban life imparted some common features to city residents as a whole.

Material Conditions

The most obvious general influence in the rising cities was the material setting. The great influx of immigrants put real strain on urban physical facilities—facilities that had often been poorly developed even before. A positive deterioration of conditions occurred in many cities during the first period of urban growth. British cities, which had been paying growing attention to street paving and to covering sewers in the late eighteenth century, could not build rapidly enough to keep pace with their rising population. An increase in urban mortality rates was the inevitable result. Rapidly growing French cities such as Mulhouse had similar problems, but centers that expanded more slowly, such as Lille, managed to improve their facilities throughout the period. Later in the century similar material pressures occurred in the cities of southern and eastern Europe.

New numbers created a great need for housing. Old buildings were divided and redivided. Cellars and attics were put to use; the poorest families had only one room or even had to share a room with another family. New buildings were hastily thrown up, providing cramped, flimsy accommodation. Rents soared, doubling or even tripling in a decade or two. Intense crowding, inadequate conditions, high prices—these were the inevitable consequences of the influx to the cities.

The expansion of cities created needs for transportation as well. New streets had to be built. Many older streets were still unpaved, and the new ones were often little more than rutted paths. Vehicular transport was in private hands and expanded only slowly; the carriages and horse-drawn omnibusses were too expensive for most of the new residents. The crowding of the cities was partly due to the need to be within walking distance of the place of work, and even so some new workers had to walk many miles each day.

New population meant increasing need for wells and for sewage disposal; these too were provided only slowly and inadequately. Many sewers remained open, and many rivers were increasingly polluted by the disposal of wastes. The poorer areas of most cities were unbelievably filthy and smelly. They were naturally subject to diseases and even epidemics, such as the cholera epidemic that raged through western Europe in 1832.

Danger from fire and from criminals was also high. Cities had few police facilities before. In 1848 Berlin had two hundred policemen for a population of 400,000—and it was one of the best-policed cities of Europe. With unlighted streets, huge numbers of new and poor inhabitants, and few regular police patrols, it was small wonder that crime rates rose rapidly. The pressure of population on already limited facilities created a vast array of material problems in the cities.

City Governments

Gradually, private groups and particularly urban governments themselves developed new concepts of what a city should be like. They tried not only to catch up with the needs created by rising population, but also to go beyond what older cities had offered. New systems of fire prevention and of mass transport were developed; new ideas of police action and government inspection arose. By the midnineteenth century in western Europe, and soon after elsewhere, new institutions were transforming urban life.

In many cases the development of new urban activities was promoted by changes in city government. New elements in the middle class, such as factory owners, sought urban political power. In Britain this change was slow. Manchester was governed as a noble manor until 1844, when the administration was opened to election by middle-class property owners. Even before then, however, industrialist groups had supplemented the manorial officials with activities of their own, especially in matters of police and hygiene. Cities elsewhere in western Europe were more abruptly freed from the control of aristocratic or church officials. The French revolution established election procedures for mayors, with the franchise usually limited to property owners. Most cities in France and the Low Countries were governed by middle-class administration. The mayors of most factory centers were usually industrialists, but older elements of the merchant class controlled other cities. In eastern and southern Europe urban administration was opened to new personnel later in the nineteenth century.

National governments, too, played an increasingly active role in the cities; in central Europe this partly continued an earlier trend.

By 1850 the British government began to suggest and then require the establishment of local boards of health and education. The French government, more active in local affairs, played a major role in such projects as slum clearance.

Municipal governments took a hand in the matter of housing. By the 1830s French cities established some inspection of houses and even closed some of the worst slums. During the Second Empire the national government sponsored housing projects in Marseilles and elsewhere. In Paris the prefect Haussmann tore down huge slum areas in order to build a network of boulevards. The object was to eliminate the twisted, crowded streets that were so easy to barricade in revolution and to replace them with avenues down which troops could march and fire. The result was a major change in the housing and transportation of Paris—and also a considerable reduction in the possibility of riot. In Britain cities were empowered to inspect houses in 1851 and to clear slums in 1865; by the 1890s minimum standards of space and sanitary facilities were established in all houses. Elsewhere in Europe, in many German cities for example, stronger traditions of government action promoted regulations even earlier.

Cities also began to build parks. Paris removed many old cemeteries, health hazards in themselves, and replaced them with parks. At the end of the century Vienna tore down her peripheral walls and substituted a ring of boulevards and parks.

Problems of transportation were attacked by private companies and cities. Increasing controls were placed on bus companies. Streets were broadened and paved. Most important, commuter trains and later subways offered rapid transport at a low price. By the later part of the century rapid transportation and municipal housing regulations had greatly reduced urban congestion; the boundaries of cities spread and suburbs proliferated beyond them.

Urban governments also attempted to deal with crime and public hygiene. Gas lighting was installed on many city streets by the 1830s. Police functions were greatly expanded. New forces, such as London's bobbies, set up in 1829, provided far more numerous personnel. Cities also established fire departments, long supplemented by private brigades such as those provided by many insurance companies. Cities built new covered sewers quite rapidly and worked to improve the water supply. They began to clean the streets. Municipal officials checked water supplies, market conditions, and slaughter-houses. Schools, factories, and hospitals were also made subject to city inspection. Many cities required vaccinations of all residents.

The result of these various efforts in housing and hygiene was a major improvement in urban health. By the 1830s French cities had a large annual surplus of births over deaths. German cities such as Frankfurt achieved a similar surplus in the 1840s. Everywhere urban mortality rates fell much more rapidly than rural, and in a few countries, such as Austria, by the end of the century they had actually dipped below the levels of the countryside.

Falling death rates produced an important natural increase in urban population. After several decades of growth by immigration, during which death rates were usually high, cities began to expand largely from within. By the late nineteenth century London's growth owed only 15 per cent to immigration; the rest was natural increase. Urban expansion had entered a new stage.

By that stage a truly new type of urban government had also been created. Particularly in many cities in Germany, Italy, and Britain, where there was important local autonomy, a complex network of urban welfare activities had been gradually created. Governments inspected and regulated most activities in local commerce and construction. They ran a growing number of schools and libraries. Urban provision of funds and goods to the poor and of public works to the unemployed greatly extended the charity resources in the cities. In some cases cities even began to take over public utilities and transport companies in the general interest. In cities such as Birmingham under Joseph Chamberlain an immensely powerful urban administration had been created. Everywhere, expanding urban bureaucracies and regulation for the public welfare represented an important response to the needs of industrial society. The concepts and methods evolved by active numerical governments were later adopted by national administrations as well. It was within the new cities that more elaborate organization and control first seemed necessary. It was within the cities that new and vigorous social classes first completely captured the government. Urban government no less than urban conditions was radically altered as a result.

The conditions of cities during the century passed through two stages. At first the massive influx of people increased the hardship of urban life. Crowding and filth added to the inevitable problems of adjustment of many new arrivals. Those who could tried to escape the areas of greatest misery. Patterns of residence changed as the rich began to build separate communities, to escape from the poor. Members of the middle class moved to the outskirts of the urban center. The development of suburbs, facilitated by improved transportation, paralleled the growth of major cities. After 1860, in fact, suburbs began to expand more rapidly than the central city itself in London and other centers. This suburban growth relieved some of the crowding of the cities, but it also increased the separation among urban social classes. At the same time, however, cities quickly began to deal with their material difficulties; the physical quality of urban life improved. A new urban society had been born, and cities increasingly adjusted to their new situation. Basic material problems were not eliminated, but they were reduced. The intense growing pains of the new cities gave way to a certain maturity.

URBAN SOCIAL CLASSES: THE WORKERS

An important segment of the urban population, particularly in the larger cities, continued to be irregularly employed. Construction projects in the growing cities drew in large numbers of unskilled. As late as 1889 in one school board district in East London, 50,000 to 80,000 people, of 450,000, were usually unemployed and depended largely on charity. A large number of Parisians, used in building projects during the July Monarchy, were unemployed during the crisis of 1846–1847. Many of these people had to beg, steal, or become prostitutes in order to live. In Berlin at the same time a tenth of the population was said to be composed of prostitutes or criminals. About midcentury virtually a quarter of the population of Lille depended on charity. Begging, though attacked by middle-class city governments and banned in some places, remained endemic in the growing cities.

Industry did not, then, eliminate the dangerous class. It did absorb a portion of it. But in early industrialization the class continued to grow in absolute numbers as the cities themselves expanded. They were the people who lived in the most crowded and filthy slums, whose food and clothing was still barely sufficient for survival. Segregated still within the city's populace, the urban poor seldom actively protested their mean lot. Some did occasional artisan or factory work, but they did not usually attach themselves to the main working classes. They remained largely uneducated and deprived throughout the first decades of industrial development. Sometimes they traveled, serving as navvies on the new railroad lines and porters for the expanded commerce of the cities. Sometimes they moved back and forth between agricultural labor and urban employment. Always they represented a large and degraded element of the rising cities.

In addition to the irregularly employed and to the artisans, a new social class of factory workers became part of the labor force of the cities. The novelty of this class was based on its conditions of work and its origins. Unlike both artisans and domestic manufacturing workers, factory labor was employed in large units. The early factories were not gigantic; often they had only twenty workers. But their size steadily increased, and they were clearly different from the tiny artisan shop. In the factory the gap between worker and employer was obvious. Sometimes there was no personal contact at all between them, and almost never was a relationship of any equality developed. The worker, unlike many artisans, owned little property and certainly did not own his tools. Furthermore, labor on large machines involved a pace and coordination unknown in artisan or rural life.

At the same time factory workers were generally new not only to their job, but also to the city. Some workers were, of course, former artisans. Individual opportunities drew some artisans into the factories. A few urban crafts were directly attacked by factory competition; some cloth printers and cutters were forced into the new plants as their processes were mechanized. But most of the industrial working class was not recruited from the artisans. Most artisan trades long remained free from mechanical competition, and the need for such trades as carpenters and bakers obviously grew as cities expanded. Furthermore, the artisans that did enter the factories usually took some of the best paying and most skilled positions. Their training and motivation still set them off from the mass of industrial employes. In Mulhouse during the 1840s, for example, few workers in the factories had been born in the city, and those who had were generally highly skilled machinists and cloth printers.

The bulk of the labor force, including many who had risen to skilled positions themselves, was drawn from outside the city and outside any urban artisan group.

Origins of the Working Class

The main source of factory workers was, of course, displaced rural labor, people who lacked land and could no longer continue as domestic manufacturers. Frequently, it was only their misery that could have induced the new workers to abandon the countryside. Peasants often resisted factories even when the conditions of labor were exceptionally favorable. Manufacturers in Décazeville, a new industrial city in central France in an area of poor agriculture but extensive peasant smallholding, found it very difficult to recruit workers locally. The methods and discipline of the factory were simply unappealing even though the wages were much higher than in agriculture. In France more generally, the lack of severe population pressure on peasant tenure made it difficult to recruit a large labor force. There were, of course, individual cases of attraction to life in the factory and in the city. Some peasants were delighted at the opportunity of leaving the economic and social limitations of village existence. More commonly, however, the labor in the early factories was recruited by no positive attraction. Often there was little conscious choice at all. The hundreds of thousands of Irishmen who crossed to English industrial cities, the Flemings who flocked to the mines of southern Belgium, and the Russian peasants who reluctantly left their villages in the 1890s were impelled by the increasing hardships of rural life. Often miserable and even more often confused, their origins were to exercise a profound influence over the early conditions of their class.

At first the separation of factory workers from their rural traditions was far from complete. Many workers retained important links with the countryside, again reflecting their reluctance to break with the agricultural life. Some could still live in a village and travel to a small factory town for work. Many of the women and children in the factories belonged to peasant households and were only trying to add to rural resources. Many male workers left their families in the villages and stayed in boarding houses during the week, returning to work their small plots on weekends. Up to 25 per cent of the labor force in the first generation of the industrial revolution returned to the countryside during the summer, when the demand for agricultural labor was highest. In economic crises as many as a tenth of the factory workers returned to the countryside to seek support from their own village and family.

Inevitably, the ties with the countryside tended to decline. Workers grew accustomed to the city, and the opportunities for rural labor continued to stagnate or decline. By the second generation of the industrial revolution the factory working class had developed independent roots and attitudes. The economic crisis of 1846–1847 in France, coming about two decades after industrialization began, marked the first time that there was no major exodus to the countryside. Even before this, the move to the factory city placed the former peasant or domestic worker in a decisively new situation.

The industrial working class was at first rather small and very unevenly distributed in a country as a whole. In new factory cities, such as Manchester or Mulhouse, the workers were a majority of the population. More traditional centers, such as Paris and London, long possessed very few factory employes; their activities were far more commercial and artisan than industrial. Other large centers did develop an industrial working class but only as one element of a diverse population. By 1902 approximately one tenth of the inhabitants of Moscow and St. Petersburg worked in factories, and they tended to concentrate in only a few sections of the cities. By no means, then, did the workers dominate urban society in the early industrial revolution.

Within a country as a whole the workers long remained a small minority. By 1848 there were probably no more than 400,000 factory workers in France out of more than four million employers and employees in manufacturing of all types. Industries such as wool spinning, with 31,000 workers, were entirely mechanized, but weaving, with half a million workers, had been scarcely touched by the new processes. In most countries once industrialization began, factory labor grew more rapidly than was the case in France. By 1850 there were fully as many workers as artisans in England, more than two million in fact. And the factory working class was the most rapidly growing social group everywhere during the first several generations of the industrial revolution.

Material Conditions

The nature of the early working class was conditioned by three primary factors. The rural origins of the class were of decisive importance. This was a group unaccustomed to city life. Psychological pressures in the factories heightened its confusion. And workers were severely limited by their material condition.

The material focus of the worker's life was his labor in the factory. Hours of work were very long. In textile factories the average was about thirteen and a half hours, but with rest periods workers spent up to fifteen hours at the plant. And a few firms required fourteen or fifteen hours of work; a few had work go on all night on Saturdays to compensate for the Sunday off. Metallurgical firms generally limited work to twelve hours so that two shifts could be set up for the whole day. Mining work varied but was usually under ten hours a day; but it was heavier work than the textile or metallurgical industries required. There were few days off. Sundays were usually honored, although some employers required workers to appear briefly to clean their machines. A few traditional saints' days were celebrated in Catholic countries, such as the festival of Sainte Barbe, the patron of miners. In Russia during the 1890s factories closed for more than forty such holidays. Generally, however, the hours and days of work were very near the limits of physical endurance. Industrialists tried to utilize their expensive machines as much as possible; and they felt that the lighter work that machine tending involved justified some increase in hours. For the workers, few if any waking hours were left after the period of work and the time taken to walk home from the job.

Women and children were used extensively in the new plants, particularly in the textile industry. They provided cheap, docile labor and were capable of handling most of the mechanical processes. Their nimbleness was in fact regarded as very appropriate for machine work. In the early textile industry women represented at least 40 per cent of the labor force, and children under sixteen another 10 to 15 per cent. Certain branches of production, such as the mechanical weaving in the early years, involved almost no adult males at all. In metallurgy and mining the heaviness of the work made women and children less useful, although some were employed in hauling coal and picking up slag. Children were rarely hired before they were eight or ten, but a few factories used even five-year-olds. Once employed, children were subjected to the same hours as the other workers. Not all working-class children had factory jobs; many families tried to keep their children out of the factories; some child labor came from peasant or urban-lower-class families rather than those of factory employes. Nevertheless, the use of many children and even more women was an important feature of factory life.

Most factory and mine work was dangerous. Machinery was unscreened and it was not uncommon to catch fingers in it. Children had to crawl under textile machines to clean them while they were in operation. Many kinds of work involved intense heat, dampness, or stench. Miners and chemical workers suffered from exposure to gases. Textile labor involved much dust because it was long believed that open windows would harm the fibers. In general, no precautions were taken that would add to the expense or difficulty of production. The health of the workers inevitably suffered as a result. Many were maimed and some were killed in accidents; and many contracted occupational diseases, particularly of the chest, due to the poor hygiene of the plants.

Standards of living outside the plant were determined by the wages workers received, and these varied considerably. Children were paid half of what women received and women about half what men received. Wages during the life of an individual worker varied considerably; rising as he grew to maturity, they would tumble as his strength failed with age. There was considerable variety among industries. Mining and metallurgy, which required substantial strength and skill, paid adult males far more than the textile industry did.

In general, differences in skill determined differences in wage levels. Mechanization by no means eliminated the need for skill; it only changed the type required. The men who built and installed machines, or who puddled iron, or who ran the more complex spinning machines required years to learn their trade fully. Their pay was from three to six times greater than that of an unskilled laborer. The factory labor force therefore included some workers paid well above the subsistence level in normal times. It also included a minority whose wage allowed only the meanest conditions of life: orphans and single females, the aged, and unskilled workers burdened with large families. Many in this group depended on charity to survive. Between these two extremes were the majority of workers, whose wages were high enough for survival and sometimes for a few relative amenities. In a family with three children, the average size, subsistence depended on the wife and one child working. Seventy-five per cent of the budget had to go for food. Life in these circumstances was without frills and without margin for bad times, but as a rule the factory workers were not the most deprived segment of the urban population.

Unfortunately, the standard of living was determined not only by the level of wages, but also by interruptions of pay. Most workers, even the better paid, faced a number of threats to their jobs. Illness was usually uncompensated and sometimes resulted in permanent loss of work. Old age might bring dismissal and certainly brought a reduction in pay. Machine breakdowns caused days and even weeks of unemployment. Most important, recurrent industrial crises plunged a large number of workers into profound, if usually temporary, misery. A crisis brought wages down, sometimes by as much as 50 per cent. In the most severe cases a quarter or even a third of the workers in the hardest hit industries and areas were thrown out of work entirely. The responses of the working class to such disaster were varied. Some returned to the countryside to seek work or to roam in bands to find food. Charity rolls expanded massively in crises, often embracing over half the working class in a city. Many workers sold or pawned their possessions. All reduced their expenses by eating potatoes instead of bread and avoiding paying the rent and all other items not essential to immediate survival. Some died; death rates always rose substantially during crises. For many members of the working class, then, life was punctuated by a number of personal and general disasters. Periods of real misery alternated with times of some comfort, creating a sense of insecurity that haunted workers even in the most prosperous times.

Patterns of consumption naturally mirrored wage conditions. The worker's diet was mostly starch, bread or potatoes. The very poorest were unable to add much to this, but most could afford a bit of meat once or twice a week, some milk products, and some vegetables. Many workers could afford occasional wine or beer or stronger drink and some coffee and sugar. The diet was usually sufficient from a caloric standpoint, but it was certainly colorless. Moreover, much of the food purchased was of poor quality; some was actually rotten or adulterated. Workers had little power to resist frauds or shoddy goods.

Housing facilities were also very limited. In the most rapidly growing cities many workers had less than a room for their families, often located in a teeming, filthy slum. Others, however, were able to afford two rooms and sometimes even a garden if they lived on the outskirts of a city or in a smaller factory town. Furnishings ranged from a straw pallet and ragged blanket to a few larger wooden pieces.

A minority of workers were literally in rags, lacking even shoes. Far more had at least one change of clothing, including a pair of leather shoes. Many bourgeois observers, with a mixture of pride and concern, noted that factory workers on Sunday were increasingly hard to distinguish from shopkeepers and clerks because of the variety and quality of their dress. The rising production and declining price of relatively stylish clothing clearly benefited factory workers quite early.

Beyond the vital trinity of food, housing, and clothes, few workers could afford any other notable expenditures. A bit of tobacco or a small contribution to a mutual aid group were all that even the better paid could afford. What variation in pay there was showed up in the essentials; a slightly more varied diet and wardrobe and a few more furnishings and utensils constituted the material range of working-class life. Even the better paid spent at least half their income on starches alone.

The poverty and the working conditions of factory employes naturally took a toll in health. Poor foods and particularly crowded, dirty housing caused much illness. Long hours and unsafe factories had a great effect. The labors of children stunted and afflicted many for their whole life. Women who worked too soon after pregnancy harmed their own health and that of their children, whom they were often unable to nurse. Many factory workers had a life expectancy at birth only half as great as that of their employers. The infant mortality rate was very high. Adult workers aged rapidly; many miners were exhausted before they were forty. Some workers were deformed; many suffered from skin ailments. Epidemics periodically afflicted the class, along with the other urban poor.

Material Conditions: Progress or Decline?

Despite their many difficulties, most workers were better off in some respects than they or their parents had been in the country-side. The question of whether conditions deteriorated or were improved by early factory employment has been hotly debated, particularly in the case of the British industrial revolution. There is evidence on both sides. Many have tried to prove that early industry was evil, while others have asserted its beneficence; even during the industrial revolution itself the question was debated with much partisan feeling. The issue is not merely an academic one. In order to understand the workers themselves, it is vital to know whether they experienced a deterioration in conditions as they entered industry. That the workers were in misery from a modern point of view cannot be denied; that they were severely limited in their conditions is obvious; but whether they felt themselves to be miserable, judging by the standards they knew, is far from clear.

Several points must be considered as a preliminary to this major issue. In the first place, there are obvious national and chronological differences to be noted. The possibility of deterioration of conditions was greatest in Britain, for several reasons. The standard of living among the British peasantry was relatively high until the early eighteenth century at least; in rates of meat consumption and quality of housing, particularly, the peasants were better off than their counterparts on the continent. Furthermore, British industrial growth and the corresponding urban crowding were very rapid, and this put pressure on the working class in the early decades that was less severe in France or Italy, where the process was slower. Also, British cities were far less regulated than those of the continent; this affected housing and hygiene significantly.

Early British industrialization stressed the textile industry. This was a highly competitive industry, with small firms battling vigorously to stay alive and grow. It involved relatively little skill and employed large numbers of women and children. In contrast, later industrialization, as in Germany and Russia, involved more employment in large firms and in heavy industry. Competition was reduced due to the size of the firms, and the greater skill and strength required of workers encouraged better treatment. Finally, countries industrializing after 1850, when the supply of money was increasing rapidly, were less pressed by falling prices than industrializing areas had been in the earlier part of the century. Working conditions in Germany in the 1850s and in Russia in the 1890s were far from good. They fell clearly within the limitations on leisure time and spending power already described. But there and even in France there can be little question of deterioration in material standards for workers entering factory industry.

Furthermore, in England and elsewhere, rural conditions had usually been declining before the industrial revolution began. This was, after all, the main impulse for peasants to accept factory jobs. Peasant standards of living were low anyway; preindustrial society was simply poor. And the people entering industry were often drawn from the lowest categories of the peasantry. These were the people who suffered most from expanding population and declining domestic industry. There was deterioration of material conditions in the early industrial period, but it occurred primarily in the countryside among the landless and the domestic producers. When they found factory employment, they seldom could note a significant worsening of their situation and often benefited from some improvements.

Standard of living did alter once a worker entered the factories. Certain features of the worker's life deteriorated, while others improved. Housing, particularly in the larger cities, was an important instance of deterioration. Rural housing was often flimsy and small, but it was seldom as crowded as the new worker quarters of the cities. There was less concentrated dirt and smell.

Hours of work were longer in the factories than in agricultural labor, and there were fewer holidays. The difference was less clear between factory hours and the hours in domestic manufacturing, for as mechanical competition increased, many rural producers were forced to work sixteen and even eighteen hours a day to make ends meet. Furthermore, machines did reduce the need for great physical effort at work. But the intensity and pace of work were greater than ever before.

Women and children, of course, worked on the farms and in domestic manufacturing as in the factories. As employers were fond of pointing out, it would have been a major innovation not to use them. There is no particular evidence that a greater percentage of women and children were used in factories than in domestic production. The hours and intensity of their work, however, were increased in the new system.

The pressures of housing and intensity of work were reflected in a possible deterioration of health. Certainly the mortality rate among workers was higher than that among peasants in general. In some instances, however, health may have been no worse than that of landless peasants and domestic workers. The rate of rejects from the army on grounds of health was higher in some of the poorer agricultural regions of northern France than it was in the factory districts of the same area. So the evidence allowing a precise comparison is by no means totally clear. In certain important respects, however, and possibly in health itself, factory workers did experience a deterioration of conditions.

Improvements also were significant. Factory workers on the whole maintained higher real wages than were offered in the countryside. Costs were greater, especially rents, but money wages were greater still. Hence workers had better diets than did peasants. In France, they were more likely to eat wheat bread instead of black bread. They had more meat, coffee, sugar, and alcoholic drink. Sales of many of these commodities rose fairly rapidly in many factory cities. Clothing was definitely more stylish and varied. There were more leather shoes, more changes of clothing, more items such as umbrellas. The resources of charity were greater in the cities than in the countryside, and crises affected agriculture as well as industry in this period. Educational facilities were better. The early workers were not well educated, but by the second generation most had been exposed to some schooling despite the evils of child labor. Only a minority were literate in the early industrial revolution, but the rate of literacy was notably higher than among the peasants. On balance, then, there were important improvements in the lot of the factory workers. This is, after all, why they usually stayed in the factories, and why increasing numbers were drawn in.

Furthermore, by the second generation of industry some of the harshest aspects of worker life were being modified. Safety and hygiene in the plants improved. Many of the early factories had been installed in old mills or even convents, which were ill-adapted to the new machines. As machines became more complex, they had to be given more space and light. And as many firms passed the initial intensely competitive period and themselves became established, they could devote greater resources to the security of machines and workers; new factories were often built, and some safety devices were installed. There was more room, more light. New machines themselves reduced the dust and odor of many operations. Accidents and occupational diseases were still common, but the rate declined.

Similarly, the use of young children in industry declined. Manufacturers developed some conscience about this aspect of industry, and laws were passed vaguely regulating the use of children. It was discovered also that young children were not particularly efficient, and their usefulness decreased as machines became more complex. Women and older children were still extensively employed, but abuses of the very young declined.

Hours were reduced a bit. Industrialists realized that long hours often curtailed efficiency; some were also concerned about undue competition through overproduction. The resulting changes were gradual and slight; over twelve hours of work remained the rule in the textile industry.

Finally, in many cases factory wages rose slightly. There was some rise in Germany in the 1850s and in Russia in the 1890s. Pay in French mining and metallurgy and in the most prosperous textile regions increased during the July Monarchy. Again, the changes were small. The period of great improvements in conditions was still in the future. But what improvements there were relieved some of the worst points of material pressure on the workers.

Gains were made, for example, in worker health. During the July Monarchy life expectancy in the largely industrial city of Lille rose from twenty-eight to thirty-two. The physical stature of workers improved during the same period, reflecting their better diet; the average worker was already taller than the average peasant. In a variety of ways, then, changes in factory conditions soon brought some slight material solace to the labor force.

Worker Disorientation

There is good evidence that workers themselves did not ordinarily sense a deterioration of conditions. In crises there were signs of collective discontent, as evidenced by food riots. But there was little agitation in normal times. Many workers were clearly grateful to their employers for their jobs and earnings.

Beyond this, many workers were not interested in maximizing their incomes in industry. Peasant expectations may have been preserved. It was quite common for better paid workers to stop work periodically to enjoy a period of leisure, instead of earning well beyond subsistence. Many French spinners and machine builders regularly worked only four or five days a week, at least until disciplined by fines and other penalties. Such workers were interested in purchasing better clothing and food, but they did not try to increase their material well-being to the greatest possible extent.

In fact, the most significant points of distress among the early workers did not result from purely material factors. Rather, they came from disorientation imposed by life in the factory cities. Material conditions played a role in this. Crowded housing made it difficult to preserve harmony within the family. Frequently crises promoted a sense of insecurity and even confusion. The greatest pressure, however, resulted from the contrast between the traditions of the new workers and their situation in the factories.

Peasant life had provided certain social and economic standards by which the rural worker could function and could understand his environment. Village and family structure had offered guidance in economic activities, in recreation, in marriage, and in the raising of children. Religion had provided comfort and explanation in bad times and good. In the move to the factory city many of these traditions and structures became irrelevant. The village was abandoned, although some workers tried to return periodically. In the cities the neighborhood and the factory were filled with strangers with whom close links were difficult to establish. Families themselves were disrupted as some members, particularly the important older ones, stayed in the village. Traditions of economic activity related to agriculture and the land were obviously irrelevant in the new situation. The worker was left at first without clear standards against which to judge and understand the urban environment.

Life in the city increased this disorientation. For example, urban crowding affected the religious life of most workers. Churches were not built rapidly enough to keep pace with the expansion of the cities. Urban churches were often too stylish and imposing for the worker; many workers cited their own shabbiness as the reason they no longer went to church. Most churchmen were unsympathetic to the problems of the workers; lacking economic training, frequently from rural or upper classes, they were far more concerned with defending the ties of the churches with conservative governments than they were with making contact with the rising working class. To be sure, some leaders criticized the greed and harshness of the industrial middle class. But no extensive effort was made to preach and minister among the workers themselves. Only in England, where the Methodists retained a specifically lower-class orientation, was real contact with some workers continued. On the continent, and ultimately in England, religious practice and feeling declined sharply among the workers.

A far greater influence on worker habits came from the factories themselves. Industrial labor cut the worker off from the out-of-doors. It stressed dull repetition of a small operation. Most important, it vastly increased the pace and discipline of work. The system of factories and machines required speed and coordination. The worker could not be allowed to set his own rate, taking breaks when he wished or absenting himself for personal reasons. These various requirements were difficult to impose on a labor force accustomed to greater independence. The fact that some workers did take extra days off reflected the clash between a traditional valuation of leisure and the needs of the factory system. A new set of work habits had to be developed for the system to succeed. Intensive supervision by the employer himself and by numerous foremen imposed the desired regularity. Elaborate factory rules were drawn up and enforced by fines. These rules forbade tardiness and faulty work; singing, whistling, talking to other workers; wandering around; and bringing strangers into the shop. The rules and the fines gradually introduced a greater discipline and precision into the labor force—but the psychological strain on the workers was great.

Factory life also disrupted the family. Work no longer centered around the home; in fact, few hours were available for home life. Husbands, wives, and children increasingly worked in different places. Women had little time for cooking and cleaning; and they had separate incomes, which freed them somewhat from their husbands' control. Children also might have independent wages, and many of them began to leave home at an early age. The material difficulties and temptations of urban life caused worker families to reduce the number of children they had, although their birth rates remained higher than those of most urban classes. Here again was an important deviation from the habits of agricultural labor, as workers tried to protect their incomes by changing their family patterns.

Finally, factory labor offered a variety of moral temptations for children as well as for adults that loosened or even eliminated many family bonds. Work involved both sexes, often in partial undress due to the heat. Long hours and a rapid pace created the need for release, which was not hard to find on the way home at night or even in the factory itself. Child workers were exposed to the rude talk and habits of adults and often imitated what they saw. Low pay drove many single girls to prostitution; in the Rheims wool factories it was called "doing the fifth quarter of the working day." In many areas little shame seemed to be attached to having illegitimate children. Some girls expected to have one or two before marrying. Many workers did not marry at all, but lived with a series of concubines. Others lived quite faithfully with one woman, but did not bother to go through a marriage ceremony. Family life continued and flourished among many workers; rampant immorality was a minority phenomenon. But the standards of family life and of morality itself were changing. Particularly when contrasted to rural customs these changes indicate clearly the novelty and confusion of worker life.

The worker had little control over his conditions, which were set immediately by the employers, more generally by abstract economic trends. The worker had no vote in municipal or national governments. He was regarded by governments more as a potential troublemaker than as an object of sympathetic concern. Only if he rioted was he likely to have any contact with the government, and then it acted as a repressive force. Nothing except his work involved him actively in a larger society. Early workers, uneducated and of peasant origin, themselves had no significant political interest. What grievances they had were economic, and they were unaware of political methods even in expressing those. Gradually, however, workers were to become aware of their alienation from established forms of government, both political and economic. Much of the later political orientation of the workers stemmed from their initial isolation.

Equally important, pressed as he was by a variety of changes in his customs at work and in the family, the industrial laborer had few outlets for recreation. Village festivals had little meaning in a strange city, although some were maintained for a time. Many urban diversions, such as the press and the theater, required funds and education, which the worker did not have. The only recreation available for most workers was a Sunday stroll, possibly to the country, and the tavern.

Bars spread quickly in working-class neighborhoods. They were mean and crowded, but they did provide some social life and escape from an ugly room. What they served provided escape as well. Many workers spent Sunday drinking, and Monday too when they could afford it; women and even children often joined in. Consumption of alcohol rose 40 per cent among Russian workers between 1904 and 1913. In Lille during the July Monarchy some parents doped their children so that they would be free to spend long hours in the bar. As with sexual immorality, by no means all workers were involved in heavy drinking. Many could not afford it, and many had no interest in it. Rates of alcohol consumption were high and rising, however, and showed the tension and novelty of factory life.

Discontent and Protest

Pressed by material hardship, and even more by a sense of disorientation, many workers were clearly discontented. The few investigators of factory conditions in the period recorded many complaints against conditions in the factories and employers themselves. A large number of workers expressed their grievances by stealing raw materials from the factory. But early industrial labor was unable to mount significant collective protests against its conditions during its period of greatest misery.

Workers were able to undertake cooperative projects on occasion. A minority of the better paid workers in Britain after 1800, France after 1820, Germany after 1850 set up mutual-aid groups or friendly societies. These groups tried to assist the sick and to provide burial expenses on the basis of small weekly fees by each member. Some of the groups were well organized and offered important aid; many others were ephemeral. Only a few regions, such as the north of France, developed an important number of aid groups of any type. Most workers were not capable of even this level of organization. Far fewer could combine for any sort of protest.

There were a variety of barriers to protest action and organization. Strikes and unions were illegal in the early industrial revolution.

The French Le Chapelier Law of 1791 and the British Combination Acts of 1799 and 1800 were typical of the measures that prohibited any association of workers. Strikes were treated as rebellions in most of Italy until 1859. Though England removed the harshest restrictions on unions in 1824, as Russia did briefly in 1906, most governments repressed worker agitation firmly in the early industrial period. Leaders of strikes were often arrested, and troops were used to break up any major demonstration. Employers also resisted expressions of discontent. They fired potential leaders and sometimes blacklisted them locally. They called in government troops when agitation was merely threatened. And if a strike did occur, they typically tried to outlast it or to retract any gains they might be temporarily forced to grant.

Factors within the working class were equally important deterrents to protest. Workers were still strange to each other. They felt no overriding common links. Some of the most vigorous agitation the workers conducted was against foreign labor in their midst.

Many workers felt no particular discontent. Some retained a peasant sense of resignation. A few hoped to rise into the ranks of foremen or even industrialists by dint of hard work. The interests of some of the most active workers were turned to leaving their social class rather than to leading it

More generally, the disorientation of the workers sapped their ability to protest. They were unable to form clear goals in their new situation. Their common illiteracy and their confusion prevented them from significant contact with doctrines of reform. Utopian socialist propagandists, for example, made virtually no headway among British and French workers before 1848. Yet by themselves the workers were incapable of assessing their position and asking for change. The little agitation that did occur was in protest against some clear deterioration, as in a crisis, rather than for a permanent improvement. Drinking inhibited protest. Many workers, discontented over some issue in the factory, typically gravitated to a bar, their natural social recourse; and very often collective protest would be drowned rather than organized.

Finally, workers lacked funds and time for firm organization. They could afford no dues, and they could not risk action that might deprive them of work for days or even weeks. They lacked time to participate in any organization apart from the factory.

Worker agitation was extremely infrequent and usually poorly organized during the early years of the industrial revolution. There was little labor agitation in Belgium until the 1860s. During the July Monarchy there were only about eight strikes a year by the whole of French factory labor. Usually even these efforts were brief and minor. The most common type was actually more a riot than a strike, involving fairly violent attacks on merchants or employers during a period of crisis. There were no strike funds, no formal leadership, no advance planning.

In only a few cases were workers able to organize a strike in good times and to continue this strike for several weeks. When they did strike for clear goals, they almost invariably sought improvement in wages and hours. There were several lengthy mining strikes for these goals, particularly in 1844 and 1846 around Saint-Étienne, and a number of efforts by the semiartisan wool workers in parts of southern France. In both cases the labor force was not entirely new to the area or the job; workers had a sense of tradition that could help them formulate goals. Their hours were shorter than average and their pay higher. Few workers had these essential advantages so the strike rate long remained low.

Gradually, more workers acquired a sense of their position and began to benefit from higher pay. Factory strikes during the Second Empire involved increasing numbers of new metallurgical and textile workers, and the rate of agitation rose. Even so, strikes remained scattered and infrequent; there were only twenty-six by workers and artisans combined from 1868 to 1870. And few permanent organizations arose within factory labor to give leadership and coherence to worker discontent.

In Britain agitation remained at a low level until about 1818, aside from riots by the unemployed as in 1815. By this time some workers were of second or even third generation in industry and were increasingly conscious of their situation. Furthermore, artisan unions and strikes provided some leadership to worker efforts. This occurred in France to some extent. Strikes by Paris artisans in 1840 had induced Parisian textile workers to come out after a few weeks. Agitation after the revolution of 1848 caused various strikes and efforts at unionization in industrial centers, though worker participation in the revolution itself had been minimal.

In Britain, with its larger and more mature labor force, the artisan example had greater effect. Strikes by bricklayers and carpenters in Birmingham in 1818, for instance, were imitated by cotton workers rather quickly; a three-month strike ensued against unemployment and reductions in pay. Union efforts led by building trades workers, such as the ambitious Grand National Consolidated Trades Union of the 1830s, involved some factory labor. Cotton spinners, who were relatively well paid and experienced, led in strikes and union efforts; under the leadership of John Doherty a minority of the spinners maintained a national union for several years during the 1820s. As in France, miners also were unusually active. A large number of factory workers, finally, participated vaguely in the Chartist movement during the 1830s and 1840s. The Chartists, under artisan leadership again, sought political reforms, especially universal suffrage. These issues meant little to factory workers, but the agitation did provide an opportunity for mass meetings and some rioting in years of economic crisis, notably 1839, 1842, and 1848. The interests of factory workers lent a tone of greater violence and less precise doctrine to Chartism in the industrial regions of England. In sum, the later period of British industrialization did see some important agitation, particularly under artisan stimulus. Workers remained most capable of violence during slumps. Organizations were small and ephemeral. Education, orientation, and resources all had to increase before Britain would enter a period of extensive agitation by factory labor.

Worker activity was limited in later industrializations as well. There were brief, unorganized textile strikes in Italy in the 1860s, but only after 1890 were there more than a few each year. Strikes were infrequent in Germany until the 1880s, and unions were small. A socialist movement attracted support from a few workers in the 1860s, but it rose to real prominence only later. Development of protest was distinctly more rapid, in relation to the beginning of industrialization, than in England or France, but it was still unimportant in the early decades.

In Russia an increase in the pace of protest was more apparent. Russian workers, like the German to an extent, had the example of organizations and doctrines developed in the west. They were organized in far larger factories; a significant portion of Russian labor was employed in factories with over a thousand workers. This may, in turn, have encouraged worker movements, whereas the small textile factories of British and French industrialization had deterred them by dividing the labor force. Also, there had been some factory labor in Russia since the 1820s; mature workers may have guided their newer colleagues by the 1890s. Finally, in the Russian case the workers were caught up in a more general movement of protest, involving the middle class and peasants as well. As a result, there were a number of well-organized strikes by Russian labor, and the union movement, during its brief period of legality in 1906, attracted 250,000 members. Factory workers also participated massively in the revolution of 1905, by a general strike.

The early industrial revolution was a formative period for the working class. A low standard of living was combined with some improvements and with a growing interest in material acquisition. An interest in leisure was even more clear, but it was asserted with greater difficulty. A new discipline and pace of work were imposed with increasing rigor. City life, while still difficult, gradually became accepted as the ties to the countryside were broken. New, generally looser, patterns of family life and religious practice were developed. Certain habits of cooperation and even organization for protest arose in a halting and limited way. All these tendencies were to be important in the later evolution of the class. During the early industrial period itself, however, the attitudes and position of the class were not entirely clear. This was a time of adjustment and confusion. Tradition and purpose were lacking. The class provided the immense labor of expanding industry. It had yet to make its mark on society more generally.

THE ARTISANS

The rise of the factory working class did not eliminate the urban artisans. Artisans remained a larger group for several decades and were far more widely distributed in cities generally. They were particularly prominent in major centers such as London and Vienna. As late as 1850 there were as many artisans as factory workers in Great Britain. In the 1860s artisans represented 60 per cent of the Prussian manufacturing force. In France artisans maintained a greater importance than in other European countries. At midcentury there were only 1,306,000 workers in firms with over ten employes, and many of these were, of course, domestic manufacturers. The remainder of the industrial population, including 1,548,000 employers and self-employed, worked in firms averaging two employes. Twenty years later, at the time of the Commune, the bulk of the Parisian workers were artisans. Of approximately 500,000 workers in a population of 1.8 million, 100,000 were construction workers; 110,000 worked in jewelry, furniture, and other luxury industries; 34,000 were printers; 41,000 worked in food processing; 115,000 worked in clothing and textiles, mainly in small tailoring and dressmaking shops. This was an unusual concentration; Paris served really as a center for craft production, exporting artisans' wares all over the world. But even factory centers in 1870 depended on artisan labor for most food processing, clothing, and construction work.

Until about 1850 in Britain and until at least 1870 elsewhere the number of artisans increased in proportion to overall population growth; for as population expanded and wealth increased with both agricultural and industrial improvements, the need for artisans rose. Industrialization itself fostered the development of some new small-shop crafts, notably in machine building. Flourishing cities required more carpenters and masons, more butchers and bakers, more tailors and shoemakers. With a very few exceptions early mechanical processes were not applicable to the kind of work done by urban artisans; in some cases they have not been widely applied to this day. A few urban branches of textile manufacturing, such as the finishing of wool cloth, were quickly affected. The printing industry underwent increased mechanization, although in this case artisan skills were not entirely displaced. Some female artisans, such as lace makers, were affected by the rise of competitive factory products. For the most part, however, it was rural home workers, not urban artisans, who were displaced by the new industrial processes. The decline of a few urban groups was more than balanced by the heightened demand for other major crafts. Only after midcentury, and then very slowly, did devices such as the sewing machine really affect key groups of artisans. Most of the history of what has often been loosely termed "the working class" in the early and midnineteenth century is in fact a history of artisans. Workers in the crafts were increasing far less rapidly than workers in the factories, but they long continued to dominate in numbers, wealth, social cohesion, and purpose.

Stability of Habits

Before 1870 artisans were fairly distinct from factory labor. They usually worked in different places; artisans still relied on traditional skills and techniques and worked on their own or in very small units. Even residentially, there was only limited contact between the two classes. There were relatively few factory workers in major artisan centers such as London and Paris and in large numbers of traditional towns. Furthermore, artisans had traditional quarters of residence, usually in the center of a city, which factory workers did not fully penetrate. Sections such as the Faubourg Saint-Antoine in Paris remained artisan preserves. However, particularly in factory cities, there were opportunities for contact. Artisans saw factory workers as important potential allies in such movements as unionization and Chartism. To some extent, they served as mentors to the new class; we have seen that workers often imitated artisan movements. But most artisans viewed the workers with some suspicion. They abhorred the factory system and its products, and they distrusted the coarseness and the violence of the working class. Ultimately, they found some kindred interests with the skilled elements of factory labor, but almost never did they identify with the working class as a whole.

Artisans remained a relatively stable class in personal habits and family structures. They had traditions in their work and in their city life to which they constantly referred. Even new artisans coming in from the countryside were assimilated to many artisan values. It is also possible that many new artisans came from more substantial elements of the peasantry than factory labor did; rural artisans, for example, would naturally drift to this group. In any case, they had a sense of status and dignity that few workers had.

Many observers noted that even poor artisans were often better off than factory labor because they avoided showy spending on drink and on clothing. Thread twisters in Lille, for example, who earned about half the wage of factory spinners, frequently had better diets and cleaner housing and depended less on charity during crises. They were thriftier in good times, worked more steadily, drank less. Artisans generally, though they earned little more than workers, were far more inclined to save money. Similarly, their family structure was tighter. Artisans retained an interest in establishing their children in their own trade and educated them accordingly. Wives worked in the home, not in the factory. Most artisans carefully limited their family size by delaying marriage until their late twenties, in the interest of maintaining their material well-being and caring properly for the children they had.

The material standards of artisans still varied greatly. Single women had to work long hours to earn enough to survive. Craftsmen facing mechanical competition received low wages for increasing hours of work. Many Lyons silk workers labored sixteen or eighteen hours a day for pay that was barely sufficient to live, though artisan masters usually had some comforts. Among the leading crafts, in which demand was rising, pay levels were high and slightly rising during the period as a whole. Carpenters or butchers could afford more stylish clothing and furnishings and could often save. They seldom needed to put their children to work until they were in their teens. In Britain and France at least, most male artisans received notably higher pay than did the average male factory worker.

There were still many hardships. Construction workers and some others suffered from long periods of seasonal unemployment. Personal disasters, such as illness or age, could reduce a family to dire poverty. Artisans suffered severely in crises. Their wages fell, and they often experienced higher levels of unemployment than did factory workers. The need for artisan products, often in a semiluxury category, fell far more rapidly than did the need for factory staples such as clothing. And this crisis of falling wages and rising unemployment was, of course, usually accompanied by rising food prices. Only bare subsistence expenditures, appeals for charity, and sale or pawning of furniture and even vital tools could permit survival in these conditions. But the leading groups of artisans were not ordinarily impoverished; they even had a rising though small and insecure margin above subsistence.

Forces of Change

Other aspects of the artisan's life were changing far more steadily than purely material conditions. In times of prosperity as well as times of crisis some of the foundations of artisan economic and social values were being undermined.

Most basically, the principles of the rising new industry clashed directly with the principles of artisan economy. Artisans relied on stable skills; industry involved rapidly changing methods and the use of large numbers of unskilled workers. Skill and training were not eliminated in industry, but the skills demanded were new and on the whole more easily learned; in few cases, for example, was prolonged apprenticeship required to enable a worker to perform his job adequately. Artisans were accustomed to a relatively leisurely pace of work. Carpenters or printers seldom worked more than twelve hours a day, and their day was interrupted by frequent breaks. There were many holidays, and large numbers of artisans worked only five days a week. In factories leisure and a moderate pace of work were incompatible with the new machines. Artisans traditionally tried to protect themselves against competitive pressure by restricting both techniques and the labor force. In industry limitations were removed; workers were hired as they were needed, machines introduced at will. The artisan interest in restraining the degree of inequality within manufacturing was also ignored in the new factories. Factory owners often acquired great wealth and tried to expand this wealth without clear limit. The gap between them and their workers was great, and it was rare for a worker to rise to the ranks of the manufacturer. The novelty of the factory system was a real shock to the artisan stress on stability.

Few artisans, of course, were directly employed by the factories. The threat of the factory system was more subtle. The rise of mechanized industry displaced artisans from a fundamental control of the urban economy. The number of artisans rose, and their wealth grew slightly, but their relative economic position steadily declined. The working class expanded far more rapidly than did the ranks of the artisans, four times as rapidly in Germany by midcentury. The wealth of the new elements of the middle class eclipsed any increase in artisan pay; some factory workers earned more than craft labor. Furthermore, factory industry was obviously dynamic and expansive. It had displaced many workers and might displace more. There was real concern among artisans, even those remote from branches of industry touched by machines, that the new principles of production might spread to their own trade.

A fear of displacement, more than actual displacement, dominated artisan activity in this period. The realization of the new challenge to artisan economic values caused many attacks on the factory sys-

attacking machiness in frustration

tem. Some artisans, directly threatened by mechanical processes, tried to destroy the factories themselves. Most areas went through a period of Luddism by urban artisans as well as some domestic workers. Nottingham glove makers destroyed a thousand new stocking frames in 1811–1812, and Yorkshire wool finishers attacked machines also. French wool finishers destroyed several machines after 1820. Craftsmen in Barcelona attacked new spinning machines between 1854 and 1856. Artisan newspapers, pamphlets, and petitions to the government often urged removal of machines. Pamphlets in Germany in the 1860s attacked the stock exchange, department stores, and the principle of division of labor. The Parisian newspaper *L'Atelier* warned constantly of the evils of factory industry.

The new economy did touch artisan conditions quite directly, affecting the leading crafts without changing the actual methods of work significantly. The preindustrial expansion of commerce and manufacturing brought an attack on the guilds. Capitalist trade could not function in a guild economy. It needed freedom to bring in new workers and new techniques. Early manufacturing firms even in the putting-out system had evaded guild control. Increasingly, entrepreneurs and the middle class generally tried to abolish guilds outright.

In Britain the process of abolition was gradual, but it was completed by the end of the eighteenth century; and at that time all other associations among workers were forbidden as well. In France the revolutionary government banned guilds in 1791. The activities of the French guilds, backed by official sanction, had been obviously limiting economic advance and innovation. Many artisans themselves had suffered from the rigid rules on methods and from the masters' manipulation of guilds to protect their own interests. The abolition of the guilds was not, therefore, directly protested by most French artisans. But the artisans did expect to be able to improve their economic position by other collective methods. The months following the abolition of the guilds saw the formation of many new unions and a large number of strikes as artisans tried to better their wages in a period of economic confusion by the cooperative efforts familiar to them. The middle-class government reacted to this by banning all unions and strikes in the Le Chapelier Law. As in Britain, artisans were deprived not only of their guilds but also of more supple methods of association. The French revolutionary government spread the abolition of guilds wherever its armies conquered, and in most cases the abolition was retained even after the revolution. By 1815 many west German and northern Italian states, and the Low Countries had eliminated the guilds. Spain abolished guilds by 1836.

Most of Germany, particularly Prussia, was slower to act. Conservative governments continued to enforce guild exclusions until midcentury. In the 1840s the Prussian government, without abolishing guilds, removed the official support from guild exclusiveness; workers could now enter crafts without guild permission. After the revolution of 1848 aristocrats tried to ally themselves with discontented artisans by restoring the legal position of guilds. Only in 1868 did the Prussian government again allow work in the crafts without guild permission. The German guilds did not therefore die; they continued privately to enforce some exclusions and to serve as centers for defense of professional interests. Their fundamental powers were nevertheless radically limited. But the tardiness of the attacks on the guilds allowed German artisans to remain attached to a traditional, even conservative, outlook that set them off significantly from artisans in the west.

In addition to the abolition of the guilds, the relationship between journeymen and masters changed rapidly during the nineteenth century. While the number of artisans grew steadily, the number of masters did not. Masters increasingly tried to protect their own social and economic position in a changing economy by limiting their ranks. Some became employers rather than masters, for they had enough workers to avoid most manual labor themselves and concentrated instead on arranging for materials and sales. In the construction industry, large crews were formed with the master serving as a contractor. Masters in this situation increased their capital for the purchase of supplies and equipment, and thus made it more difficult for a journeyman to rise. The social relations between artisan and master were changed. It became less common for journeymen to be housed and fed by the master. The gradual development of a purely and permanently wage-earning status for journeymen, though not entirely new, was a profound shock to artisan tradition.

In other instances, masters and journeymen alike were forced into virtual employment by merchant capitalists. This was particularly common in the textile industry, where industrial capitalism was spreading rapidly, but it also occurred in some construction work and in some branches of metal work. Embroiderers, knifemakers, and the like were increasingly assigned tasks by a foreman employed by a large merchant. They might work in their homes or in a master's shop, but their conditions were set outside the artisan system.

Finally, many new employers, whether merchants or masters, showed some tendency to neglect traditional methods of apprenticeship. If they hired children, they expected them to work more than to learn. Journeymen themselves, involved increasingly in a wage system, were often reluctant to delay their work by training a child. Apprenticeship continued except in a few decaying trades such as lace making, for the old traditions were not entirely violated. In a limited way, however, aspects of industrial organization were being applied to the crafts without a real introduction of a factory system.

The social as well as the economic position of the artisans was changing. The artisan lost the social contact of the guilds at the same time that his links with his master were declining. His place in the city was also slipping as factory workers became more numerous and as new elements of the middle class rose to prominence and took a growing role in city government. Neither destitute nor uprooted, the artisan was nevertheless faced with major challenge.

The Reactionary Impulse

Artisans reacted to the challenge to tradition in a number of ways. There were some efforts to retain the old customs. The various attacks on machine industry, sometimes physical but more often verbal, were an important sign of traditionalism. A number of groups tried to maintain the guilds. British joiners and shoemakers retained some guild structure into the nineteenth century. This retention was primarily for social purposes, as the organizations raised few economic demands. Similarly, French carpenters formed secret groups called *compagnonnages*, which were really extensions of the guilds. The *compagnonnages* dealt with matters of apprenticeship and working conditions but again were primarily social organizations. They arranged for the traditional tours of France by young journeymen and provided an elaborate ritual for the entertainment of their members. The importance of these various guild remnants gradually declined and never involved more than a minority of the class as a whole.

Only in Germany was there a persistent effort to preserve the guilds, for only in Germany did conservative classes have sufficient power to allow some hope of success. Hence the major demand of German artisans in the revolution of 1848 was for full restoration of the guilds, which had after all only recently been threatened in states such as Prussia. The German artisans, spurred by two previous years of intense economic crisis, rioted in many cities, petitioned the revolutionary government, and even assembled a national congress of their own in June, 1849, in an effort to win their demands. They wanted guilds to restrict the number of workers, wanted regulations and taxes to limit the output of factories, and wanted the state itself to guarantee work. In Prussia during the 1850s the restoration of the guilds simply encouraged the artisans' attachment to a conservative social order. Having been rebuffed in their revolutionary demands by the middle-class assemblies, which sought economic freedom instead of guild restrictions, they turned against middle-class liberalism. The attacks by artisan pamphleteers on new industrial and commercial methods increased even in the 1860s; and as they acquired the vote, many German artisans attached themselves to conservative parties.

The German case represented an extreme of the general suspicion of modern trends. Even in Germany artisans west of the Rhine, where guilds were abolished during the Napoleonic period and where regimes were relatively liberal, did not concern themselves greatly with restoration of the guilds. There and elsewhere in the west there were some signs of attraction to past structures and a widespread distrust of recent changes in the economy, but artisans also tried to adapt to a new situation in new ways.

The Impulse to Self-Help

One of the most common impulses of artisans in industrializing Europe was to seek individual improvements in social and economic status. Some simply abandoned their craft to seek more lucrative work as skilled factory operatives or as foremen. Others entered the industrial system as owners of small manufacturing enterprises.

More commonly, artisans attempted to earn more money by working harder and improving themselves within their craft. Many artisans developed a great interest in education, and artisan groups and publications commonly stressed the importance of education as a means of self-improvement. In Britain, Mechanics' Institutes were established to provide a variety of technical and commercial training. Courses in accounting, chemistry, practical mathematics, and the like established in most French cities were attended particularly by artisans, although often intended by their middle-class founders to benefit factory workers.

The vast majority of urban artisans were now literate, and some purchased and read books and newspapers fairly regularly. By the 1840s a number of artisan newspapers were appearing in Britain and France, often with great stress on political and social problems. Artisans sought entertainment above all from their reading, however, and cheap novels and periodicals were more popular. They stressed sentiment and sensation, and they purveyed tales of supposedly aristocratic immorality.

Artisans also tried to improve themselves by saving. Savings banks spread fairly widely during the period, and artisans and servants were their principal patrons among the lower classes. Many artisans undoubtedly banked the funds that in an earlier period they would have devoted to buying a master's position. The saving habit was not a new one, but it now took a new form, much as the tradition of vocational training was now expressed in a desire for formal education. At the same time, elements of the artisan class were undoubtedly patterning themselves upon the values of the rising middle classes. The interest in self-improvement, education, and saving was frequently urged by the middle class, in speeches and in pamphlets, as the path to happiness and success. These recommendations undoubtedly caught the attention of a class that had a sense of pride and that sought a respected place in a society increasingly dominated by the middle class.

A desire to uplift personal character permeated a wide variety of artisan efforts. A number of artisan groups and papers urged temperance and morality on the artisan class, just as middle-class organs did. Some artisans were active in formal temperance movements, particularly in Britain. Again the impulse was to perfect the individual so he could rise in society. Many artisan unions encouraged temperance; the Amalgamated Society of Engineers in Britain, for example, had rules against drinking and swearing. Most mutual aid funds forbade assistance in cases of illness or accident resulting from drink or to victims of venereal disease.

Many artisans adopted the self-help approach so completely that they simply entered the lower middle class. Their earnings were sufficient for this; artisan masters were increasingly small employers anyway. But most important, artisans of this type felt they were part of the middle class; they found middle-class values appropriate. By 1870 German artisans not only regarded themselves as middle class, but were so regarded by the rest of society. Elsewhere, though less massively, many artisans underwent the same process.

Political Interest

Artisans also tried to raise their political and social status. They increasingly wanted the vote, particularly in western countries where the middle classes possessed or actively sought suffrage. In Germany, where political interest even in the middle class was relatively low, artisans were also less active. During the revolution of 1848 they made some demands on the government, including free state education, provision of credit for artisan shops, and support for the ill and maimed; but they showed little interest in political rights or in changing political forms. Even so, there was political consciousness: in the city of Halle in 1848, 81 per cent of the artisan masters and 71 per cent of the journeymen voted, compared to 46 per cent of factory labor.

In France, where the revolution had provided a brief experience of universal suffrage and political action, especially in Paris, and in Britain, where the middle class sought and gained the vote in 1832, political activity made even more sense to many artisans. French artisans who filled the streets in 1830 were acting specifically against the existing monarch and for a change in the political system. During the July Monarchy some artisans joined republican groups and pressed for universal suffrage. British artisans were even more persistent before 1848 in seeking the vote. Before the Reform Bill of 1832 many joined with middle-class elements in associations and meetings to promote an extension of the suffrage. After 1832 artisans, particularly in London, took the lead in forming the Chartist movement to seek universal male suffrage and other political reforms. They held meetings, passed resolutions, sometimes threatened violence, and circulated gigantic petitions to further their cause. On three occasions, in years of economic crisis, the movement drew a great following, including factory workers as well as artisans. In 1839 a Chartist petition was signed by 1,280,000 people, and in 1842, 3,317,702 signed a new appeal. After a final abortive effort in 1848 the movement collapsed, and artisan organizations turned away from politics. For three decades, however, the political consciousness of many artisans had been quite high in a variety of forms, and their efforts to win a place in political life extensive.

The artisans sought political change for many reasons. They wanted the state to aid their self-improvement efforts by providing educational facilities. They hoped that their votes would induce the state to take economic action in their behalf. The Chartists, for example, had a vague belief that political reforms would result in the ending of poverty. Parisian artisans in 1848 felt that their control of the government would bring a new organization of work that would restore artisan forms of production and eliminate unemployment. Finally, artisans sought political participation as one means of obtaining respect from other elements of society. The German artisans in 1848 who insisted that they be addressed with the formal *Sie* instead of the familiar *du* were expressing a general desire to be treated as equals by employers and other members of the upper classes. The search for political equality was an important effort along the same lines. In an age when established social positions were eroding, the artisans attempted to assert their place in new ways.

Mutual Aid

In addition to efforts at self-improvement and at political reform, artisans utilized a variety of methods to better their economic position and provide greater social cohesion. These efforts continued some of the artisan economic traditions but in a new framework. They involved cooperation in the interest of collective economic security. They were organized along craft lines and were usually local.

The simplest and earliest form of artisan cooperation was the mutual aid group or friendly society. Most major cities had a variety of such groups for the leading crafts, which grew up quickly after guilds were abolished. The groups were far more extensive among the artisans than among factory workers. They provided aid in sickness and in death and often established technical courses, libraries, and recreational programs. Occasionally, aid groups conducted strikes as well.

Many crafts also formed unions to protect their economic interests, usually a few decades after aid groups began to form. Artisan union movements waxed and waned in most countries according to economic conditions. However, some individual locals persisted from the 1820s or 1830s in Britain and France. Groups such as printers' and carpenters' unions began in Paris in the 1830s and in London even earlier. Lyons silk workers had several large unions in the early 1830s, but government repression eventually reduced the movement. Printers and hatters formed short-lived associations in Italy in 1848, and in the 1860s more permanent unions grew out of aid groups.

In Britain artisan union efforts were unusually elaborate, aided by the easing of legal restrictions in 1824. In the early 1830s about half a million workers, led by members of the building trades, joined the Grand National Consolidated Trades Union under the leadership of Robert Owen. This group went well beyond the purposes of ordinary artisan unions and tried to reconstitute the economy on cooperative lines. A smaller effort at a national union, the Association for the Protection of Labour, was formed in the 1840s, again with artisan participation predominant. Finally, after the failure of Chartism in 1848 and with the rising economic prosperity of the 1850s, the union movement among artisans and skilled workers increased substantially. Carpenters, iron founders, engineers, and the like dominated this movement, known as New Model Unionism; and they intentionally ignored the mass of factory workers. These unions attempted to be respectable and solid. They had large funds and professional officials. They urged temperance, saving, and hard work on their members and provided the benefits of a friendly society. They preferred to negotiate with their employers for improvement of wages and hours and conducted strikes only with reluctance. This was a quiet, exclusive movement operating on principles of collective benefit for members—very much in the artisan tradition.

The New Model Union movement was the most extensive and elaborate union effort developed among artisans before 1870 and the only one that went beyond purely local associations. But the methods of New Model Unionism were quite common. Parisian groups and the shorter-lived Lyons unions tried to establish solid gains for their members in terms of wages and hours. They attempted to bargain collectively with their employers and in a few cases did succeed in winning contracts that set the conditions for the whole profession in the city. The more enduring artisan unions, then, worked carefully for major general gains within the existing system. They tried, with some success, to win a voice in craft conditions to compensate for the loss of guild controls.

One other form of organization elicited considerable artisan interest, but again only a minority of the class was involved. By midcentury a cooperative movement of some importance had developed in western Europe. There were two hundred cooperative associations in Paris in 1851, principally among artisans. A number of similar groups existed in Britain, particularly in London, and involved tailors, hatters, and the like. These groups tried to establish a new system of production based on artisan principles. They stressed the need for a period of apprenticeship and limited entrance to their group. They hoped to eliminate competition and mechanization at the same time. Some of the groups collapsed, and even the successful ones failed to gain control of the economy as their founders had often hoped. Many groups did provide economic assistance and social contacts to their members.

Protest Movements

Much artisan action, including efforts at self-improvement and mutual aid, were primarily intended to improve positions within existing society. In prosperous times artisans saw no reason to challenge their legal order directly. There were occasions, however, when direct action seemed necessary even for limited goals such as wages. Furthermore, aside from any interest in maintaining or restoring a guild system, many artisans were concerned about the basic direction of society. The cooperative movement expressed such concern and frankly hoped to restore a more artisanal system of production. The Chartist movement vaguely sought a new organization of the economy. Movements such as the Grand National Consolidated Trades Union intended to take over the whole of industry and organize it on a cooperative basis; government itself would be put into the hands of the unions. These various movements enlisted only a minority of the artisans, for challenges to established order are always difficult to follow. They represented, nevertheless, a significant impulse within the whole class. And there were many occasions when artisans defied the legal order by action as well as by doctrine.

Artisans conducted a number of strikes during this period. Even unions that sought respectability did not completely shun the strike. The strikes in which artisans participated differed from strikes by factory workers in several ways. They were more frequent. The first strike movements in Italy during the industrial revolution, in the 1860s, were almost entirely artisan; the first strike organization was formed by Siena printers. During the July Monarchy French artisans struck half again as frequently as factory workers, in proportion to their numbers. The strikes were better organized and larger, although they never went beyond a single locality. The strikers often had a fund to support a major effort.

Artisans' strikes generally sought explicit improvement in wages and hours. Commonly they sought collective agreements, as in the Lyons silk strikes of 1831 and 1833, to provide a minimum wage in a whole area for a given industry. Once again the artisan tradition of stability through joint action was reappearing. Some artisans also urged the establishment of permanent groups in each shop to make sure that conditions remained acceptable.

Artisan strikes were characterized by their sense of timing. Unlike workers, artisans did not usually agitate during the peak of a crisis. They knew that employers were unlikely to grant any gains on such occasions. Rather, their strikes reached the highest levels in the year or so after a crisis, when business was good but wages were not yet back to normal. The chances of winning in this situation were considerably greater. This was the background to the wave of strikes that swept Paris crafts in 1840 and to the strikes in Birmingham in 1818. Artisans did not strike heedlessly; the majority never struck at all. Strikes were illegal, expensive, and risky. Nevertheless, elements of the class did defy legality on occasion with solid efforts.

Artisan strikes were rarely violent. Artisans were less likely to break windows or attack stores than were workers, for their strikes were not simply an outburst of anger and frustration. On occasion, however, artisan action could go beyond clear economic goals to a broader challenge to existing society, involving violence and even a revolutionary effort. During the Lyons strikes of 1831 and especially

1833, government efforts at repression and a certain interest in republican principles led artisans to go beyond mere strike activity and actually take over the town for a brief period. The repression of the 1833 rising in turn led to violent protest riots by Paris artisans.

Most important, artisans provided the street fighters in the three French revolutions of the nineteenth century, all of which were centered in Paris. Parisian artisans were distinguished from others in France and elsewhere by their number, their revolutionary tradition, and their exposure to the doctrinal and political ferment of the capital. In 1830, 1848, and after the siege of Paris in 1871 they rose in revolt. The 1830 revolution, though sparked by middle-class protest against the Restoration government, was manned by artisans. Members of the leading crafts composed the bulk of the street fighters, with carpenters and masons playing a particularly large role. During the 1848 revolt artisans rioted not only in February, but also in the succeeding four months; and they manned the barricades during the bloody June days. Finally, in 1871, artisans and some small shopkeepers provided both the troops and the government personnel during the Commune.

Artisans played a major role in the rioting in Vienna and in Berlin during the 1848 revolutions there. Fighting in Berlin during March was concentrated in the artisans' quarters. Only a minority of artisans were ever revolutionary; of about 350,000 artisans in Paris in 1848, only 50,000 were on the barricades in June. Few other French cities stirred significantly during the same year. Nevertheless, the artisans provided a greater number of actual revolutionaries than did any other urban class.

Artisan revolutions occurred shortly after a major economic crisis, though usually after the worst point was past. In Paris before the Commune, 90 per cent of the workers in some major crafts were unemployed. The 1848 revolution followed two years of intense hardship.

The goals of artisan revolutions were quite broad, in the economy and usually in politics as well. In 1848 French artisans clearly pressed for the establishment of a democratic republic and in the Commune sought a new political regime for the city of Paris. In the economic sphere artisans sought protection from unemployment and government sponsorship for small artisan shops. In Paris in 1848 a significant number of artisans were acquainted with utopian socialist doctrines, particularly those of Louis Blanc and his book *The Organization of Work*. Blanc, like most other socialists of the day, offered doctrines with distinct appeal to artisan traditions. The stress of utopian socialism was on small, cooperative units of production working without elaborate equipment and distributing wealth equally among members of the unit. This was not the old guild system restored, but it urged some similar principles. Hence, when Parisian artisans shouted for the organization of work in 1848, they were shouting for more than a system of relief from unemployment through public works. Public works were all they received, however, in the form of National Workshops; and even these were abolished in June, touching off the June Days. The leaders of the Commune, finally, were largely in the tradition of Proudhon, himself an artisan and a socialist. There again the stress was on small, cooperative, egalitarian units of production and in this case also the abolition of the state in favor of self-government by these units.

In times of unusual hardship, particularly in France, there was in the artisan class some desire for a radically new social system, a system that would return to the idealized traditions of the artisans. In France, and to an extent in Germany and Austria, this resulted in revolution. In Britain it went into the Owenite union movements, into Chartism, and even into the cooperatives, without coming to major violence. Generally, the movement tended to die after midcentury as artisans found new ways of dealing with their economic situation. In France, and later in Barcelona and parts of Italy, a utopian feeling lived on and was to reappear even after 1870. These were countries where industrialization had begun but proceeded slowly and where artisans were caught in the pressures of the industrial revolution for many decades without losing their sense of strength and tradition. A minority of them could continue to hope for radical change. Before 1848 this utopian hope influenced artisans more generally in western Europe. It represented one aspect of the complex process of artisan adjustment to industrial society.

At the end of the first decades of industrialization the artisans remained a distinct and growing class. They had fairly firm personal goals and had developed important collective institutions in their effort to adapt to change. A minority was periodically interested in more than this, in remaking the whole of society in the artisan image.

THE MIDDLE CLASSES

The rise of the middle class and its values was the most important single development in western European society before 1870. Even in eastern Europe a small, preindustrial middle class developed.

In western Europe control of manufacturing and commerce was firmly in the hands of the middle class, and the class extended its influence into other aspects of national life. It increasingly gained control of political functions, and its interests and attitudes dominated cultural life. Most of the intellectuals and artists of the nineteenth century came from the middle class. The leading artistic rebels against bourgeois culture and the leading intellectual socialists themselves came from this dynamic class. The prominence of the middle class and the intensity with which it promoted its values influenced elements of other social classes as well. Many aristocrats, artisans, and workers blended their own traditions with a middle-class sense of respectability and interest in personal advancement.

Growth of the Middle Class

The nineteenth century represented a second formative period for the middle class. The numbers of people in the class increased substantially; the wealth of the class grew. The balance of subgroups within the class changed, and behavior patterns were gradually altered under the spur of greater wealth and social position.

All segments of the class expanded. The growth of urban population and of wealth called for more professional people. New government activities, both national and local, increased the number of professional positions also. A distinct lower middle class arose as retail shopkeeping expanded everywhere. The upper middle class grew with the broadening of economic opportunities. In Paris the wealthiest segments of the middle class rose from 2.4 per cent of the population in 1820 to 3.6 per cent in 1847, and the population of the city had itself risen during the same period. Most important, a new group of factory owners was added to the middle class during this period. The number of firms rose rapidly in the early stage of industrialization, bringing many new owners into the middle-income group.

The growth of the middle class as a whole was greater than the national population rise, but it did not keep pace with urban expansion. The class was not a tiny elite.

Nevertheless, there were significant barriers to entry into the class. Educational opportunities increased, but higher education could be acquired by only a minority. Few middle-class positions in business were open to people without some capital. And the middle class itself often drew together to restrict new entries. Established firms tried to preempt the field; they were aided by the fact that within a generation or two of the mechanization of any branch of industry the number of firms began to decline. Social lines were drawn; intermarriage was often limited to a particular level of the middle class. Hence in many textile cities the personnel of the industrial group was largely developed within twenty years. On a higher level, the Parisian upper class, quite open in early industrialization, tended to close during the next thirty years. During the Restoration only 25 per cent of the group had originated in the upper middle class; by 1848 the majority had been born to their wealth. Never were opportunities for mobility totally cut off; in Paris they were to reopen in the 1850s. But there were limitations, and in some localities they could be overwhelming.

Patterns of middle-class growth reflected both the new opportunities and the continuing barriers of wealth and education. The class as a whole grew principally by an influx from below. Little growth was generated from within the class particularly because most segments of the class limited family size. But the major influx came at the shopkeeping levels, where capital needs were relatively low. The growth of other middle-class levels, particularly professional and industrialist groups, resulted primarily from mobility within the class.

There were workers and even more artisans who bettered themselves according to the best bourgeois tradition. Some of the very wealthy had started in factory labor. A number of artisan masters converted their operations into small businesses and entered the ranks of employers. More important, many rural residents possessed sufficient capital to take advantage of the new economic opportunities of the cities. Sixty per cent of Parisian shopkeepers had been born in the countryside, some as peasants, some as well-to-do farmers. At the lower reaches of the middle class a majority were new men.

The upper levels of the middle class were largely new, as in Paris during the Restoration, but their numbers were drawn mostly from existing middle-class families.

The industrialist group was recruited mainly from other elements of the middle class. Families of established merchants provided relatively few industrialists. The solid wealth and social position of this group made the risks of early manufacturing seem pointless; merchants long looked down on industrialists as upstarts involved in a rather degrading occupation. A larger number of professional people entered industry. In France during the Restoration many former army officers used their capital and their sense of discipline to exploit the new possibilities of industry. Many shopkeepers also seized on industry and related commerce as a means of bettering their economic and social position. Approximately one fifth of the middle ranks of the Parisian bourgeoisie came from shopkeeping families, while 30 per cent were of rural origin. Well-to-do farmers often entered industry; in Lille independent farmers provided more industrialists than any other group. Most of the manufacturers in Mulhouse and many in Switzerland came from families who had previously directed artisan manufacturing and local commerce. During the eighteenth century they extended their operations into domestic industry and developed factories as an expansion of that. In Britain a large number of industrialists were originally foremen in the putting-out system. They had some capital saved from earnings and a certain technical knowledge. It was a group eager to improve its position.

During the early industrial revolution, then, the middle class underwent a dual process of rapid expansion and great internal change. Older elements of the class were increasingly challenged by new men who consciously sought advancement. The traditional social structure of the class was broken by this extensive mobility.

The wealth of the middle class expanded greatly at the same time. In Britain the number of taxpayers earning over £5000 quadrupled between 1801 and 1851. In Paris the average wealth of an upper-middle-class family rose during the same period. Many industrialists gained great fortunes, and others steadily augmented their earnings. The very successful, such as Krupp in Germany or Wedgwood in Britain, were extremely rich. Even a more modest manufacturer could steadily increase his standard of living. The Alsatian Thierry-Mieg began with a small textile operation and within twenty years was earning about three hundred times as much as the average worker he employed. But the new profits of commerce and industry were unevenly distributed within the middle class. Important sub-groups persisted, based on differing functions, traditions, and incomes. In fact, different patterns of income created certain tensions within the middle class.

Middle-Class Structure

The shopkeeping elements grew to almost half the whole middle class by 1850; but despite the many new opportunities in cities and towns alike, the small size of most shops limited average earnings. About 15 per cent of the group was in a really marginal position with earnings little above those of artisans; some shopkeepers inter-married with artisans and sent their sons into the crafts. Such tiny shopkeepers hovered near the brink of ruin and had little beyond the bare necessities. The average shopkeeper was considerably more affluent; in Paris or London he possessed at least twenty times as much capital as the 80 per cent of the population not in the middle or upper classes. His standard of living was comfortable but not luxurious. He could keep a servant and send his sons at least to primary school. This was a group solidly in the middle class.

Most members of the lower middle class had a fairly firm sense of status in the period. They felt keenly that property ownership, relative wealth, and avoidance of manual labor separated them from lower elements. Hence they usually married within their own group; in Paris approximately 80 per cent of the daughters of shopkeepers married shopkeepers during the period 1820–1848.

At the same time the economic position of this group tended to stagnate. Those who rose into the ranks of shopkeepers usually improved their economic position, but the group itself made no major gains in average wealth. In a city like Paris the average shop-keeper was no better off in 1848 than his counterpart in 1820. And this was in a period when other business groups were gaining rapidly in wealth. The relative economic standing of shopkeepers was slipping, yet it became increasingly difficult to rise into the groups with greater earning power. Some economic operations of the merchants and industrialists competed with those of the lower middle class. In the textile industry small entrepreneurs who in the early years of the industrial revolution had bought a few looms or spinning machines often struggled for years in great hardship, but ultimately had to yield to the greater efficiency of larger competitors. Most retail transactions still took place in small shops, but shopkeepers in big cities did face some competition from new commercial outlets such as department stores.

The lower middle class often suffered burdensome political restrictions not applied to wealthier business or professional men. In France during the July Monarchy the upper-middle class alone could vote; property qualifications limited the suffrage to approximately 250,000 males. Later in the century property qualifications and class voting systems deprived all but the upper-middle class of effective political participation in Italy, where only 2 per cent could vote, and in Prussia. The lower middle class gained the vote in Austria only in the 1880s. The lower-middle class tended to be more radical politically than other elements of the middle class because of its political and economic disadvantages. In France, the group became republican in the late 1840s. After the hardships of the siege of Paris in 1870 shopkeepers joined artisans to form the revolutionary Commune. There was substantial democratic sentiment among shopkeepers in Germany in 1848. Only in Britain, where shopkeepers received the vote along with other elements of the middle class in 1832, was this sort of political division avoided. Generally, the lower middle class proved unable to take full advantage of the opportunity of industrialization and political reform. Its isolation within the middle class increased.

The professional group was distinguished in the middle class by its level of education. In western Europe it represented about 10 per cent of the whole middle class. In the east, particularly in Russia, a new professional group was arising by midcentury, largely for government service; until the 1890s it represented the greater part of the middle class.

The growth of the professional group was based on an extension of educational opportunities at the upper levels. Governments everywhere expanded higher educational facilities in the first part of the nineteenth century, largely to support their growing need for bureaucrats. Not only lawyers but also doctors and writers were trained as a result. Between 1809 and 1842 attendance at French *lycées* doubled. Russian university attendance rose from 1,700 in 1825 to 4,600 in 1848.

For the most part jobs kept pace with the increased production of professionals in this period, but in western Europe there was a decline in the relative status of professionals. The prestige of professional work, including government service, declined as industry rose, and the group did not share in the growing wealth of the business elements. There were a few very wealthy, but many poor professionals; average incomes did not rise sharply. The political role of professionals was often threatened. Factory owners sought control of municipal governments, which lawyers had often controlled before, and some national administrative posts were being offered to the masters of industry. Factory owners partially displaced professional people as the leaders of local social groups. Professionals in local artistic and philanthropic societies had to pay increasing deference to the power and wealth of businessmen. Professionals sensed the challenge to their status and often tried to compensate by new forms of political activity.

In eastern Europe there was no business group to rival the professional element, yet professionals had grievances which they often tried redress through political activities. These people, who had been trained for administrative efficiency, resented the backwardness of their governments. Suppressions of liberty, of the press, and of teaching were matters of immediate importance to the professional group. By midcentury Russian middle-class professionals were taking an increasing role in the intelligentsia. And whereas gentry intellectuals had spoken mainly in liberal terms, the new professionals were often more radical. Nowhere else in Europe did educated professionals feel themselves so distinctive and isolated as in Russia. Nowhere else did so many turn so radical. But everywhere an unusually intense political activism pervaded the professional element in the nineteenth century.

Everywhere professionals were distinguished by their advanced education and receptivity to new ideas. Universities were a principal center of political agitation in western Europe in the early nineteenth century and in Russia by the 1860s; student riots could assume considerable importance. Even outside the university professionals remained the most self-consciously political element of the middle class. Lawyers particularly espoused political causes, but professors and doctors also played a role. Businessmen, of course, had

a political interest and often acted as a pressure group to win governmental economic assistance. For the most part, though, their
politics were more occasional and more limited to the economic
sphere than were those of professional elements. Much of what is
termed middle-class politics was the activism of professionals. Politics
of various sorts constituted a channel for the energies and goals of
professionals during the century. Through politics jobs might be
found, ideals expressed and new status achieved.

The majority of the members of political societies such as the
Carbonari were from the professional element, and middle-class
revolutions were led by professional people. Journalists directed the
French revolution of 1830. Professors led the delegation to urge reforms on the king of Prussia in 1848, and lawyers took the major
role in the activities of the Frankfurt assembly. As parliamentary
regimes spread, professional people again took a leading role as
middle-class representatives. In all these activities the professional
group worked for interests that the business elements also supported;
but it continued to be the most politically conscious segment of the
middle class.

A few professional men were unusually interested in social
reform, although they often sought business support for their efforts.
British doctors like Edwin Chadwick and several doctors and teachers in French cities were among the earliest advocates of labor
reform. Many of the most active and articulate critics of business
life came from the professional group. They were not representative,
but their professional position was directly relevant to their reformist and revolutionary efforts. Most of the initial socialist leadership was derived from the professional class. Early Russian socialists,
both Marxist and agrarian, were drawn from the professional intelligentsia.

Leadership within the middle class rested with the larger merchants and industrialists. Within this group there was a fairly clear
upper element, for a segment of the economic middle class possessed
extraordinary and increasing wealth. In Paris during the July
Monarchy 1 per cent of the middle class controlled 30 per cent of
the wealth of the class. In 1848 there were only 712 really large
merchants in Berlin out of a population of 400,000. Members of
this upper middle class had a truly luxurious standard of living.

They alone could maintain private mansions in major cities such as London and Paris. They alone could rival the style of life of the wealthy aristocracy. Toward the end of the century, in fact, they increasingly intermarried with the aristocracy, though this was not common before 1850. The economic interests of this group were diverse. Some men started out as industrialists or bankers or large merchants, but most members of the upper middle class steadily diversified their interests, acquiring holdings in industry and commerce and often in banking as well. Most owned some landed property too. The wealth of the group brought it great political power. In many cases this was almost the only middle-class group that could vote, as in Italy after 1861 or France during the July Monarchy. Even in more democratic systems the group had disproportionate political influence. Generally, the upper middle class was the most conservative segment of the bourgeoisie. It had the greatest stake and power in the established order and tried most actively to preserve that order.

Most industrialists and merchants were considerably less wealthy than the upper group. Owners of medium-sized factories, particularly in the textile industry, managers of plants in heavy industry, and many others could afford a high but not luxurious standard of living. They had large apartments or, particularly in factory cities, private homes. Some had country houses as well. The average businessman owned furniture worth half the entire capital of the average shopkeeper. Such businessmen had several servants and a private carriage, but usually not a coachman. They could afford good education for their children. However, many business families went through a period in which they had to restrict their spending in order to build up capital. Often it took almost a generation for successful industrialists to enter a period of substantial expenditure on private consumption. The business group, like the middle class generally, valued material comfort and did not glory in self-denial. As soon as they could, businessmen did increase their spending, particularly on housing. Their diet and clothing were from the first superior to those of the lower classes, and their health was correspondingly much better. However, spending was not unrestrained; the highest levels of luxury were inaccessible to most of the business element.

Basic Middle-Class Interests

Work and the family continued to provide the primary focus for the middle class in the early industrial period. Both the daily life and the principal values of the class revolved around these two interests.

The middle class saw work as a panacea for social ills and the basis for personal success. Few early industrialists took regular vacations and those who did often felt uncomfortable until they could get back to their jobs. These same industrialists and the shopkeepers worked long hours, sometimes longer than those they imposed on their workers. Children were expected to help in shop or factory at a relatively early age, though only after some schooling. Wives helped regularly with the accounts and were also responsible for the direction of a rather complex household. The life of most members of the middle class in this period was full of labor, and they gloried in this fact.

The middle class frowned on expenditures and urged close accounting. Even industrialists who spent heavily on housing and other items typically kept careful daily budgets. The traditional virtue of saving was urged as a salutary discipline and a vital provision for the future. Saving was essential to maintain and perhaps increase the property on which the economic security of the class depended and to provide suitable education and dowries for the children. Savings might be invested in bonds, in land, or, most commonly, in the shop or factory itself. In addition to suitable savings the middle class expected sufficient profits for substantial consumer spending to increase comfort and to demonstrate a secure social position. This meant particular attention to home and furnishings. Shopkeepers often furnished a living room elaborately, even when they could afford almost nothing for their other rooms. Successful industrialists showed their wealth, as quickly as possible, in new houses on the outskirts of factory towns.

In spending and in saving alike, members of the middle class tried to promote the position and expectations of their families. The majority of the middle class was new to its economic situation in the early industrial period. Many new industrialists and merchants were scorned not only by aristocrats, but by some older members of the middle class. One industrialist newly arrived in Rheims, where there was a traditional merchant group, noted bitterly that he had almost no social contact with the established middle class. Even in newer factory centers, where there were fewer local social distinctions, industrialists felt a need to establish their families' social position in the country at large.

The family orientation of the middle class not only provided goals for the economic effort but also set the framework for most enterprises in the early industrial period. This was obviously true in retail shops, but a familial tone dominated many factories as well.

Family funds, including dowries and loans from relatives, provided the initial capital of most firms. Borrowing was necessary but was resented because it involved dependence on outsiders. Many partnerships were terminated as soon as the firm was well established; loans were repaid as quickly as possible. Further investment was provided, as far as possible, from the earnings of the firm; thus family control could be maintained. Staffing of the enterprise was often a family matter too. Industrialists directed their operations as much as possible by themselves, with their wives and children providing additional managerial assistance. In larger operations brothers and cousins were often called on, although outsiders were certainly used. Most important, merchants and industrialists intended to provide definite employment for their sons in the firm. In large families great efforts were made to extend the firm in order to give respectable jobs to all. Sons were trained to specialize in sales, accounting, design, or industrial chemistry in addition to general management. The enterprise was intended to perpetuate the family and to be perpetuated by it for an indefinite future.

The association of family and economic effort determined many other aspects of family life. Marriages were carefully arranged to promote economic success. Most members of the middle class married locally and within their own economic stratum. Some marriages were designed to add directly to the operations of a firm. It was not uncommon for a spinning mill, in essence, to marry a weaving plant. More generally, large dowries were given to daughters to set a young couple on a solid economic footing. Parisian shopkeepers, for example, often devoted as much as 20 per cent of their capital to the dowry. The age of marriage was also determined by economic considerations. Most members of the middle class married late, between twenty-five and thirty, when the man should be well established economically. Professional people married even later so that their vital education could be completed and a start made in a career. Finally, family size was carefully limited in most cases, for too many children would be impossible to place satisfactorily.

Education was stressed as a means of promoting the family's future. Many families spent up to 25 per cent of their capital on education. Professionals expected to provide good educations for their sons as their main contribution to the boys' successful futures. Industrialists and shopkeepers more commonly stressed technical training. Several years, usually into the midteens, were devoted to good primary education. After formal schooling boys were given some special technical education for the family business and then were trained in the firm itself. Girls were given education in morals, in household tasks such as sewing, and sometimes in music. They needed no elaborate technical skill, and their education was often quite rudimentary.

As the members of the middle class became more established economically, they broadened their interest in education. It was possible by the second or third generation for many industrialists and merchants to give their sons classical training at the secondary as well as the primary level. Scores of new secondary schools were founded in northern England after 1800 to educate the sons of industrialists, and after 1850 the most successful families began sending their children to the great public schools. In France business families relied increasingly on tutors or private schools for primary education after 1850 and after 1864 insisted on sending their sons to the prestigious *lycées,* even though they were the most expensive secondary schools. There was a clear interest here in providing an education that would increase the social standing of the family by imitating the sort of training professional groups and even aristocrats received. The association of education with family interest, now social as well as economic, was maintained.

The family ethic of the middle class stressed discipline and control. Women were subject both legally and by custom to the guidance of their husbands. They were not expected to appear as social equals, though they were often freely consulted by their husbands on major decisions. Children were guided with a strictness that was usually benevolent. They were expected to be respectful toward their parents—many were not allowed to address their parents by the familiar form—but were given great care and affection. Family gatherings provided most of the social life in many new factory centers. Family reading and church attendance represented the major cultural interests. The middle class constantly praised the family, organized with proper discipline and restraint, as a crucial element in social life. Sexual morality was urged, and middle-class men may have been unusually faithful to their wives during the nineteenth century. Mention of sexual problems was taboo; even the House of Commons was criticized, during an investigation of working conditions, for asking a female laborer about so personal a matter as a miscarriage. Restraint within the family was also regarded as essential. Excessive drinking was condemned because it jeopardized the family's position. Excessive procreation was deplored. Family life was to provide the framework for a strict discipline as well as for successful economic effort.

There was, clearly, a certain narrowness and severity to the life of the middle class during the early industrial period. Contacts and interests were largely restricted to work and the family. Pleasure for pleasure's sake was discouraged. Even clothing, though of good quality, reflected the sobriety of the class. Self-restraint was a key element of bourgeois morality. This was, after all, a class engaged in vast and novel economic effort. A strong will was necessary to take advantage of opportunities and to avoid the many chances for failure. The standards of the class, particularly the insistence on wealth and property, were rigid and demanding. The dynamism of the middle class was due in great part to the willingness to work and associate its ethics and the family with this work. It was natural that concern for economic success and family life dominated, in turn, the attitude of the middle class toward culture, politics, and society generally. With some wealth and education, the class did possess and express views on larger issues. Given the power of the class, these views were often extremely influential in religion, government, and economics. For most of the middle class these same issues were, however, secondary to the fundamental purpose of productive work within the framework of a closely knit family.

Middle-Class Economics

Based on their individual purposes, members of the middle class made certain general assumptions about the economy in which they operated. They desired a fluid and open economy in which the individual could develop his own enterprise. They were optimistic about the results of such individual efforts and about the trends of modern industry generally. They pointed out that the combined activities of thousands of entrepreneurs were producing growing quantities of goods of increasing quality and at steadily falling prices. They noted the employment potential of the industrial economy. They praised the effects of mechanization in lightening the physical strain of the worker as well as in creating new wealth. They were convinced that the middle class was responsible for this progress, and they saw no reason to stint on self-congratulation. In many respects they shared the views of the liberal economists whose theories dominated formal economic thought during the early nineteenth century. These theories were reproduced, in popularized form, in many middle-class journals, from which businessmen picked up key ideas and slogans.

The class heartily praised the virtues of competition as the motive force of progress, the impulse to individuals to improve their methods and cut their prices. Competition forced the individual to develop his industry to the limits of his ability. Most members of the middle class were highly competitive. They tried to keep any technical advances secret for as long as possible in order to increase their own opportunities for profit. They competed actively for markets by developing new products and methods. In prosperous times most members of the middle class resisted any interference with their individual economic activities. They refused to cooperate with each other or with governments in limiting frauds on the public or abuses of labor. An optimistic individualism pervaded much of the middle-class economy of the period.

Optimism was not always realistic, however. The middle class did not blindly follow liberal economic theory or indeed any theory. This was a pragmatic class, interested in personal rather than theoretical goals. And it did not love risk. For the few businessmen of great daring there were many more who took risks reluctantly if at all. Hence the adoption of new techniques often came only as a result of economic crises, when costs had to be cut; in prosperous times the majority of industrialists were content to rely on routine.

Along with competitive individualism, then, the middle class was interested in promoting security. This interest was most intense in crises; it tended to fade with prosperity, when goals were being met. It was greater on the continent than in England, partly because of traditions of strong government, partly because English competition was faced and feared from the first. But even the English tried to modify competition.

Cooperation was one means of reducing competitive pressure. Industrialists' associations developed early to share technical information or even to allocate markets and supplies. The middle class also sought government encouragement for the economy. Except in Britain almost all entrepreneurs insisted on tariff protection. They might feel that internal competition was valuable, but they certainly had no desire to face foreign goods. Most businessmen also sought government encouragement of exports, provision of better transport systems, and the like. A smaller number of manufacturers sought government controls on quality and on conditions of work in the interest of modifying excessive competition. There were even proposals, fairly common during the July Monarchy, for example, for a system of government licensing aimed at restricting overproduction and crises. The middle class remained fundamentally optimistic about the course of the economy, for usually its purposes were being realized; but it was not wedded to a concept of complete individualism.

Politics

The middle-class view of government also maintained a certain flexibility. This was a class with a high level of political interest. Even business activities required some attention to politics at times. Furthermore, certain fundamental assumptions of the middle class had obvious political repercussions. The middle-class tenet that the individual was responsible for his own fate contributed to a desire to secure the protection of certain liberties even aside from economic freedom. Middle-class reformers sought government aid to liberate men from the thrall of ignorance by providing education, from slavery by abolishing the slave trade, and from abusive child labor by humanitarian legislation.

In addition to a general desire for freedom, the middle class sought order. This class, which prided itself on the order it created in home and business through proper discipline, had a great deal to lose in the event of disorder. Riots ruined shops and factories, strikes impeded the conduct of one's business, and prolonged periods of chaos inevitably produced a business slump. The middle class expected the government to provide the order necessary to preserve economic prosperity and the safety of property. It also expected the government itself to be orderly. It disliked aspects of the government that were inefficient or irrational. It disliked the cost of inefficiency in taxes and found it offensive in principle. It criticized aspects of the government that were justifiable only in terms of tradition, particularly since the tradition was usually aristocratic. It expected government to be open to new ideas and competent personnel.

Most basically, the middle class felt that government should be subject to middle-class participation and even control. The middle class had a dynamic belief in its own worth. Like the aristocracy, but for different reasons, it felt itself singularly qualified to rule. Wealth measured worth, and the middle class now had the wealth. Discipline, temperance, and a firm will measured moral fiber, and the middle class alone possessed these virtues. Middle-class governments would also favor economic prosperity, but this was not the only interest. The middle-class politician Guizot wrote histories showing that middle-class rule represented the highest stage of social evolution, a stage that would henceforth be permanent. This sentiment was more high-flown than the feelings of businessmen, but it expressed a common principle.

In cities and in whole nations the middle class sought political power for itself alone. It wished to displace the aristocracy and prevent lower-class participation. Property qualifications for suffrage were almost everywhere introduced to express the middle-class belief that wealth guaranteed political competence. Wealth meant a proper interest in order, it meant education, and it meant personal merit. Bourgeois revolutions such as that in France in 1830 brought an extension of the vote—to 250,000 people in all. The British electoral reform of 1832 gave suffrage to a sixth of the population, embracing almost the entire middle class and little beyond. To obtain participation in government the middle class was sometimes willing to sacrifice order and rise in revolt. To maintain control it sometimes sacrificed freedoms, as in the measures taken against the press and the right of assembly during the July Monarchy. These exceptions to common purposes were justified by the principle that rule by the middle class meant rule in the best interests of all.

The fundamental political goals of the middle class led to a somewhat ambivalent view of government itself. There was a profound suspicion of government within the middle class, particularly in the west. During the era of aristocratic control governments had been motivated by principles the middle class found incorrect. They had directly interfered with and hampered the conduct of business through guild restrictions and other regulations. The middle classes felt that they and, by an extension of principles, all men could handle their own affairs best if free from this sort of government control. The class also resented having to contribute to the expenses of government activity, and its general interest in liberty demanded limitations on government.

The middle class also saw positive roles for the government. The members of the class were attached to no theoretical view of politics, even though their impulses did coincide to a degree with liberal writings. There was some division within the class on proper functions of government. The German middle class, accustomed to strong and relatively efficient government, was less interested in restrictions on government than were its counterparts in France or Spain. In a given area, even in the same individual, sentiments on the proper power of government varied according to the time and the issue.

Governments could promote the economic interests of the middle class by positive action in providing tariff protection, transport facilities, and the like. Urban administrations were urged to build streets, drainage systems, parks, libraries, and schools. The growing vigor of city governments was, after all, due primarily to middle-class demands and interests.

Governments could promote humanitarian projects. There was an important strain of reformism in the middle class, based on the belief that the individual was basically good and responsible. Where evils existed, they were assumed to be environmental and so correctable. Only a minority of the middle class actively worked for major reforms, but they often had broad support from the class. Many reform societies were strictly private, hoping for voluntary gains; this was particularly true in England. But the government clearly had a role to play. Reform societies urged regulation of evils ranging from gambling to child labor, and public aid for education was almost always sought.

Finally, the middle class saw a positive role for government in the preservation of order. The class wanted protection against crime in the streets and protection against riots and strikes. For a variety of reasons the interests of the middle class promoted government activity in many spheres, some of them new. As the class gained increasing participation in government, its distrust of the state gradually lessened. First at the municipal level, later on the national level, middle-class regimes promoted a wide range of activities. The interest in liberty and restriction of governmental activity was not abandoned, but a positive view of the state gradually gained in importance.

Middle-class political groups had firm convictions about the best form of government, which followed from the political interests of the class. The middle class sought constitutional government based on an orderly and rational statement of the form, functions, and limitations of government. Most middle-class revolutions produced not only a constitution, but also a bill of rights protecting freedom of religion, of the press, of property, and of economic activity. In revolutionary periods freedom of assembly was also established, but was often restricted after the danger of lower-class agitation was realized.

The middle class sought a parliamentary regime, usually with limited suffrage. Parliaments would provide a salutary check on arbitrary action by the monarch or any other executive. They would also supply the forum in which representatives of the middle class could exercise power in government. In the demand for the establishment of parliaments the middle class most clearly showed its intention to alter the class basis on which governments rested. Parliaments were installed in all middle-class revolutions, from France in 1789 to Russia in 1905 and 1917, and the power of parliament was jealously protected and promoted by all major middle-class parties, such as the Prussian Progressives in the 1860s. Only with a constitutional, parliamentary regime did the middle class feel that its political interests could be realized.

Middle-class political interest was increasingly attached to the concept of the nation as well as to the ideal of parliamentary rule. This was the class to which nationalist doctrines particularly appealed. The middle class saw the nation as a vital economic unit. It needed a national market for its goods and national protection of its economic interests. Nationalism also gave the class a focus distinct from attachment to traditional dynasties and aristocratic political principles. In the revolution of 1830 the new king, Louis Philippe, ruled not by hereditary right but as king of the French. In Britain, France, and Belgium, where national existence was established by the 1830s and where the middle class participated in government, nationalism was expressed in pride in existing national institutions and the belief that one's own nation was morally superior to others. Elsewhere, as in Germany and Italy, the middle-class interest in nationalism obviously worked for political change. Middle-class political groups sought national unity along with constitutional, parliamentary regimes. In parts of eastern Europe a small middle class was often instrumental in introducing nationalism. Greek and Serbian merchants were exposed to nationalism in trade with the west during the French revolutionary period. Bulgarian merchants, a new group after 1850, inspired much nationalist activity. Middle-class intellectuals spread nationalist ideas in many areas. Here again, a passion had been aroused in the middle class that was to have profound political consequences.

During the first half of the nineteenth century, and later in parts of eastern Europe, the middle class was dissatisfied with existing regimes, although few members of the class agitated actively. Where there was sufficient liberty of the press, middle-class newspapers attacked governmental conservatism and aristocratic rule. In Restoration France and before 1832 in England, meetings were held and groups formed to agitate for reform of the suffrage, greater protection of liberty, and real limitation of the role of the aristocracy in government. In Spain, Italy, and Germany middle-class activity could not be so open, but there were some publications and discussion groups that condemned the established order. A minority of the middle class, drawn particularly from young professionals and students, went beyond discussion and actually joined groups for agitation. Masonic groups in Spain, the Carbonari in Italy, and the Burschenschaften in Germany drew significant numbers into vigorous political discussion and sometimes direct action.

In certain circumstances the middle class countenanced direct action, even revolution, in pursuit of its political goals. It is incorrect to say that the class itself revolted. Businessmen were seldom on the streets in revolutions, although they might shut their shops and encourage their employes to riot. The interest in personal security was too great for participation in actual disorder; and after revolution broke out, the class was quick to form and join national guard units to preserve order. There was, nevertheless, a series of middle-class revolutions in the first half of the century in most western and central European countries. Middle-class intellectuals prepared the doctrines for these revolutions, doctrines that were accepted quite widely in the class. Middle-class groups typically provoked the revolutions and controlled the revolutionary governments, which sought liberal parliamentary and nationalist goals.

Most of the revolutions failed to establish a government wholly conforming to the middle-class ideals, but even where revolutions were directly defeated, as they were in Germany and Italy in 1848, the succeeding years brought some of the reforms the middle class desired. Parliaments were established, although their powers were limited. Middle-class economic interests were promoted, and national unities were achieved. The middle class did not rule in its own right; it shared power with the aristocracy and compromised its principles with those of the old regime. Nevertheless, a major political role was now assured.

After 1848, in fact, the era of middle-class revolutionary activity was over in western and central Europe. The class had made sufficient economic and political gains that it could be relatively content and the revolutions themselves had heightened its interest in order. Particularly in 1848, the agitation by the urban lower classes, culminating in such bloody riots as the June Days in Paris, attached the middle class to existing governments even when such governments were not fully satisfactory. The class did not lose an interest in parliamentary rule and other reforms, but efforts at reform worked within the legal structure. In most countries the class had won some freedom of the press, through which opinions could be expressed. It had won a parliament, albeit often a weak one, in which further changes could be proposed. It had dislodged the aristocracy from total control. It could now defend its interests in a calm and orderly way.

Middle Class and Working Class

As employers and as political leaders, members of the middle class had direct contact with the working classes. They had to develop policies to guide and explain the treatment of workers. The middle class lacked a reasoned social theory, but there were some generally held assumptions that determined and explained the social behavior of the class. As the class rose to economic and some political dominance, its social attitudes were crucial for society as a whole.

Middle-class knowledge of the life of the lower classes was in many respects very slight. Increasingly, the middle class lived in separate areas of the city in order to avoid the worst urban problems. Many members of the middle class never penetrated the poorest quarters. They saw some workers and some beggars, but knew nothing of their life, so it was easy to accept general stereotypes. There were other gaps between the middle class and the urban lower classes. Speech was different. Many artisans and workers had distinctive accents or dialects; some were even foreign. The middle class usually prided itself, after the first generation at least, on pure pronunciation. The middle class stressed cleanliness and respectable clothing. Workers, in contrast, were often dirty, ragged, even diseased, and to middle-class eyes they were unpleasant to look at. The middle class urged hard work, while many workers valued leisure and took time off when they could. The middle class valued saving; the lower classes had little to save and often preferred to spend any margin for enjoyment. The drinking of many workers contrasted with middle-class sobriety. Family ties among the lower classes were loosening at a time when the middle class regarded a solid family as essential. The lower classes seemed often disorderly because of their penchant for rioting and the roughhousing and fighting in which many workers engaged. Some members of the class feared the enmity and violence of the workers. More commonly, the middle class regarded workers as alien and inferior because of the obvious differences in economic achievement and in attitudes.

A combination of ignorance and congenital optimism colored the middle-class view of the conditions of the poor. Improvements in clothing or diet were often exaggerated. Great stress was laid on political reforms that freed the workers from the restrictions of guild and feudal lord. Technical developments such as gas lighting were assumed to be of benefit to all. Many observers claimed that workers could always earn enough in good times to cover their needs in bad. Others noted the beneficence of the factory system in giving work to women and children, who would otherwise be left without resource and without proper discipline. Mine owners might claim that their employes gloried in the possibility of working in a soothing pit, sheltered from the glare of sun and the beating of rain. The tendency to see a silver lining in every lower-class cloud relieved the consciences of the middle class and dulled any willingness to take positive action for reform.

However, optimism was not the only reaction of the middle class to the problems of the poor. The class could not be blinded to some of the horrible features of working-class life. Employers, after all, did see their own workers in the plant at least. Crime, riots, and begging indicated that all was not well. Government investigations of the conditions of child labor, carried on in Britain and France in the 1830s and 1840s, were covered by the press, and private reports by doctors like James Kay in Britain and René Villermé in France received considerable publicity. Local middle-class groups also sponsored surveys of labor conditions. Only the most fatuous members of the middle class persisted in asserting that all was well.

Confronted with the evidences of lower-class poverty, the middle class sought a scapegoat. Some said the fault was with the cities; others blamed foreign countries or distant regions for unfair competition that forced conditions down. Some maintained that poverty was inevitable; did the Bible not say so? Many employers were honestly if occasionally saddened by their workers' lot, but felt powerless to do anything about it.

Many blamed the conditions of the poor on the poor themselves. There was a deep-seated belief that poverty must somehow be the result of moral inadequacy. Anyone with merit could rise in middle-class society. Commentators were fond of pointing to manufacturers who had come from the ranks of the poor. Often employers favored particularly talented workers by giving them special training or using them as foremen. The sympathy here was for the worker who had essentially middle-class ambitions; he was the worker who was easiest to understand according to the middle-class values by which the great body of the poor had to be condemned. If workers would save, they would be protected from misery and could even rise; middle-class pamphlets pointed out how easy saving was. If workers would stop drinking, they would have both more money and more energy. Some manufacturers in France claimed that workers spent a quarter of their income on drink and that if they gave up drink they might be rich. If the poor had a decent family life, they would work harder, train their children better, and avoid the exhaustion of sexual debauchery.

The view that the poor were immoral justified a great deal of neglect of social problems—why help those who would not help themselves? In 1834 the British Parliament passed a new Poor Law designed to make poor houses as unattractive as possible. As the poor were to blame for poverty, they should not be encouraged to take charity. The same belief in the immorality of the poor justified such political measures as restricting the vote to the well-to-do. Society was fundamentally a hierarchy with the meritorious rising to the top. The same view of the immoral poor conditioned many of the reform efforts that were made.

Some elements of the middle class were not content to leave the problems of the poor unremedied. Individual employers were often disturbed by the plight of their own workers, even if they might regard them as inferior. There was some feeling that the worker was really a less civilized being, capable of being content with hard work and simple pleasures such as drink and sexual indulgence. However, many employers believed that hard work did deserve reward. Particularly as long as workers were uncomplaining, as long as they were resigned and grateful, there was a feeling that they deserved sympathetic treatment. Some employers were also impelled to better treatment by a lack of sufficient labor, particularly skilled labor. Many improvements were introduced to attract and retain needed workers. Even arguments by critics of industry, such as aristocratic reformers or utopian socialists, impressed some members of the middle class with the need and possibility of reform. Religion motivated many, including some of the leading industrial reformers, to a sense that the poor were God's creatures and deserved real assistance. Finally, the middle class belief in progress and in individual opportunity caused much interest in improvement of conditions. Only the blind could claim that there was progress in a society when little children had to work in giant factories or that such children had decent opportunities.

Middle-class values, often combined with a religious or even socialist impulse, drove some individuals to a life of devotion to reform. Some industrialists, such as Robert Owen and Daniel Legrand, worked persistently for radical change. More generally, similar motives impelled members of the middle class in more modest efforts that did not distract the class from its primary devotion to personal goals. The middle class, responsible for much harshness toward the poor, was responsible also for many efforts at amelioration.

The middle class contributed substantially to charity. Most cities had annual balls and other social affairs for the benefit of the poor, and the middle class played an increasing role in these. Especially in economic crises, contributions were extensive. In 1847, for example, employers in Lille grouped together and collected two million francs to buy wheat for the poor. Individual employers and merchants often left grants for hospitals or pensions in their wills. Charity was one of the most general and traditional responses to the problem of the poor, but it was uncongenial to certain values of the middle class. It degraded the recipient and did nothing to improve his future opportunity. Characteristically, reformers in the middle class sought measures beyond mere charity.

Individual companies played a leading role in effecting reforms, particularly the larger companies, which had greater resources and a greater need for labor. As the number of large companies increased with time, so the efforts at reform expanded. During the July Monarchy at least a sixth of the French companies with more than fifty workers offered their employees something beyond work and a wage, ranging from provision of an hour of schooling for child workers to elaborate housing and health services. The mining concern of Decazeville, for example, built housing for half its 6,000 workers. Groups of industrialists set up schools to give technical training and sometimes advocated reform legislation as well. Local booster groups and even artistic societies, containing many merchants and professional people, concerned themselves mildly with the problems of the poor.

The middle class was particularly interested in measures that would encourage workers to help themselves. These measures had the dual advantage of coinciding with middle-class interest in individual opportunity and of being relatively inexpensive. Many middle-class groups offered prizes to diligent and moral workers, while others set up and administered savings banks for the poor as a means of providing moral discipline as well as material support. Many companies and organizations promoted friendly societies. They often contributed to these insurance funds, but again the basic contribution was to come from the worker, who would be taught the dignity of providing his own support. Some companies conducted extensive campaigns against drunkenness and immorality, chiefly by fining or dismissing offenders. Many groups were organized to issue tracts urging temperance and the family virtues.

The greatest concern was for formal education. Companies and societies often established schools, with particular interest in technical and moral training. The British Sunday-school movement taught middle-class morality to over a million and a half workers and artisans. Many groups urged extensions of state school systems. The middle class believed that education would create better workers and would even allow some to rise out of the lower class altogether. One English observer noted:

> Virtue is the child of knowledge, vice of ignorance: therefore education, periodical literature, railroad traveling, ventilators, and the art of life, when fully carried out, serve to make a population moral and happy.

In addition to encouraging self-help, some members of the middle class sought legal reforms for the poor. In many countries individual manufacturers and chambers of commerce urged legislation on hours of work, on factory safety conditions, even on minimum wages. Reformers particularly sought protection for child labor. In France the first proposal for a child labor law was made in 1827 by an industrialist in Mulhouse. In the next decade the Mulhouse Industrial Society backed the proposal, as did a number of other groups. Many manufacturers resisted it, claiming that children were vital to industry and that the government should not interfere with working conditions. Nevertheless, support from elements of the middle class brought about the passage in 1841 of a law that regulated the age and hours of the employment of children and required that child workers under twelve go to school. The law was poorly enforced and often resisted, but it represented an important step toward the principle of government regulation in industrial society. The British government enacted a child labor law in 1833, and in 1847 passed a ten-hour bill for women and children. Middle-class society proved capable of taking some steps toward self-regulation.

Efforts by companies, societies, and cities to improve education raised the literacy of the lower classes, and efforts to improve hygiene in factories and cities and to provide better medical care for the poor reduced illness significantly. In general, however, the efforts at reform had little effect on the difficulties of working-class life and for the most part were undertaken in a paternalistic manner. The middle class professed interest in creating more equal opportunities, but still believed that the poor were an inferior group that needed middle-class leadership. Institutions such as schools or friendly societies were kept under middle-class administration and taught a combination of middle-class morality and grateful resignation. From the middle class itself, quite understandably, would come no revolution in the social relationships of industrial society.

Cultural Interests

The middle class had sufficient funds and education to develop cultural interests, and the middle-class values accordingly had great influence on the general development of the arts in the nineteenth century.

At the beginning of the industrial revolution the cultural interests of the middle class were relatively simple. The tastes and habits of many members of the class reflected those of their parents in lower levels of the middle class or in rural society. Few businessmen had substantial resources for cultural activity, and fewer still had time. In London, for example, even substantial businessmen could not afford to attend concerts regularly until after 1840. On the continent, particularly in the larger cities, there was a tradition of theater-going even for the lower middle class. But in industrial cities, and in Britain generally, simple amusements were the rule.

Cultural activity centered around the home and was largely confined to furnishings and decorations, items useful in daily life that provided some status among friends. The middle class sought comfort, neatness, and some sentimentality in its decorations. Typical of this taste was the Biedermeier style, which dominated German bourgeois furnishings and paintings during the midnineteenth century. The Biedermeier style stressed simple, manageable furnishings that would not take up too much space, decorated without great imagination or luxury. Wallpaper was crowded with picturesque designs; it was cheaper than it had been in the eighteenth century and became common in middle-class homes for the first time. Paintings in middle-class homes were generally either portraits or sentimental country scenes. Again, the interest was in a setting that would be at once comfortable and respectable. The class had neither the time nor the background for ostentatious designs.

The reading interests of the middle class also centered in the home. Men kept up with political and economic news in their newspapers and journals. Both newspapers and magazines increasingly stressed accounts of technical and scientific developments. Many middle-class views on progress were reflected in and furthered by this reading. Beyond this, there was a general interest in stories suitable for family reading. Families often read aloud in the home. Newspapers and magazines provided serialized stories for such reading; authors such as Charles Dickens derived most of their income from these stories, sentimental narratives that were particularly pleasant for the women, whose formal education was slight. Such a magazine was *Die Gartenlaube* in Germany, which jumped from 5,000 subscribers in 1853 to 225,000 in 1867, as the middle class rose to greater prominence. *Die Gartenlaube* offered articles on science and education, the paths to progress; it editorialized against traditional superstition and for humanitarian causes. Its stories stressed the moral value of family and property. It condemned the aristocracy and often in stories portrayed the idleness and immorality of nobles as a shocking—but somewhat exciting—contrast to bourgeois virtue. Novels for the lower middle class in Germany went even farther in sensationalism, as well as sentimentality, although they too were always careful to let morality triumph.

Apart from home decoration and reading, the principal cultural interest of the middle class in the early nineteenth century was religion. In cosmopolitan centers such as Paris, where educational levels were unusually high, the middle class inclined to skepticism in matters of religion. Generally, however, the class maintained a firm tradition of church attendance and religious interest. Some industrialists came from intensely religious backgrounds. The Nonconformists in England entered industry in large numbers and long preserved their religious fervor. Protestant leaders of industry in Alsace and Switzerland tried to combine work and prayer. Some began each workday in the factory with collective prayer and Bible reading; many attributed their economic success to the will of God. Catholic manufacturers in northern France displayed similar religious intensity. Later, fervent Old Believers played a major role in early Russian industrialization, again combining religious zeal and economic activity. Church attendance was important to the middle classes during the early industrial period; for women, par-·ticularly, religious practices provided an important outlet. Children were trained in the principles of religion and often were sent to church schools.

The middle class had little interest in theology and ceremony. Doctrines of sin and the afterlife were accepted, but were not the focal points of middle-class religion. In fact, the middle-class values of material success and the ability of the individual to improve himself tended increasingly to contradict the traditional stress on other-worldly goals and original sin. Beyond this, the middle class was generally opposed to the political powers of established churches. In countries where there was a tradition of a dominant state church, as there was in France and the Scandinavian states, the middle class proved particularly hostile to religion generally. In Britain and Germany the multiplicity of religions reduced the political issues surrounding the churches, although even there important conflict arose. The middle class resented religious intolerance and its en-forcement by a state. It resented the power of aristocrats in the established churches. Neither traditional theology nor church politics attracted the middle class to religion.

Religion did fulfill three vital functions for the middle class. It provided a social focus; for most women church attendance was the only regular contact outside the home. Religion was regarded as use-ful for the masses; it promoted morality and the acceptance of hardship on earth in the expectation of reward in heaven. This feel-ing of the social utility of religion increased with time, particularly among the upper levels of the class, and caused a great deal of middle-class support for religious endeavors. Most important, religion served as a source and sanction for morality for middle-class families themselves. The class sought sermons and religious reading that would explain the beauty and utility of moral behavior.

Outside of home and church, the cultural activities of the middle class were few. Some women did a bit of painting and took music lessons, but this was rare. Music was not widely known except as part of church services or family entertainment; by 1800 most Eng-lish middle-class homes had pianos. Theater attendance was gener-ally uncommon; in England many businessmen felt that it was a waste of time, and some regarded it as immoral. Not until 1850 did the British middle class begin to show an interest in drama. When it did, it applied to the theater the tastes it had developed in reading. It wanted sentimental and instructive plays—and it insisted on more comfortable theater seats. In this early period the middle class shunned dancing and cards as wasteful and immoral. Such activities were not part of the respectability the middle class sought in its entertainments.

These early trends in middle-class culture were not permanent. They did, however, contain certain durable principles. The class demanded that literature and art be moral. Erotic references were unacceptable, and governments during the period often tried to ban works such as *Madame Bovary*, which seemed too daring. Sensationalism was frowned upon, although it did appear in discussions of aristocratic behavior and elsewhere. Literature was to portray the value of hard work and thrift and show how these qualities allowed men to rise in society. It was to avoid subjects such as crime and was not to dwell on life among the poor, for such topics could not offer proper lessons for family reading.

Cultural products were also to be useful. They should provide information. The class did not care for flights of fancy; it preferred moderately realistic portrayals. Purely aesthetic experiences were not sought; art should decorate and represent, or it was a waste and perhaps a temptation. Sentiment was entertaining and informing, but great emotions were dangerous.

Scientists were particularly esteemed among intellectuals because their functions were so obviously useful; in fact, the middle class tended to confuse science with technology and praise both as motors of progress. Other intellectuals and artists were regarded with some suspicion, for they seemed preoccupied with abstract theories and were not motivated by a proper respect for wealth. Middle-class reading often contained portrayals of the wild life and subversive quality of some artists. The legend of the Bohemian artist was being born and would increase middle-class doubts about the morals and motives of writers and painters.

The middle-class cultural canons of utility and respectability both reflected and caused its educational interests in the early industrial period, for most members of the class had only primary schooling, and some technical training. By the second or third generation of the industrial revolution, however, the cultural interests of the middle class broadened notably. By midcentury in Britain and France and a bit later in Germany the intense efforts of the middle class to found businesses had paid off in secure and rising incomes. The class had more leisure, for many businesses now had large staffs, which reduced the time required at work. The class developed the inclination to enjoy itself, although the stress on hard work and saving did not disappear.

The religious interests of the class tended to decline as material success became greater and as other opportunities for recreation arose. The class did not abandon the churches. It still regarded them as morally and socially useful, but its religious zeal abated. By the second generation it was noted that manufacturers in Zurich had become somewhat apathetic in religious practice; the same trend appeared later in Russia among middle-class Old Believers. In the second half of the nineteenth century some churches tried to accommodate the new interests of the middle class. Modernist movements in Protestantism and the rise of Reform Judaism were attempts to harmonize religion and science and deemphasize unappealing doctrines such as original sin and the possibility of damnation. These trends reflected not only the continued attachment of the middle class to aspects of religion but also their lack of traditional piety.

After the first generation or two of industrialization, the wealthier elements of the middle class began to patronize music, art, and literature extensively. New forms of education played a great role in this process. Sons of successful business families were given more education and were sent to more traditional schools. In the early nineteenth century the middle class derided the classical stress of traditional secondary schools. Middle-class magazines urged the importance of science, modern languages, history, and other useful subjects, and the class sent its sons to schools that provided such subjects. About midcentury, however, the focus changed. Business families in France began to abandon the cheaper *collèges* in favor of the more prestigious and more classical *lycées*. The great British public schools were investigated in the 1860s and did introduce some modern subjects; but although they changed only slightly, the upper middle class supported the schools eagerly now that its sons could enter them. The educational interests of the upper business group, the leading professional families, and the aristocracy increasingly merged. The lower middle class could not follow this pattern; its education remained more limited and utilitarian. In fact, it was cut off from the leading middle-class families by the new educational gap. The upper middle class was developing cultural standards that would reflect its established economic power.

To demonstrate their social prestige middle-class families sought clear, almost official canons of taste. They shunned cultural innovations that might prove socially unacceptable in favor of firm, respectable standards. As vacations and travel became fashionable, travel guides were printed, and travel agencies formed to arrange safe and respectable itineraries for the increasing numbers of eager but inexperienced middle-class tourists. In the 1840s Thomas Cook opened in London the first major travel agency. Spas such as Brighton and Folkestone were patronized in imitation of aristocratic resorts. They might be dull, but they became symbols of status.

The middle-class interest in creating socially acceptable institutions led to growing support for opera companies and symphony orchestras, institutions that enjoyed aristocratic patronage as well. Permanent symphony orchestras were established in many cities for the first time. Concert prices were reduced, which allowed many middle-class families to attend, and the new numbers and wealth of middle-class patrons increased the professionalization of concert music. German symphony performances even in Beethoven's time had usually involved a temporary collection of semiprofessional musicians, and the quality of playing was often very poor. The change in middle-class culture promoted a real change in musical performances.

The new patrons of art preferred works that met the conservative standards set by established academies, such as the British Royal Academy. Aside from portraiture, middle-class purchases of art were concentrated on the old masters, whose paintings had clear prestige and would be trophies as well as decorations. The new interest in the old masters was so intense that the forgery of masterpieces became a substantial business.

Middle-class libraries, similarly, were heavy with the older, safer works. The upper middle class in Paris in the 1840s bought more eighteenth- and seventeenth-century classics than contemporary works.

Magazines and books like J. C. Louden's *Encyclopedia* in Britain gave guidance for taste in furniture. The interiors of wealthy homes were elaborate and often showy. They scorned unity of design for an interest in accumulating decorative objects. Heavy furniture and fringed curtains were combined with Chinese figurines. An impression of wealth and profusion, with a continued interest in comfort, dominated many middle-class homes.

In many ways the architectural standards of the nineteenth century best exemplified the taste of the rising middle class. Expensive, ornate mansions became badges of middle-class wealth. Standards were again sought in the past. Imitations of classical and even byzantine style rivaled recreations of the Gothic. These imitations, however, were usually modified to reflect a new interest in massive form and luxuriant detail. The French architect Viollet-le-Duc restored many Gothic buildings in France and in England. He often added battlements and ornamentation unknown to the middle ages but appropriate to the new age of luxury. Public structures such as the Albert Memorial in London and small, castlelike houses had the prestige of an established style and the gaudiness of middle-class wealth. Renaissance classicism was copied yet made more grandiose in Napoleon III's extension of the Louvre. If the nineteenth century cannot be viewed as a triumph of taste, it can be seen as a vast development of a self-conscious interest in culture. The middle class, massive in numbers, rose from simple, traditional taste to an eager search for cultural prestige.

The expanding power of the middle class affected all areas of social activity. The class developed on the basis of individual interest in the economic and social advance of self and family. Members of the class denied themselves much in the quest for personal progress. Their denial and hard work often brought success. Many rose to middle-class ranks for the first time; even more rose within the class. This rise, although intended primarily to establish the individual and his family, had larger effects. As numbers and wealth increased, the middle class developed new demands for political power. Their economic and political advance extended their power over other groups in society; the class increasingly tried to justify and in some ways reform this power. They also tried to protect it. New wealth and a desire for social prestige brought new interests in art and literature. These interests affected not only the life of the class but also the cultural tone of the age. For this was a dominant class.

Wealth, numbers, and a sense of virtue and vitality gave the class and its values real leadership in society.

CONCLUSION: CHURCH, STATE, AND THE NEW SOCIETY

The expansion of population, the spread of a market economy, and early industrialization profoundly altered European social structure. Traditional classes were challenged, and new ones arose. There was social ferment everywhere. Peasants and artisans tried to adjust to novel forces, and the rising middle class tried to expand its influence on the basis of new economic power. The resulting situation was obviously revolutionary. One class alone, even the middle class, might have been withstood by a combination of repression and compromise. The coincidence of agitation from a variety of classes could not be resisted and could be diverted by nothing less than basic changes in the structure of society. At the same time the class that led the resistance effort, the aristocracy, was being steadily weakened by changes in the economy. Its resistance could delay change but could not repress it. Undue resistance would, in fact, produce direct, revolutionary attack.

The initial period of social adjustment to the economic and demographic change was therefore a period of political upheaval. From 1789 to 1848 western Europe underwent an amazing series of revolutions. Almost every country, from giant Prussia to tiny states like Switzerland and Belgium, experienced at least one major revolution. France, which came to be something of a specialist in these matters, produced three. Only a minority was actively revolutionary, and subversive organizations were small, but the minority could win far larger support at certain times. The two leading institutions, church and state, were the principal targets for the rising current of discontent.

The social changes in nineteenth-century Europe posed great problems for the major churches. These churches were not merely religious bodies; they were also political institutions largely under aristocratic control. The churches therefore drew the wrath of the middle classes as one of the bastions of noble privilege. The middle classes tried to reduce the power of the churches by establishing religious liberty and in some cases showed an interest in separating

education and charity from church control. The optimism of the
class, the belief in the capacity of the individual, implicitly countered
a belief in original sin and the possibility of damnation. The interest
in education and science diminished the credibility of miracles and
even of faith itself. After 1859 the popularization of the theory of
evolution raised even greater doubts of and disinterest in Christian
tradition. The middle class, in sum, challenged certain important
features of the political powers of the churches. Their interests also
reduced the vitality of some fundamental principles of the Christian
religion.

The churches encountered problems with the lower classes as
well. The peasantry had little contact with new secular principles
and remained generally religious. The peasant attack on feudalism,
however, altered the economic position of many churches substantially. Peasants in Catholic countries had paid dues to the church as
well as to the manor lord, and when they sought to rid themselves
of feudal obligations, they often attacked the tithe as well. Peasant
hunger for land also put pressure on churches where, as in France
and Spain, they were major landowners. In the cities the wealth and
conservatism of these same churches alienated many of the poor and
could even cause direct attacks as part of general revolutionary
efforts. Some artisans espoused new beliefs in science and reason
that were developed in their education and reading. The churches
faced rising indifference and some outright hostility among most
urban groups.

The greatest attacks on the church occurred in France. The revolution of 1789 deprived the church of both its land and its tithes
and declared full liberty of religious belief. The church was subjected to new state control, which involved state appointment of
higher clergy, provision of church funds, and insistence on loyalty
to the government. The government of the Restoration was more
generous in its treatment, but it did not restore the previous wealth
and position of the church. The revolution of 1830 saw renewed
attacks on the church, including a number of riots against church
buildings in Paris; for many weeks priests dared not appear on the
streets in clerical garb. Under the Second Empire state protection of
the church was renewed, but this antagonized most urban groups
all the more. The stage was set for further attack on the much-
reduced institutional power of the church.

The Spanish revolution of 1820, supported by middle-class elements, seized many church lands and established religious liberty. The power of the church was restored after the defeat of the revolution, but urban hostility to the church remained. The later spread of anarchism among the southern peasantry involved a great hatred of the church and its attachment to conservatism. The Spanish church retained many political privileges during the century and grew in wealth after losing its land in 1835; but it was under serious attack. Belgian liberals, drawn largely from the commercial middle class, cooperated with Catholics in the revolution of 1830 against Protestant Holland but were soon at odds with them in the new regime over the usual issues of the church's efforts to retain government support in education and other matters. In Germany firm state control of the major Protestant churches and efforts by Prussia to dominate Catholicism minimized popular antipathy to the church. Even so, one of the first acts of the revolution of 1848 was to declare religious freedom. In Italy, where the hand of the church lay heavy, middle-class liberals tried to curb the political powers of the Catholic Church. Risings in central Italy in 1830 and 1848 attacked the government of the papacy directly. Even in Great Britain issues concerning the established Anglican Church were numerous. Many leading industrialists were Dissenters and resented the power of the Church in matters of education and the financial aid which the state provided. The establishment of a substantial public education effort was in fact long delayed by disputes over the role of the various churches. The last political privileges of the Anglican Church were gradually removed during the century as tolerance was extended to Catholics and admission to Parliament and the universities opened to members of all religions. Nowhere by 1870 were the churches in a settled position. Most had already seen their political and economic powers curtailed and all were still under attack by elements of the urban classes.

The reaction of the churches to these various attacks on their political position and their doctrines was almost uniformly conservative. Pressed by changes such as those brought by the French revolution and by increasing intellectual criticism by scientists and other scholars, the churches tried to preserve as much as they could of their old status. Aristocratic prelates saw in organized religion an important bulwark against social unrest. They attached religion to traditional monarchical governments and used governments to ward off attacks on the churches. Leading French churchmen were long devoted to the cause of the Bourbons and resisted efforts of liberal priests to free the church from state control. They rejected liberty and liberals and largely ignored the social problems of the new cities. In Britain Anglican leaders opposed legislation extending religious liberties. German Protestantism docilely accepted control by the Prussian state and was rewarded by continued state pay and protection. There was little effort to come to grips intellectually with scientific and other attacks on aspects of religion. In general, the established churches tried to ignore new trends by clinging to tradition and political defenses. In 1864 Pope Pius IX issued a Syllabus of Errors that summed up the position of Catholicism; he condemned liberalism and the idea of freedom of worship, modern science, socialism, and nationalism. He claimed that the church should control all education and scholarship. Effectively, he declared war on some of the most dynamic principles of nineteenth-century society. Six years later he tried to strengthen the church's organization by proclaiming papal infallibility, but this separated the Church still further from the advocates of freedom of conscience and parliamentary government. The gulf between the churches and much of European society was widening.

Like the churches, the states of Europe sought refuge in conservative policies, and the aristocracy again stood behind a major institution and used it to maintain the status quo. Middle-class demands were largely ignored by the states after 1815. In Britain and France small elements of the class were represented in the government, but they had little real power. Eastern and southern European governments remained almost totally closed except for a small and conservative middle-class element in the bureaucracy. Even middle-class economic interests were partially thwarted by official protection of guild restrictions and the like. Furthermore, middle-class political agitation was directly repressed. Press censorship and limitations on the right of assembly were rigidly enforced in most countries. Governments were even more repressive of the lower classes. Prohibitions on unions and strikes were rigidly maintained, and many labor leaders were arrested. The British government moved troops against large political meetings and passed acts in 1817 and 1819 to curtail public meetings and even suspend *habeas corpus* temporarily, for the first time in English history. European governments emerged from the French revolutionary period in a mood of stern conservativism. Despite tremendous social change, they chose to repress rather than to adjust.

The result of repression was the series of revolutions of the early nineteenth century. Britain alone of the major western nations avoided revolution, but it did not escape major agitation. Before 1832 political ferment among the middle classes was intense, particularly in the disenfranchised industrial centers. Mass meetings were sponsored and sometimes led to violence. Inflammatory pamphlets and newspapers were widely circulated. The middle class did not stand alone. Elements of the working class struck occasionally, and many artisans were quite active in movements for economic and political reform. The peasantry also rioted on occasion, but never with great force or persistence; this was one feature distinguishing the British from most continental movements. Further, the middle class won its major demands without revolution, for the electoral reform of 1832 removed the major reason for protest. Some organizations continued to agitate for other gains, such as repeal of the Corn Law, and this led to ferment on occasion; but the mood of sharp grievance was gone. Artisans and some workers continued their efforts alone, in movements like Chartism, but they lacked the resources and organization to launch real revolution.

On the continent middle-class discontent was more enduring. The class faced a far more obdurate aristocracy and, in the case of France particularly, possessed a more definite revolutionary tradition. Other classes, such as artisans and peasantry, frequently offered important support and conducted their own agitation as well. Many revolutions burst forth: in 1820 in Spain and the Kingdom of Naples, in 1830 in France, Belgium, and parts of Germany and Italy, in 1848 in Switzerland, France, Germany, Denmark, Austria, and Italy, and in 1871 in Paris. A few revolutions failed completely; those of 1820 were repressed by Austria and France. Many more achieved only partial success; feudal obligations were abolished in Austria and Germany after 1848, and universal suffrage was established in France in the same year. Some, including the 1830 revolutions in France and Belgium, placed the leadership of government in new hands. None was entirely successful for all the classes involved; none could be, for the classes sought mutually contradictory goals.

Most revolutions progressed according to similar patterns. They were typically foreshadowed by a period of rising written attack on the governments, distributed particularly within the middle class. The major nineteenth-century French revolutions, for example, were prefaced by a spate of histories of the great Revolution, comparing the contemporary government unfavorably with certain key revolutionary principles. A wave of opposition newspapers helped prepare the revolution of 1830. Opposition groups, not always overtly revolutionary, were also formed in advance and often in secret. Usually they were composed of members of the middle class, particularly professional people. Some, such as the democratic clubs in France during the July Monarchy, dipped into the artisan class as well. Such groups kept alive discussion of political grievances and often guided actual revolutionary effort. Leaders of the Carbonari played a key role in the Neapolitan government of 1820, while French republican clubs helped guide the Parisian masses during 1848.

A major economic crisis preceded the most important revolutions. The years 1828–1829 and 1846–1847 brought hardship to many in the middle class and misery to large numbers of peasants and artisans. Food riots and other risings usually indicated the temper of the masses even before the revolution broke out, and the middle class became increasingly critical of the established order.

A specific issue then triggered revolution itself. In 1820 the issue in Spain was the imminent dispatch of many reluctant troops to South America. The army began the revolution, and the middle class provided most of the other support for it. The rising in the Kingdom of Naples imitated that in Spain, with the army taking a lead and providing the necessary force and the middle class supplying vital support and guidance. Elsewhere, the events triggering revolution were usually more directly political. The desire of Charles X to impose new curbs on the press and on parliament moved middle-class journalists to urge the Parisian masses to come into the streets. The government used force against the masses, largely artisans, only slowly and ineffectively, and the revolution was won. Other revolutions in 1830 were spurred by the news of the rising in Paris. The wave of protest in 1848 again began in Paris. Middle-class politicians embarked in 1847 on a campaign of political banquets, urging extension of the suffrage against the conservatism of the government of Guizot. The government's confused effort to prevent a major banquet in Paris in February, 1848, triggered the rioting that finally drove the monarchy out of France and inspired rioting in Berlin, Vienna and other cities.

Once the revolutions began, the middle class retained basic control. The class possessed the education and resources to provide leaders and had fairly definite goals. The same journalists who called the people of Paris into the streets in 1830 arranged for the new government of Louis Philippe. The Frankfurt parliament was called and staffed by members of the middle class, particularly lawyers. The Paris government of 1848 was composed of middle-class politicians. These middle-class governments, as well as the revolutionary army governments of the 1820 risings, were interested in political reform. They sought constitutional, parliamentary regimes and drew up bills of rights to establish basic liberties of religion, press, and assembly. In some cases they sought nationalist goals as well. Revolution in the Hapsburg lands in 1848 was badly split as Czechs, Germans, and Magyars sought separate nationalist goals and refused to cooperate with one another. The risings in Italian cities were overlaid by an effort on the part of the state of Piedmont to drive Austria out of Italy. The German revolutions were aimed at political reform within the various states, but also produced a national parliament committed to national unity. To the middle class the national effort was a logical complement to the political. It too involved overthrow of the existing government and freedom from unwanted control. It too would promote middle-class economic interests by providing a larger market.

Peasants were uninterested in political reform and were apathetic or even hostile to revolt when they had no grievances of their own. The Spanish peasants who tore down revolutionary posters in 1820 or the French peasants who sent conservative representatives to parliament when they voted in April, 1848, were expressing their typical dislike of urban political agitation. Urban risings did trigger rural rebellions in Germany and Austria in 1848, but the peasant revolts were against feudal restrictions alone. Never did peasant rebellions operate in real harmony with middle-class purposes; nor were there any real organizational links between the classes. There was a common enemy, the feudal aristocracy, but the grounds for enmity were vastly different, and elements of the middle class who backed revolution were often disturbed by peasant attacks on rural property.

Within the cities middle-class revolutionary effort depended on support from the artisans. The middle class rarely took part in street fighting; the artisans manned the barricades. Their purposes differed from those of the middle class. They were impelled by recent, severe hardship and wanted government help. They hoped for some new economic system, either a revitalized guild system or some form of cooperative structure that would replace middle-class capitalism. The goals of the middle class were meaningless to many artisans and insufficient for all of them. To keep firm control of a revolution middle-class leaders tried to persuade the artisans of the importance of limited political reforms, as they did successfully in Paris in 1830. But where the risings were of greater substance, this sort of control could not be maintained. Parisian artisans forced notable concessions in 1848, particularly the establishment of national workshops, by their massed presence in the streets. German artisans attempted independent action also. Typically, middle class leaders faced steady pressure to move the revolution to the left.

The last act of most revolutions, then, was the effort of middle-class leaders, sometimes backed by peasants, to return to order and to quell the artisan threat. In Paris this was done gradually after 1830 by growing governmental repression of artisan groups and agitation. In 1848 it was done suddenly by the use of troops against the barricades in June. Leaders of the Frankfurt assembly called on Prussian troops to end the artisan rising of 1849. The revolutions in Germany, Austria, and Italy ended with middle-class acceptance, however grudging, of a return of the old regimes, backed by military force. The revolutionaries had not succeeded, nor even particularly attempted, to establish their own force or to destroy the existing ruling class. They had simply ruled briefly on sufferance, unwilling to make a fully revolutionary effort, except in the case of some Italian cities. The middle classes in Germany and Austria were politically timid anyway, and the fear of lower-class agitation added to this timidity.

In a formal sense, then, the revolutionary period might seem a study in failure. This was not the case. Two classes made major gains in most areas. The peasants won emancipation, as they had earlier in France and adjacent areas. Within two decades, new parliaments were established in Germany, Austria, Italy, and in them the upper middle class had substantial representation. National goals were also largely fulfilled in Germany and Italy. Civil and economic liberties were increasingly provided. The middle class still had less political power than in Britain and France, but it had made major gains. For two major classes, then, the need for massive protest had been removed in western Europe by 1870. A substantial segment of the peasantry had property and wished to defend it against social chaos. The middle class had not only property but also growing political and social power. It had no desire to see a renewal of the revolutionary threats by the urban lower classes.

Even the artisan class in western and central Europe remained largely quiescent for several decades after 1848. In Germany it was attracted back to the guilds; in Britain it developed calm methods of action. Everywhere, two decades of considerable prosperity helped ease discontent, and the postrevolutionary arrests of many agitators helped inhibit it. Discontent and agitation were to return to western Europe after 1870 and were to gain the fringes of eastern and southern Europe. Except on the fringes the renewed agitation would take a new form and involve different classes.

The period 1850–1870 represented something of a transition in western Europe. The first wave of changes had been met, and the most obvious ferment had ended. The population boom was slowing down, industrialization was established, and governments had partially, often reluctantly, responded to the need for change. At the same time new developments in the economy, particularly the rise of heavy industry, prepared further developments in society. By 1870 the basic class structure of industrial Europe was established, and each class had made some adjustments to industrial society. But the implications of a mature industrial economy were only beginning to emerge.

4

THE RISE
OF THE MASSES

By about 1870 the character of industrial society began to change in western and central Europe. Industrial organization was altered significantly, political systems changed, and states assumed important new economic functions. Wealth rose for most groups. New cultural institutions were developed through universal education and the mass press.

These developments touched all groups in society. The political changes weakened the aristocracy and certainly required new political behavior. Changes in the structure of industry created new opportunities for the middle class. But, more than before, important segments of the class were disturbed by industrial trends, and diversity of behavior increased within the class.

Most important, economic and political changes gave new opportunities to the various lower classes, the members of which became increasingly self-conscious and assertive. The role of the masses as consumers, voters, soldiers, and even as students and readers grew. The masses were not a unified social element, for major class distinctions continued to exist among the lower classes and were even increased by the formation of a new clerical lower middle class. From patterns of consumption to political behavior, the various lower classes differed greatly. The concept of "the masses" is realistic only as a collection of quite diverse groups that had great numbers and relatively low incomes and status in common. The concept is useful for two reasons. First, the various lower classes were subjected to some common experiences and opportunities, although they used them differently. Second, the middle class and aristocracy became increasingly aware of the rise of the lower classes, and the growing importance of these classes posed new problems for all established groups and institutions in industrial Europe.

In eastern and southern Europe the end of the century brought the first stages of industrialization and attendant changes in agriculture. These were the decades of massive peasant unrest in southern Italy and Spain, in the Balkans, and in Russia. These were also the decades of the formation of an industrial working class and of a business element. In many ways developments in this period resembled those of the earlier nineteenth century in the west.

At the same time, there were points of contact between mature and newly industrial regions. Rural societies differed enormously, although there was an agricultural crisis common to the whole of Europe. In the cities, however, there were some significant parallels. Governments copied some of the economic and welfare measures of the west, such as the extension of public education. Business structures were created on western models. Russian manufacturing was organized in large corporate units with substantial clerical personnel, although there was far less industry than in the west. The small working class in Russia, Sicily, and the Balkans produced waves of strikes similar to those elsewhere. This was partly because most workers everywhere did work in large units and partly because labor movements that developed in the west, such as socialism, could provide leadership and doctrines to workers elsewhere. Rates of unionization and agitation generally remained lower than those in the west; but there was far more activity than there had been in France or Germany during the first generation of industrialization.

For most groups, however, differences outweighed similarities. Eastern workers lacked the education and resources of their western counterpart, and the business middle class remained rudimentary. Agitation among professional elements can be noted in both east and west, but it had different bases. Again, in some ways similarities with the early nineteenth century were clearer; the activities of Russian professionals in the revolution of 1905 bore definite resemblance to earlier western patterns. Certainly, it is impossible to discuss eastern Europe in this period in terms of industrial maturation.

ECONOMIC STRUCTURE

In western and central Europe major changes in the economy altered the balance of social classes and changed the character of every class. Except in England it was only after 1870 that industry superseded agriculture as Europe's economic base and that the full impact of industrialization was felt.

More important, in England as well as on the continent the character of industry itself was changing, a process often described as a second industrial revolution or the attainment of industrial maturity. Neither of these descriptions is altogether apt for in many ways industrial changes were simply extensions of trends apparent earlier. And if industry matured in some senses, it created new problems that foreshadowed further change. However, with all the qualifications, a new stage of industrial development had been reached, with far-reaching social implications.

Machine technology now spread to virtually every branch of production. Between 1870 and 1890 the application of inventions such as sewing machines transformed many craft industries. After 1890 utilization of electric and gasoline motors made it possible for virtually every form of production to utilize mechanical means. And during the whole period agricultural producers increasingly applied mechanical equipment to their work.

In the major branches of industry new methods of capital information allowed the development of units of unprecedented size. The initial stages of industrialization had seen only halting innovation in the structure of enterprise; now innovation became massive. Relatedly, the old emphasis on the industrial pioneer was replaced by the development of organized bureaucracy.

Finally, changes in technique and business organization greatly increased agricultural and industrial production. Wealth grew rapidly. New marketing structures were developed to handle the new levels of production and consumption.

Yet here lay a major difficulty; the power of consumption, despite its great expansion, did not keep pace with the power to produce. The spread of machines and the new techniques of management were not matched by sufficient changes in the distribution of goods. The result was a serious economic crisis in each decade after 1870 and, after 1900, some reduction of the over-all pace of industrial growth.

Each aspect of the new stage of industrialization touched several social classes. The spread of machines vitally affected artisans and small businessmen, and the rise of big business had obvious impact on the middle class and factory labor. The increase in total wealth and recurrent economic crisis reached every segment of society.

The Spread of Machines: Light Industry

By 1900 almost all forms of production were mechanized to some degree. Most clothing and shoes were now made in factories. In the food processing industries machines prepared, processed, and canned many products. Even the baking of bread was partially mechanized, although factory production was not installed. Printing developed automatic compositor machines. Cranes and electric saws were introduced in construction work.

The spread of machines affected new regions as well as new industries. The new motors made mechanization possible in regions distant from a coal supply, although the heaviest concentrations of industry were still attached to mining centers. Areas with potential for hydroelectric power, such as the Alpine regions, experienced a real burst of industrial development after 1890. But all areas were touched. Ribbon makers around Saint-Étienne, in France, saw their industry transformed by the introduction of electric motors. Construction work everywhere was aided by new methods.

Finally, technical change also affected textile production, the one light industry in which mechanization was already substantial. New mechanical looms, for example, increased productivity per worker by as much as four times. Yet the market for new textile goods was distinctly limited, for earlier industrialization had already exploited many sales possibilities. Hence, although production as well as productivity increased, the relative position of textiles inevitably declined. Fewer workers and fewer firms could survive in the industry.

The changes in the various light industries had various social effects. Increased production of shoes and clothing reduced prices. Machine methods standardized products, but for the poorer classes at least they improved average quality.

Some categories of workers were definitely displaced by technical advances. The decline of employment in textiles was obvious. The industry still used many workers, but it was no longer the major employer of factory labor. As a result, conditions in the industry no longer dominated the labor force. As before, textile wages were below those of heavy industry, although they improved somewhat. As before, the industry employed many women and youths. But the bulk of the labor force was now engaged in other types of industry.

The mechanization of many crafts, notably shoemaking and tailoring, displaced artisans, and after 1870 the total size of the artisan class began to decline in both Germany and France. Shoe factories needed some skilled labor, but not the skills of artisans, and the factories themselves were usually located far from customary artisan centers. They created a new labor force for the most part, including many women and children.

Other artisan trades maintained or even improved their position. Bakers and construction workers were not put into factories. Even there, however, there was some fear of displacement by machines; and certainly new methods of work had to be learned. On the other hand, many artisans survived only because they could use motors appropriate for small shop production. Finally, some new industries were developed on an artisan basis. Automobile production before 1914, for example, took place mainly in small shops and used thousands of former coachmakers and blacksmiths.

In sum, displacement of some workers in light industry was partially compensated for by new opportunities in other branches and even artisan forms survived. However, total employment in light industry declined. Purely traditional skills were at least modified by new techniques. And there was justifiable fear of further displacement in the future.

These same trends obviously affected the middle class. The relative decline of textiles was clearly important, for the industry had offered a haven for family firms. A family structure remained in textiles; firms grew, but did not alter their basic organization. But a number of individual firms failed, and even those that survived were eclipsed by the growth of other industries.

Outside of textiles, the new developments in light industry offered many opportunities for small firms. The mechanization of crafts might displace artisans, but by the same token it allowed entrepreneurs with a little capital to set up a shoe factory or a shop producing automobile parts. Many new entrepreneurs entered the middle class by taking advantage of these possibilities. The number of shops employing one to five people increased 24 per cent between 1882 and 1895 in Germany, while companies with six to ten workers increased 66.6 per cent. The relative importance of small business was declining, but the number of firms engaged in small business clearly expanded. Small businessmen remained an important part of the middle class, and new opportunities provided significant mobility at the lower levels of the class.

Big Business

The average size of industrial and commercial firms had grown steadily since the beginning of industrialization. After about 1870 the rate of growth soared, and the ownership and management of large firms changed in character. Big business was born and quickly dominated major segments of industry.

There were several leading causes of the development of really new business forms. Most obvious was the rapid development of heavy industry after 1850; vast quantities of coal, iron, and steel were needed for the expansion of railroad systems, metal ships, heavy industrial machinery, and more massive weaponry. These needs catapulted heavy industry into a leading position in terms of the value of its product and the number of its workers. But heavy industry had, even before, been characterized by relatively elaborate business organization. As heavy industry rose, it would obviously impel changes in the general structure of enterprise.

Furthermore, after 1850 new technical developments altered heavy industry. Inventions such as the Bessemer process expanded the possible size of blast furnaces and allowed the reintroduction of carbon to make steel. The Gilchrist-Thomas process, developed in the 1870s, allowed the utilization for the first time of iron ore rich in phosphorous; this opened the iron ores of Lorraine to industrial exploitation and impelled the metallurgical industries of Germany and France to unprecedented heights. Such technical developments vastly increased the potential output of metallurgy and at the same time raised the capital needed by any metallurgical firm; the new devices were extremely costly. Here, clearly, was a direct impulse to changes in business structure.

During this period, however, firms grew well beyond the levels required by new technology. The chemical industry, for example, developed gigantic firms at least a decade before extremely expensive equipment was introduced. There was a new spirit in many branches of industry, a spirit that tried to use size to modify competitive pressure and even to reduce risks of failure during business crises.

A big firm with extensive capital at its disposal, could afford a research staff; technical improvements could be produced more regularly, and the dependence on competition for occasional inventions could be reduced. A large professional sales force decreased the hazards of the market. Greater size allowed the integration of more operations to assure supplies and to eliminate dependence on any single product for profits. Finally, a firm sufficiently large could have direct control of much of its market. It could partially dictate terms to its buyers rather than rely on the forces of supply and demand, which were so difficult to predict and control.

By the 1890s well over half the labor force in Germany, Britain, and Belgium was employed in firms with more than twenty workers. By 1910, 88 per cent of Russian manufacturing labor worked in firms with more than fifty employes. Everywhere the number of large companies increased at a far faster rate than did the number of small enterprises. The trend of expansion touched virtually every industry, but the most significant development was the giant firm. In an extreme example of size, the German electrical industry was dominated by just two firms, the Allgemeine Elektrizitäts Gesellschaft and the Siemens concern, which controlled over 90 per cent of German production, and had important international links as well. Each firm could set the terms for many leading buyers on the strength of its great size; beyond this, the firms made agreements with each other on market allocation, which made price-fixing even simpler. In the German chemical industry the I. G. Farben company possessed a tremendous influence over its own sales due to its size alone. Few firms approached outright monopoly, even in Germany; and the concentration of German industry was greater than that of Britain or France. Nevertheless, the trend was general. The steady growth of firm size allowed the utilization of more massive and efficient equipment. It also allowed a greater possibility for profits, even aside from efficiency, by permitting greater control of research, supplies, sales, and position in the market.

The development of huge firms was significant in itself. The position of labor in such firms inevitably differed from the situation in small factories. New techniques of management had to be devised to administer the giants. Equally important, the large firm required new methods of finance. These methods altered the nature of industrial ownership and increasingly encouraged the formation of still larger economic units.

A few firms grew large and wealthy by judiciously plowing profits back into the business. Old metallurgical companies such as Le Creusot in France expanded and developed a variety of new operations without changing their fundamental structure of family ownership. Even there dependence on bank loans increased, and the prodigious expansion of industrial banking aided capital formation of all sorts. With the rise of railroads and heavy industry, the association of the financial power of banks with industry became absolutely essential. During the 1850s Napoleon III encouraged the *Crédit mobilier* as an investment bank to support the development of ports, railroads, and urban clearance. The bank ultimately failed, but in the next decade similar banking enterprises, such as the *Crédit lyonnais*, were formed to channel funds into industry. In the German areas the association of banks and industry was even closer. The Vienna *Kredit Anstalt* was formed in 1856 specifically to lend to industry. The German Darmstädter Bank and *Diskontgesellschaft* arose in the same decade, along with a number of less solid banks that collapsed after contributing to a speculative mania. Other investment banks, such as the Deutsche and the Dresdener, arose in the prosperous period of the early 1870s, when the French war indemnity was filling German coffers. The Dresdener Bank developed close ties with the Krupp industrial complex and served as a major source of Krupp's funds. In Germany particularly, but to some extent everywhere, industrial investment banks greatly increased the amount of capital available and thereby promoted the development of larger firms.

The most important source of funds for large enterprises came, however, from the growing use of the corporate form. Banks might contribute to stock purchases, but funds could be drawn from an even broader base, from hundreds and sometimes thousands of investors, large and small. Corporations spread rapidly in every area toward the end of the century, and the rate of corporate formation increased as well. In France corporations required special authorization from the government until 1867, when a change in law encouraged a first burst of corporate growth; but the slow pace of French industrial advances restricted the number of corporations until the 1890s. By then the expansion of French heavy industry required massive financial support and so required extensive use of the corporate form. During the 1890s up to a thousand corporations were formed every year in France. Rates of corporate formation in Germany and elsewhere were rising in the same period, although Great Britain maintained a lead in the sheer number of corporations.

The use of corporate forms greatly increased the size possible for an individual enterprise, either new or old, by extending the amount of capital available. It also changed the nature of ownership, reducing personal control over a firm and substituting divided and substantially anonymous ownership and responsibility. Along with investment banking, the growth of corporate organization tied industry to essentially novel financial forms. This development was almost as important as the growth of the sheer size of firms.

Capping the growth of big business was a search for organizational forms that could bridge the gap even among giant firms. Lobbying associations were formed, such as the *Comité des forges* in France, to coordinate the relations between a major industry and the government. More important, cartels were developed to restrict or eliminate competition within an industry. The *Stahlwerkverband* in Germany, created in the 1890s as a successor to several smaller steel cartels, allocated set market quotes in some goods for each member of the association and fixed limits on all other types of production. In the 1890s a cartel was established among coal producers in the Rhineland-Westphalia region. Each company had votes in the cartel proportionate to its output, and a central commission was established to set production quotas and to determine prices. By 1900 there were three hundred cartels in Germany, and many more were created before World War I. A similar, if less intense, movement developed in Britain, Russia, and elsewhere.

Many governments favored cartels as a means of providing more rational direction to industry. Big investment banks encouraged them; many cartels and even trusts were formed by banks that owned shares in several concerns in an industry. Most important, however, the cartels were formed because manufacturers increasingly realized that they could control market conditions through association as they never could in isolation. The movement began in Germany as a result of the crisis of the 1870s, which provided a clear motive to seek more rational organization in industry. The movement was taken up almost exclusively in industries dominated by large firms, hence cartels were common in coal, steel, and chemicals but literally unknown in textiles. Large firms could make contacts easily because of the small number of units in the industry. Their owners recognized the value of size and coordination and were not committed to a system of family control and mutual rivalry. Increasingly, the principal branches of factory industry were dominated by a small number of giant firms with various mutual links. Coordination and control rather than competition provided the motive force for much of the economic activity within most industrial countries.

Big Business: Some General Social Effects

The rise of big business was obviously important for the working class. Growing firms needed new workers, often in tasks requiring considerable strength and skill. Reduction of competitive pressure gave many large firms greater margin for increasing wages and other benefits to their workers. With the great growth of heavy industry up to 1900, those same firms had to offer better conditions to attract the quality of labor they required.

The attraction of new workers into industry produced some of the same symptoms of disorientation that had developed during the initial stages of industrialization. Italian miners in Lorraine, who had the added burden of living in a foreign country, had particular difficulty in putting down roots. Their rates of crime and drinking were high. Many were simply transient, and family life was rare. The creation of new, sometimes confused, factory labor was a leading result of the dynamism of big business in the period.

More generally, the development of large units of employment removed any opportunity for personal contact between workers and owners. It was easier for workers to see the owners as enemies than it had been in the days when the character and even the hard work of owners had been personally known. The benefits of industry, the rising wages and growing welfare programs of large firms, no longer elicited loyalty and gratitude from workers, for they were given impersonally. The huge profits of big corporations invited attack in the hope of obtaining a larger share for labor. At the same time, workers became increasingly accustomed to large organization. They learned to abide by certain rules; they learned to operate as part of a mass of fellow workers. Many of the causes of new unions and other groups among factory labor can be directly attributed to experiences in huge enterprises which encouraged both the ability and the motivation of workers to take action to improve their lot. But the power of the giant firms was such that successful action would be difficult if the firms chose to resist. The resultant conflict contributed to the rising tide of social tension before World War I.

Big business created new groups of employes during this period. Huge firms, directed by professional managers, required large bureaucracies and growing numbers of clerks. In commerce, large enterprises required clerks and salespeople. A new lower middle class was being formed that neither owned property nor worked as manual labor and whose members were salaried, but did not work with their hands. This new class was one of the most important social results of the development of large economic units dependent on masses of paperwork for their successful administration.

For the middle class, particularly the industrialists, the most obvious result of the new business structure was a great increase in profits. Larger enterprises and larger investments permitted an unprecedented concentration of profits. With the reduction of competitive pressure, the bulk of the vast new wealth industry was creating went to the owners of big business. Wages rose, to be sure, but not nearly so rapidly as production increased. During the period 1870–

1900 the workers' share in the gross national product declined by 26 per cent in Britain and by 55 per cent in Germany. But the owners of industry had larger incomes than ever before. Their investments rose; giant firms became even more gigantic. And their standard of living became more luxurious. The middle class attained the highest level of material prosperity it had ever known.

Many members of the middle class welcomed and profited from the new system of industrial control. There were others, however, who were disturbed by the trends toward concentration and impersonal ownership. They harked back to the pioneering days of industry, when a man could be personally associated with every phase of his enterprise, when his economic effort had a direct relation to his family and the other purposes of middle class life. For the trends of modern industry left some members of the middle class by the wayside. Certain industries, such as textiles, preserved the older forms of organization, but instead of being industrial leaders, the owners of textile firms were now insignificant and unnoticed beside the new economic giants. The power of big business forced many manufacturers to abandon their individual efforts, under pain of ruin. Some might be driven out of business altogether. Others would be given an opportunity to merge with a larger enterprise and might profit financially from such a deal; but their personal economic life would be disrupted.

The trends of industrial organization enriched the middle class as a whole. They created a new group of industrial managers who thought in terms of coordination rather than competition and who looked to the organization of masses of workers and of products. These same trends, however, worried and even harmed certain more traditional elements of the middle class.

New Goods and Markets

The technical changes in both light and heavy industry, in firms both small and large, obviously quickened the pace of industrial production. Older products, such as textiles, continued to increase; Great Britain, for example, expanded her equipment for the production of cotton goods by a third during the last three decades of the century. Heavy industry grew far more rapidly. World pig-iron production tripled between 1870 and 1900. French production of iron and steel expanded four and a half times between 1890 and

1913. Coal output soared; Britain doubled her already massive production, France tripled hers, and Germany raised hers fifteen times in the last three decades of the century. New products were added to the industrial list. Electrical equipment and chemical goods became major industries for the first time. New needs for acids, dyes, fertilizers, explosives, and even synthetic cloth caused a rapid boom in chemical production. Germany's output of sulphuric acid increased three hundred times by the end of the century. Expansion of older areas of production and the addition of new branches created an unprecedented, though not uninterrupted, industrial boom during the latter part of the nineteenth century.

Many new products were designed for individual consumers. The chemical industry began to discover new kinds of cloth. Novel products such as bicycles, telephones, and automobiles began to flood the market. That was an extremely significant development; the early industrial revolution had concentrated primarily on goods already in use. The nature and amount of these goods had changed with their mechanical production, as in the growing use of cotton cloth. The growth of general wealth and of technical knowledge now allowed the development of totally new consumer items. Some, such as automobiles, were reserved for the wealthier classes. Others, such as telephones and electrical lighting, were seldom purchased by the lower classes but affected their way of life as public telephones and lighting systems developed. Finally, some items, such as bicycles, were purchased by many members of the lower classes.

The expansion of industrial and also agricultural production spurred new developments in marketing and transportation. In these areas the industrial trends of spreading mechanization and creation of more complex forms of business organization were also apparent.

Railroads were extended. Western and central Europe, having completed the development of trunk lines, began to concentrate on local lines. The speed and capacity of railroad transport were brought to increasing numbers of small towns and even villages, expanding both market opportunities and social contacts for rural residents. In eastern and southern Europe trunk lines were now built; the completion of the trans-Siberian railroad in the 1890s was the most notable example of the spread of railroad transport to the European hinterland and beyond.

Oceanic shipping expanded greatly in the same period. Metal

steam-driven ships dominated ocean transportation for the first time, raising the capacity and speed of shipping. The development of refrigeration allowed perishable items to be sent long distances. Oceanic cables and, late in the century, the radio combined with new shipping to allow increasing international trade. Exports and imports rose massively. European business sought, and often found, new markets in all parts of the world.

Even within cities, transportation facilities increased greatly. Electric subways and trams speeded the movement of people. New techniques for hauling goods depended on the full development of gasoline engines. But larger trucking companies were developed for horse-drawn transport, and employment in urban hauling expanded and became more regular.

New marketing methods followed naturally from the increase of production and the expansion of transportation and communication facilities. Large wholesaling firms arose to supply major cities with consumer products, including foodstuffs. Department stores and even chain stores played a growing role in retailing. Expansion of business structure was a vital part of commerce as well as of industry. Advertising increased, particularly in the mass press, as a means of speeding the circulation of goods. Newspapers and other publications were filled with large, presumably eye-catching notices.

In a variety of ways, then, more care was being given to the distribution of goods. A growth of transportation facilities and sales outlets was a vital concomitant of the new levels of production. A change in the habits of buying was the inevitable result of new sales techniques. Industry increasingly looked to a mass market for its sales and even tried to influence taste through advertising.

New Wealth

The expansion of production and of trade had an obvious and beneficent impact on the wealth of Europe. Both profits and wages rose significantly during the latter part of the nineteenth century. At first this rise was spurred by an increase in the supply of precious metals. By the 1880s, however, money supply was again beginning to lag behind economic activity, but profits and wages continued to increase on the basis of expanding production. During much of the period those increases were accompanied by a fall in prices. Between 1870 and 1884, for example, the wages in French industry rose 14 per cent while prices dropped by the same amount; the result was a major expansion of purchasing power. The cost of housing continued to mount because cities remained crowded, but the declining prices of food and clothing more than compensated for this change.

In Britain real wages rose by a third between 1850 and 1875; between 1870 and 1900 they rose 45 per cent. German real wages increased 30 per cent in the last three decades of the century; French wages rose 33 per cent, and Swedish workers benefited by a 75 per cent gain. The expansion of purchasing power for workers was a general phenomenon even in Russia, where industrialization was just beginning; major differences in standards of living remained, of course, and the older industrial countries offered far higher standards than did newer arrivals, such as Germany.

For the first time in human history real poverty, life on the margins of subsistence, was a minority phenomenon in the industrial regions. In Britain only a third or less of the population lived really near subsistence by 1900; a century before two thirds had done so. This decisive change developed particularly in the latter part of the century. Wealth remained unevenly distributed; in fact, disparities between the middle and lower classes increased as the profits of industry soared. Nevertheless, the masses had gained.

The rise in real wages was translated into a number of improvements in living standards for the lower classes in the countryside and particularly in the cities. Diets became more varied. Consumption of starches tended to stabilize, and the quality of starch improved, especially through the growing use of wheat for bread. Milk and milk products came into greater use. In France the consumption of butter rose 50 per cent between 1870 and 1884. Meat consumption increased notably. In Britain meat consumption per person rose 20 per cent between 1880 and 1900, while the rate of bread consumption remained unchanged. Germans bought an average of 59 pounds of meat per person in 1873; by 1912 they were buying 105 pounds per person per year. The consumption of tobacco, tea, coffee, and sugar increased. British consumption of sugar rose 33 per cent between 1880 and 1900, while Germans tripled their average annual consumption (from 12 pounds to 34 pounds per person) between 1870 and 1907. The use of drinks such as beer increased; German consumption of beer rose from 78 liters per person per year in 1872 to 123 liters in 1900. There were still cases of grossly inadequate nutrition, particularly among some agricultural workers and the large group of irregularly employed in the major cities. For the majority of the lower classes, however, diets were well above the levels of mere subsistence. This was an important precondition for the new vigor that elements of the lower classes showed in many aspects of behavior.

With rising wages and declining food prices, the masses could devote less of their budget to food and still purchase more and better food than ever before. By the 1890s in France only about 60 per cent of the average budget was used for food instead of the previous 75 per cent. The amount and stylishness of clothing reflected the greater resources that the masses could devote to their attire. Furthermore, prices of shoes and clothing fell rapidly. Cotton goods in France cost 50 per cent less in 1896 than they had in 1873. By the late nineteenth century it was virtually impossible to determine a man's exact station by his clothing. The steady democratization of costume, though by no means complete, was an obvious symptom of the rising purchasing power of the masses— and of the growing willingness of the upper classes to relax their peculiarities of dress.

Housing for the masses was still cramped and expensive, after 1870, especially in the larger cities. An increasing portion of the budget had to be devoted to rents, but the teeming tenements of the early industrial period were gone from the more advanced industrial nations. In Prussia over 6 per cent of the families had only one room, but only 1.6 per cent of British families lived in one room, and only 4.42 per cent had two rooms. Clearly, housing construction had begun to catch up with the worst needs of the new cities even though rents rose.

Even with all the significant gains in food, clothing, and shelter the masses increasingly had money left over for other expenses. Purchases of newspapers and inexpensive novels became common among the masses. Many workers could now pay union dues and contribute a portion of their wage to insurance programs. Popular theaters and music halls arose in the cities to attract the masses; after 1900 moving pictures provided entertainment as well. Sports events, such as soccer football, became commercialized in this period because the urban masses could afford tickets. Railroads offered

Sunday excursions for a clientele drawn from the lower classes, and hundreds of thousands of workers and clerks in western Europe bought bicycles, the most expensive consumer good not related to basic needs that had ever been available to the masses. At the same time small savings accounts increased rapidly, and new facilities such as postal savings systems were established to handle them.

The rising average wealth of the masses undoubtedly brightened the lives of most people. The increasing opportunities for diversion were a major new element for the masses in the cities. With more wealth, there was less chance of absolute economic disaster, even during a depression. Savings accounts and sometimes insurance programs provided some protection against illness and old age. There was still great economic insecurity but no longer so many risks of absolute destitution. Better housing and food promoted noticeable improvements in health. This was the period, after all, in which declining mortality rates provided the bulk of the continued expansion of population in western Europe.

Finally, the fairly steady increase in well-being developed a new interest in material enjoyments among the European masses. The masses, particularly in the cities, began to expect further improvements in the standard of living. They developed a concern for new technical devices that would make their lives more pleasant. They were gradually affected by the same attachment to material and technical progress that the middle class had developed earlier. The popular press, even the union movement, both encouraged and reflected this attachment. On the other hand, the rising standard of living, significant though it was, did not take the European masses into an era of abundance. A substantial minority remained desperately poor. Many others had only a small part of their budget free for expenditures beyond the necessities. The conflict between rising expectations and continued limitations on means was to affect both social and economic developments for many decades.

Weaknesses in the Economic Structure

To many observers, particularly in the middle classes, the economy seemed stronger about 1900 than it ever had been before. However, the new economic trends brought with them certain major difficulties. The fundamental problem was that the opportunities for production were not matched by consistent and comparable oppor-

tunities for sale. Production was expanding mightily as new countries joined old in industry, and everywhere improved equipment
steadily increased possible output. In a real sense the industrial
revolution had removed, for the time being at least, any major problem in the production of goods. What remained difficult was the sale
of goods produced in growing profusion. Improvements in sales
outlets and in transportation were a great help, and trade increased
steadily. Nevertheless, there were real weaknesses in the available
markets that affected economic conditions and attitudes.

In the first place, this period of massive economic growth was
also the period when the rate of population expansion slowed in the
industrial nations. Population growth continued, but no longer
provided the tremendous and almost automatic extension of the
internal market that had existed during the earlier period of the
industrial revolution.

Furthermore, important elements of the existing population were
severely limited in their ability to buy. Despite rising wages workers
could not increase their purchases so rapidly as production itself
was rising. At the same time, the income of agricultural producers
was relatively stagnant. Agricultural prices were falling as competition from fertile new regions increasingly pressed farmers. The
price drop was partially compensated by major improvements in
agricultural equipment and methods during the period, but the incomes of peasants and other landowners did not rise significantly.
It was difficult, then, to extend the sales of industrial products
among this group. Some new tools and machines were sold because
farmers often went into debt to try to improve their production. But
again, there was no increase in buying power comparable to the rise
in industrial output.

In fact, the only major social class whose income was growing
at a huge rate was the middle class itself. This class increased both
its consumer and investor purchases during the period. However,
the middle class did not spend its money so rapidly as production
rose, for it was not pressed by primary needs and was therefore inclined to hold much of its income for a time before deciding to
spend. The wealth of Europe as a whole was rising rapidly, but its
distribution was such that the principal gains in purchasing power
fell to groups that spent rather slowly. Europe had developed the

capacity for massive production but had not yet made the change to a mass-consumption economy.

The disparity between production and market was by no means constant. Utilization of new export opportunities, the high rate of investment in new productive facilities, and the expansion of population and purchasing power allowed a rapid increase in sales. However, there were periods of slump even before 1900. Each of the last three decades in the century saw several years of depression in most areas. The crisis of the 1870s was particularly severe because it came after a period of great confidence induced by the building of basic railroad lines and other outlets for heavy industry.

The slumps of this period were new in some respects, reflecting the novelty of industrial development. They were triggered not by agricultural failures, but by financial crises. The increasing investment of banks and private individuals in stocks could create an artificial speculative mood. The values of stocks would soar not because of any corresponding increase in the possibilities of production and sales but because of the rising demand for the stocks themselves. Eventually the speculative bubble would be burst, sometimes by a failure of a major firm or even of a bank. Investors would become more cautious and funds for further investment harder to obtain. Firms producing capital goods, which depended on investment for their sales, would be forced to reduce their production and employment. This would affect other industries in turn, as the purchasing power of workers and others declined, and the spiral of depression would take its course.

Although levels of unemployment rose during every crisis, suffering among workers was not as intense as it was in earlier depressions. More workers had some savings, and they were not plagued by a concomitant rise in agricultural prices. The inevitable fall in industrial prices made life easier as well. Nevertheless, living standards did decline during the major slumps. And many depressions, such as that of the 1870s, lasted for several years. If crises were not so intense as they had been before, they were more prolonged. Only gradually would the level of investment be built up again as capitalists tried to dispose of their funds; only gradually would sales recover, spurred by lower industrial prices.

The frequency and duration of economic crises was an important symptom of the weakness of the industrial market. It was far easier to invest in industry and produce industrial goods than it was to find corresponding sales opportunities. The growth both of investment and of production continued at a high rate during the period as a whole. Tremendous boom periods, such as much of the 1890s, compensated for periods of difficulty. Nevertheless, a certain structural imbalance in the economy was not removed.

After 1900, in fact, even industrial production faltered in some areas. Growth by no means ceased, but it did proceed more slowly. Coal production in Britain and France rose as much between 1895 and 1900 as it did during the next ten years; Belgian coal production remained stable during the first decade of the twentieth century. Metallurgical production also slowed, although France was engaged in a major boom as she began to utilize her vast ore resources for the first time. Labor suffered from the decline in economic vitality. British workers were hardest hit because Britain failed to keep full pace with the newest technical developments. There was a high level of unemployment in Britain after 1900, often reaching 9 per cent of the labor force. And real wages fell by about 4 per cent even for the workers who were employed. Money wages rose, but prices increased more rapidly. In France real wages lagged also, although there was little unemployment. Germany and other regions also experienced growing stagnation of wages. Profits did not suffer so greatly. Before 1900 profits had held up better than wages even in actual economic crises, although they declined too. After 1900 profits actually rose significantly, because there were few years of actual depression. The greater size and strength of economic units allowed sufficient control over prices and wages that growing profits could be found even though the opportunities for increasing production were somewhat limited. Hence the gap between the incomes of labor and the middle class widened, and workers assumed most of the burden of the new economic difficulties.

However, even the industrialists showed some concern about the tightness of the market for industrial products. Well before 1900 it was clear that many felt that international competition was increasing and that economic activity was becoming more difficult. The feeling of growing pressure was deliberately exaggerated to obtain public support for the demands of the industrialists, but there was real and growing worry. Industrialists and their lobbying associations began to demand new political measures to protect existing markets and promote other sales. They sought tariff protection with greater insistence than ever before. In Germany groups such as the German Industrialists' Union joined hands with protectionist Junkers to press for tariffs on both agricultural and heavy industrial goods. Their greatest success came with the Bülow tariff of 1902, which put a 25 per cent duty on many foods and metal products. France passed a high tariff in the 1890s, and Russia, Italy, and most other countries increased or established high levels of protection. Only Great Britain resisted the new wave of economic protectionism, despite the growing demands of British industrialists for high tariffs. There was a general desire to mark off national economies and protect the internal market, but in practice tariffs often worsened the situation by making exports more difficult. The pressure for tariffs, however irrational, was symptomatic of the growing anxieties for the future that prevailed among the captains of industry.

The owners of industry urged other panaceas for their marketing problems. Industrialist groups were among the principal promoters of imperial expansion. They argued that colonies would provide both protected sources of raw materials and great markets for finished goods. These arguments were also largely incorrect. Some raw materials were drawn from the new colonies, and certain firms profited hugely from empire. Most of the colonies cost more than they earned, however, and almost none provided useful markets. Trade continued to be most active among industrial countries rather than between an industrial nation and a poor, semipastoral colony. Nevertheless, the intensity of the desire to find secure supplies and markets was another indication of the changing attitudes of industrialists.

Certain industrial groups were also active in promoting increased military expenditures by their governments. This was another, and very realistic, effort to obtain new markets for goods, particularly the products of heavy industry. In Germany owners of metallurgical firms joined with military leaders in the Navy League in a successful effort to stir up public support for the creation of a large navy that would both reflect Germany's national greatness and use an encouraging amount of iron and steel.

Finally, even the investment policies of the middle class showed a clear realization that economic opportunities at home were less enticing than those elsewhere. More and more, investors poured their funds into foreign enterprises, where interest rates were higher and the chances of major economic advance more abundant. The end of the century saw a significant movement of capital abroad, especially from Britain and France. The movement was not entirely new, but the pace increased notably. By 1900 over a quarter of British assets were invested abroad. Fifteen per cent of the total French capital and 7 per cent of the German were invested in foreign countries or in the empires. Many of these investments brought handsome returns, helping the middle class to maintain and even improve its economic position during the period. There remained, nevertheless, a certain loss of confidence in the internal economy.

Markets were found for both goods and funds as the industrial nations spread their operations ever wider in the world and sought a variety of political measures to bolster their economic efforts. The middle class largely evaded the consequences of economic difficulties during the period. It did not solve the difficulties, and in some cases it increased them by artificial political measures and by withdrawing capital from the domestic economy. Furthermore, the class itself did not escape a sense of pressure as economic activity became more complex and more difficult.

Conclusion

The economic trends from 1870 to 1914 had a variety of social effects. They strengthened the wealth and position of the middle class, but changed the nature and values of the class to some extent as managerial skills replaced the individualist spirit of the pioneer industrialists. The size of the urban lower classes was greatly increased. New workers were demanded as industry expanded, particularly before 1900, and the numbers of clerks and sales people increased even more rapidly. Further, the material resources of the lower classes were increasing as wealth and wages rose. Industrial trends not only heightened the numbers and concentration of the masses but also increased their economic power. These were primary ingredients of the rise of the masses in society more generally.

At the same time, the trends of industry roused new grievances on the part of the lower classes. Crises, although different in character now, remained a severe economic threat. The gap between the masses and the middle class increased. And after 1900 the economic gains of the lower classes ceased and even receded in some places. The period during which the masses were rising in numbers and resources was also a period during which discontent was considerable. Both the dynamism and the weaknesses of the economy found expression in the attitudes of the urban masses.

POLITICAL CHANGE

The Rise of Democracy

Paralleling the new concentration and resources of the masses, major alterations in political structure greatly increased the participation of the masses in government after 1870. The most fundamental change was the establishment of universal male suffrage for the first time in western and central Europe. The revolution of 1848 had extended the vote to all males in France and, temporarily, in Germany. French voters had little real choice, however, during most of the Second Empire. Only in the 1860s was there any real opportunity to vote against official candidates; with the establishment of the Third Republic during the 1870s the choice became even more free. The new German Empire, created in 1871, granted universal suffrage for the lower house of the national parliament. Great Britain extended the vote to urban workers in 1867 and to most other males in 1884. Belgium established universal suffrage in 1892. Italy extended the vote in 1882 and made it universal for males in 1912; Austria established universal male suffrage in 1907. Finland and Sweden even allowed women to vote in the 1900s, although female suffrage was not yet a general movement. What was quite general was the establishment of parliaments with at least one house elected by universal suffrage.

Furthermore, the powers of elected parliaments tended to increase, and parliamentary bodies were established in many nations where no regular instrument of popular representation had existed before. In 1911 the British House of Lords was stripped of the power to veto legislation, fully establishing the House of Commons as the basic authority in British government. The formation of the Third Republic during the 1870s established the supremacy of the French parliament over the executive branch. Elsewhere parliaments were less powerful. In Germany, especially, the functions of the elected Reichstag were severely limited. An upper house had equal powers, and that house was effectively dominated by Prussia, whose parliament was elected on the basis of a class-voting system that allowed the upper classes to control the bulk of the seats. Most other German states established universal suffrage for their parliaments by 1900, but Prussia did not yield. Moreover, the national cabinet was appointed by the emperor of Germany, not by the parliament. The opportunities for the masses to exercise political influence were therefore considerably more restricted in Germany than elsewhere. Even in Germany, however, the government paid careful heed to the political composition of parliament, and the masses received increasing attention. They did not rule, but they did not rule in other countries either. It remained generally true, except in Spain and eastern Europe, that the masses gained a regular political voice for the first time during this period; the spread of democratic parliamentary structures was the basis for that voice.

Other reforms promoted effective mass political power. Ballots were made secret in most countries, making it less easy to control votes. Parliamentary representatives began to receive pay, so poor men could serve. By the 1870s most parliaments contained a small number of representatives of working-class origin, and by the 1900s in most parliamentary countries a few such representatives had entered the cabinets, usually in a minor capacity. For the most part, government posts remained in the hands of aristocrats and members of the middle class; even the leaders of working-class parties were usually from the middle class. Nevertheless, upper-class politicians of all political persuasions increasingly had to seek mass support for their persons and their policies. The ruling group did not change radically, but the activities of governments and the political consciousness of the lower classes themselves were significantly altered as political structures changed.

The political reforms, including the extension of the suffrage, were largely the work of middle-class and even aristocratic politicians. Few elements of the lower classes had real political consciousness, although the rising of Parisian artisans in 1848 was the direct cause of the establishment of universal suffrage in France. Intensive political agitation by the masses, often under socialist leadership, promoted voting reforms in Italy, Belgium, and Austria later in the

century, after universal suffrage had already been established elsewhere. Government fear of mass agitation promoted many political
reforms, but the major steps were usually taken for other reasons.

Conservative-liberal rivalries prompted politicians of both persuasions to broaden the vote in the hope of finding support among
the masses. Most important, middle-class political interests continued to stress effective parliaments and even universal suffrage.
The class modified a desire for a political hierarchy based on wealth
with some sincere interest in equality of political opportunity. And
lower elements of the middle class actively supported voting reforms as a means of obtaining political rights for themselves as well
as others. Middle-class parties in Italy, for example, were sympathetic to the idea of political reform and gradually sponsored democratic measures. Democracy resulted only indirectly from the power
of the masses. Democracy created, rather than followed, political
consciousness among workers and peasants.

Hence there was usually a conspicuous lag between the extension of the suffrage and the development of any clear new political
trends. The masses were not accustomed to the vote, and political
rights remained meaningless for many. Even in 1900 only about
65 per cent of the urban lower classes, and an even smaller portion
of the peasants, usually voted, in contrast to over 80 per cent of the
middle class. Those of the lower classes who did vote naturally
turned at first to established political parties and leaders. In France
the crisis of the Franco-Prussian War caused many elements of the
masses, especially in the countryside, to turn to local nobles or
members of the traditional middle class in the election of 1871; the
result was a royalist parliament. In Germany newly enfranchised
voters supported established aristocratic and middle-class parties for
more than a decade after 1870. Gradually, however, the masses developed political independence and a sense of their own distinctive
interests.

Existing political groupings obviously had to change their approach in order to win the mass support they needed after universal suffrage was established. By the 1880s conservative parties
had begun to beat the drum of nationalism, an appeal that caught
the fancy of many elements of the masses but one that altered
the nature of conservatism. Even in dealing with the peasantry,
which remained largely attached to conservatism, conservatives had

to promise some attention to peasant economic interests. And active campaigning among all groups was necessary for the first time.

Middle-class parties were also altered by the need to obtain mass backing. Liberal parties obtained the support of many elements of the lower-middle class, artisanry, and even the working class by offering support for the extension of free education to the masses and many important measures of industrial legislation and social welfare. The parties were still committed to the protection of middle-class economic and political interests. These interests were not totally inflexible, not totally opposed to the desires of the urban masses. The policies of middle-class parties changed considerably, nevertheless, as they too were opened to the political pressure of the masses.

The most distinctive result of the new political power and consciousness of the masses was the rise of the socialist parties, an obviously new political force that was at least partially representative of the interests of the working classes. The socialist parties appealed to few members of the lower-middle class, although they drew votes from some professional groups, notably teachers. They appealed to only a minority of peasants and artisans. By no means, then, did the socialists represent the masses as a whole, but the socialist parties did gradually become the expression of the political interests of most factory workers and some other groups. On this basis alone, given the numbers involved in factory labor, socialist parties rose quickly to great importance.

The rise of socialism did not follow immediately from the extension of the suffrage, for socialist leaders were not always ready to take advantage of the new opportunities, and the industrial workers were certainly not prepared for such a novel use of their new political rights. In Britain the Labour Party developed real strength only after World War I, although it had eighty representatives in Parliament after 1906; the Liberal Party continued to win the support of most workers before the war. German socialist activity began in the 1860s but was slow to attract voters until the 1890s, when it regularly polled about a million and a half votes. By 1913 the party received four million votes and had 110 deputies in the Reichstag; it was the largest single party in Germany and the strongest socialist party in the world. French socialists, split into several groups, had forty-nine representatives in parliament as early as 1883 and about a hundred by 1913; a socialist had even entered the cabinet in 1899. Socialist parties in Italy and Austria remained smaller because the laboring class was smaller and gained the right to vote only after 1900. Nevertheless, in those countries and where-ever democratic suffrage existed socialist parties rose from nothing to massive political strength during the period.

The new political power of the masses altered existing parties and created a major new element in the political spectrum. Every major social class developed distinctive political interests and expressed them actively. Changes in governmental structure had added a new element to the lives of the masses, revised the party systems of Europe, and brought further changes to governments themselves in the form of new policies and functions.

Mass Education

The spread of political democracy formed the most notable new link between the masses and government, but it was not the only one. The new importance of the masses caused governments to seek increasing contacts with them, and those contacts in turn affected the lives of the masses significantly. Impressed by the power of Prussia's conscript armies, most continental governments instituted systems of universal military conscription during this period. By the 1900s most young men of all classes spent two, sometimes three, years in military service. This service gave the masses experience in discipline and organization and provided important training in national loyalty. The Russian army even taught its recruits to read and write. Everywhere military service provided new experiences for many individuals and tended to unify and standardize certain habits regardless of class or region. Particularly for the peasantry, it loosened the force of localism and tradition. Just as military life and tactics changed greatly due to the development of massive conscript armies, so the military experience became an important, if often resented, part of the lives of the masses.

In most countries governments took over functions of record keeping and even marriage from the clergy, usually during a time of church–state conflict. The state registered births, deaths, and weddings for all its citizens.

Most important, the state in all western and central European countries developed free universal public education systems during the period and required school attendance by every child. Education had, of course, been increasing steadily among the masses even before 1870; government expenditures on schools had risen. But many schools remained in the hands of private groups, particularly the churches, and the quality of education before 1870 had been spotty. Many teachers were ill-trained, and there were only loose regulations for entry into the teaching profession. Many children who attended school retained little from their experience, often not even the ability to read, and many children could not attend at all because of long hours of work in the city or their distance from schools in the country. Most schools charged small fees, which deterred many parents. Literacy rates rose in industrial countries, but a large minority still could not read.

By about 1870 this situation began to change rapidly. Governments developed a great concern for the education of their citizens, as part of the growing consciousness of the importance of the masses. If the masses were to vote, and serve in armies, they would have to be educated. It was vital to attach the loyalties of citizens and soldiers to their governments through education. Middle-class politicians supported educational improvements actively, and the middle class had increasing political influence in this period. The interests of industry also created a greater need for mass education. Industry required growing numbers of people who could read instructions and do simple calculations. It also increasingly needed a population that could read advertisements. Like the state itself, industry required some participation by masses of people who had a basic education. Finally, groups within the urban lower classes, such as artisan unions, pressed for the extension of public education. This was an old demand given greater force by the new political power of the masses.

For a variety of reasons, then, the nations of western and central Europe developed systems of universal primary education during the 1870s and 1880s. Even in Russia primary schools spread rapidly though only 5 per cent of the children attended by 1881. In the west schools were available for all. They were quickly made both free as in Britain in 1891, and compulsory. Furthermore, compulsion was usually extended beyond mere primary education. By 1900 most of western Europe required school attendance until fourteen years of age, and states were providing technical and secondary schools

for the last years of education. There was even a small movement to
broaden university education. New provincial universities were
established in France. University extension-course movements and
institutions such as Britain's Ruskin college were set up in the hope
of drawing talented workers to the universities. These movements
had little effect except to extend university training to more members
of the middle class. They were symptomatic, nevertheless, of the
interest attached to the education of the masses. And the extension
of primary and secondary systems, with the element of legal compulsion, did have great effects on the lives of the masses.

The most important result of the spread of education was the
extension of literacy to virtually the whole population of industrial
countries. In 1900 four fifths of the Russian population was illiterate.
Two thirds of the people in Spain and Portugal, half of those in
Italy and Hungary, and a third of those in Austria still could not
read. In all those countries education and literacy were spreading,
but the development was too recent to have eliminated extensive
illiteracy. Often it required a generation of schooling for a family
really to absorb education to the point of being literate, and this
generation had not passed in these areas. In the west, however,
nearly universal literacy was obtained. Britain rose from 66 per cent
literacy in 1870 to 95 per cent in 1900, France rose from 60 per cent
to 95 per cent, Belgium from 55 per cent to 86 per cent, and so on.
The masses could read, and they did so increasingly. Newspapers
preferred by the masses attained circulations sometimes in the
millions. Inexpensive books and other publications were widely
read also. Mass education, simply by creating the ability to read, was
fundamental to the new interests and activities of all the lower
classes.

Mass education required significant changes in the organization
and curricula of education, which in turn guided the cultural development of the lower classes.

In the first place, the educational systems were increasingly
standardized under the control of the state. Central bureaus developed uniform course programs, textbooks, and teacher's qualifications for use in all public schools throughout the nation in countries
such as France, where the government was highly centralized, or
throughout a state in a federal nation such as Germany. The French
ministers of education boasted that at any given moment the same

lesson was being taught all over France. Local dialects and other parochial interests were specifically fought. One French minister stated that "for the linguistic unity of France, Breton should disappear." Not only Breton, but also Basque, Flemish, Provençal, and, after World War I, Alsatian were attacked by the French school system. Local customs as well as languages were attacked by an educational program consciously designed to provide uniformity. Peasants, obviously, were most affected by these trends, as their localism had been most intense, but all classes were involved. An expectation of uniformity and some cultural guidance from above were among the most important products of the new public education.

The systems of public education also encouraged secularization of the attitudes of the masses and the reduction of religious influences. In most countries the period was marked by major conflict between church and state over the degree of religious influence permissible in the schools. In Germany education was largely secularized during the *Kulturkampf* of the 1870s. Priests and pastors were removed from the schools, and a number of Catholic teaching orders were suppressed, although Bavaria continued to give public support to church schools. Teaching orders, especially the Jesuits, were suppressed in many other countries during the 1860s and 1870s. Belgian Catholics lost a long and bitter political struggle with middle-class liberals for control of education. In France laws establishing public primary education in the 1880s banned priests from teaching in the public schools and closed all Jesuit schools. The state in most countries sought full control of the education of the masses. It was supported by large elements of the middle class who traditionally combined an interest in education with a dislike of religious influence. The result was an educational experience for the masses that was largely secular in all countries and entirely, even militantly, secular in some.

In place of localism and religion in education, the new systems promoted useful patriotic subjects. Courses in civics and national history were intended to provide the knowledge necessary to a good citizen and particularly to encourage national loyalty. Systems of public education were one of the most important forces in the development of mass nationalism during this period. Training in the national language and literature supplemented the nationalist orientation of the social sciences.

Mathematics, particularly arithmetic, some technical and scientific training and sometimes a smattering of classical languages and literature completed the typical curriculum. This was an education designed to be useful.

There was some tendency also to develop a new discipline in the schools. Leading educational theorists, such as Froebel in Germany, urged that children be allowed to learn by doing, free from severe regulations by the teacher. It was, after all, unnecessary to train lower-class children to conform to strict patterns of behavior and to develop an interest in subjects as distant from daily life as those of the classically oriented schools for the upper classes. Discipline in the public schools was usually strict, but there was some interest in recognizing the special needs of children. In subject matter and to an extent in discipline the public schools were designed to fulfill the needs of the lower classes and to train those classes in a manner useful to the state. The result was a significant departure from the educational principles of the upper classes.

Upper-class education was also extended during the same period. The educational differences between the middle class and aristocracy on the one hand and the lower classes on the other were not allowed to disappear. The masses might obtain the rudiments of education, but they had neither the interest nor the resources to enter the higher levels of education save in a few individual instances. At the same time, the interest of the upper classes in extensive education increased. The growing wealth of the middle class and the continued desire to use education to advance the future of the family were joined with an interest in maintaining educational distinction from the masses.

In Great Britain the middle class and aristocracy continued to patronize private and secondary schools where the curriculum was rich in classical training and lightly seasoned with modern languages, science, and the social sciences. French and German upper-class children either had tutors or attended special public primary schools that stressed the classics and at the age of ten or eleven entered public university preparatory schools—the *lycée* or the *Gymnasium*. Enrollment in these schools was restricted to 10 to 15 per cent of the population and was drawn primarily from the upper classes. The restricted enrollment was easy to achieve; these schools still charged fees, and their entrance examinations were too stiff for children who had not been given a suitable primary education and who lacked the cultural background and interest of the upper classes.

In many secondary schools training was built around Greek and Latin, mathematics, and some philosophy—the traditional curriculum. This curriculum remained popular with the aristocracy and upper middle class. Most of the middle class still sought a more pragmatic training in science and modern languages; in Germany, for example, the *Realgymnasium* provided precisely such a program. Even there students remained educationally distinct from the masses. They completed their secondary education at eighteen or nineteen, instead of twelve or fourteen, and their training was radically different. The education of the masses, important as it was, did not disturb the pattern of class distinctions in Europe.

Nevertheless, the vast improvement of educational opportunity, along with new political rights and economic resources, changed the life of the lower classes significantly. More contact with ideas was possible for the masses than ever before, and there was more political and economic opportunity to work for the implementation of relevant ideas.

Conclusion

At the same time that their political and economic opportunities increased, many elements in the lower classes were finding their life in industrial society less bewildering than they had at first. The shock of novelty had worn off. The rise of the masses was partly due to their growing consciousness of the nature of industrial society. Grievances continued and sometimes increased, as in the case of factory workers. But even protest was largely based on an understanding of industry rather than resistance to it in the name of past traditions.

Peasants in the west were accustomed to a market economy and the decline of village agriculture. Artisans largely ceased to insist on a restoration of the guild system. Most important, industrial workers became increasingly accustomed to their lot. There were new workers in the period, even in western Europe. But the majority of the labor force was now of second or third generation and was familiar with urban and factory conditions. Material improvements, such as alleviation of residential crowding, aided the process of adjustment. Family life became more stable. Theft was less common. Rates of alcohol consumption declined. It was notable that in a period when the lower classes increased their consumption of most items, per capita sales of hard liquor declined. In Britain, for example, 1870 represented the peak of alcohol consumption.

In a number of respects the principal symptoms of confusion and individual hostility within the working class became less acute, enabling the class to take constructive action to better its lot.

Much of the impetus toward the development of new activities among the masses came from the outside. Economic developments, sponsored by the industrialists, accounted for increasing concentration of labor. The general expansion of industry supported the increasing well-being among the masses. Political changes were influenced by the potential power of the masses but were adopted by the active decision of established groups and leaders. All of this provided the background to the rise of the masses. As time went on, the new opportunities were supplemented by a new will to action among elements of the lower classes. Increasing levels of education and increasing consciousness of position and purpose in the economy promoted numerous organizations and movements with mass participation. The initial rise of the masses did not depend solely on the masses themselves; but further gains were largely the result of conscious effort on their own behalf.

THE PEASANTRY

Change in the circumstances of the peasantry in western Europe was a significant aspect of the growing importance of the masses. Contacts between peasants and the broader society increased. Peasants by no means lost their identity or distinctiveness, but their local isolation did decline.

The spread of education and military service exposed the peasantry to new ideas and new environments. In the armies peasants could meet people from the cities and learn something of their goals and conditions. Among other things, they could learn that their own standard of living was inferior to that of the urban masses. The schools preached loyalty to the nation instead of to the locality. The lessons in citizenship provided the tools of political consciousness and participation. They exposed peasants to a literature, sometimes even a language, that had not been known before. They brought ideas about the importance of science and technology that were unfamiliar to most peasants but which began to affect the economic life of the countryside. The schools were a new source of authority for young peasants. They did not eliminate the older sources, such as parents or village, but they did reduce their importance. For peasant women contact with authority outside the home was particularly novel.

At the same time, formal education prepared peasants for other types of contacts with their broader society. They shared some ideas and ways of thinking with other groups because of a common education. Their ability to communicate and to receive communication was increased. By the 1900s the younger peasants in southwestern France could speak French, although their parents still required translations to and from Provençal. This sort of unification of speech was occurring quite generally. Peasants could now read publications and understand speakers from the cities. Travel to the city increased as local railroads facilitated short trips. Growing purchases of equipment and sales of specialized agricultural produce made dealings with urban agents more necessary. In some cases peasants even began to use the city's facilities for entertainment and recreation.

And most peasants now heard appeals by urban political leaders. Representatives of all parties sought the peasant vote, and many began to speak in the villages during election periods. Union leaders also sought peasant support for their causes. Exposure to unfamiliar ideas, methods, and even people became increasingly common for the peasants. Already shaken from their traditionalism, peasants now proved open to further change.

The Crisis in Agriculture

An unprecedented crisis in agriculture helped to determine the courses of action taken by the peasantry after 1870. Beginning in 1873 huge imports of grain, especially wheat, from areas outside Europe reduced grain prices steadily and so reduced the earnings of all segments of the peasantry.

Agricultural labor was near the borderline of subsistence even before then. Wages had risen slightly during the two prosperous decades after 1850, but diets were still poor, clothing ragged, and housing crowded and mean. Then wages were reduced. British landowners cut the pay of their agricultural workers in response to the crisis, and German Junkers tightened their grip on their labor force, already held in conditions of extreme poverty and submission.

For peasant landowners the situation was only slightly better. Their earnings dropped and the value of their land decreased, a major blow not only to peasant economy but also to peasant values. Many were able to survive only by borrowing; everywhere the number and size of mortgages on the land increased. Natural disasters in the 1870s and 1880s compounded peasant difficulties. Heavy and untimely rains ruined several crops in Britain during the period. No one starved, and food prices did not rise because of the possibility of importing cheap grain; but the agricultural population suffered severely from additional loss of income. French peasants battled during this period with diseases that attacked silkworms and ravaged the vines. Disaster was piled upon disaster for most agricultural producers.

Response to the Crisis

In eastern and southern Europe, the effects of the grain crisis, the pressure of rural overpopulation and the vexation of remnants of feudal obligations combined to promote massive peasant unrest. In the west there were a few attempts to unionize among agricultural workers, and there were some major rural strikes, particularly in France; but peasants for the most part remained calm. The principal responses of the western peasantry to the crisis were more subtle. Peasants altered their methods far more than they had in the earlier response to market agriculture. Some interest in political defenses developed, again providing novel experience. Both economic and political action proved effective in alleviating the crisis. By the 1890s the worst was over, although land values were still shaky and debts still high. But peasant habits had been substantially altered. Even interests developed earlier in the century were modified.

Most notable, the earlier reaction of acquiring more land was now restricted. Peasants in regions pressed by population growth, as in Russia, still sought land above all. In western Europe, however, land declined in importance for the peasantry—just as it declined in economic worth. Many British farmers preferred to rent land rather than buy so that they would have capital available for other purposes. Quite generally, mere possession of land no longer seemed to be a sovereign remedy.

All over western and central Europe peasants tried to counteract the agricultural crisis by improving the efficiency of their methods. Never before had peasants been so eager to try technical innovations. They purchased new tools, including seed drills and even threshing machines. After 1892 most wheat fields in France, large or small, were cultivated and harvested with machines. Danish dairy farmers began to use cream separators after 1870. Everywhere the utilization of fertilizers increased. The result of the quest for efficiency was a general and significant improvement in yields. French production of both wheat and wine increased after 1890 even though the amount of land devoted to each of those crops declined. An interest in technical advances began to penetrate the peasantry, promoted both by education and economic pressure, and the spread of new methods definitely helped the peasants to improve their economic position in the face of falling prices.

Peasants also began to change the crops they raised. They increasingly abandoned grain, in which competition was most intense, in favor of meat, dairy, and truck products. In Germany the raising of animals, particularly hogs, increased rapidly, especially in the smallholding areas. Danish peasants intensified the specialization in dairy farming they had begun before the crisis. British farmers curtailed the amount of land devoted to arable farming, and their production of wheat actually declined. They concentrated instead on meat and dairy goods, as did farmers in Normandy. The peasants of Britanny and several other regions of France specialized in truck farming, but France as a whole retained a higher level of wheat production than any European country except Russia. Generally, the conversion to more marketable crops was an important result of the agricultural crisis. The growing demand of the urban masses for meats and dairy products assured an excellent market for the new specialties. Peasant attunement to the market, already well developed, was clearly increasing.

Most peasants converting to mechanized farming or to a specialty crop ran into important difficulties. Mechanized equipment was beyond the means of many individuals. Conversion to stock raising or dairy farming required far more capital than was necessary for grain production. The growing dependence on the market posed certain problems in itself. Peasants were economically weak in comparison with the producers of agricultural equipment and fertilizers; they could easily be victimized in their transactions. They were weak also in relation to the wholesalers who bought their crops. Some peasants entered into contracts with breweries, sugar refineries, and canneries in an effort to assure their sales; too often these contracts left the peasants in virtual servitude to the manufacturer. Peasants who borrowed money to buy new equipment or stock were often exploited by the lenders. For a variety of reasons peasants found it difficult to respond to the agricultural crisis and adopted new equipment and crops only hesitantly, despite the great need for change. Many peasants sought devices for avoiding the need to change at all. At the same time, a movement arose in the period that provided an answer to many of the problems of individual peasants. By a new organization of the peasantry, by a combination of peasant resources, capital could be provided, supplies purchased, and even marketing arranged to the advantage of each producer. An extensive cooperative movement arose in direct response to the new economic needs of the peasantry.

Cooperation and Peasant Politics

The first cooperatives were established before 1850 as savings banks and lending agencies for the members. The Raiffeissen banks in Germany, begun in 1846 as a response to the agricultural crisis of that year, and the Schulze-Delitzsch credit cooperatives did a great deal to reduce interest rates on loans and provide more ample funds for German peasants. Savings and loan organizations were the most popular rural cooperatives, and their membership grew rapidly after 1870 in Germany and elsewhere. Purchasing cooperatives were also formed to buy expensive supplies and even heavy machinery for shared use. After 1870 Danish cooperatives helped purchase cream separators; the first French cooperative was founded in 1881 to buy fertilizers. Other groups in France were established to acquire vines from the United States to replace the diseased French stock. Cooperatives extended their purchasing functions even to consumer goods such as clothing. By grouping the purchasing power of individual peasants, cooperatives lowered prices, assured high quality, and allowed technical improvements impossible to the individual peasant. Finally, some cooperatives developed storage and processing facilities for agricultural goods and served as sales agents for their members. Again, the cooperative organization had far greater power in the market than did individual peasants.

The cooperative movement spread widely; 750,000 French peasants were in cooperatives of some sort by 1910, while over a quarter of the German peasantry was enrolled. In Denmark, which adapted most successfully to the new agricultural situation, cooperatives played a major role.

Nevertheless, cooperatives demanded important sacrifices from the peasants. They violated the individualism many peasants had developed during the earlier period of adjustment to market agriculture. Cooperatives also demanded administrative skills that few peasants possessed. The movement, although it spread constantly, did not touch the bulk of the peasantry during the period. In France, where peasant individualism was unusually intense, no more than a tenth of the agricultural population joined cooperatives before World War I, and many who did only joined credit cooperatives, which were in business to finance individual, not collective effort. The cooperatives offered great assistance in adjusting to the new needs of agriculture, if only to a minority of the peasantry.

Peasant political consciousness inevitably rose in the period as voting rights were extended. In a few cases peasants used their vote to express radical discontent. There were isolated pockets of socialist voting in southwestern Germany. Around Bologna, where large estates were formed in the 1860s on newly drained land, peasant support for socialism developed before 1900. Generally, however, peasants in industrial countries were not attracted by extremes of this sort. They developed new political interests, but remained conservative. In France peasants traditionally had supported monarchist notables and Bonapartists; they had never developed an interest in republicanism. During the 1870s republican campaigners, led by Léon Gambetta, tried to persuade peasants that a republic could maintain order and protect private property; most French peasants therefore became firm republicans. Elsewhere, traditionalism was not modified even to this extent. Peasant voters in Austria rejected the political control of the landlords by voting for the

Christian Social Party, but they were still supporting a conservative party favorable to religion. Many German peasants still voted as the landlords told them to. Gradually, however, peasants did become aware of the possibility of using their votes, always in a conservative way, to win economic assistance from the government.

Governments offered various assistance to farmers during the period. They extended advanced technical training in agriculture. German universities offered night courses to peasants, in the villages, on the principles of scientific agriculture, and the British government established similar training after 1900. In 1900 the British government also allowed county councils to buy land for rental in plots of moderate size in an effort to encourage small farming. The German government promoted consolidation of land and also purchased some estates to assist small farmers. The French government lent money to the cooperatives, and governments generally tried to develop the credit facilities in the countryside.

Of greatest interest to the peasants was the possibility of establishing tariff protection for agricultural goods. Most countries had abandoned significant duties on food prior to 1870. Agricultural producers who depended on exports, such as the Junkers, supported free trade, but the peasants took little interest in the issue. As the crisis in agriculture began, pressure for tariff protection rose. The peasants did not initiate the pressure; issues of this sort were unfamiliar, and peasants were not accustomed to political action of any kind. In Germany the Junkers launched the agitation by forming the Union of Agriculturalists to spread propaganda for tariff protection and to serve as a vigorous lobby. In France not only large landowners but also some industrialists pressed for new agricultural tariffs; the industrialists hoped to promote a general return to protective policies. These various interests began to appeal to the peasants for support in their campaigns. Conservative politicians sought peasant votes by pointing to the need to defend the nation's agriculture against foreign competition. Propagandists from the German Union of Agriculturalists talked of the unity of agricultural interests and the need to defend agriculture as a whole. The group persuaded many peasants to urge tariffs that were often against their own economic interest. German peasants who were converting to hog raising and who therefore needed to buy feed grains, nevertheless proved willing to back tariffs on grains. The traditional political prestige of the aristocracy and the idea of defending agriculture were the magnets that attracted peasants to the protectionist cause.

More generally, peasants supported tariffs, once the idea was presented to them, as a means of reducing the need for change. With high duties on food imports, old methods and traditional products could still be profitable. In France, Germany, and elsewhere tariffs undeniably protected methods and crops that were economically wasteful. The French tariff of 1892 returned France to a position of almost complete agricultural self-sufficiency, despite the fact that French peasants could not produce grain so economically as farmers in the New World. The main victims of this system were urban buyers of food, however, not the peasants themselves, who saw their incomes and habits alike defended by the tariff system.

Peasant attachment to tariff advocates was intense. Along with continued political traditionalism, it helped maintain the conservative political orientation of most peasants. Peasants in France voted generally for moderate republicans because they offered tariffs, governmental sympathy for the church, and a firm defense of private property. German peasants usually voted either for the Catholic Center Party, urged on by their priests, or in Protestant areas for conservative groupings controlled by the Junkers. Both of the parties receiving peasant support in Germany were staunch advocates of agricultural tariffs. Protectionism had considerable effects on the political as well as the economic action of the peasants. In turn, the conservative politics and protectionism peasants came to support had considerable effects on the economic and political structure of society generally.

Peasant Standards of Living

The various responses to the crisis in agriculture succeeded in bringing some improvements in peasant standards of living during the period. The slump in earnings was most acute before 1890. After that the wages of agricultural labor began to rise, and landowners made sufficient adjustments to allow better conditions for themselves as well. Standards of living were varied, ranging from the meager diet and housing of much agricultural labor to the substance of many peasant landowners. Generally, the diets of peasants improved and included more items purchased in stores. Clothing was almost entirely factory made and was similar to the attire of the urban lower classes. Many peasants could afford tobacco, coffee, and new entertainment in the towns for the first time. The improvements in conditions generally brought peasants closer to urban patterns of spending.

There were a number of signs that most peasants were becoming actively interested in improved standards. The most bitter rural strikes occurred not during the agricultural crisis but after agricultural wages had begun to increase. After 1904 a number of strikes by winegrowers and others in France involved more than 20,000 peasants. Far more generally, peasants increasingly took care to limit their birth rate in western and central Europe, in order to protect their incomes against the pressure of too many children.

The new interest in consumption also helped promote a new exodus to the cities. The movement was not so massive as before, but it continued. The crisis in agriculture naturally prompted many departures, and conversion from grain production to stock raising reduced the need for labor. But there was more than crisis involved here. The peasants who moved were not always driven by economic desperation but rather by a desire to taste the delights of urban life. Many substantial landowners in France abandoned agriculture for work in the cities. In France and Britain the absolute number of peasants began to decrease for the first time. Previously the great migration from the countryside had been, in effect, the surplus of population growth. Now a minority of peasants wanted to abandon farming even though they could easily subsist by it. To be sure, most of those who left the countryside were landless laborers. In Germany the two and a half million landowners remained, but the figure of three and a half million laborers began to decline. But even the laborers were not goaded by dire necessity. In France and elsewhere so many laborers left the land that agricultural wages began to rise, but the exodus still did not cease. Desertion of the countryside by an important minority of the peasantry was a significant indication not only of agricultural difficulties but also of changing peasant values. Contact with the cities through marketing, military service, and education altered the standards by which many peasants viewed their life.

Despite all this, the incomes of most peasants remained noticeably below those of urban workers. The gains in consumption did not match those of other lower classes. Wages for agricultural workers were at best half the average levels in the factory. Peasant owners earned more but still not usually at the urban rate, and their rising debts were a constant burden. Yet despite the new interest in consumption there were few signs of active discontent over the inferiority in income. Strikes, though important, involved very few peasants. The most dissatisfied peasants simply left. For those who remained largely traditional standards still sufficed. Customary attachment to work and the land and devotion to religion and village recreation still gave satisfaction.

For western peasants, then, the period brought alterations in methods and outlook and certainly many new contacts with outside influences, but the main lines of adaptation to market agriculture still sufficed. Political consciousness spread, but it was not particularly vigorous. Family size was limited but not so radically as in the cities. New organizations were developed but were of active interest only to a minority. The need for innovation was not so great as it had been before or was to be in the subsequent period.

In the east and south, of course, these were the decades of massive upheaval. Population pressure was intense; the need to adapt to the market was heightened by agricultural crisis; large estates kept many in semiservitude. Substantial agitation was the principal peasant response. Only in Russia did the spread of smallholding and the beginning of industrialization suggest a further stage of adaptation after 1906; and there the war plunged the countryside into renewed turmoil. The calm of western peasants was in total contrast to the persistent rioting in the east and south, despite some common economic pressures.

THE LOWER MIDDLE CLASS

Urban Class Structure

By the end of the nineteenth century urban lower classes represented a far more numerous segment of the masses than did the peasantry in the older industrial countries. Only a third of the German population was peasant, only a seventh of the British. Over a third of the populations in each country worked in industry, and many more worked as employes in commerce or banking and constituted part of the urban masses. From the standpoint of numbers

alone, the rise of the masses in this period was largely a rise of
urban lower classes. The urban lower classes were freer from the
hand of tradition than were the peasants. Their material resources
were greater. They were better educated and they had such items
as newspapers in far greater quantities. Urban life, due to its concentration of people, facilitated organization and contacts among
the lower classes, through which ideas, methods, and even leaders
could be found. In Europe, cities had always been the main source
of novel intellectual, social, and political movements. What was
new by the end of the nineteenth century was that the majority of
the population was now directly affected by the dynamism of the
urban environment. The cities provided the principal setting for
the development of new activities and attitudes on the part of the
masses.

The balance among the urban lower classes shifted rapidly. A
minority of irregularly employed still existed in most cities. These
people were part of no clearly defined social class save that of the
poor. Their apathy, their dependence on charity, their lack of
resources set them apart from the other lower classes. The position
of this group was changing, however. The numbers of the desperately poor were shrinking in the cities. The rise of industry increased
the opportunities for factory employment and created more and
steadier jobs for the unskilled in construction and transportation.
A number of professions whose members had previously been in the
category of occasional workers developed a new confidence and
ability to act during the period. Dockers, wagon drivers, and ditch
diggers began to participate in the same sorts of organizations as
factory workers and for the same reasons. Though still suffering
from some irregularity of employment, they entered into the general
working class. This alteration in the resources and attitudes of many
unskilled was a major social development in the cities.

Two other traditional urban groups were declining in numbers,
although both remained important; the servants and the artisans.
Opportunities in factories and stores made recruitment of servants
increasingly difficult. At the same time the factory labor force began
to assert direct influence over political and economic life; it became
the most obviously important element of the masses.

The most novel element of the urban population, the only one
that arose during this period, was the clerical lower middle class.

This was the most rapidly growing group in western Europe after 1870. The working class expanded, but its rate of growth had slowed. New machines increased production without major additions to the labor force. The needs of the economy centered increasingly on bureaucratic and commercial development, and this impelled the numerical burst of the lower middle class.

Sources of the Lower Middle Class

The lower middle class expanded in two directions at the end of the century. The numbers of small businessmen and property owners increased. A rapid rise of small investors, particularly among widows and retired persons, accompanied the development of the stock markets. However, the principal growth of the lower middle class was not among the property-owning element. The need to increase sales outlets created more sales personnel than shopkeepers, and clerks in private and public bureaucracies swelled the ranks of white-collar workers. A nonpropertied, salaried lower middle class was an important addition to European social structure.

The continued development of small businesses with one or two employes steadily expanded the numbers of small employers and shopkeepers. The growing importance of manufactured goods in the agricultural economy created new needs for village stores. Where agricultural populations remained large, particularly in smallholding areas, the small town or village shopkeeper played a major role in the development of the lower middle class. This was the case in France. Owners of village bakeries, hardware stores, and the like were numerous and increasing. On the other hand, in Britain where there were few agricultural producers, the rural shopkeeper constituted only a small part of the lower middle class.

There were definite limitations to the expansion of small property ownership. Small businesses increased but could not match the rise of giant concerns. Most notably, competition from department stores and other large commercial units reduced the significance of the small shop in the cities. Shops continued to handle most foods and many other goods, but the expansion of the shopkeeping element was relatively slight in the cities despite the growth of urban populations. This was, of course, in marked contrast to the earlier industrial period, when the need for new retail outlets was filled almost entirely by small shops.

In general, then, the property-owning element of the lower middle class was rising in numbers but at a moderate rate. There were important national differences. France, with more shopkeepers and more tiny manufacturing firms than most western countries, had a property-owning group unusually large in size and unusually important in politics. More fully industrialized nations, in which large firms predominated, had correspondingly fewer shopkeepers and small employers. Everywhere the property-owning element of the lower middle class could not match the growth of newer segments of the class.

There were several major sources of white-collar employment. The new wealth of upper and lower classes alike increased the demand for services not connected with manufacturing or with manual labor. Services such as teaching, the staffing of hotels and resorts, barbering, and banking expanded rapidly in the period and played a major role in the extension of lower middle class jobs.

The expansion of large organizations required a vast number of lower-level bureaucratic personnel. Huge corporations needed quantities of secretaries, clerks, and other white-collar workers. The spread of large factories increased the demand for foremen to supervise and direct the labor force. In earlier industry many of these tasks had been handled by employers and their families. Wives had often done accounting and secretarial work for their husbands, while manufacturers had supervised workers directly in many small plants. With the expansion of firms, bureaucratic personnel became absolutely essential. Furthermore, this new bureaucracy was not confined to private enterprise alone. Governments also expanded their administrations during the period; they too participated in the movement to develop more massive organization, particularly in the economy. Expansion of government functions created thousands of new jobs. New taxing powers, including tariffs and even income tax, required massive paper work and the clerks to handle it. Government education systems demanded teachers. New factory inspection laws called for inspectors and their clerks to execute them. By 1900 at least 5 per cent of the labor force in France was employed by the government in white-collar jobs. The expansion of bureaucracy, both public and private, was the most important single source of the growth of the lower middle class.

The expansion of white-collar employment was extremely rapid.

Britain had 7,000 female secretaries in 1881, 22,200 in 1891, and 90,000 in 1901. By 1871 the lower middle class constituted about 10 per cent of the British population, up from roughly 7 per cent in 1850. By 1900 the British lower middle class was a full 20 per cent of the population. Comparable development took place in other industrialized countries. A significant clerical class began to rise with the spread of corporate bureaucracies even in countries such as Russia, where 3.5 per cent of factory employment was in the white-collar category by 1900.

The lower middle class drew its new numbers from several social classes. To displaced businessmen, professional people, and artisans white-collar positions seemed relative attractive alternatives, befitting their educational levels and sense of respectability. Displaced artisans were particularly numerous and welcomed the chance to avoid factory work, and of course many artisan masters entered the lower middle class as small employers. The thousands of women who found white-collar employment came from a wide variety of social groups, including factory workers, for clerical positions were far less demanding physically and far more respectable socially than factory labor. Certain white-collar positions were filled by male members of the working class; foremen, particularly, usually rose from the ranks. Sometimes they retained the attitudes and interests of the labor force, but more commonly they assumed a lower-middle-class orientation. Many lower-middle-class jobs were filled by peasants newly arrived in the cities. It was, after all, increasingly difficult to enter the ranks of factory workers as the rate of growth of manu-facturing labor slowed. Factory workers themselves, accustomed to their work and realizing the importance of their class, tended to pass their attachment to their jobs to their sons, so that relatively few openings were created by men leaving the factories for other em-ployment. Further, there were many features of white-collar employ-ment that appealed to peasant immigrants to the city. The fact that white-collar workers were not unionized appealed to peasants who were politically conservative and inclined to resist formal organiza-tion where possible. The attachment of the lower middle class to the idea of property, even when no property was owned, was also attractive. And the prestige and respectability of the class were important to people seeking a place in a new environment.

The sources of the lower middle class were thus diverse. There was a traditional element, which held positions or owned shops that had long been in the family. Far more members of the class were newcomers and showed some of the confusion of goals that was common to recent entrants to a social class. At the same time, many of the newcomers brought to the lower middle class certain attitudes that helped develop the values of the class itself. The period was a formative one for the lower middle class, and the orientation of the class was not fully clear.

Economic Position

Earlier in the nineteenth century the lower middle class had been set apart largely by economic factors. It had been a property-owning group for the most part, considerably wealthier than workers and artisans but poorer in income and capital than the rest of the middle class. In this new period the criteria of membership in the lower middle class changed significantly. Property ownership was less common, although a minority of the class still had capital and many clerks and foremen invested in a few stocks or bonds. Most members of the class maintained savings accounts, for the class remained oriented towards the accumulation of capital.

In over-all earning power, however, the lower middle class was no longer radically distinct from other elements of the lower classes. Some shopkeepers and small employers earned substantial incomes. Foremen were paid more than ordinary workers, but large numbers of clerks and salespeople were paid less than many skilled laborers. Many members of the lower middle class had diets, dress clothing, and housing no better than those of the workers. At the same time, the gap between the lower middle class and the rest of the middle class widened, for the profits of the bulk of the middle class were rising rapidly. Both in property and in earnings, the association of the lower middle class and the middle class was far less clear than it had been previously.

The material goals of the lower middle class differed considerably from those of the working class, even if its earnings were often scarcely different. Workers tended to spend any extra money on present enjoyment by improving their diets and seeking new recreation. The lower middle class, in contrast, spent more heavily on items that improved social status. Clerks and shopkeepers bought stylish clothing, for they could wear it on the job. This distinguished them from factory labor and provided an outlet for considerable attention and expense. Members of the lower middle class also spent more on housing than did the working class. A higher percentage of their incomes was devoted to rents, furnishings, and the like. They wanted to live in suitable neighborhoods, often in the suburbs, and in a type of dwelling that would gain general recognition for its respectability. At the same time, urban crowding and rising rents in cities like Vienna and Paris forced many members of the lower middle class to accept inferior housing. Here was one of several matters in which the expectations of the class could not be fully realized.

Status

The lower middle class was set apart particularly by its intense concern with status. Its members were proud that their work involved their minds, not their hands. In the Balkans many clerks let the nails on their little fingers grow as long as possible to make it obvious that they were not manual laborers. Elsewhere the sense of status was displayed in more subtle ways, but it existed quite generally and shaped such basic aspects of life as consumption patterns and many other activities.

The lower-middle-class belief in distinctive status was asserted primarily against the working class, whose improving economic position seemed to pose a growing threat, and most members of the lower middle class lost no opportunity to demonstrate their separateness from, and even their hostility to, labor. With few exceptions they did not vote for socialist parties, which were favored by workers, and they abhorred unions. Although their economic position was often no better than that of workers and although they were commonly merely employes, they fought to preserve their sense of being economic individualists. They resisted any organization tainted with working-class participation. The large number of women among the clerical forces also impeded unionization because women in any class proved unusually reluctant to join organizations of combat. There were, to be sure, some unions established among sales personnel, teachers, and postal workers. Except in Germany they were uniformly small and ineffective in this period. The German Federation of Salaried Commercial Employees, formed in 1893, attracted a quarter of all private salaried employees by 1914 and actively sought favorable legislation on hours and wages for white-collar work. It was not a worker type of union, however, and was based in large part on hostility to the labor movement. It was intensely conservative, antisocialist, and antisemitic. It shunned the undignified proletarian weapon of strikes and desired above all to promote its members' sense of status. The Federation showed that the German lower middle class was unusually self-conscious and that even new clerical workers were quickly drawn into this consciousness; it also revealed the pervasive desire to resist worker movements in the name of lower-middle-class superiority.

This desire was commonly manifested in personal contacts too. Clerks treated workers in their firms with scant respect. Foremen were careful to preserve their superiority not only on the job but also in social gatherings. Foremen were generally opposed to strike and other union activities in the factories and often acted as strike breakers. Other elements of the lower middle class had only infrequent contact with labor and found this a blessing. For its part, the working class often realized and reciprocated the indifference or hostility of the lower middle class. For workers and clerks alike there was little question of the separate status of the lower middle class.

As the lower middle class shunned working-class movements and attitudes, so it clung to middle-class patterns of behavior. Businessmen did recognize that clerks and small shopkeepers were far more respectable than ordinary workers. They agreed that manual labor was essentially degrading. The lower middle class in turn adopted many typically middle-class attitudes. This was quite natural to the shopkeeping element, part of which had long been on the margins of the middle class; but it proved common also among newcomers to the lower middle class. The class often tried to copy middle-class styles in clothing and furniture, although differences in means made it impossible to imitate fully. Middle-class fads such as the popularity of Chinese *objets d'art,* real or mass produced, spread quickly to the lower middle class.

The lower middle class was ambitious. It believed in the possibility of rising economically and socially; it believed in the legendary self-made man. A substantial minority did improve themselves. Far more people from this class than from the working class rose to professional or managerial groupings. Thirty-five per cent of the managers of British industry named between 1900 and 1920 came from the lower middle class but only 25 per cent from the far larger laboring classes. The interest in mobility, which penetrated many clerks who never actually advanced themselves, led to adoption or maintenance of many traditional middle-class values suitable for economic advancement—hard work, thrift, cleanliness, and respectability. The importance of education was widely recognized, and members of the lower middle class were more likely to go beyond minimal education requirements than workers were. Finally, the value of property was asserted. This was of direct interest to shopkeepers and even those who had savings; it also attracted clerks and others who simply hoped to own property in the future.

Politics

The attachment to middle-class values influenced the political behavior of the lower middle class, and in many instances the classes supported the same political parties. The lower middle class was a bulwark of political conservatism or moderation in the period. It cultivated political behavior that would seem respectable in middle-class terms, that would be distinct from working-class political patterns, and that was firm in defense of the values of property and order.

The political interests of the two classes were not identical, however, and in France and Austria they supported different parties. In France shopkeepers were more radical than the leaders of big business. They supported the republic more firmly and with elements of the peasantry supplied the principal backing of the Radical Party, which developed in the 1890s. The French lower middle class had an old tradition of supporting the political left, and it continued its attachment to democratic political institutions and hostility to the church. Nevertheless, even in France the concerns of the class remained socially conservative. It wanted no tampering with the freedom of property, and it resisted government measures that might lead to heavier taxation.

The Austrian lower middle class, which gained the vote in 1882, quickly turned toward the new Christian Social Party, which won clear majorities in Vienna by 1895 and in the whole country by the 1900s. The upper middle class abhorred this party, with good reason, and continued to vote for liberal groupings; it actually preferred the

socialists to the Christian Social Party. The lower middle class, unlike its French counterparts and unlike the Austrian middle class,
had no liberal tradition. And it grew increasingly resentful of big
business, which the liberals supported; its hostility was heightened
by the fact that, as in Germany, most artisans regarded themselves
as part of the lower middle class, but still detested industrial capitalism. So the lower middle class supported a party that attacked big
business, promised to protect the artisans and the "little man," and
blasted the Jews and foreign capitalists as exploiters. Once in power
in Vienna, the party did make life easier for the lower middle class
by taking control of the public utilities and reducing their rates
and by various social welfare measures. Here was an interesting
point: the middle class tended to resist welfare programs, and so
did the lower middle class in France, where shopkeepers feared
taxation; but the support for the Christian Social Party in Austria
and for the employes' unions in Germany showed that the central
European lower middle class welcomed government action so long
as it offered real protection for the class and so long as it was undertaken by an antisocialist party. The political behavior of the Austrian
lower middle class also showed that the class was not wedded to
middle-class politics, that it could turn against the middle-class
economy. Even here it was politically conservative and certainly
antilabor, but its conservatism was a new variety.

Everywhere, the lower middle class had some distinctive political
and economic grievances. Attempts to develop essentially bourgeois
patterns of behavior were difficult for the class. The goal of respectable housing, for example, was hard to maintain with the slender
earnings of clerks or secretaries, and housing costs were rising
significantly in most cities as crowding became more intense.

Many of the economic goals of the lower middle class were more
appropriate to the earlier industrial period than to the end of the
century. Ideals of economic individualism and competition, for example, were current within the lower middle class at the very time
that industrial leaders were developing collective ownership and
trying to limit rivalry. And direct competition by big business made
conditions for lower-middle-class property owners more difficult in
many cases. The economic situation seemed hostile to lower-middle-
class interests in various ways.

This did not lead to direct political protest except to a degree in

Austria. The lower middle class tried to preserve its respectability and interest in social order, and a sweeping protest against big business would be against the middle class itself, a group on the whole venerated by the lower middle class. Furthermore, the class was not radically discontented. It was gaining in numbers and position; it was interested in individual improvements in status and confident that these could be attained. The individualism of the lower middle class was hostile to formal, separate class organizations. Many clerks and others were too new to their position to have developed a clear sense of common concern with shopkeepers or to have acquired any organizational ability. As with factory labor earlier, the newness of much of the lower middle class impeded definite action in the class interest. Nevertheless, the discontent and economic difficulties of the class, the rapid and confusing change in numbers and in types of work within the class, did find some expression.

Signs of Grievance

The lower middle class was unusually attracted to nationalism after 1870. The relative newness of the class and its lack of established loyalties encouraged receptivity to the nationalist urgings of the schools, the military, and the popular press. A substantial segment of the class was directly employed by the national state. Nationalism made sense in terms of many lower-middle-class values. It was clearly respectable and was preached by many members of the middle class and even the aristocracy. It opposed the internationalism of working class socialism. Nationalism provided a great deal of interest and satisfaction but in a socially acceptable way. Accounts of national power thrilled people who were somewhat concerned about their personal status, for national greatness seemed to rub off on individual citizens and gave them a sense of belonging to a higher unity. Reports of imperial conquests were satisfying demonstrations of the superiority of the national civilization, and they made exciting reading for people whose jobs were often rather uneventful. Finally, certain forms of nationalism could even be used to express some of the specific grievances of the lower middle class. The class was not alone in its growing enthusiasm for nationalism and imperialism; all elements of society shared it in some degree.

The lower middle class was, however, the class most clearly associated with its values.

The new nationalism of the lower middle class, on the continent particularly, often manifested itself in the form of anti-Semitism. Jews, quite simply, were not part of the nation. They were racially different and therefore subversive. Anti-Semitism was not peculiar to the lower middle class, for it spread to segments of the middle class and elsewhere, but it did have peculiar value for the lower middle class. As with nationalism generally, it seemed to support the respectable status of the class. By pointing to an inferior group, by attaching oneself to the true nation, a shopkeeper or a clerk could show his superior social position. Furthermore, Jews could be blamed for much that was disturbing to the lower middle class. The prominence of Jews in finance and as owners of department stores made them a target for the growing hostility to big business. Many shopkeepers in Paris, for example, belonged to the Merchants' Antisemite Leagues, which worked to limit the commercial competition of Jews. That was a way to express economic grievance in the eminently respectable form of interest in racial purity, and without attacking the whole upper middle class.

Intense nationalism generally and anti-Semitism in particular occasionally led elements of the lower middle class to precipitate disorder. A number of riots occurred over imperialist crises, such as those in London in 1898 over Fashoda and Rome in 1911 over the issue of conquering Tripoli. These riots were stirred up by the excitement of the popular press and were often led by professional nationalist agitators; but they attracted a certain number of shopkeepers and clerks, who provided the bulk of the popular support for the agitation. The large riots over the Dreyfus case in Paris in 1898 drew more participation from the lower middle class than from any other group except students, and many students were of lower-middle-class backgrounds. The initial riots over Zola's letter claiming that Dreyfus was innocent were spurred by the desire to protect the honor of the national army against an officer assumed to be traitorous partly because he was a Jew. The popular press was uniformly hostile to Dreyfus, and some anti-Semitic papers, such as Drumont's *La France Juive*, called for riots. Students answered this call first, but they were not alone. Riots in January and again in October called forth many grocers, pastry-shop owners, waiters, and small investors in stocks and bonds. Along with medical and law students, these groups provided most of the participants in the riots and drew most of the arrests. This sort of nationalist and anti-Semitic agitation was not typical of the lower middle class as a whole. Only a minority participated, largely in capital cities, and only infrequently. Most members of the class were content to work individually for acceptable status and material well-being and supported nationalist causes only with their votes and their reading. Nevertheless, the rioting did express an important current of discontent within the class, which found an outlet in vigorous nationalism.

THE WORKING CLASSES

Composition

Despite the numerical decline of the artisans and the displacement of some whole crafts by machines, artisans still formed an important part of the labor force. Some crafts, particularly in the building trades, were in greater demand than ever before; and some countries, notably France, maintained an unusually large number of artisans in small firms and luxury production. Many artisans retained the special traditions of the class or developed distinctive reactions to the new threat of mechanization. After 1881 artisan conventions in Austria regularly called for restoration of the guilds. German guilds continued as social organizations. Many artisans resisted the organized, disciplined quality of working class protest. Most did not protest at all, but those who did often preferred local, individualistic forms. Anarchist movements drew much of their small support from watchmakers in Switzerland and artisans in northern Italy, whereas they almost never attracted factory labor. In no country was there a total merger of artisans and factory workers by 1914.

In most industrial countries, however, artisans were vastly outnumbered by factory and unskilled labor. And artisan conditions increasingly resembled those of other workers. The introduction of new machinery in artisan shops changed the nature of skills and curtailed traditional apprenticeship. The employment of construction workers and other artisans by large contractors created obvious similarities between them and the rest of the labor force. And many artisan organizations realized that they needed the numerical support of the whole working class. Artisans had ceased to exist as a fully independent social class. Many of them attached themselves to the lower middle class, but in western Europe the majority identified with the working class.

The great working-class growth at the end of the century was in the ranks of transportation workers and factory labor. Booming trade required more railroad labor and more dockers than ever before. Heavy industry increased its employment, and new branches of production such as the chemical industry recruited a substantial force of workers. Only in textiles did the number of workers decline significantly. By the 1890s a third of the population of Germany and England was in the industrial labor force, the largest single segment of the lower classes in the most advanced industrial nations. Elsewhere, of course, in Russia and even in France, the working class had not attained this size, but it was increasing steadily. From the standpoint of numbers alone, the advance of factory labor in the period was a notable social fact.

Conditions of Life

In the more developed countries the rate of growth of industrial labor was declining by the end of the century. Gains continued, but they no longer significantly increased the percentage share of factory workers in the total population. The steady advances in production did not require massive numbers of new workers; greater mechanization and the transfer of workers from more stagnant industries, such as textiles, were sufficient. In other words, the formation of the working class was now roughly complete. The majority of the industrial labor force were the sons and grandsons of factory workers. This was truest, of course, in Great Britain, where industry had developed most extensively at an early date. By the 1890s it was also true of Germany, Belgium, and even France.

The greater maturity of the working class had significant social effects. It meant that most members of the class had some sense of tradition in their work and residence. They were accustomed to the factories and to the cities. Instability remained, of course. Many workers changed jobs frequently as crises struck their factories, or they sought some temporary relief from the harshness or boredom of a given job. Some workers floated from city to city in quest of a change. Most factory workers, however, were stable employees who led stable lives. The pace of work could no longer surprise men whose parents had worked in the factories and who had worked there themselves from a young age. Equally important, the city was no longer a strange environment. There was no major tendency now among workers to try to return to the countryside; many workers in fact shunned rural life as backward and unattractive.

Many of the earlier symptoms of disorientation disappeared or declined. Individual acts of grievance such as thefts in the plant were reduced. Drinking of hard liquor decreased, although the taverns remained important social centers for people whose apartments were small and who enjoyed the company of their fellows. Family life became more stable. The establishment of civil marriage procedures provided a useful alternative to religious ceremonies and marriage rates increased. Many workers did not possess the middle-class ethic on marriage and sexual morality. They were more tolerant of immorality, even when they themselves remained faithfully attached to their family. The reading, including the newspapers, of the class more often dealt with themes of sex and immorality than did the reading of the middle class. Working-class leaders, as in France, frequently had mistresses and displayed them publicly without losing their followings. Within families sexual pleasure was more openly and possibly more frequently sought than was true in the middle classes. At the same time, the confusion of the earlier period with regard to family life was substantially reduced, and a stable family structure was quite generally developed.

The position of workers was altered not only by growing adjustment to factory life, but also by the significant expansion of material standards. The working class, including artisans in the leading trades, benefited from the rising real wages in the last decades of the nineteenth century. Improvements in diet increased the physical vigor of most workers, as did the general decline of major disease. Better housing made life more pleasant and contributed to the stabilization of family patterns. Many workers sought better housing and lower rents by moving to the suburbs and commuting to the cities on the newly extended railroad, subway, and tram services. Workers devoted most of their new resources to fairly immediate pleasures and recreations. They spent more on better food than on better housing. They flocked to theaters and music halls, sports events, and after 1900 to motion pictures. The desire for enjoyment was a significant aspect of the lives of the working class in this period and colored the class demands for more leisure and more money to improve the opportunities for recreation. There were still important differences in standard of living within the working class. Textile workers earned far less than labor in heavy industry. Construction workers had relatively high wages but continued to suffer from substantial seasonal unemployment. Unemployment also reduced the standards of many dockers and truckers to low levels. Nevertheless, the general trend of rising wages affected almost all categories, and the desire to use these gains for enjoyment, for compensation for the strain of work, spread widely also.

Workers benefited during this period from other material improvements. Welfare legislation provided new protection in the factories and in other aspects of life. Safety and hygiene conditions were inspected. Hours of work were limited for women and children. Other welfare plans provided insurance against illness, accidents, and old age for many workers. Workers furnished the bulk of the contributions to these plans but derived considerable benefits from them, especially in Germany where the programs were first established. Certain categories of workers, such as miners, received an unusually high level of government protection. The risk and difficulty of their work and the fact that their union organization was particularly active combined to promote growing government interest in their lot.

Municipal governments set up minimum standards for housing and food markets. Many private companies increased their own welfare programs in the period. Mining and metallurgical concerns often had systems of pensions and medical care, housing, and recreational programs and facilities. Railroad companies, in addition to the usual fringe benefits, provided free trips for their employes. As before, the larger firms offered the widest variety of assistance, but after 1870 the number and size of the large firms were far greater than ever before and their resources correspondingly more abundant. They contributed to the well-being of workers and their dependents and, along with public programs, provided an important supplement to the earning levels of labor.

Aided by legislation, working conditions improved during the period. New safety devices were invented, and direct contact of workers with the operation of machines was reduced. Technical improvements also lightened the physical burden of many kinds of work. A combination of laws, technical changes, and humanitarian concern of some employers eliminated the employment of children under twelve, except in newly industrializing nations.

Most important, the length of the work day declined. Hours of work varied considerably in different regions and in different industries. In Britain workers had Saturday afternoon and all of Sunday free. This "English week" was eagerly but on the whole unsuccessfully sought by continental labor. Sundays were increasingly protected by law, a measure beneficial especially to artisans such as bakers and barbers. The number of workdays in the year declined on the average, and some highly skilled workers, such as electricians and railroad employes, received annual vacations. The workday itself was seldom extended beyond twelve hours. Most construction workers labored only ten hours a day and some only nine. Workers in heavy industry seldom worked more than ten hour days, and many countries legislated eight-hour days for miners during the period. Textile labor had longer hours on the whole, but even there changing customs and new laws reduced hours to ten by 1914. Quite commonly then, workers had more leisure than ever before. This contributed to the growing elaboration of their recreational interests. It also contributed to their new activities in other fields.

The various improvements in material conditions of the working class obviously reduced some of the worst pressures and made life more pleasant. They also encouraged the development of new interests in material acquisitions. Religious concerns faded still further, although a minority of workers retained active religious faith. Christian, particularly Catholic, unions formed in the period to hold worker interest in religion, drew a membership of over fifty thousand in Germany, somewhat less in France. A number of workers still attended church and contributed to religious institutions. However, the general decline was clear. In Britain, Methodism had developed expressly to appeal to the lower classes, but workers began to drift away from it around midcentury. The new opportunities for material advance seemed more meaningful than concern for the future life, and secular education encouraged doubts about aspects of traditional Christian doctrines. New loyalties, to class and to nation, competed with religious concerns. Secular unions and parties provided substitutes for churches as social centers and even offered some ritual satisfactions. These groups had the merit of being under some working-class control, which most churches still were not, and they focused on the material problems which were moving to the fore-front of the interests of the class.

The growing materialism of the class was apparent in the willing-ness of many to work long extra hours for overtime pay. There was a desire for more leisure, but, on the whole, it could not com-pete with the desire for higher earnings. Many workers sought lower hours not only for lighter work loads but also for greater opportunity to earn overtime pay. Union leaders, who usually agitated to reduce the hours of work, struggled in vain against the desire of many workers for overtime. Certainly the earlier subsistence mentality of many workers was now gone. Absenteeism among better-paid operatives, who wanted to use excess income in the form of leisure, was a thing of the past. There was an interest in shorter hours and in reduction of the pace of work. There were many pro-tests, for example, against the system of pay by piece of production rather than by hours. Most workers felt that this system was manipu-lated by employers to make the labor force work too hard to complete the piece, and they wanted the system replaced by hourly or daily pay. On the other hand, in almost all demands of this sort they insisted equally on maintenance of existing levels of wages despite reduc-tions in hours or in output. When laws curtailed the hours of work for various categories of the labor force, workers demanded that pay not be reduced as a result. And the most vigorous and general action by the working class aimed at the raising of wages. This was the clearest and most important expression of the new material expecta-tions of the class.

Discontent

The new expectations produced something of a paradox. Although material standards were improving, particularly before 1900, the level of discontent on the part of the working class was constantly increasing. In the earlier period factory labor had taken collective action only infrequently. The action had been confined, with very few exceptions, to years of economic disaster, when conditions fell below even subsistence levels. By the end of the century this trend had been almost completely reversed. Worker demands were highest at times of rising or at worst stagnant wages. In years of crisis labor agitation declined, for high levels of unemployment meant that it was risky to court the displeasure of employers. Falling wages made it difficult for workers to raise funds for collective action or to take time off from work to conduct any sort of agitation. The membership of working-class organizations almost invariably fell off in times of crisis. Discontent might be high, but it was expressed only when conditions improved, and then it was directed not simply at restoring old standards, but at attaining absolute improvements. This goal motivated several important forms of working-class action after 1870.

One of the earliest and most pervasive new organizations in the later nineteenth century was the cooperative movement. Consumer and credit cooperatives spread widely among the working class. Some of the early efforts, like the British Rochdale movement, which was initiated in 1844, were intended to remake society. It was felt that cooperative principles of buying and production would prove sounder than the system of capitalist ownership and would gradually, peacefully replace that system. Those hopes were not fulfilled and were abandoned within a decade. From the first, regardless of their doctrines, the cooperatives concentrated on wholesale purchasing, which lowered the price of food and other items, and on protection of the quality of goods.

After a period of very limited membership the cooperative movement spread to large numbers of people in various classes. In Britain and Germany two million people belonged to consumer cooperatives by 1900, and the groups continued to spread. Cooperatives developed considerable membership in the Scandinavian countries and in Holland; even in France, where resistance to organization was widespread, consumer cooperatives boasted 850,000 members by 1900. Cooperatives lowered prices and improved the quality of goods and also gave workers some experience in organization by urging membership participation in elections and administrative duties. Cooperatives promoted a realization of the power of combination, which was to typify other efforts of the working classes.

The cooperative movement was the mildest of the movements in which the working class participated during this period. Its development had important features in common with the other movements. The labor movements were intended for the lower classes alone and relied on the economic and organizational power of large numbers of people. They typically began with some general hope for a new economic system, based on the elimination of capitalism. The initial ideal attracted few workers, although they were often intensely devoted; but the immediate and substantial material benefits of the labor movements attracted millions. Larger ideals were not totally abandoned, but they faded in importance with the development of greater interest in immediate gains.

The Development of Worker Unions and Parties

The rise of the socialist and union movements were the most important outgrowths of the new interests and abilities of the working class. They had great impact on society generally; for the first time factory labor made more than occasional impressions on the consciousness of the ruling groups. Both movements developed strong organization and a vigorous sense of purpose. Both constituted a major departure for factory labor. Workers were unaccustomed to political interests and rights and were unskilled in developing permanent organizations. With help from other classes, they developed those skills as their education increased and their resources expanded. Their material expectations provided important motives to participate in movements of action. Nevertheless, neither movement ever included the class as a whole. Only a minority of workers joined unions during this period. A far larger number came to vote for socialist parties, but by no means all did so.

A substantial number of workers, including many women, actually resisted socialism and the unions. Some were intimidated by the opposition of employers and others to these movements. Others sought a rather middle-class respectability without ever rising out of the working class. They went to church, worked regularly and hard, and saved their money if they could. For such workers specifically working-class movements were irrelevant and risky. If they voted, it was for conservative parties. If they joined a union, they picked yellow or religious unions pledged not to strike and backed by the favor and funds of employers. In some cases they did active battle with their more radical brethren, serving as strike breakers or goons to break up union and socialist meetings. More commonly, they simply ignored the ferment among the rest of the working class. No picture of the great agitation conducted by workers in the period should create an impression of uniform motive and method. Fear, a desire for respectability, satisfaction with the status quo, even gratitude to employers created an overriding desire for stability and calm in many workers and artisans. Workers in isolated towns and factories were largely ignorant of the activities of their class; it was not always easy, even now, to spread information. Movements of protest and agitation did not, then, touch the whole working class; and the most active efforts involved only a minority.

Even the workers who espoused new political and economic organizations were involved only gradually and, at first, on the initiative of outside leadership. More than twenty years passed between the foundation of a socialist movement in Germany in the 1860s, and the development of mass support for it. In the meantime, workers voted for traditional, rather conservative parties. These parties made increasing efforts to offer platforms appealing to the workers but did not develop elaborate programs for them. In France a socialist movement began in the 1860s but was firmly established only in the late 1870s. There support came more quickly. The working classes, particularly the artisans, had considerable political experience and interest. Even so, the movement gained only gradual headway among the masses. A substantial British labor party was founded in the 1890s; it too expanded steadily, but most workers ignored its appeal for over two decades.

The union movements also caught on only gradually. Although artisan unions made fairly steady gains in Britain after 1850 and included some elements of skilled labor, massive industrial unions developed only in the late 1880s. French and German unions rose significantly only in the 1890s at least ten years after unions had been legalized and initial unionization programs launched. It took time for workers to learn the advantages of positive, collective action. It took time for them to become acquainted with the literature of the new organizations and to shake off their traditional apathy and hopelessness.

Both socialism and the unions were initially brought to the workers by outside leaders. Socialist parties were almost uniformly led by members of the middle class. Guesde and Jaurès in France, Liebknecht in Germany, Turati in Italy were all lawyers or journalists with advanced education. The Labour Party in Britain had more working-class leadership, but its ideology, which developed only gradually, came from the eminently middle-class Fabian society. Middle-class leaders alone had the understanding of doctrine and organization that could impel a political movement. Even anarchism was founded by a Russian military officer, Bakunin, not by a worker. Members of the working class developed important subsidiary roles in the socialist movements as local deputies and administrators. In a few cases, such as that of the artisan Bebel in Germany, they even rose to national prominence, but generally the socialist leadership remained in middle-class hands. Workers influenced the movement, supported the movement; but they did not found it.

Unions, too, had important assistance outside the factory labor force. Again, dissident members of the middle class played some role. Middle-class socialist leaders, particularly in Germany and Austria, played a vital role in stimulating the initial union movement. In Britain one of the first strikes by unskilled labor, a strike by female watch workers, was instigated by the middle-class reformer, Mrs. Besant. One of the early leaders of French unionism, Fernand Pelloutier, was of middle-class origin—his family was traditionally monarchist—and was initially a radical journalist by profession.

The guidance of artisans played a key role in the union movement. Artisans were a class that had maintained an ability to organize. Most artisan unions were initially uninterested in rousing industrial labor, but a minority of leaders provided vital guidance. Two agitators from the Amalgamated Society of Engineers in Britain, Tom Mann and John Burns, helped organize one of the first strikes and unions among unskilled workers and continued to play a major role in British union formation after 1889. French leaders of artisan background, such as the shoemaker Victor Griffuelhes and numerous construction workers, dominated the largest union movement of France. Unions in the Balkans were introduced by typographers, often from Austria or Italy; they spread only slowly to new factory labor.

Once the movement toward industrial unions was initiated, many workers formed their own organizations. Miners, with their tradition of collective action, developed solid unions quite early. Nevertheless, in the industrial-union movement the first impulse was commonly provided from outside the factory class. Unions were closer to workers than were socialist parties, in terms of activities and leadership. Their goals seemed more real, and they commanded more active support. Unions, however, like the political movements, required significant initial assistance from people more skilled in doctrine and in organization. They needed time to win massive support, though often less time than working-class parties. Their ultimate importance within the working class should not obscure their novelty or their difficulties.

Early Socialism

Before the 1880s labor movements were extremely limited and involved few members of the working class. Socialist parties existed in most industrial areas. They maintained a strong interest in doctrinal purity although the doctrines differed from country to country. There were usually rivalries between Marxist and other groups, which encouraged attention to ideologies. Most socialist leaders were intellectuals, devoted to ideas. Those ideas were of great importance. Marxist doctrine, particularly, was to guide many socialist parties for decades. It attracted a number of articulate workers, many of whom became leaders in spreading socialism. Yet the stress on doctrine drew only a tiny minority of the working class, which gave its support to socialist parties only when they developed pragmatic interests as well.

The earliest socialist movements began in France and Germany. Marxist groups formed in both countries in the 1860s, but they drew only a few thousand followers. They emphasized the need for class warfare and revolution to rid the working class of capitalist control. A proletarian dictatorship could then install a perfect society based on freedom and equality. In both countries non-Marxist socialist groups competed for working-class support, and intense doctrinal quarrels developed among the factions. Outside of France and Germany only rudimentary socialist parties were established before 1890. Limitations of suffrage and of industrialization in Austria and Italy confined socialist support to a minority of the middle class that wished to protest the actions of the government. These people were often sympathetic to the workers, but their interest was a bit abstract and their approach to worker problems doctrinaire. Efforts to establish a Marxist group in Britain failed almost totally. A few intellectuals and others were attracted, but the working class remained untouched.

This early period of socialism was not directly decisive or important for the working class. Parties and doctrines had been established that tried above all to win the working class to their banners. The idea of remaking society and the state to correspond to worker interests, the intense desire for economic equality, the bitter condemnations of the present system and its miseries—all these were potentially popular doctrines. And they attracted during this period a group of leaders whose doctrinal devotion could lead to vigorous activity. An important, though small, second echelon of local working-class support had been developed. From this nucleus more and more workers could be drawn to the movement. As this occurred, however, the movement itself would change. The revolutionary, doctrinal fervor of a minority of the labor force would remain; but it could not be transmitted to the class more generally without major change.

Early Unions

The socialist parties were not the only form of working-class activity in the period before 1890. There was a significant development of unions as well. The socialist groups themselves attempted to establish some unions. Before 1870 both the Marxist and the Proudhonist movements in France developed more as unions than as political parties, although their orientation was highly political. These unions, which largely died in the repression of the Commune, attracted some Paris artisans and construction workers, some textile labor in Rouen, and scattered other workers. In Germany the Lassalleans tried in 1868 to form unions to support their political efforts. Interestingly, the leaders felt that some union movement, working for immediate improvements in conditions, was needed to attract significant worker backing. But the unions were regarded by many leaders as betrayals of Lassallean purity, and they drew only 35,000 members. German Marxists also formed small unions. This was done primarily under the leadership of Bebel, himself an artisan, again from a realization that socialist doctrine by itself was too abstract to appeal to workers. In the 1880s French Marxists showed some interest in unions, although as usual they feared that unions might spoil the ideological purity of the party by working for limited reforms. Generally, a specifically socialist impulse was not significant in the union movement before 1890. Only in Germany was it of major importance, largely because there was no strong alternative movement other than the mild Catholic unions, but even in Germany mass unions developed only after the Marxists modified their approach. Elsewhere, a substantial union movement arose independent of socialist direction.

There were in western Europe a large number of unions of artisans and skilled workers before 1890. These unions were strongest and most extensive in Britain, but they had arisen elsewhere as well and exhibited a number of common features. They were organized rather strictly by craft. This coincided with artisan tradition and enabled the unions to deal with employers of labor as homogeneous groups with certain common interests and problems. Many artisan unions were confined to a given locality, and few craft unions in France and Germany had national affiliations. In Germany the Hirsch-Duncker movement was of national scope, but had attracted only 66,000 members by 1892. In France the moderate Barbaret organization of the 1870s was a congeries of scattered artisan groups. Only in Britain were national organizations at all strong. There groups of engineers, carpenters, and other skilled workers had professional leadership in national movements, and this leadership had real power of direction. In France some national units did develop, as with the printers, but later and less completely than was the case in Britain.

Local interests and jealous guarding of craft lines prevented much cooperation among artisan unions and led to a great proliferation of individual organization. There was a loose linkage among the major unions in Britain in local trades union councils, which provided forums for discussion of common problems; the London council served somewhat as a national organ. In 1868 a more formal national Trades Union Council was established to deal especially with the political problems of the union movement, but it too remained a loose body; the major power rested in the craft organizations. In France labor exchanges, the Bourses du Travail, were formed in the 1880s as discussion centers for local unions, particularly craft groups. The Bourses had a national organization that was quite revolutionary, and many locals became centers of agitation. Some, however, served the intentions of many moderate craft unions, and in any case the craft groups had almost total effective autonomy.

The focus of the artisan unions was on the craft and usually on the locality. Generally, craft unions had little concern with other unions and no concern for the working class as such. They sought gains for themselves and made no effort to organize the far larger mass of unskilled and factory labor. Because of their superior tradition, resources, and education artisans were capable of developing considerable power in their trade, which they did not care to jeopardize by more extensive efforts.

The purpose of the craft unions was to win immediate material improvements for their members. They shunned politics, for the most part, as irrelevant to their function. The British movement even opposed the extension of the suffrage to workers. The Trades Union Council only gradually developed a political concern, based primarily on the need to resist legislation hostile to union formation and activity. Most French artisan unions were too small to have any political influence, and they made no attempt to develop any. The craft unions also opposed any revolutionary sentiment or effort. They accepted the existing system and simply tried to make gains within it. They avoided violence, avoided even strikes where possible. Their methods were designed to be respectable and calm.

Many unions developed benefit funds to help members in sickness, old age, and unemployment. Some French unions provided travel funds for members so that artisans could move from an area of unemployment to an area of demand for workers. Many unions, especially in France, had only tiny funds, for artisans were not always willing to pay substantial dues. Others, such as the French printers' union, were able to offer subsistence support to any member during the first weeks of unemployment or illness. Between 1851 and 1889 the British Amalgamated Society of Engineers paid out £3,000,000 in benefits—while it spent only £88,000 on strikes. The old principle of mutual aid was one of the main interests of the crafts union. It included material aid but also libraries, some technical courses, and pamphlets urging temperance and morality.

The craft unions also tried to bargain with employers directly to obtain collective agreements. They wanted collective contracts for members of a given craft in a given locality that would guarantee a minimum wage for each type of work, a maximum level of hours, extra pay for overtime and travel. They attempted also to regulate apprenticeship in their craft in order to make sure that youths obtained proper training and to limit the number of new craftsmen. The desire for collective protection, for defense of the skill, and for limitation of membership continued old artisan traditions. These demands could, on occasion, win important benefits for the union members, for many craft unions were successful in establishing collective contracts.

On occasion unions resorted to strikes to press for gains or to defend established positions. The artisan unions used the strike only sparingly and tried to prevent undue violence; they viewed the strike only as a means to impel negotiation. Usually they provided funds for their strikers so that the strike would be popular and so that there would be no misery to induce violence.

The rate of strikes by craft unions in this period was low. The unions were usually willing to negotiate peacefully on the basis of the importance of their members' skills and the unexpressed possibility of a strike. They could endure setbacks in negotiations. Their members were not impoverished, they often were unwilling to risk loss of income and the displeasure of employers by striking, and they were reluctant to jeopardize the benefit funds of the unions. There were a few major strike movements by craft federations, such as that in Britain during the depression of the 1870s. But many unions never struck at all, and most did so only with reluctance and for very specific purpose. The craft-union movement was an important expression of the position and traditions of skilled workers at the end of the nineteenth century.

Skilled workers were, of course, only a minority of the labor force as a whole. In Britain they represented at most a quarter of the total working class. Furthermore, many skilled workers were content to strive individually for gains and ignored the union movement altogether. The craft unions, then, were small, though extremely significant in western Europe. But the artisan-union tradition did not die after 1880, and it provided an example and some leadership to industrial unions. The moderate craft approach was still favored by most skilled workers. New local unions were formed in France, and the British unions extended their membership. The structure and purpose of artisan unions spread to new regions, such as Italy and the Balkans. When typographers in Bosnia, for example, established their union in the 1900s, they ignored the rest of the labor movement and sought a collective contract, without striking, that would set minimum levels of pay and a nine-hour day; they obtained such a contract in 1905. The craft-union movement remained important and even spread as the opportunity and advantages of unionization became increasingly apparent.

Nevertheless, the most dynamic union movements departed to some extent from the craft approach. The factory labor force was incapable of maintaining the calm of skilled workers, and it could not seek exactly the same types of gains. Many artisans, particularly in the Latin countries, themselves developed new forms of union organization and approach in this period. Beginning in the 1880s, both in the political and economic spheres, a new wave of working-class action arose and expanded steadily until World War I and beyond. It spread beyond the boundaries of the mature industrial countries into eastern and southern Europe. The awakening of the workers created organizations and doctrines that dominated the class from that time onward.

The Bases of Worker Agitation

The causes of the increase of working-class movements included greater resources, leisure, and education of the labor force. Dedicated propagandists, though handicapped by lack of funds, worker apathy, and government hostility, had been at work for over a decade. Personal visits to working-class areas proved particularly important, for workers were still unaccustomed to rely on the written word.

Legal changes were also of vital significance in developing mass movements among the workers. These changes resulted from extension of suffrage, for politicians sought the favor of the lower classes; but they largely preceded massive pressure by the workers themselves. Limitations on the socialist parties were largely removed. Germany dropped the legal ban on socialism in 1890. Italy, after arresting many socialists during the riots of the 1890s, developed greater tolerance in the next decade. Only in eastern Europe was a prohibition maintained, and there a formal socialist movement did not fully develop. In Russia socialists operated primarily underground and from abroad and had only limited support. Elsewhere the removal of legal limitations on socialism was a vital factor in the spread of socialist parties.

Equally important was the elimination of major restraints on unions and strikes. France loosened the restrictions in the 1860s and removed them finally in 1884. In 1874 Britain repealed the laws making strikers liable to arrest. Germany withdrew similar limitations in 1881, and Belgium did so in 1868. There were still some legal barriers to the union movements. The British courts attacked the right to picket and the political activities of unions in the 1900s, and only after some difficulty were those rulings rescinded by legislation. French law forbade any interference with the right of individuals to go to work, which made it difficult for unions to compel obedience to strike calls. The result was frequent arrest of strikers and recurrent conflicts with police. Many workers still found it necessary to violate the law in their protest efforts. Nevertheless, the worst barriers had been removed, and this facilitated attack on the difficulties that remained. In combination with the new resources, motivation, and leadership of the working class, legal changes opened the way to the development of massive action by labor.

Worker Socialism

Socialist parties grew everywhere. The British Labour Party was formed in the 1890s to represent the working class specifically, although it cooperated with the Liberals to fight for welfare legislation and other government assistance to labor. On the continent socialist parties were larger than in Britain. France had more than a hundred socialist deputies by 1913; the German party was receiving almost a million and a half votes by the mid-1890s and four million by 1913. The Austrian socialist party rose to a similar position of strength, and socialist movements in Scandinavia, the Low Countries, and even Italy drew the support of increasing numbers.

Most of the continental socialist movements were Marxist, although some native traditions, such as the French, did persist. In Germany and Austria the socialists were characterized by tight organization and strict control from the top, after the pattern Marx himself had established in earlier stages of the movement. Elsewhere, in France, for example, there was a constant tendency to splintering within the movement, although a Marxist orientation was accepted by most socialists at least in theory.

Under Marxism the continental socialist parties rose to great prominence; they were supported by most of the working class and urged the abolition of capitalism by means of revolution and the establishment of a new working-class society. Without doubt, many workers found the existing economic and political system unacceptable. Many found the idea of a radically new society based on worker rule and on equality of wealth extremely attractive. Most workers had not developed their criticisms and hopes very explicitly, but they were certainly susceptible to conversion by Marxist leaders.

There is evidence, however, that hopes for revolution and for a future utopia were not dominant in the minds of most working-class supporters of Marxism. Those hopes continued to influence many leaders. This was particularly true in areas such as Russia, where government restrictions prevented the development of a regular party. Elsewhere, however, the socialist movement changed significantly as it developed mass support. These changes reflected the new position of the leaders of the movement and the interests of most supporters.

By the 1890s most socialist parties began to desire to work for reforms than revolution. In the 1880s a Possibilist party split from the Marxist movement in France, specifically renouncing revolution and proclaiming the possibility of reforms through parliamentary means. In Germany a bit later Eduard Bernstein stated that Marxist predictions of increasing poverty under capitalism were not true and that the revolutionary approach in general was inaccurate and needless. He too urged cooperation with middle-class parties for reform.

The socialist movements in general renounced these new doctrines, known formally as revisionism. Both the German and the French movements asserted the continued validity of Marxist teachings. In practice, however, socialist behavior became increasingly revisionist. German socialists worked primarily for new welfare measures and for political reforms, especially in the Prussian voting system, that would increase democracy. They talked of revolutionary Marxism, but they did nothing. In France, similarly, socialists such as Jaurès struggled to defend the republican form of government against attack. French socialists talked of the principles of the new society, but their efforts were increasingly bent toward welfare legislation, laws protecting unions and strikes, and other measures that would aid labor. A similar reformist approach developed in most continental countries.

Socialist leaders found that they could gain significant power for themselves and for the workers through the present system; revolution was not necessary. And the specific measures of reform that the parties advocated appealed to the working class. The labor force wanted the sort of welfare protection that was being developed, with socialist support, during the period. They wanted hours limiting laws and regulating safety measures in the plants. They wanted assistance in old age, illness, and accidents. The growing worker interest in socialism during the period was primarily the expression of the desire to use the government to bring material protection and greater dignity to the working class.

The workers felt the need for a political force that represented their interests alone; they were drawn away from older parties, just as they felt themselves separate from other classes; the reforms they sought were substantial. Their political discontent was high, but they did not work for revolution. In Britain their party was not even revolutionary in theory; on the continent it was, increasingly, revolutionary in theory alone. Only in Russia, where political participation was denied to the workers, did an active revolutionary tone remain.

The Unions: Socialist and Syndicalist Impulses

The industrial-union movement developed along with socialism and represented many of the same interests of the labor force. The union movement also was based on the collective power of masses of workers. Unlike the artisan unions, which relied on the force of skill and exclusivism, the new unions wanted to organize and direct masses of workers. Like socialism, the union movement represented a sense of class consciousness on the part of labor, a feeling of being separate from the rest of society, and a realization of common interests within the working class itself. Even more directly than the socialist efforts, unions attacked the middle class, or at least the employers of labor. The unions shared some of the revolutionary overtones of socialism; this was particularly true in France and Spain, although the type of revolution sought was rather different. Generally, however, the unions shared with socialism the desire to win immediate collective gains for the working class, to bring both greater material well-being and greater dignity. Finally, the union movement, along with socialism, resulted essentially from a vigorous desire for change on the part of the workers. This change did not have to be revolutionary, although many workers were not repelled by the idea of future risings. It was conceived largely in immediate, fairly practical terms—higher wages, shorter hours, more worker voice in the conditions of labor. A large minority of workers, at least, wanted major improvements quickly. Their votes for socialism and their action in unions both worked for this goal.

There were important direct links between socialist parties and unions in many countries. The union movement in Germany stemmed from groups set up by the socialists and retained friendly ties with the party, although it moved away from close association. Many industrial unions in France, such as the largest mining union, the textile federation, and the railroad union, had close links with the socialists; some union leaders were also socialist deputies. In Britain the unions were somewhat suspicious of the Labour Party but gradually came to support it. The links between unions and parties were based on common interest in reform. Socialist parties could help protect unions against hostile legislation and could press for legislative gains, such as legal limits on hours, that had the same purpose as much union action.

Nevertheless, the union movements had a significantly different approach from the socialist parties. Their methods were economic, not political. They relied on their ability to supply aid through collective funds, on their bargaining power with employers, and on the ultimate economic weapon, the strike. Their arena of action was clearly different from that of socialism, even though their fundamental impulse was similar. In Germany the union movement did not prosper in the period of direct socialist control. During the 1890s the unions had only 350,000 members—a fraction of the socialist electorate. As a result, the unions gradually broke away and developed their own goals and methods; their break was made formal in the Mannheim agreement of 1906. When the unions did begin to support the immediate economic wishes of labor, they grew greatly in popularity. By 1906 they had 1,345,000 members. British unions were never under socialist party dominance, for they were created independently. Some French industrial unions had been founded under the socialist aegis but quickly broke away.

There was in France, in addition, an important union movement that was specifically hostile to political action and to the idea of government itself. This movement, known as syndicalism, influenced

some industrial workers and their leaders but was primarily confined to artisans. Most artisans were hostile to the syndicalist approach. They either belonged to no union or to a local union that
was separate from the major syndicalist groupings. French printers,
for example, resisted syndicalism except in Paris, where the syndicalist atmosphere was very heady. And certainly the major
industrial unions remained largely apart from the movement. Syndicalist organizers were unable to penetrate the area of greatest
concentration of miners, the north. The textile federation was
hostile to syndicalism, although some local unions proved sympathetic. The railroad federation was also hostile, although syndicalists
captured a small minority on occasion. Dockers stayed largely apart.
Most metallurgical workers were not organized at all. Syndicalism
should not, then, be confused with the majority of the labor force
in France, and particularly not with the industrial union movement.
Industrial workers, though occasionally touched by syndicalist ideas,
did not depart from the patterns of unionization developed in other
countries. Nevertheless, syndicalism was an important impulse in
the union movement. It dominated the major federation of unions in
France, the *Confédération générale du travail* (C.G.T.), of which
many industrial workers were members. It affected workers in Italy
and in Spain, particularly in the Barcelona region, where many
workers had been influenced by Andalusian peasant anarchism.
And it touched some union leaders elsewhere especially in Britain.

The syndicalist approach insisted on the necessity of abolishing
the capitalist system and government in any form. It advocated an
economic structure organized by local unions and run on principles
of cooperation and equality. All forms of exploitation and coercion
would be abolished. To achieve the new society, syndicalists looked
to the general strike as a weapon. Revolution was too difficult now
that the ruling classes had the might of modern military apparatus
behind them. But if all workers everywhere stopped work, capitalist society would collapse. Syndicalists preached the general
strike, planned for it, even tried to launch it on occasion. They
promoted such major strike movements as the May strikes of 1906
in France for an eight-hour day; hundreds of thousands of workers,
particularly artisans and particularly in Paris, participated in this
movement. Syndicalists also urged sabotage as a method by which
even small groups could damage the capitalist system. Acts of

sabotage were not infrequent, although they usually involved nothing more than cutting telephone wires.

Syndicalism had many bases for appeal, especially to groups that were radically dissatisfied with the reformist approach of socialist politics. It appealed to many union leaders because it stressed the importance of a union method, the strike, as the means of achieving the new society and the importance of local unions as the permanent basis for the new society itself. It appealed to many workers who found their lot unacceptable and who were engaged in bitter conflict with their employers. For example, although French metallurgical workers were generally untouched by syndicalism, they accepted syndicalist leadership and doctrine at least temporarily in some bitter strikes.

Primarily, however, syndicalism appealed to certain artisans. The principal syndicalist unions were composed of construction workers, bakers, workers in small machine shops, some printers—they were the backbone of the movement in France and Italy, countries where artisans were still numerous enough to maintain a separate sense of identity. In France they had an important tradition of revolution, especially in Paris, where the movement was strongest. They felt increasingly threatened, for the organization of their work was changing. Many were faced with new machines, like the cranes now used in construction work, and they feared displacement. They feared also the growing trend of organization in large firms, to which they were unaccustomed. They feared loss of skill, as traditions of apprenticeship steadily lost their force. These artisans saw in syndicalism a radical reassertion of their ideals of cooperation, organization in small units, and equality. Syndicalism represented one of the last expressions of these ideals in countries where factory industry was gaining but had not yet dominated the labor force. But like the artisan class, the movement was declining even before the war; the *Confédération générale du travail,* for example, progressively modified its syndicalist approach after 1908. And it largely died during the war, although workers in Barcelona maintained the movement into the civil war of the 1930s. It was an important, if limited, expression of artisan fervor that found outlet in major union movements and even in fairly formal doctrine.

Syndicalist ideas of general strike penetrated a number of union organizations. General strikes were attempted in Italy, Belgium,

Holland, and Sweden during the period, and British leaders seriously considered using the method. But many workers were repelled by the ideas; one of the reasons for the relatively small size of the French union movement was the fear of syndicalist doctrines. The majority of the members of unions in France did not belong to the C.G.T., and the majority of the C.G.T. was not syndicalist, although the syndicalists controlled the organization. British leaders might be touched by syndicalism, but union membership was not. The German federation specifically voted down the idea of general strike. Syndicalist ideas were in the air, they had influence. But they were not responsible for the main development of unions in the period or even for the most massive strikes that occurred. Far more significant was the rise of mass industrial unions for the first time.

Industrial Unions

Unions of factory workers developed by the 1890s and increased their membership steadily until 1914 and beyond. They arose first among the older categories of workers, in textiles and in mining especially. But the movement spread widely. In 1889 the successful London dockers' strike by thousands of unskilled workers made it clear that even the poorest elements of the labor force could organize with success, and the union movement caught fire and spread quickly to most types of workers in industry and transport. Large groups were formed in mining, metallurgy, railroads, docking, and among maritime workers. Textile unions grew in size, although they were limited by the greater dispersion of their workers in small firms and by the large numbers of women used.

Some of the early industrial unions fluctuated in size and success, as members feared to use the novelty of collective action against their employers. An unsuccessful strike, such as the railroad strike called in France in 1898, could drive membership down almost to nothing. Gradually the movement gained greater stability, although some workers still remained loosely attached. A vigorous loyalty to the union arose among much of the labor force that became a focus for social life as well as an instrument for economic action.

Industrial unions were huge. National mining federations had more than a hundred thousand members. By 1910 the French railroad union had 80,000 members. British unions collectively had more than a million members in the 1890s and more than three million a decade later. Germany had almost a million and a half members by 1906. France lagged a bit with a smaller labor force and smaller firms, but French unions had half a million members in the 1890s and twice that many a decade later. Newer industrial countries, such as Italy and Russia, where unions were briefly legal, developed a smaller but still substantial movement. Nowhere did unions embrace more than a minority of the labor force. Some workers objected to the movement because of its risk; others, who approved of unions but resented their dues, found they could benefit from union action without joining. However, the unions became the largest active organizations ever developed in Europe, and they reflected the attitudes of a large segment of the working class.

The industrial-union movement brought important changes to the organization of unions. Local unions embraced all types of workers in an industry, not just a single skill, and the locals were joined in a strong national federation within the industry. Sheer weight of membership was the key to union power. The industrial federations linked into a national union organization, which brought in many craft unions as well. The German and Austrian movements, influenced by the Marxist stress on organization and by the concentration of industry, were particularly centralized. Links among British unions, which centered on the Trades Union Congress, were looser but still significant, and individual industrial federations had considerable central power. In France the C.G.T. was founded in 1895 and embraced the *Bourses du Travail* movement in 1902. Never did it manage to include the majority of French unions, and its central powers were relatively weak. Too poor to lure many union managers, it relied on syndicalist tactics partly because it lacked the power to engage in more practical movements. Many industrial federations in France, however, had effective central organization with substantial funds and strong professional leadership. This was true of the northern miners' group, the railroad union, and the textile federation in the north. In Italy the *Confederazione generale del lavoro*, formed in the image of the C.G.T., was limited in power, but some federations had great central strength. Massive membership and considerable direction from the center characterized the industrial-union movement. The federations developed funds, information and propaganda programs, and a wide variety of professional services; and their organization tended to grow stronger as time passed.

Unions assumed numerous functions. Some arranged insurance and benefit schemes, after the pattern of the craft unions. Union locals served as social centers for their members, organizing dances, lectures, and picnics; unions were part and parcel of the personal lives of the members. Unions also tried to offer some educational facilities for workers, especially in the form of libraries. They hoped to teach workers their economic position and persuade them to pin their faith on union activities.

Most of all, however, the unions existed to improve the wages and working conditions of their members and to protect against abuses by employers. Unions formulated general goals for their efforts with the stress on better pay, lower hours, a reasonable pace of work, and recognition of the unions as bargaining units. They preached such goals to the workers in an effort to gain support. They urged them on employers and, where possible, bargained in behalf of their members. They requested government assistance in the realization of their goals in many instances and sometimes promoted programs of legislation on matters of hours and wages as well as more usual welfare measures.

Most important, the unions conducted strikes for their demands. They had far less compunction about striking than the earlier artisan unions had felt; and many artisan unions themselves struck with increasing frequency during this period. Many important unions were born in strikes; many union members regarded their organization primarily as a basis for battle with employers, so the rate, size, and duration of strikes increased tremendously in conjunction with union growth. Not all strikes involved unions, and in Russia a high rate of strikes was maintained even though unions were usually illegal. But strikes were easier when formal organization existed, for unions could provide some funds to support the strikers, could help formulate sensible goals, could time many strikes to coincide with the greatest opportunity for success. The wave of strikes that hit Europe after 1890, essentially a part of the union movement, was the best indication of the desire for action that had developed among many workers.

Strikes

The frequency of strikes increased steadily in most areas from 1890 until at least 1910. Russian workers struck 1,765 times between 1895 and 1904; and in 1905, as part of the revolution, there were 13,995 strikes recorded; after that the rate declined to an average of almost 2,000 strikes a year. In 1892 French workers struck 261 times against five hundred companies. Most of the strikes were small and local, often affecting only one company; but 50,000 workers were involved. By 1897 there were 356 strikes involving 68,875 workers; in 1904 there were 1,026 strikes involving 271,097 workers; in 1906 there were 1,309 strikes with 438,466 participants. Not only the number of strikes but also their size in terms of both numbers of workers and numbers of companies affected were increasing. Germany experienced an average of 2,000 strikes a year between 1902 and 1906. British labor maintained a similarly high rate, as did most industrial countries. There were major strikes also in Italy, Spain, and eastern Europe. Growing indoctrination by union and socialist leaders combined with a rising sense of the power of unions and of the working class to produce an ever greater willingness to strike. After 1900 the growing stagnation in wages, and in Britain an ominous level of unemployment, heightened the active discontent of many workers without robbing them of the means to strike. The result was the greatest wave of strikes Europe had ever known or was to know in later decades. All types of workers were involved —construction workers, various artisans, factory and transportation labor, unskilled ditch diggers. As usual, only a minority of the working class participated, but it was a large segment. The workers who struck, often many times, had an unprecedented sense of purpose and a level of grievance that would not easily yield.

Many strikes in crafts and in relatively dispersed industries such as textiles were quite local, often involving only one firm. At the other extreme there were efforts to organize strikes throughout a whole industry. Most of the major industrial countries saw at least one general strike by miners, railroad workers, and dockers on a national level. These were industries in which the unions were powerfully organized on a national basis. They were also dominated by gigantic firms, which could be fought most easily through an industry-wide effort. They were industries, finally, in which employer resistance was often intense, for big employers had a sense of their own power and a desire to avoid all interference with their management. In some cases they tried a new, more conciliatory approach to labor as the result of an initial major strike, but in others they maintained their opposition to any real concession. They represented, then, an obvious target for worker hostility and for generalized strikes. In other fields, such as the electrical and chemical industries, management showed a greater desire for harmony, and the level and size of strikes were correspondingly lower.

In addition to industry-wide strikes involving tens of thousands of workers, there were a number of efforts at generalized local strikes. Waves of strikes often touched almost all categories of workers in a region, sometimes in a whole country, as in Holland, Belgium, and Sweden. The result could be, again, a strike involving tens of thousands in cities as diverse as Paris and Sarajevo, both of which witnessed such movements in 1906. The generalized local strikes were often led by construction workers, who were active in strike movements but who found it difficult to organize national efforts in their trade because of differences in local conditions and a tradition of local autonomy in labor activities.

The duration of a strike varied greatly in accordance with conditions in the industry and in the area. Strikes might last less than a day, less than a week at most, if an employer yielded quickly or the workers had no means to hold out. Well-organized strikes more typically lasted several weeks, even months; a few dragged on for over a year. Duration depended on the intensity of the feeling of grievance, on the funds the strikers possessed, and on the employers' will to resist.

Methods of strikes differed also. Some began with a burst of angry attacks on employers and their property. This was particularly true in cases of unusual abuse, as in factory towns where employers had long maintained low material conditions and had also controlled the political activities of their workers. There was occasionally violence against new machines that seemed to threaten conditions; dockers, for example, dumped cranes in the water in several strikes. Strikes very often involved violence against nonstrikers to prevent them from working. Such violence was almost certain if employers imported special labor to break the strike. Many strikes also brought clashes with police who attempted to quell demonstrations or to help nonstrikers get to their jobs. But many strikes were conducted in complete calm. A quiet procession might occur, and some would gather outside the workplace to urge their fellows to join the effort. On the whole, however, the level of excitement in strikes was high. There was resentment against employers and sometimes against the government for any efforts to resist the strike. Violence did not always result, but there were usually angry murmurs and threats of violent action.

Strikers also sought public support, particularly the aid of shop-keepers who might extend credit. Very commonly, important segments of the middle class found the demands of the strikers just and provided moral and financial assistance. Funds were also contributed by other workers and by the union conducting the strike. Union leaders usually tried to keep their charges busy to avoid the twin evils of abandonment of the strike and violence, which might bring police repression. They led marches, made daily speeches, and held picnics and other social events.

Strikes were busy occasions in the lives of workers. They provided entertainment and considerable education in the purpose of working class effort. They could bring hardship as well. A few might be arrested, many might be fired. Prolonged strikes brought economic hardship, for few unions had the funds to offer more than bare subsistence. Only the excited sense of grievance impelled workers to strike despite the difficulties.

Strikes occurred for a wide variety of reasons. Sometimes they arose spontaneously, at the announcement of a change in working conditions, the introduction of a new machine, or after some real or fancied insults to a worker by an employer or a foreman. Many strikes, particularly the national ones, resulted from long planning. Most strikes arose from immediate material interest, such as hours or pace of work. The most common demand was for an increase in wages, whether the strikers were poor ditch diggers or highly paid skilled metallurgists. As workers gained experience, they often demanded a set, contractual wage covering the entire labor force in a given area and industry.

There were rare strikes directed at government legislation, particularly by categories of labor in which the government took most interest. In Russia the strikes of 1905 included major political demands for freedom of the press, universal suffrage, and an effective parliamentary regime; but such generalized demands were rare. However, the many strikes involved more than a protest over material conditions. Aided by their unions, workers sought dignity and control of their lives. Many strikers protested against acts that were insulting to one of their members on the job. Many insisted on employer recognition of the union as a means of obtaining greater equality between labor and management and an opportunity for workers to have some control over their conditions. The frequent insistence on written, general contracts expressed a similar interest in regulation in which workers would participate and which would bind the employers.

The development of unions and of strikes was, then, based on a dual sentiment, the desire for immediate improvements in conditions and the impulse to express the collective dignity of labor in forms that would give workers a greater sense of control over their lot. The combination of these sentiments gave the working class ample motive for their numerous efforts during this period.

Conclusion

The various forms of action of the working class had many fruitful results before 1914. Socialist parties helped encourage many legislative measures that aided the labor force; and they expressed clearly the power and distinctiveness of the class. Unions provided some internal aid for their members and offered an important social focus. Unions and strikes together produced many improvements in wages and other conditions. They were not the major force in determining wages, but they contributed now to wage policy.

Perhaps most important, the unprecedented levels of unionization and strikes gradually created a genuinely new relationship between management and labor in many cases. The insistence of numerous workers that they share in the determination of conditions was realized through collective bargaining. Decisions on wages, hours, and other matters became the products of joint discussions between employer and workers, represented by the union. Systems of collective bargaining covered a million British workers and one and a half million German workers by 1914. The system was not general; only a minority was affected. But this minority included such huge groups as coal miners in all the major mines of France. It included many artisans as well, far more than had previously been involved in collective agreements. This new and growing system of collective bargaining could lead to significant improvements in conditions and to a greater sense of worth and participation on the part of the workers involved. In many industries it reduced the rate of strikes, particularly after about 1910; for the level of grievance had lessened.

The rise of working-class activity was not simply a manifestation of new sentiments and abilities on the part of labor. It had effects on society more generally. It changed the political party structure and even the functions of governments. It influenced the organization and policies of industry. Workers did not obtain all they sought. Many strikes failed, and the majority won only a compromise settlement. The demands of the socialists went largely unheeded. But there had been major gains. The worker no longer felt powerless in his society. He had made important strides and had created organizations that promised further progress in the future.

THE MASSES AND SOCIETY

The activities of the various lower classes began during the period to have regular influence on the institutions of society as a whole. The new purchasing power, the sense of purpose, and the ability to take collective action had obvious general effects. Attention was given especially to the workers, for this was the largest and most vigorous group; but various programs were designed for all the lower classes. Organs of culture and recreation were created to cater to their wishes and interests. Local and national governments took increasing action to benefit them. Even churches began to abandon their earlier conservatism in the hope of establishing some relationship with the new, rather material concerns of the masses.

In no sense did the masses take control of society. They had political influence, but the leadership of governments and parties came from the middle class and the aristocracy. Cultural institutions developed for the masses were primarily controlled by members of the middle class. The education and reading of the masses was, to a great extent, directed from a small number of central sources that were in turn dominated by the upper classes. Certain middle-class values, such as the importance of national loyalty, were transmitted to large segments of the masses through these sources. However, the lower classes made their mark on established institutions even if they did not control them. Recognition of some of the interests of the masses became part of the religious, cultural, and political life of western and central Europe.

Cultural Outlets

Nowhere was the new position of the masses more apparent than in the field of journalism. As the lower classes gained in literacy and income, it became possible to address newspapers to them for the first time. This possibility attracted two types of journalistic effort. One, quite naturally, came from the leaders of working-class political and union efforts. A wide variety of socialist and syndicalist papers were created, which contributed to the great increase in the numbers of newspapers during the period. These papers provided political information and guidance to their members and maintained a high level of excitement about current problems. However, those were not the papers that appealed to the lower classes; their circulations were limited to a small number of the faithful.

The truly mass press had a two-fold basis. First, it was able to lower prices drastically. This was partly due to major improvements in printing, but particularly to the development of huge advertising revenues. Second, the new press catered to the interests of the masses. Those were papers designed for people whose reading habits were not sophisticated and who sought entertainment in what they read.

Older journals of course continued, appealing to the upper classes with their serious accounts of political and cultural events; but their readership was limited. By 1900, however, *Le Petit Journal* in Paris sold two million copies a day. The Berlin *Lokal-Anzeiger* had a million readers, as did both the *Daily Mail* and the *Daily Express* in London. The size of these giants allowed steady reductions in cost and development of various new features to keep the readers entertained; both tended to increase the readership even further.

The entertainment function of the mass press was expressed in many ways. Stories of crimes and of personal melodrama proved increasingly popular. This contrasted with the older bourgeois press, which had devoted space to short stories with a moral message and to comments on theater, music, and the like. Special features were developed to appeal to the interests of various groups. Women's sections discussed social news and other matters of concern to female readers. Accounts of sporting events were greatly expanded. And in all the features of the paper, writing was simplified, headlines made more sensational.

The political content of the new papers differed from the older middle-class press and from the working-class press. Little attention was given to internal politics. The great interest in editorializing, which typified older middle-class papers, declined as the enlarged reading public showed little concern for elaborate discussions of issues. However, the papers did have a political tone, almost uniformly conservative. The publishers and the advertisers were businessmen; they had a definite interest in turning the masses away from social discontent. And they discovered quite quickly that appeals to national loyalty, particularly in accounts of imperial ventures, appealed to readers. Stories of national empire could be filled with excitement and the lure of the strange and promoted a comforting sense of importance among readers who saw their nations dominating inferior peoples.

Mass journalism was an important social development. It showed the possibility of offering the masses relatively standardized fare. The mass papers were few in number and similar to each other in approach and style. The papers reflected the interests of the various lower classes in exciting news and entertaining special features. They furthered these interests, but they did not create them; the masses themselves, by choosing this journalistic approach over others, had a direct role in changing the character of journalism. At the same time, the press did promote certain interests within the masses. It began to shape buying habits; it encouraged national loyalties. The behavior of the masses was susceptible to some control from above. Nationalistic sentiment, promoted by schools and military training as well as by newspapers, was not uniformly felt by all the lower classes. The working class was less attracted than the lower middle class, partly because working-class leaders often preached against national loyalties. Nevertheless, as the widespread loyalty to nation during the First World War was to prove, even the working class was quite firmly attached to the idea of nation. Newspapers and the equally centralized organs of mass education played a major role in cementing this national feeling. The mass press, by both guiding and responding to the interests of the masses, was an important part of the culture of the lower classes during the period.

Other outlets for entertainment developed characteristics similar to those of the mass press. Spectator sports developed into a big business by appealing to the desire of the masses for entertainment. Sports became increasingly standardized as professional firms took advantage of the new opportunities. This standardization seemed necessary to develop leagues and facilities that could cater to mass audiences at a sufficiently low price. Popular theaters and, after about 1900, motion-picture houses provided the excitement and spectacle that appealed to the tastes of many in the lower classes. As in sports, these facilities offered the sort of crowd diversion, outside the home, that had long been characteristic of the recreation of the urban lower classes.

Furthermore, the various outlets of mass entertainment had some effect even on the upper classes. Many members of the middle class were attracted by the excitement and the low prices of professional sports or the mass press. The recreational interests of the middle class were changing and broadening for various reasons, but the influence of mass taste played a definite role. Mass audiences cut across local differences as well as across class lines. The diversity of popular culture in Europe was reduced. At the same time, many people in both lower and upper classes found more opportunity for enjoyment and recreation than ever before.

The Churches

The interests and resources of the masses had considerable influence on religious bodies. Christian churches had traditionally appealed to the masses, but during the nineteenth century their hold had been notably loosened. Toward the end of the century many churches tried to develop programs that would have greater appeal to the lower classes in the cities.

Many Protestant organizations established settlement-house facilities to aid the poor. They sponsored scouting groups and various efforts in social work to offer recreational facilities and material assistance to the lower classes. In Britain a new Protestant movement, the Salvation Army, was founded in 1880 to provide material as well as spiritual solace to the poor and downtrodden.

A variety of Catholic programs were also developed to promote material well-being and thereby attract working-class groups to the Church. Many Catholic unions were founded in Germany, France, and elsewhere. Far more moderate than other union movements, they stressed mutual aid and bargaining without strikes. They won few members but they revealed the new level of Catholic interest in the needs and demands of workers. More generally, Pope Leo XIII tried to modify the Church's earlier opposition to modern political and social movements. He admitted the acceptability of democratic and even republican regimes, urging French Catholics, for example, to rally to the support of the French republic. Further, while attacking socialism and insisting on the importance of private property, he urged greater attention to social justice. In the encyclical *Rerum novarum,* issued in 1891, he approved of the union movement and of government welfare programs and recommended that employers better the conditions of their workers.

On the whole, however, the churches had just begun effective adjustment to the new position of the lower classes. The decline of religion continued. Some few workers were attached more firmly to the church by the new programs, but far more were left untouched. Important rural and aristocratic elements in the churches resisted many of the programs of modernization, so efforts to woo the masses were small and were often contradicted by conservative action by Christian leaders. Many French Catholics, for example, ignored the pope's appeal to support the republic and seized on the Dreyfus affair as an excuse to attack republican principles. Catholic army officers, aristocrats, some members of the upper middle class, and certainly many members of the hierarchy continued to view religion as a force for social conservatism. It was significant, nevertheless, that the efforts by both Protestant and Catholic churches to woo the masses were based on recognition of the need to combine religion with social reform. The working of religion in the world, beyond mere charity, became an increasingly important part of church activity.

The hold of religion on the urban lower classes was weakened by developments in church–state relations and in intellectual life. The middle-class political attack on church privileges continued, and middle-class parties had greater power than ever before due to the rise of parliamentary structures. And they were aided by the new socialist parties, which were almost uniformly hostile to Christianity. Together the parties launched a major attack on the churches, especially the Catholic Church, in most countries. The

German *Kulturkampf* of the 1870s suppressed many religious orders, partially secularized the educational system, and established civil instead of religious marriage. In Italy and France the government and the liberal parties were in a virtual state of war against the Church; many religious orders were suppressed, and the Church's role in education was curtailed. After the Dreyfus affair the attack was renewed in France, for the Church seemed attached to the enemies of the republic. Religious orders and schools were weakened further, and in 1905 the Church was separated from the state; state funds and protection were entirely withdrawn.

The political clashes weakened the churches in several ways. The churches lost institutional power and many traditional functions. Their educational role was reduced; traditional charity was diminished by the advance of secular welfare efforts. The Christian marriage ethic and influence over the family were hampered by new laws permitting divorce and civil marriage. Furthermore, the political disputes distracted many Christian leaders from the pressing problems of dealing with the newly awakened lower classes. The continued concern with defending institutional privilege often heightened the impression that the churches were conservative, out of date.

This impression was heightened, finally, by the spread of new scientific doctrines, such as the theory of evolution, and the popularization of attacks on the historical veracity of the Bible. These new doctrines were published widely in the press and were often taught in the school systems; they confirmed many members of the middle and working classes in their view of religion as superstitious and irrelevant.

Despite the decline of religious interest, the churches showed considerable vitality during the period. The new scientific doctrines were answered by a revival and revision of Christian theology. The churches gradually accepted new political regimes; Catholics adjusted to the new German state after the 1870s and even to the separation of church and state in France. There was a huge burst of missionary activity from Catholics and Protestants alike. Many churches were gaining in wealth; the Irish and Spanish churches, particularly, were richer than ever before. The decline of religion was thus ambiguous; the churches were still receiving support and seemed to be gaining in vigor despite growing indifference among major groups.

The power of the churches came largely from nonindustrial classes, many of whom turned to religion with renewed interest in reaction to hostile modern trends. Peasants remained loyal to the faith and were often guided politically by local priests. The churches were vital to aristocratic conservatism and, in most countries, to shopkeepers and other traditional elements of the lower middle class. Largely nonindustrial regions, like southern Germany, or whole countries, such as Ireland, were the bastions of religious fervor. Religion was increasingly a refuge for people who were being reduced in status by the classes most directly associated with the leading economic forms. Where anti-modern political movements developed, they usually had Christian overtones and appealed to many Christians. The conversion of many French priests to anti-Semitism, in the 1880s, or the association of many German Protestant pastors with anti-Semitic movements, were extreme forms of Christian protest against the modern world.

The decline of religion was not, then, a uniform process. It touched mainly urban groups and the workers most of all. For those groups, however, alternate loyalties were arising that could replace religion altogether, loyalties that seemed more appropriate to modern life. Socialist or syndicalist beliefs were often held with religious-like intensity. It has often been pointed out that these movements had religious overtones, with formal doctrines, ceremonies, even martyrs. More generally, national loyalties developed that could replace religion or at least reduce its importance. The masses did not stop believing after 1870. Some elements believed in Christianity because of traditional attachment or a new sense that an anchor was needed in troubled times. Increasing numbers transferred their faith to new doctrines.

Toward a Welfare State

The masses, particularly factory workers, had a significant impact on the functions of the state in the period. Governments were now faced with a "social question," which meant not that social problems were new but that they now had to be consistently recognized. In general, governments tried to meet the challenge by expanding their role in the economy to protect at least the most politically active elements of the lower classes.

Workers put direct pressure on the state, as socialist and union representatives pushed for welfare measures. And politicians tried to forestall strike waves and compete with socialism by promoting government assistance to workers. Without working-class pressure the early spate of social legislation could not have occurred.

However, there were other sources of support. Conservatives introduced many leading measures, such as the German insurance laws of the 1880s. A clerical, royalist majority in the French parliament passed in 1874 the first effective factory inspection law. Conservative parties hoped by these measures to win working-class support, and the idea of regulating middle-class business and extending paternal assistance to the poor still had some appeal for conservative aristocrats.

Far more support for welfare functions came from liberal middle-class politicians. There was opposition, of course. The liberal tradition was opposed to expanding the functions of government. Many businessmen feared the expense of welfare programs; German industrialists, for example, opposed the initial social insurance laws of the 1880s. However, there was much middle-class support as well. Many came to see that welfare measures did not harm business interests; in Germany the business community supported some later welfare laws. Many saw welfare measures as a necessary response to the agitation of labor; the middle class was not inflexible in its attitude toward working-class desires. Finally, the humanitarian traditions of the middle class prompted some to see the justice of welfare measures, the need to eliminate some of the worst forms of material insecurity and abuse. Knowledge of the conditions of the poor was promoted by various public and private reports and by the propaganda of socialists and union leaders. There was some realization that reforms were needed not just to assuage labor but also to approach more closely middle-class ideals of general prosperity and opportunity.

Many elements of society, then, could see some utility in the development of at least limited welfare programs. There was opposition, and few extensive measures were adopted. The working class did not, after all, hold primary political power; their hopes for government help were only partially realized. And the form of wel-

fare legislation was guided by the interests and values of the middle
and upper classes.

Prior to 1870 or 1880 relatively little had been done by national
governments to meet the social problems of industrial societies. There
had been minor protective legislation, covering particularly the
field of child labor. National laws had permitted action, sometimes
by localities, to protect certain minimal standards in health, housing,
and education. Food and drug inspection began in the 1860s in
much of western Europe. Municipal governments had led in developing new functions by providing parks, libraries, effective
sewage disposal and a wide variety of other facilities for their
citizens. But the total amount of welfare activity was small and
limited in concept. Most of it involved simply an extension of the
middle-class idea of the state as policeman, removing abuses but
not engaging in positive action to construct new conditions. Vigorous
protection was extended only to categories of people, particularly
children, who were clearly incapable of defending their interests.

After 1870 many older welfare concepts were drastically extended,
and new principles were developed, especially in the field of social
insurance. Even relatively new industrial countries participated in
the movement toward some welfare legislation, in imitation of the
more extensive programs of the mature industrial countries. Governments came to assume growing responsibility for the conditions
of the lower classes. Poverty and economic insecurity were no longer
regarded as the just deserts of idleness or immorality, although these
ideas persisted in some segments of the middle class. It was recognized that, even with the best of will, the lower classes faced difficulties beyond their power to master and that society owed a
minimal level of protection to all of its citizens.

Germany was the first nation to develop a comprehensive welfare
program. In 1883 a compulsory insurance program against illness
was established for most industrial workers; up to thirteen weeks of
sickness were covered. Both workers and employers contributed to
the program, which was administered by local groups, including
some old mutual aid societies. In 1884 accident disability insurance
was passed, paid for entirely by the employer—novel recognition
that the employer, not the worker, was responsible for accidents in
the plant. Finally, in 1889, a program was passed to support the
aged and invalid, with premiums paid half by employee, half by

employer, with government subsidies if necessary. These three laws established the basic welfare program for Germany in the period. They were extended several times to cover more people, including agricultural workers. Between 1885 and 1900 fifty million Germans received from the program benefits worth $750 million—$250 million more than the workers had contributed. Germany also passed various laws regulating hours of work and conditions of pay; even domestic workers were protected. The state also promoted industrial courts to arbitrate disputes between employer and worker. With a massive program of social insurance and various other protective measures, the German state offered the most complete welfare program of any nation in Europe.

Britain, somewhat later than Germany, developed a series of measures almost as comprehensive. There was a great deal of regulation of sanitary conditions, of hours for women and children, even of the conditions of children in schools and in homes. In 1909 an eight-hour law was passed for miners, the first law directly regulating the hours of work for adult males. In 1912 a new type of protection was added, again for miners, with the establishment of a minimum wage. A 1905 law, passed by a Conservative administration, admitted new state responsibility for unemployment by establishing state funds for the relief of deserving unemployed, and in 1908 a tax-supported pension plan was established. In 1911 the National Insurance Act was passed, the most extensive scheme developed in Britain before the war. It covered both sickness and unemployment and was compulsory for those categories of workers to whom it applied. A third of the funds for the program came from workers, a third from employers, and a third from the state.

Other European states developed welfare programs, often patterned on the German. Austria passed an accident-insurance plan in 1887 and a sickness-insurance scheme the next year. Denmark created similar programs between 1893 and 1903. Italy passed legislation providing insurance against accidents and old age in 1898, and Norway, Spain, and Holland established accident compensation in the 1890s. Most European states also passed laws limiting the hours of work, regulating the labor of children, setting minimum standards of ventilation, light, and sanitation in factories, and eliminating abuses in fines imposed on workers and in payments of wages in kind. In France insurance against illness and accident was passed, but coverage was voluntary rather than compulsory. A ten-hour day for factories employing both men and women and a six-day week were established by law. In 1910 a pension plan was set up by the state. The movement toward a variety of welfare measures was quite general, although the elaborate insurance schemes of Germany and, later, Britain were nowhere fully duplicated.

The welfare programs set up during the period all followed several general principles. They extended the concept of the state as policeman on guard against abuse by regulating many new aspects of factory and market activity. Some traditional limits on regulation remained, however, as in the general avoidance of direct regulation of the hours of adult males. Another middle-class principle, self-help, guided the insurance programs of the period; participants in most of the programs paid most of the costs. This self-help feature was acceptable to many workers, who could thereby regard the programs as something other than charity, and it helped make the programs more compatible with middle-class ideals, for it seemed to encourage self-reliance and also did not threaten to cost much in tax money.

Many of the insurance programs went beyond the self-help feature by making them compulsory for the categories of workers covered and by adding state or employer contributions. Compulsion was necessary to spread the risks from an insurance standpoint, but it did reduce the liberty of workers to go their own way. Few programs depended on workers' contributions alone. The 1908 pension plan in Britain relied entirely on general tax funds. There was an embryonic concept of the state as a redistributor of income through taxes, and most states established graduated taxes, although mainly to support military expenditures. The Lloyd George budget in 1909 established special taxes on land, raised the taxes on upper incomes and lowered them for the poor, and provided some deductions for children. The British tax schemes, in combination with tax-supported welfare programs, effectively set aside 1 per cent of the national income each year for redistribution. This was only a halting step, but it was the most novel extension of state responsibility during the period. More generally, the growth of the functions and personnel of the state was unprecedented, in part due to the new operation of the state in the fields of education and welfare. The expansion of government was an important aspect of the increasing political attention to the needs of the masses.

The early welfare laws did a great deal of good. In Germany and elsewhere insurance programs contributed significantly to the resources of many workers in times of misfortunes. Regulations of conditions eliminated countless abuses in factory conditions and were responsible for many of the gains in leisure time and in health by the working classes.

However, most of the plans were quite limited. Regulations often applied only to factories and left artisans and rural workers unprotected. Insurance schemes, even where compulsory, often covered a minority of workers. The National Insurance Act in Britain was intended to be experimental and applied to only two and a quarter million men. None of the plans covered dependents, widows, and orphans. The poorest people, such as rural labor or single women working at home, were left almost untouched by these various schemes; only in Germany did measures go significantly beyond factory workers alone.

Even those who did benefit received relatively little. Pensions and insurance payments in Britain were set deliberately low to discourage idling. It was assumed that these plans would merely supplement other savings; but other savings did not necessarily exist. The little redistribution of income that occurred was more than offset by the growing gap between profits and wages that developed everywhere after 1900.

The welfare programs, particularly in their insurance aspects, were important indications of the new political power of the masses and the flexibility of the upper classes in response. They showed that some new ideas of government function were developing. They were not, however, major contributions to the well-being of the masses. They did not notably stem the discontent that had arisen among factory labor and even among some segments of the peasantry during the period. In Britain the significant innovations in government functions after 1900 coincided with, and did not diminish, the waves of strikes. The measures taken obviously accorded with the expectations of the masses for direct government aid; but they did not yet go far enough to assure contentment.

A Mass Culture?

It is possible to cite the real pressure the lower classes put on the state and, less clearly, on cultural and religious institutions. Yet the growing awareness of the importance of the masses did not give way to a common mass interest or culture. A number of worried intellectuals talked of mass culture and its barbarity, but they saw only superficial characteristics of the lower classes.

To be sure, most elements of the various lower classes were developing increased interest in material well-being and enjoyment. There was a common subjection to some guidance from above, from both public and private sources. The lower classes did depend on outside leadership for most of their political and educational activity. Finally, workers and some peasants had a growing realization of the power of collective action, of the force of numbers. Certainly, the methods of many lower-class groups differed from patterns of upper-class action.

Still, the diversity among the lower classes overshadowed any general points of similarity. Political interests were obviously varied, often totally opposed; the growing radicalism of the working class was directly opposed to the conservatism of the peasantry and lower middle class. If there was a rise in collective action, there was also a clear assertion of the individualism of the lower middle class and most of the peasantry. There was growing materialism, to be sure, but each class had different standards of living and each put its resources to different uses. The lower classes were exposed to schools and a mass press, but clearly this had not produced uniformity in behavior or attitudes.

In terms of the concerns of the lower classes themselves, then, a search for a common mass culture is off the mark for this period. It remains true that, for different reasons and in largely separate ways, the lower classes exerted growing influence. It is also true that to the upper classes an impression of a rising and undifferentiated mass could be increasingly vivid.

ARISTOCRACY AND MIDDLE CLASS

The rise of the masses and the profound economic changes that conditioned this rise obviously had great effects on the upper classes in society. The middle class adjusted to the various changes without huge difficulty and certainly without loss of political and economic power. There were elements of discontent, however, and differentiation within the middle class, initially on the basis of income, increased. At the same time, aristocrats encountered growing difficulties from several sources; one of their responses was the formation of alliances with the upper-middle class.

This period, in fact, marked the development of a new upper class in western and to a degree in central Europe, a class that included both aristocrats and the leading businessmen. The alliance was based on extensive intermarriage and a sharing of economic interests such as tariff protection. Even in eastern Europe many aristocrats abandoned the land and entered middle-class professions such as law. The political powers of the two groups coalesced. The upper class gained control of positions in the state bureaucracy, including the military, that had previously been largely an aristocratic monopoly. New civil-service standards opened the bureaucracy to the upper middle class but barred the entrance of people who could not afford the most expensive education. Finally, the educational and recreational patterns of the upper class increasingly united rich businessmen and wealthy aristocrats.

The upper class was not fully formed by 1914; distinctions still existed between the aristocracy and the upper middle class. But the distinctions were fading. This is the last period in which a separate aristocracy can be noted in western Europe. For the middle class changes were equally decisive. Approximately 5 per cent of the class was clearly set apart by great wealth and links with the aristocracy. It is still valid to look at aristocracy and middle class separately for this period, but the designations are far less satisfactory than they were in earlier periods.

New Threats to the Aristocrats

The decline of the aristocracy was accelerated after 1870; remaining positions were defended with increasing bitterness. An active sense of grievance developed among some aristocrats during the period, which led to direct political moves and to a feeling of frustration and pessimism. Yet by no means was all lost; major political and economic power remained.

The increasing importance of elected parliaments and the rise of mass parties cut deeply into aristocratic political traditions. Remaining privileges of upper-class houses were bitterly assailed by representatives of labor and the middle class. Socialists even threatened to divide landed estates and eliminate the aristocracy. At the same time, the aristocratic role in state bureaucracies declined. In western and central Europe the use of civil-service examinations spread rapidly. Along with the expansion of higher education, this opened many of the top administrative positions to nonaristocrats for the first time. Again, all was not lost. The class retained many positions in diplomacy and the military, although even there outsiders gained steadily. Traditional prestige and, in some countries, class voting systems maintained disproportionate power for the aristocracy even in parliaments. Yet the political challenge was unmistakable.

There was growing social challenge as well. In western Europe the consumption levels and the educational opportunities of the upper-middle class were indistinguishable from those of the aristocracy. After 1870 in France, when legal protection for noble titles was withdrawn, a significant number of business and professional people even adopted the noble preposition "de"—and who was to deny their right to do so?

Finally, the crisis in agriculture posed an unprecedented economic threat. The new competition was all the more severe in that the nobles had stressed the raising of grain, precisely the crop under greatest pressure. The rapid decline in grain prices and the resultant decrease in the value of land posed great economic problems for the aristocracy. Even British landowners, long successful in market agriculture, now faced major difficulties. There was a general increase in indebtedness. Large numbers of aristocrats were forced to sell their estates to middle-class buyers or, as in Russia, sell portions to the peasantry. On the whole, the aristocracy proved incapable of making an effective adjustment to the new crisis. Baltic aristocrats switched to stockraising and hired experts to increase efficiency, but most aristocrats were slow to alter methods and crops, and their position constantly threatened to deteriorate still further.

Aristocratic Responses

If the economic adaptability of the aristocracy was slight, its political flexibility was considerable. Several political responses were open to the class. Some nobles simply gave up in the face of novelties beyond their comprehension. They huddled on their estates or in their clubs and tried to ignore the world around them. There was some interest in the possibility of a conservative revolution that would return society to its proper, aristocratic bases. Many Junker groups talked of the need for a strong leader to keep the masses in their place and defend traditional values of status and honor. Some aristocrats in France abandoned their monarchism because it was hopeless but sought a strong leader who would restore the essential features of the old regime. Potential strongmen such as Boulanger were supported by many aristocrats. Some aristocrats in France and elsewhere even fomented strikes and other agitation in the hope of embarrassing existing regimes. A sense of revulsion and futility dominated many aristocrats during the period.

At the same time, the class as a whole showed an active interest in using the state for the defense of aristocratic interests. The state might protect jobs and values in church and army. It could offer other jobs in expanding imperial bureaucracies, which were popular for noble younger sons. It could provide direct subsidies to large estates. The Junkers managed to obtain state payments for rye; along with the high tariff protection they also won, this allowed them to continue their traditional agriculture and keep some hold over the large estates. In Russia a Nobles Land Bank was established in 1885; by 1900 aristocrats had borrowed 660 million rubles, much of which they used for consumption. Some influence in the state was vital now not just for prestige or sense of power, but for economic survival as a class.

Three basic approaches, often used in combination, allowed aristocrats to retain substantial political influence. One was a growing opposition to proposals for further political reform. The Russian gentry, previously ambiguous in support of autocracy, now allied with the state for the sake of economic aid and jobs in local government. Aristocrats in Britain and France abandoned their earlier, paternalistic attitude toward the working class and furnished the most bitter resistance to labor's political demands. French aristocrats provided most of the opposition to the legalization of unions in 1884. The British House of Lords tried to prevent laws increasing the political power of unions; it was rewarded in 1911 by the loss of its power to veto laws. Everywhere there was vigorous defense of church and army. During the Dreyfus affair in France many aristocrats tried to defend the military against political control and against the admission of Jews to the ranks of officers.

Much of this conservative action was undertaken through the aristocracy's established positions in the state. But there was a need in parliamentary countries to develop other political resources. Increasing cooperation with the upper middle class developed. The 1902 Bülow tariff in Germany resulted from cooperation between Junkers and industrialists. Military spending could also appeal to both groups, as did resistance to lower-class demands. As we have seen, an upper-class establishment was arising in many countries that combined aristocracy and upper middle class in distinction to all other groups. This could bring needed resources and vigor to the aristocracy, although it involved obvious weakening of exclusivism.

Finally, the aristocracy helped to develop mass conservative parties, particularly by appealing to the peasantry. Individual aristocrats appealed for peasant support on the basis of tradition, defense of agriculture, and defense of the church—often with great success. Larger groups, such as the Union of Agriculturalists in Germany, worked to the same end. The use of nationalist arguments proved exceptionally fruitful; they could be invoked in defense of military traditions, of empire, of tariff protection. Aristocrats were not alone in using nationalist arguments, but they did play an active role. Significantly, nationalism represented a new approach for most nobles; earlier attachments had usually been local and dynastic, as in Prussia, or international for the upper magnates.

On the whole, the aristocracy found political means to retard its decline. The methods used affected both politics and the aristocrats themselves. In the west the class became almost indistinguishable from a general upper-class establishment. Elsewhere nobles had more independent power; but they had to rely increasingly on a sympathetic state for their very survival.

The Middle Class: New Opportunities

Unlike the aristocracy, the middle class as a whole faced no economic crisis. In fact, opportunities for accumulating wealth steadily increased with the vast expansion of industry, commerce, and banking. With the spread of corporate forms even those with moderate incomes could profit from industrial growth by purchasing a few shares. Investments in stocks and bonds, including those issued by foreign firms and governments, became an important part of the revenues of the middle class during the period, as the class gained in wealth over all other large social groups.

Political changes too were largely favorable to the middle class. Freedoms of press, religion, and assembly were broadened during the period, and extensive censorship was practiced only in eastern Europe. Most important, the spread of parliamentary systems expanded the role of the middle class in government. Legislatures were filled with members of the class. Improvements in education and the development of the civil-service examinations allowed increasing penetration of administrative posts as well. These developments more than offset the political gains of the masses. And even the political representatives of the working class, as socialism became more revisionist, supported political and welfare reforms with which elements of the middle class could sympathize. Middle-class parties in fact cooperated with socialists in France, Britain, and elsewhere, though only to a limited degree. Certainly, the political developments in the period were not seen as unduly threatening by most of the middle class. To a great extent they seemed to confirm middle-class political values and participation in government.

Other important values were still being served during the period. Most notably, it was still possible to rise into and within the middle class. Advancement in government bureaucracy was a major channel for mobility. The continued formation of small businesses drew active elements of the lower classes into industrial or commercial ownership. The extension of industry to new areas, such as Russia, created a new business group. The rise of new major industries, banks, and trading companies allowed new men to come to the very pinnacle of economic power.

Most important, the development of corporate structures, which separated ownership from direction, and the expansion of firms beyond the point of individual control caused a need for a new group of managers. These people did not have to have significant capital, although some had certain investments. They often needed a relatively high level of education, but this was fairly easy to acquire. And many managers in the period simply rose from the ranks of workers and, more commonly, clerks.

The development of a managerial class opened some new mobility in industrial society. This mobility was at its peak at the end of the century, when the functions of managers were becoming increasingly important. By no means all managers, or even the majority, had risen in status. Many were displaced owners whose firms had been ruined or swallowed up by the new industrial giants. In Britain in 1899 about 40 per cent of the managers in industry had approximately the same status as their fathers; of the remainder, only 43.1 per cent had improved their status. Mobility in this period involved deterioration for many. At the same time, the large number who had been able to better themselves gave new vigor to the middle class and confirmed the belief in expanding opportunities for advancement. The manner of advancement might be new; no longer could primary attention be given to formation of one's own firm. But there was no general sense of stagnation of opportunity.

Style of Life

The gains in wealth and the new structure of industry created important changes in the habits of the middle class. The stress on productive work began to decline. The hours of work were reduced, for the development of bureaucracies allowed division and regularization of the directive functions, and relatively fixed hours could be kept by the staff of an enterprise. Increasing numbers derived at least part of their income from investments that did not require direct administration of a firm. The investments themselves had to be attended to, but there was no need for constant supervision of a complex enterprise. Leisure time increased for many. Work was still valued, and elements of the old productive ethic remained, but the extremes of self-restraint were abandoned.

The behavior of the middle class became more relaxed, and the old standards were loosened as the class took advantage of its new leisure and increased resources. The very wealthy spent more heavily and more conspicuously than ever before. Newly rich Germans built huge mansions and even castles in medieval styles. Many purchased aristocratic estates and houses and became patrons of culture. Artistic and musical events drew much of the time and interest of the wealthier members of the middle class. Resort areas, such as the Riviera, were increasingly popular as places for enjoyment and also for status. Travel in general became more extensive. New items of consumption began to attract attention. The automobile, most notably, became a standard possession for many members of the middle class after 1900; and telephones and electrical lighting systems were common in middle-class homes. The middle class became attuned to the effects of technical advance on patterns of consumption and comfort. This supported the optimism of the class and increased its interest in spending and in enjoyment.

The new interests of the middle class were related to changes in educational and family patterns. Advanced education, including university training, was sought by more members of the class, although the majority still stopped with secondary schooling. Many children of business families now entered the professions after attending the universities, and many more took advantage of the new possibilities in government work. And many returned to business but with a desire to continue interest in reading and the arts as part of business life. The interest in more advanced education, then, reflected the desire of the middle class to acquire greater cultural respectability, to broaden its horizons.

The family life of the middle class was altered and relaxed during the period. Economic life no longer centered on the family, for enterprises increasingly surpassed the family boundaries. As bureaucratic staffs were developed, there was no need for the wife to assist in the administration of the firm. Children were brought into the firm at a later age than before, and some chose other professions entirely. The use of leisure time was broadened beyond the confines of the home. Family reading and visits were replaced by more general entertaining and by attendance at opera, the theater, and other events outside the home. These new outlets were of particular significance in broadening the cultural and social horizons of women in the middle class.

Finally, the new interest in enjoyment inevitably loosened some of the strict controls of family life. Patriarchal authority decreased. Rates of divorce and, possibly, of sexual immorality rose within the middle class. Discussion of moral problems became less narrow. Public consideration of matters such as prostitution became possible; in Britain, legal changes in prostitution laws could even be recommended by a woman, Josie Butler, without raising a vast outcry. Novels read by the middle class, such as those of the French naturalists, were increasingly frank in their presentation of sexual problems. The theater too reflected the loosening of standards, by using themes such as premarital love and even adultery. Many members of the middle class protested against what seemed to be an atmosphere of license, for the old moral ethic was not entirely abandoned. But both in behavior and in culture the middle class as a whole was clearly relaxing its earlier standards of family and of sexual morality. The family remained an important institution for the class, but the intensity and strictness of family life were now reduced.

One important aspect of the change in middle class family life was a gradual alteration in the position of women. Women were less confined to the home than ever before. The steadily declining average number of children released women from purely family duties in all classes, but especially in the middle class. The extension of educational facilities and requirements for women created new opportunities and demands. Job possibilities outside the home for women included not only factories but also clerical positions, which a middle-class woman might fill without great loss of status or danger to health.

Finally, legal reforms both reflected the new position of women and promoted further changes. Most countries allowed women to own property and control their earnings; this was of primary importance in protecting women from the domination of their husbands. In Sweden and Finland, and in Britain for local elections, women were granted the vote. Barriers to women in higher education and in the professions were steadily lowered. Universities were opened to women in the 1870s and 1880s. France in 1900 and Britain in 1903 admitted women to the practice of law and medicine.

These changes affected women in all classes to some degree. Women in the working class had long maintained jobs outside the home. Educational facilities, on the primary level, benefited all. It was in the middle class, however, that the position and expectations of women changed most radically. The small number of women who took advantage of the possibility of higher education and entry to the professions came almost entirely from the middle class. In Britain a large number of women, led by middle-class people such as the Pankhurst sisters, agitated actively for further advance, particularly for female suffrage. The suffragette movement obtained hundreds of thousands of signatures on petitions before 1900, from men as well as women. After 1900 the movement stressed massive demonstrations and even violence to further its goal. Nowhere was the restiveness of women, especially in the middle class, more evident.

On the continent women were not so assertive, especially in political matters. But everywhere they displayed a growing independence of behavior. Costumes for women in the upper classes became far less severe toward the end of the century, reflecting the relaxation of middle-class standards. Dresses were gayer in color, looser, and less concealing. The social position of women improved. Women participated more actively and on a more equal footing in social gatherings. Feminist groups were formed in every country, although they did not usually stress political goals. German feminists pressed such causes as the promotion of birth control and the elimination of the double standard of morality. Even aside from the extraordinary outbursts of British suffragettes, women in the European middle class were obviously developing new attitudes and roles.

Most men in the middle class accepted the modifications of the older standards for female behavior, and some urged further reforms. A minority, however, protested in the name of traditional values. Some professional men, including secondary school teachers, feared competition from women. A number of anti-Semitic movements included criticisms of modern women in their general condemnations of modern life, and urged that women stay in the home where they belonged. The gradual change in the expectations and roles of women was an important part of the alteration of the middle-class style of life, but not all members of the class could accept the loosening of traditional standards.

Sources of Discontent: Western Europe

Although the changes in the attitudes and economic structures of the middle class increased the wealth and confidence of the class as a whole, they caused some concern to important elements in the class. The rejection of older values inevitably shocked many traditionalists. Developments in the economy directly contradicted much of the traditional middle-class ethic. The separation of ownership from management, essential to the corporate form, was unacceptable to many industrialists who had always associated the enterprise with the work and property of a single family. The decline of competition in fields dominated by large corporations and cartels obviously vitiated traditional beliefs in the possibility of rising to ownership of an enterprise. The very idea of limited liability, also vital to the corporation, was considered by many to be a device for evading payment of debts. The increased involvement of banks and speculative finance in industrial control and investment contradicted older ideas about the need to avoid dependence on other people's money. The waves of speculation that could sweep over stock exchanges were viewed with some suspicion by middle-class people who defined income as the fruit of productive work.

In a variety of ways, then, the economy seemed to be developing new values to displace the old. Some members of the middle class tried to adhere to more traditional forms. The textile industry did not abandon its essentially family structure, nor did it participate extensively in the new methods of finance. Yet the owners of the industry could not fail to realize that their place and their economic values were declining in the economy as a whole. In other cases, some of the people who participated in the new forms, as small stockholders at least, could share a concern about the novelty of their economic role. The older middle-class values were not totally contradicted; the nature of property ownership might change, but ownership was still possible. Nor was the class as a whole repelled by the new opportunities. There was, nonetheless, an undercurrent of discontent about the fundamental trends in the economy.

Furthermore, some elements of the middle class saw their actual economic position slip during the period. Many owners of small industrial and commercial firms were inevitably displaced by the growth of larger units. Many of the managers in industry came from this group and could only regard their new positions as inferior to their former ownership status. Although the opportunities for investment and speculation could bring great profit, they occasionally led to ruin or hardship for small investors. Financial crises, like that of the 1870s, ruined many who had, in effect, invested more than the economy could bear. Fraudulent investment schemes robbed others of their savings even in prosperous years. The Panama Canal scandal in France affected almost half a million investors.

These various losses underlined the concern that many felt about the soundness of the economy. It also turned many to a search for scapegoats. Jews seemed to be involved in high finance and were prominent in some of the frauds; anti-Semitism could therefore be a vehicle for protests against the economic situation. Big business and the government itself came in for more generalized criticism. Some members of the middle class voted socialist, as an expression of protest against big business and sympathy for the hardships of the labor force. Many in the middle class supported working-class strikes by financial contributions or by extending credit to strikers; again, rifts within the middle class could cause direct attacks on the economic leaders. Active sympathy with the cause of labor was extended by only a minority, just as demonstrations against Jews involved only a small group, mainly young students. They were symptomatic, nevertheless, of the insecurity of segments of the middle class.

One portion of the middle class developed particularly active economic grievances. More than any other middle-class group, many professional people were in economic difficulty during the period. As university training became more common, the numbers of graduates increased more rapidly than their opportunities. Certainly, few doctors or lawyers kept pace with the increasing earnings of businessmen. Many lived in near-poverty. Journalists were badly paid, and there were many unemployed in the larger cities. In 1901 it was estimated that only half the doctors in France could be considered, or considered themselves, prosperous. As a result, French medical students grew increasingly restive. They sought legal limitation on the admission of foreigners in medical schools, hoping to reduce the size of the medical profession in order to increase their own opportunities. They also participated in some actual rioting. Along with some shopkeepers and clerks, many students from law and medical faculties in Paris joined anti-Semitic groups and participated in street demonstrations over the Dreyfus affair. Jews were again blamed for economic trends, most notably the rise of big business, which seemed hostile to the purposes of other segments of the middle class. And there was growing Jewish competition within the professions. In Austria, where Jews were free to enter the professions after 1867, 33.6 per cent of university students in Vienna were Jewish by 1890.

In many ways, then, the middle class in industrial countries seemed increasingly fragmented at the end of the century. The small upper element merged increasingly with the aristocracy into a new governing elite. Most businessmen prospered and many new men could rise into the ranks of the successful. But some traditional business elements were harmed in the process. The professional group grew rapidly, but opportunities did not keep pace with this growth. Finally, the lower middle class, though attached to many bourgeois values, was increasingly separated by the types of work and income involved.

Nevertheless, a mood of confidence did prevail in the middle class as a whole before 1914. Newspapers and other publications, looking back in 1900 to the developments of the past century, could only be impressed with the progress that had been achieved. The economic situation had been transformed by the revolution in technology and the massive increase in production. New products were available to almost everyone. Advances in health and increases in population were evident. Political changes had brought new liberties and opportunities for participation to the middle class and even to the masses. Knowledge had advanced as education spread, and scientific discoveries challenged the forces of ignorance and superstition. In terms of the values held by most of the middle class, progress seemed undeniable, and there was little doubt that further advance would come. The class could expect further increase in its profits and the maintenance of its political gains. There was some concern about the rising levels of international competition and the demands of the working class, but these problems seemed within reach of satisfactory solution. New economic devices seemed to assure profit levels despite competition. The gains of the working class were not regretted, and methods of collective bargaining and welfare legislation seemed to promise greater social harmony in the future. The economic and political dominance of the middle class was not yet seriously threatened.

For most members of the class, in fact, the decades before the war were almost a golden age. In later decades, too, many would look back on this period as "the good old days" or "le bon vieux temps." For changes were to come, based in part on currents developing in the period itself, that were to alter the character of European society and especially the position of the middle class. At this point, however, these changes were only dimly foreshadowed. The mood of western Europe, of its leading class particularly, seemed unalterably confident.

Sources of Discontent: Eastern Europe

Outside of western and central Europe the same feeling of satisfaction could not prevail, for the position of the middle class remained insecure. A business element was arising, such as that in Russia, and growing in wealth; but the bulk of the middle class continued to be employed in professional pursuits. Professional opportunities themselves were expanding, but they could provide no sense of real control in society. Hence, among professionals particularly, an active sense of grievance persisted.

These grievances were expressed in outright agitation in several places. Nationalist ferment in the Balkans had a strong middle-class element. The leadership of professional people helped produce the insurrections of 1875 in Bosnia and Bulgaria. Most important, the participation of segments of the middle class was vital to the Russian revolutions of 1905 and 1917.

University education expanded substantially in most areas of eastern Europe in the last decades of the century. By 1881 a third of the Russian secondary school and university students were of middle-class origin, and by 1897 more than half a million people belonged to the professional group. Newspapers grew, offering both employment and information; if their subscribers numbered only a few thousand, they were still an important innovation. Teaching naturally expanded, and employment for lawyers and doctors in local governments increased. In Russia particularly this was a period of expansion for the professional group.

Yet grievances remained. The state was autocratic; it interfered periodically with the schools and newspapers on which professionals depended. Society was backward, and professionals in Russia and elsewhere saw clearly that the conditions of the peasantry had to be remedied before real modernization could take place. A minority felt that revolutionary means were necessary to correct the evils of the existing system; from professional, university-trained groups came the leaders of socialism and anarchism in Russia. Most professionals, in 1890 at least, were not so radical. A wave of liberalism spread, urging civic freedoms and parliamentary government with wide suffrage as well as agricultural reforms. As before in western Europe, this impulse could lead to revolution.

In 1904, as Russia suffered in the Japanese war, groups of authors, teachers, lawyers, and doctors formed unions to work for liberal political reform. They countenanced and helped guide the revolution of 1905 and formed the liberal Kadet party to push for effective parliamentary government. The role of liberal professionals was less great in 1917, although again they took the lead in the early stages of the revolution. Certainly middle-class discontent played an important role in the general agitation in eastern Europe.

With all this, the position of the middle class remained extremely weak. It constituted only a tiny percentage of the total population, and there was no large business element to lend support to the political activism of professional people. And the existing regimes, particularly in Russia, remained extremely oppressive. Educated people could agitate, but by themselves they could effect no major change. They could countenance revolution, but they might be swept away by it.

CONCLUSION: SOCIAL PROTEST

Western Europe

The period 1870–1914 saw no direct attempt at revolution in western and central Europe. Established governments retained their great power, and improvements in military technology, notably the repeating rifle, made revolution difficult. Police forces learned better methods of crowd control. Most important, large elements of the population were apparently satisfied with their lot. Most peasants were content, and the bulk of the middle class, even many workers, saw opportunities for steady progress under the existing system.

Yet there was discontent, although it was not strong enough to shake the foundation of society. The massive agitation of workers could not be ignored. Sometimes it had revolutionary overtones; certainly it sought major change. Nowhere was the social question solved in the period, although welfare measures and collective bargaining satisfied some. In countries where economic conditions deteriorated significantly for the working class, notably Britain and Belgium, discontent grew to alarming proportions.

Only in the working class were there huge organizations of protest. However, signs of uneasiness were developing in various elements of the population. At the extreme, a wave of anti-liberal, anti-modern intellectual protest developed at the end of the century. It had roots in earlier intellectual and artistic movements, notably Romanticism, and in the theory of evolution; but it had a social basis as well. Artists rebelled against middle-class standards of taste, and rejected the official canons of the rich patrons of art, the desire for clarity and social utility. Instead they asserted that the artistic experience was aesthetic and arational. There, clearly, a gap developed between many intellectuals and the bulk of the middle class. At the same time, social scientists began to emphasize the irrational elements in the human mind. Certain philosophers, notably Nietzsche, developed a total criticism of existing society; democratic parliamentary structures, based on human rationality, were held to be worthless and dangerous, and middle-class materialism was bitterly attacked. What was needed was a new ethic that only a few could achieve, an élitist code based on emotion and on recognition of the importance of violence and expressed particularly in war. Philosophical systems of this sort obviously undermined many of the premises of existing society, particularly those of the middle class. Such systems had growing currency among students and second-level intellectuals. Their influence, however, was not widespread. Few people had yet heard of Freud or of doctrines of the irrational and the violent. The new intellectual currents seemed largely irrelevant to the primary purposes of most social groups. At any rate, the intellectual ferment of the period was not translated directly into social ferment.

There were points of contact, however, between major developments in society and some of the new intellectual concepts. Most notably, an atmosphere of violence did seem to be developing. Workers, although not directly touched by formal doctrines of violence, did engage in violent agitation over economic grievances. Growing interest in sports, in hiking, and in scouting movements showed an increased attention to physical activity. Even more important, doctrines of violence were used and accepted as part of the nationalist current of the period. Newspapers stressed the need for force in the imposition of imperialist aims. Business groups talked of national competition in their efforts to obtain tariff protection and encourage military purchases by governments. Small but vigorous groups were formed to urge national expansion, such as the pan-German League, whose members were mainly professional people. When World War I came, whole populations marched off to war with at least a superficial joy. Although it was assumed that the war would be short and would end in national victory, it was also assumed that the combat would be glorious. Clearly, the doctrines of struggle had won considerable influence.

In the same period the ideas of violence and of irrationality led to certain political movements that, although small, won some support from various groups hostile to the leading trends of their society. A new radical conservatism arose that argued for authoritarian government instead of parliamentary democracy. Intellectuals, such as Langbehn in Germany and Maurras in France, bitterly criticized the materialism of their era. They condemned both big business and the movements within the working class. They sought instead a new, united nation that would devote itself to the spiritual needs of man, including the need for violence. They pointed to the responsibility of certain groups, notably the Jews, for the evils of the existing system. These ideas, and political movements based on them, won some support from elements of several social classes. Certain aristocrats backed them as their class declined. Some members of the middle class, particularly professional people, found the doctrine appealing; some in the lower middle class were also attracted. Membership of radical conservative movements remained small; the political party formed by the anti-Semite Stöcker in Germany received only one hundred thousand votes in the early 1890s; riots led by authoritarian nationalists such as d'Annunzio in Italy were small though violent and influential. The anti-Semitic French paper, *La France Juive*, had only one hundred thousand subscribers. In no sense, then, were these new movements massively popular. They appealed to grievances shared by several large groups, but they won active support only from a minority. They did correspond to some of the leading intellectual trends of the day; their leaders, in fact, were often primarily intellectuals, as were the poet d'Annunzio and the writer Maurras. They expressed clearly the gulf that had formed between many intellectuals and the leading groups in society. Their period of primary social influence, however, was yet to come.

Eastern Europe

In the non-industrial areas of Europe a clearly revolutionary mood prevailed at the end of the century. Peasants were everywhere restive because they suffered from the pressures of agricultural crisis, overpopulation, and, often, the dominance of large landowners. In Spain, particularly, their agitation took on an unusually doctrinal tone. Everywhere, peasant risings recurrently threatened established society.

Urban workers were also discontent. Their numbers were not yet large, but they could dominate the cities. Socialist and anarchist doctrines spread, and the harsh working conditions and brutal police repression gave a revolutionary cast to strikes and riots in Catalonia, Sicily, and Russia. Unlike most strikes in western Europe, these often raised direct questions about the nature of the political regime.

Finally, middle-class grievances swelled the tide of agitation. Middle-class agitators played a role in most urban unrest. Bolshevik leaders, Balkan nationalists, Sicilian socialists, and Catalonian separatists generally came from the educated group. Beyond this, the middle class often looked with favor on agitation against the established regime, and in Russia professional groups attacked it directly.

As in western Europe earlier, the discontented classes could not easily cooperate. Peasants usually agitated separately; and their risings, although massive, were usually sporadic and disorganized. The middle class could easily come to fear lower-class ferment. In Spain and the Balkans many businessmen joined the aristocrats in urging the repression of these outbursts; even in Russia there was some impulse to use the state to maintain order.

Only in Russia was there outright revolution during the period. The grievances of peasants were great, all the more because partial reform had whetted the appetite for more; peasant risings in 1905–1906 were unusually persistent. There was a substantial working class capable of repeated strikes. The autocratic character of the regime drove professional people to unusual activity. Finally, two wars galvanized and coordinated the various currents of discontent into two revolutions, the second successful.

The societies of western and eastern Europe remained largely separate in this period. Class structure and conditions were vastly different in the two areas. The revolutionary mood in eastern Europe contrasted vividly with the relative contentment in the west. There were grievances among professional groups in both areas, but they sprung from largely different causes. There were important links between worker movements, particularly in doctrine, but again the bases of protest were generally distinct. Nevertheless, much of the ferment of eastern Europe resulted from efforts at modernization in western terms and, often, a desire to imitate the west more fully. In turn, the revolution in Russia was to play a significant role in western society in future decades.

5

EUROPE BETWEEN
THE WARS

WORLD WAR I

Morale

World War I precipitated a variety of changes in European society. It heightened certain trends evident in previous decades and brought developments of real novelty as well. Most generally, the war constituted a massive shock to European morale. On both sides most people had expected an easy victory, and celebrations marked the departure of troops in the early days of the conflict. Disillusionment soon set in. The war proved to be one of the most frustrating and certainly one of the most brutal encounters in European history. On the western front particularly the lines established within the first few months shifted only slightly during the next four years.

The battle lines were dug with trenches, and troops settled into a situation in which little advance was possible and only at fantastic cost to life. Day-long battles could result in the loss of tens of thousands of lives. New war machines were introduced that were unprecedented in their destructive power. Submarine warfare attacked even civilian shipping. The use of gas, tanks, and flamethrowers provided awesome proof of the power of technology to injure and destroy. Airplane warfare, including some bombing of major cities, brought the horrors of war directly to some civilians. Destruction seemed endless and without clear purpose.

The people most affected by the shock of the war were, of course, the fighting men themselves. The armies on both sides embraced millions of men; in war as in other activities the age of the masses had clearly arrived. These millions were directly faced with the daily pressures of shelling and with the frequent anguish of bloody but inconclusive battle. An attitude developed among the troops that was to endure long after the war was over. Soldiers felt that their efforts deserved some sort of special recognition from society, that their hardships should result in a changed world and a better life. During the war itself many troops believed that civilians, particularly politicians and war profiteers, were not responding properly to the situation at the front. Important mutinies by troops, from 1917 until well after the war's end, indicated the discontent of the fighting men.

After the war troops returning to civilian society continued to feel abused and somewhat separate. They faced inevitable problems of adjustment to civilian life after the bloody stress of war. Many were wounded, others psychologically marred. Veterans also faced economic difficulties, for the national economies adapted only slowly to the influx of returning workers and peasants. The problems of veterans were heightened in some countries, notably in Germany, by the reduction even of professional military ranks, in which officers as well as troops were thrown out of their accustomed positions. Again, it proved easy to focus the frustrations of peacetime on civilian society, on the politicians, on the capitalists.

Some of these frustrations very early assumed a political form; veterans formed organizations designed to remake society. Many supporters of communist groups in the postwar years were veterans, and the founders and followers of rightist movements were veterans who could not find a suitable place in civilian life. General veterans' groups grew to considerable size and importance in all countries and demanded special benefits for their members. They, too, could easily develop political overtones, because they tended to be hostile to parliamentary rule and anxious to support national honor. Veterans' organizations such as the German *Stahlhelm* or the French *Croix de feu* became active proponents of radical and nationalist conservatism. Quite generally, then, the bitterness of many veterans played a significant role in shaping the political tone and the morale of postwar society. This bitterness extended to men in all social classes and took various political forms. It encouraged strike movements and even led to attempted revolutions by returning workers in the immediate postwar years. It encouraged the formation of conservative, even fascist, paramilitary groups.

The shock of the war affected civilian populations as well as fighting men. Civilians in front-line areas, such as Serbia, Belgium, and Poland, were subject to the same pressures of bombardment and attack as soldiers themselves. Civilians everywhere were actively involved in the war effort. The economies of Europe had to convert almost totally to wartime production. Rationing of foods and some other products was introduced. Most countries suffered from a lack of consumer goods, particularly food. In Germany and eastern Europe the conscription of peasants into the armies and the difficulty of importing food led to real hardship for most civilians by 1916. Diets were reduced to subsistence levels, with primary dependence on potatoes and other starches. In Russia outright famine reappeared in some areas. These reductions in standards, coming after a period of rising material expectations, produced a psychological as well as material shock to the millions affected.

Involvement in war economy was not confined to consumption patterns. More and more people were drawn and even forced into war industries. Many countries, including Britain and Germany, set up compulsory labor procedures to channel workers into the most vital branches of production. This brought new experiences to many people, including large numbers of women who found jobs of unprecedented importance open to them. It also brought a sense of involvement in the war itself and in its frustrations.

Moreover, governments were not content with requiring economic participation of civilian populations; they insisted on moral participation as well. War in industrial Europe brought not only the creation of armies of unprecedented size but also the subjection of civilians to centrally directed propaganda designed to instill uniform and active loyalty to the war effort. Censorship of all forms of publication and arrests of dissidents became commonplace. Governments also planted news in various media, without particular regard for truth. The German government tried to instill firm belief in German victory and war aims and in the evils of the opposing powers, with such success that many Germans were unaware that the tide had turned against them in 1918. British and French propaganda painted the Germans as barbaric Huns whose defeat was essential to western civilization. All governments tried to promote a constant sense of excitement and tension that would lead to more vigorous support of their cause. The propaganda efforts were not totally successful. Particularly among the working classes, partially hostile to the established order before the war, movements of protest developed as material conditions deteriorated. On the whole, however, extraordinary loyalty was developed. After the war was over, the emotional and economic involvement with the war brought to civilian elements some of the frustrations that afflicted veterans.

Finally, partly because of the tension and expectations developed during the war, the aftermath disillusioned most people everywhere. Some had put faith in Wilsonian principles of a democratic society free from war. They were quickly disillusioned, because Wilson's efforts were partially thwarted. Far more people, spurred by government propaganda, had expected massive national gains. Frenchmen hoped not only for the return of Alsace-Lorraine but also for permanent protection from Germany; they were disappointed. Italians dreamed of great acquisitions in the Balkans and the Near East; they were frustrated. Germans had expected huge gains in both east and west; instead they lost much of their own land in both areas. Newly created states in eastern Europe, though excited by their existence, were almost uniformly discontented about territory that they did not receive.

For various reasons, then, there was a widespread feeling that the war and all the strain it involved had led to failure. Radical socialists gained mass support by pointing to capitalists as the scapegoats. German nationalists began to preach that revenge was necessary, that Germany had lost only because of the disloyalty of politicians or labor leaders or Jews. Italian groups, including the new fascist party, made rapid gains by citing the failures of the parliamentary government to win significant new territory. Even in a less agitated nation like Britain many leaders urged that the war had been a mistake and that Britain should pull out of its continental involvements; again, these views corresponded to sentiments held by a wide public.

To the horror of the war itself, then, was added a widespread disillusionment about the peace. It became more difficult to maintain the confidence and optimism that had dominated much of the prewar mood. The bloodshed and the apparent futility of the war efforts helped to change the tone of European thinking. Some groups, particularly in the defeated countries, preached the need for revolutionary change to right the wrongs of the war. Far more people, in most social classes, were vaguely bitter and confused as a result of the shattering conflict, and their uncertainty about traditional goals and principles dominated much of the behavior of the interwar period.

Demographic and Economic Effects

The war brought direct changes in the economy and in population structure that helped shape society for the next decades. The population losses in the war were great. They included not only the deaths caused by the war itself but also a drastic decline in birth rate arising from the absence of young males. The result was a creation of two hollow generations, one in the group of twenty to forty years of age, from which the war took its greatest direct toll, and the other in the generation that would have ordinarily been born during the war and reached maturity in the 1930s. In most countries the absolute population loss was made up by a spurt in the birth rate right after the war, but the lack of two vital age groups could not be immediately compensated.

Furthermore, certain groups of society suffered disproportionately. The aristocracy, which had supplied many officers, saw its numbers drastically depleted. Professional men of good education, who also generally became officers, suffered greatly; the death rate among lieutenants and captains was severe because those ranks had led the futile and bloody charges against opposing trenches. In terms of age groups, education, and social standing the greatest population losses were suffered by those elements of European society that were most needed to assume positions of leadership in the next two decades.

Most important, however, was the magnitude of the total death rate in the war. Germany lost two million people; France lost 1.7 million, one twentieth of her total population. Italy and Britain lost a million each, while Russia was to lose a full seventeen million in war and the revolution and famines that followed. In all, sixteen million men died or were lost during the war. Twenty million more were wounded and in some cases proved to be a permanent drain on the resources and morale of postwar society. Finally, the transfers of territory resulting from the war, especially in eastern Europe, led to some massive migrations that added to demographic and economic dislocation. The exchange of more than a million Greeks and Turks after 1923 was the most notable case of forced migration, but there were others.

In sum, the war contributed to a significant deterioration in the population structure of Europe. Recovery from this blow varied, depending on the demographic vitality of the region, but in no case could complete recovery be immediate. War deaths and injuries conditioned economic development and morale during the next two decades. And the losses were deeply personal; the majority of families mourned the loss of at least one relative.

The economic impact of the war was less clearly harmful, but it opened certain structural weaknesses that were to dominate the succeeding period. As in demographic matters, some of the economic difficulties were not new. Inability to sustain previous rates of population growth had already afflicted western Europe; the war simply but massively aggravated the problem. In the economy a slowing of the pace of growth, especially in the mature industrial countries, had already been apparent; but the war increased the problem and added several new elements of concern.

Actual devastation in the war was considerable, but it did not prove to be permanently incapacitating. Approximately one thirtieth of Europe's assets were destroyed during the war. Physical damage was greatest in France, Belgium, Serbia, and eastern Europe. In general, this damage was relatively quickly made good. Reparation payments and government financing enabled France and Belgium to restore damaged factories, mines, and fields, sometimes with a bonus of modernized equipment that their economies had sorely lacked before. By the early 1920s, after a severe but brief depression as industry reconverted from the war, European production as a whole had mounted not simply to prewar levels but to the level that could have been expected at uninterrupted prewar rates of growth. Most of the continent, in fact, was on the verge of a period of unprecedented, if superficial, prosperity. In countries such as France the war had stimulated new attention to industry, particularly in metals and armaments. Certainly the technical and managerial ability that had already been developed seemed fully capable of surmounting even the major handicap of a world war.

There were, however, several points of weakness. The war ultimately added to the maladjustments of European agriculture. During the war many workers and considerable land were taken out of agricultural production on the continent. The resultant demand for food stimulated production elsewhere, in the United States, for instance, and even in combatant nations such as Britain, which reversed its earlier tendency to abandon farming. Those who could farm during and immediately after the war benefited from the high levels of demand for their goods. By the midtwenties, however, traditional producers had for the most part returned to their earlier patterns of production. Although some land was abandoned, particularly in France, the levels of agricultural production on the continent returned to normal within a short time—but the new productive capacities of the other regions were not eliminated. There was a greater surplus of agricultural goods than ever before, and farming income suffered accordingly. This was to affect not only farmers themselves but also the economy as a whole, for agricultural earnings proved insufficient to support significant increases in the production of manufactured goods.

The war also drastically altered the economic position of Europe in the world. The diversion of production and shipping to war needs made it impossible for European industry to supply its export markets. Non-European powers, led by the United States and Japan, entered these markets and retained part of their hold on them after the war. To these material difficulties was added a blow to morale as traditional views of European superiority were weakened.

Europe's credit position was also drastically altered. The need for foreign supplies, especially from the United States, compelled many countries to abandon their investments abroad in order to pay for needed materials. Foreign investments were also lost, particularly by France, when the Russian revolutionaries renounced their foreign debts. For both Britain and France the loss of those investments was accompanied by new borrowing. Germany also borrowed significantly during and after the war; her debts also were increasingly owed outside Europe, especially to the United States. Thus Europe was transformed from a creditor continent to a continent considerably in debt.

The war also dislocated the internal finances of many European countries. The war and production for it proved expensive, calling for resources far beyond the ordinary governmental budgets. Yet, except to a limited degree in Britain, the European states did not increase their levels of taxation; they financed the war through loans and the printing of new money. Both methods increased the amount of money in circulation at a time when production of consumer goods was falling. Inevitably, the result was inflation. The extent of inflationary pressure was indicated by the growth of the German national debt from four billion to 99 billion marks and of the French debt from 34 to 144 billion francs. During the war itself inflationary pressures were limited by rationing, international loans, and the pegging of currencies at artificial levels. The real effects of the financial crisis were to be felt only later. Even during the war, however, inflationary pressure was clear. Prices rose two and a half times in France and Italy, one and a half times in Britain. And in all cases, a legacy of monetary weakness and instability was bequeathed to the postwar economy.

Finally, the peace settlement was economically disruptive. A few nations profited economically from the settlement, notably France, which gained the remainder of the iron ore resources of Lorraine. Even for the victors, however, the new boundaries were drawn on the basis of nationalist impulse rather than economic reality. The new states in eastern Europe were for the most part economically weak. They were too small, and they quickly increased their economic isolation by a nationalistic policy of high tariffs. The states of the former Hapsburg empire were particularly handicapped; Austria lost its traditional iron and coal resources and its agricultural hinterland, and Hungary was severed from the traditional markets for its agriculture in industrial centers. Russia lost Polish industry and the oil resources of Bessarabia. Germany lost part of her coal resources in Upper Silesia and was deprived of the coal fields of the Saar for fifteen years; and she lost three quarters of her iron reserves as well as merchant shipping, railroad rolling stock, and cash in the various reparation exactions imposed upon her. The various deprivations of markets and resources, heightened by the protective tariffs adopted by all European states immediately after the war, decreased the economic possibilities for mature and emerging industrial nations alike.

The Social Classes

The general effects of the war on morale, economic prosperity, and even population touched all the major social classes. Some of the barriers among the various classes were reduced by common experience in military service or in war industry, and certainly material hardship and government propaganda touched wide sectors of the population without regard to class. Class differences remained, however, and the precise effects of the war varied with each class.

Peasants, for example, were used more extensively in military service than were the urban working classes. Many were killed; in France 53 per cent of the war dead were peasants. Those who survived retained both the sense of shock and the broader horizons they had experienced in the war. Many peasants in Germany stopped going to church when they returned. Some peasants did not return to agricultural life at all. Many veterans led in new peasant political movements and in other new forms of behavior. The peasants of eastern Europe sustained the additional impact of the Russian revolution. Russian peasants were roused by the hardships of the war and the risings in the cities to seize new land and to expect some political reforms. Many of their expectations were disappointed. But for a time the prospect of a new land system in Russia affected peasants in neighboring countries as well. Peasants returning from the armies provided much of the leadership for the agitation that resulted.

The aristocracy was also changed by the war experience. The population loss of the class during the war was significant; in Russia revolution and counterrevolution took a further toll. In Germany some of the territory of Junker holdings was transferred to new nations by the peace settlement. The settlement also provided new regimes that were to influence the political behavior of aristocrats in Poland, Hungary, Rumania, and other states. The parliamentary, democratic structures the victorious powers promoted in eastern Europe contradicted traditional aristocratic political ideals and even threatened the integrity of landed holdings. Except in Russia, however, the class was nowhere eliminated. It was weakened, increasingly menaced, but it still had a source of power in land and in its sense of social tradition.

The position of urban groups was modified by the war. During the first years the demand for workers caused a rise in wages that in turn promoted a significant degree of contentment. Furthermore, traditional working-class parties and unions cooperated with the war effort in spite of theoretical hostility to existing structures, and this too encouraged worker participation in war industry and in military service.

With increasing material hardship, however, as wages lagged behind prices after 1916, some discontent did arise and was expressed in the form of strikes. A minority of political and union leaders reverted to older doctrines and tried to dissociate themselves from cooperation with their belligerent governments. This trend was encouraged by the Russian revolution of 1917, which showed the possibility, in theory at least, of working-class revolution and of separation from the war effort.

By the end of the war a new split in working-class organizations was clearly developing. On the one hand, the majority wing of labor parties and unions remained tied to the existing structures. These groups had gained in respectability by their association with wartime governments, for socialists had participated in coalition cabinets more than ever before, and unions were given official encouragement. Realizing the need for organizations that could discipline and control the working class, governments had favored collective bargaining and other improvements in union status, and in return most unions had worked to prevent strikes and demonstrations that might disrupt production. The bulk of the labor movement was clearly inclined to modify its earlier methods of protest and had won vital official sanction in return. Votes for moderate socialist parties and membership in union movements soared during and immediately after the war because of the improved status of the labor movement. On the other hand, the minority faction of vigorous protest that had developed during the latter years of the war was fed by the theories of revolution maintained in earlier years, by the dissatisfaction the war itself bred, and by the fact of proletarian revolution in Russia. Both wings of the labor movement were to survive and were to influence subsequent attitudes of the working class.

The middle class was, of all groups, most shaken by the experience of the war. This was the class that had most firmly held to a mood of confidence and optimism before the war. The harsh realities of the conflict and the peace settlement were most dispiriting to this group. The extension of government action in the economy and in propaganda also contributed to a weakening of middle-class values.

The Russian revolution and the rise of communism in most countries soon after the war provided a further shock. Attempted communist revolutions in Germany and Hungary and the development of communist parties and union movements in Germany, France, and elsewhere supported the impression of a growing wave of working-class discontent. Communism seemed more menacing than previous working-class movements for several reasons. It was not initially modified by elements of compromise and revisionism as the socialist parties had been when they reached general notice in the late nineteenth century. Communist movements were well organized and capable of creating agitation far out of proportion to their numbers. Their domination by a foreign power, Russia, offended middle-class nationalism and made the movement generally more ominous. The mere fact that a working-class revolution had succeeded in a major state made revolution seem really possible elsewhere. There was tremendous hostility in the middle-class press to the Russian revolution, with accounts of communist atrocities appearing quite frequently. Many European governments took action, however ineffective, against the new Russian regime. Internally, many middle-class parties played on the communist threat; conservative groups in France during the early twenties had great success with a poster showing, without verbal comment, a red hand holding a dagger dripping with blood. The threat seemed real, particularly in the context of the general loss of confidence of the middle class.

Not only did the values of the middle class seem under attack, but its fundamental economic position was menaced as well. Certain members of the middle class made healthy profits during the war on the basis of war industries. Nowhere did governments radically limit profits and fundamental private ownership during the war. On the other hand, many middle-class people lost their investments abroad, and many more saw profit opportunities limited by the new stress on war industries. Those who relied on savings and lower-middle class clerks who depended on wages were hurt by the war. Inflation cut the value of savings, and prices rose much more rapidly than clerical incomes. In fact, workers during the early years of the war gained on the lower middle class because their incomes increased more rapidly because the demand for their services was greater.

The blow to middle class morale and economic standing, the interruption in gains for the class, was to influence much of the character of succeeding decades. The middle class did not lose fundamental dominance in western and central Europe, and it seemed to gain in eastern Europe outside of Russia through the liberal political and economic reforms. But the class as a whole felt increasingly threatened, and its attitudes changed accordingly.

GENERAL CULTURE BETWEEN THE WARS

When the war ended, there was a general sense of emotional release, at least in the victorious countries. In Britain victory celebrations included some sexual affairs with strangers in parks and shop entrances, which showed the emotional strain the war had imposed and foreshadowed to some extent the looser behavior that was to develop in the interwar period. There was general profession, in some countries, of a desire to return to normalcy, defined in prewar standards. Nowhere, however, could prewar canons of behavior be restored. Certain earlier trends in intellectual and artistic development continued, but even they went farther than their predecessors. There was a new sense of conscious criticism of older cultural values that went beyond artists themselves. And there was a broad change in the standards of popular behavior, and some lower-class values increasingly penetrated the upper classes. These changes had some relationship to cultural trends in that they stressed novelty and conscious abandonment of older values. They also emphasized sensual enjoyment in a manner not dissimilar from the teachings of some of the new intellectual leaders. Although some of the alterations in intellectual outlook penetrated only a small number of the highly educated, there was a more general cultural change that was not without consistency. The basic trends both in intellectual life and in popular culture had been prepared before the war, but the impact of the war heightened their popularity and quickened their influence.

The interwar period, especially before the dampening effects of the depression and the Nazi takeover, was one of immense artistic creativity. New artistic movements developed and received far wider attention than ever before. Novel styles were created in painting and sculpture, in which the trend to abstraction continued. Novelty also spread to fields such as architecture, where a "modern" style was elaborated by schools such as the Bauhaus in Germany. In literature, also, there was a growing distaste for conventional form. There was a new desire to express irrational impulses in writing and also to some extent in behavior. Writers such as Joyce and Proust employed complex symbolism to convey the obscure but basic elements of human personality and particularly of their own personalities. The morality, or at least the public morality, of artists was consciously defiant of established standards. New and intense artistic centers, such as Berlin, were the scenes of various forms of deviant behavior among artists. Individual writers such as André Gide felt compelled to announce personal characteristics such as homosexuality. In conduct as well as in actual artistic endeavor there was an air of creative if somewhat frantic experimentation. Older assumptions of optimism and rationalism were directly challenged and were found, if not erroneous, at least irrelevant. The doctrines of Freud and even new scientific theories that stressed terms such as relativity won new currency among intellectuals. Some philosophers of history, notably Spengler, were elaborately pessimistic about the future of civilization itself and directly critical of the canons of nineteenth-century middle-class life. There was a general feeling that Europe had entered a new period in its history. Some traditionalists bemoaned this; other writers found the opportunities exciting. No one, however, saw any way to return to the past, and no one developed totally clear intellectual standards for the future.

The prewar gap between artist and society was not fully bridged in this period. The most popular books and artistic styles were not those of the modern school. The reading public still preferred realism and entertainment in literature. Home furnishings remained predominantly heavy and elaborate. Middle-class and popular journals and papers ridiculed some of the abstract styles and criticized the moral behavior of some artists. Fascist leaders, especially in Germany, directly condemned the new intellectual movements as degenerate and vowed a return to healthy national tradition.

There were, nevertheless, important points of contact between the new artistic movements and more general attitudes. Certain terms, such as relativity and the unconscious, received growing currency in the popular press. There was some discussion of the theories of people such as Spengler even by groups who did not read their works directly. Exhibitions of modern art drew larger crowds; many members of the upper classes particularly began to build up collections of modern paintings, and many of the new homes of the wealthy were constructed in modern style. An obvious search for new stylistic values, and a decreasing dependence on past standards became apparent among the most direct patrons of culture.

Finally, the immorality, in traditional terms, of many intellectuals was more publicized than criticized. There were no crises over such behavior comparable to the trial of Oscar Wilde before the war. Gide's announcement of his homosexuality, for example, caused no stir. There was a new freedom of discussion, formal and informal, about sexual matters. Popular cultural idols as well as more obscure artists received great attention and considerable admiration for their physical attractions and for their willingness to display their independence from narrow family morality. Accounts of the divorces and amours of film stars became commonplace yet perennially interesting to the public. The distrust of natural appetites that artists and intellectuals condemned as a vile relic of the Victorian era was clearly declining in society as a whole, and the search for new standards of behavior was the clearest link between the experimentation of intellectuals and the attitudes of the major social classes.

The loosening of traditional restrictions was reflected in concepts of marriage. In the upper classes chaperonage and arranged marriages declined drastically. As had long been the case in the urban lower classes, it was increasingly assumed that young men and women should form their relationships on their own. Divorce rates rose among all classes, reflecting this new freedom.

The position and behavior of women changed as they were admitted to increasing social equality, and the feeling that they needed to be shielded from certain topics of conversation declined. They began to smoke and drink in public. Again, their freedom in these forms of behavior had long been greater in the lower classes than in middle-class society, and certain restraints did continue in some groups; but the increasing liberty was a general phenomenon.

Fashions became less formal and less restrictive. Women wore shorter skirts than ever before. Dancing styles altered; they too became less formal and allowed far greater motion. The new relaxation of behavior was reflected in the conduct of large numbers of people and dominated organs of mass cultures such as the press and films. On various levels, then, the movement was widespread.

A new desire for enjoyment was clearly abroad. Newspapers found that only their frivolous articles attracted readers. They provided intensive coverage of particularly interesting crimes, the activities of the socially fashionable, sports, and phenomena that were diverting in their peculiarity, such as nudist movements or the tales of the Loch Ness monster. New professional sports received wide attention; to professional football were now added boxing, cycling, and auto racing. Gambling increased among most groups, and mass outlets were organized by the state in the form of lotteries and football pools. These attracted attention and considerable spending from the middle class and the urban lower classes alike. New outlets for entertainment were developed. Some, such as night clubs, were particularly for the wealthy and reflected the increased desire for enjoyment on the part of the middle class. Most, however, attracted all elements, including some in the upper classes. The film and the radio rose to tremendous popularity because of their relatively low cost and their obvious entertainment value. Those institutions, along with the growing standardization of the press, provided an increasingly common culture for all groups, urban and rural, rich and poor. Rural groups were in fact brought closer to urban culture by the extension of bus service to even tiny villages. Class lines were not eliminated and seemed more tightly drawn than before in many respects; but a desire for enjoyment transcended their boundaries. The tensions of the war and steady economic and political pressures afterwards affected European society generally and caused a common desire for release. Not all found the sort of diversion they sought; rates of suicide and of mental illness rose in all groups during the period. But the quest for pleasure led clearly to new and important cultural institutions and patterns of behavior.

ECONOMIC TRENDS

New Opportunities

Developments in popular culture, along with more general social changes, were clearly related to economic development in the period. Technical changes promoted new cultural patterns as inventions such as radio and film rose quickly to prominence. A rise in prosperity prompted some of the new forms of recreation by providing more means and greater leisure than ever before. Areas and groups that did not participate in this increased prosperity, such as eastern Europe and the unemployed in the West, shared only partially in much of the new popular culture. Finally, the evolution of the economy provided much of the pressure that was reflected in the search for pleasure. The European economy, profoundly shaken by the war, remained fundamentally weak during the succeeding two decades. There were important gains, but they were balanced by difficulties in basic structure. Economic changes and economic difficulties dominated the position and attitudes of the major social classes during the period.

The productive capacity of the economy steadily increased. Technical improvement continued to raise productivity per worker. Automobile manufacturing, for example, changed from a largely artisan basis to assembly-line systems. Other products were developed, such as the radio, that opened new possibilities for manufacturing and for consumption alike. On the basis of new machinery and types of goods, production increased during the 1920s. After the brief postwar depression production rose quite noticeably during the 1920s. The French economy, particularly, entered a period of substantial boom. Standards of living improved for most elements of the population. There was more money for recreation, which was reflected in the popularity of radios and films. Clothing became increasingly varied with the addition of artificial fibers such as rayon.

Cosmetics were more widely sold than ever before, reflecting the growing resources of the lower classes and the interest of women in developing their own pleasures. Diets remained varied and were supplemented by some new processed foods. There were some gains in housing, although the lag in construction during the war and destruction in some areas created problems. Major developments, such as the "Siemens city" in Berlin, allowed some industrial workers to buy or rent private houses in the largest centers for the first time. In the wealthier classes purchase of items such as automobiles became even more common. To an extent, then, during the 1920s the economy seemed capable of continued gains.

The rationalization and concentration of economic organization continued, as before the war. Giant new combines were developed, such as the *Vereinigte Stahlwerke,* which controlled almost half of the German steel industry. The formation of cartels, some on an international basis, reached higher levels than ever before. Industrial investment and control by banks also became more extensive. These developments naturally increased the managerial and bureaucratic element in European society. There were more jobs for men with technical skills in administration of firms and factories and in development, through research, of new methods and products for the giant enterprises. Some managers might, through their dominance of a large organization and ownership of at least some stock, rise to the upper class. Others, whose duties were limited to managerial assistance or to research, remained at a modest level of income. And of course the clerks, salespeople, and technicians remained essentially at a lower-middle-class level. All were involved, however, in functions of direction and service far more than in ownership directly. They were part of the middle class in their incomes, attitudes, and even clothing, but their growing importance and their distinctive position increasingly altered the character of their class.

Structural Weaknesses

The increasing organization of the economy and the utilization of more massive financial instruments encouraged economic development in several respects. As before, they increased the opportunities for profit by reducing competition. The new enterprises had greater resources for investment and for technical research, both of which helped stimulate economic advance for the firm and for society as a whole. The boom mentality of Germany in the midtwenties was based in large part on the investment possibilities of the new combinations.

In many cases, however, the spread of investment and of the formation of huge economic units went beyond the point of real economic value. In Germany particularly, where the boom seemed greatest and where investment was most intense during the decade, actual production and sales potential did not correspond to the developments in organization and finance. Many combinations were formed for their speculative possibilities, their potential drawing power for investments, rather than for any improvements they would make in production or distribution. New promoters such as Stinnes found it easy and profitable to buy firms of extraordinary diversity as vehicles for attracting speculative investments. This development was possible, again especially in Germany, for two related reasons. First, the rapid inflation of the early 1920s made it easy to borrow with the expectation that the sum would be less valuable, and therefore less onerous, when the time for repayment came. Second, massive American capital was available for speculative investment in Germany, Austria, and eastern Europe. American funds were not always directed to projects of real productive possibility, but this of course simply heightened the speculative spiral. Investments stimulated production without developing a certainty of sales; production could be maintained only if further investment created a market. Also, soaring stock values on German and Austrian exchanges depended on continued bidding by investors. Ample profits could be made by elements of the middle class, but those profits were not fully translated into increased demands for goods. In fact, the widening gap between rich and poor in Germany heightened the basic difficulty of developing sufficient markets. The result was an economic structure highly vulnerable to shock. When American capital was withdrawn after the 1929 financial crash and when the faith of European investors and financiers in their own holdings was correspondingly reduced, collapse of the speculative structure was inevitable.

Even before this collapse there had been important limitations on real economic advance in Europe as a whole. The inflationary trend severely shook the economic position and confidence of many groups. Except in Britain, where the government deflated the currency by returning to the gold standard, inflation hit hard at some point during the decade. Inflationary pressures were based on the increase in money supply during the war and were heightened by borrowing and new printing by governments in Germany and the states of eastern Europe. In Austria the cost of living was 2,645 times higher in July, 1922, than it had been in 1914. In Germany the inflation of the early 1920s made money virtually valueless as prices rose to astronomical heights. The process was stopped only in 1923 when the government set the mark at a more realistic, but far lower, level than ever before. In France inflation later in the decade was ended only in 1928 by pegging the franc at a quarter of its previous value.

Inflationary pressures affected most groups. Some elements of the working class suffered, for their wages rose less rapidly than prices. Unions were massively damaged as their treasuries were depleted both by the inflation and by the subsequent government devaluation of money. Members of the middle and lower middle classes suffered even more. A few, to be sure, seized on the inflation as a chance to borrow money cheaply for speculative investment, but the larger element that relied on savings and previous investments saw their holdings virtually wiped out. This encouraged an interest in enjoyment rather than in saving. But the price rises during the war itself, the new taxes imposed by many governments, and the postwar inflation severely reduced opportunities to spend. The loss of savings was also a blow to the confidence, to the very sense of identity, of many in the middle class, which relied on property ownership to provide wealth and status. A new fearfulness arose in the class, which could be translated into active discontent. The class did not lose its esteem for property and its sense of separate status, but it recognized that these values were increasingly threatened by the workings of the economy itself.

Inflation was the most obvious sign of economic disruption during the 1920s, but it was not the only one. Equally important was the economic stagnancy or decline of many important groups. Agricultural incomes remained low as competition reached new levels. Elements of the working class suffered from unemployment or poor wages. In the aggregate, there was little new demand for workers during the period. Production was rising only slowly, and technological innovations easily provided for the small increase. There was some transfer of workers from old industries to new ones, particularly to fields such as chemicals and electrical equipment: but on the whole, the period of expansion of the working class seemed over. In addition, some key industries were clearly sick. Shipbuilding declined as international trade proved sluggish. The textile industry was faced with overwhelming competition from areas of cheap labor, particularly outside Europe, and those firms that survived did so only by reducing their work force and introducing new machines. Coal production fell everywhere, because oil provided cheaper and more efficient fuel; but oil could not provide direct alternate employment for coal miners, for it required less labor and its sources were outside Europe. Some of the most traditional industries and the largest users of labor were declining. In Britain this led to economic depression even during the 1920s. Levels of unemployment stood at 10 per cent even in the best years and at 16 per cent in mining and textiles. Whole areas of traditional industry, such as Lancashire and South Wales, seemed permanently blighted. On the continent as well there were substantial though less massive pockets of unemployment. Although wages rose for many categories of workers during the decade, the gains were counterbalanced by the dire poverty of other groups.

On the whole, the level of demand for goods was relatively low well before the great depression. Some workers, certain elements of the lower middle class, and the agricultural community generally were actually earning less, or at least no more, than they had before the war. Two other traditional sources of demand were now limited. Population growth was slowing everywhere after the brief compensatory spurt following the war. In France birth rates fell below death rates, and the population would have declined except for immigration from Italy and eastern Europe. British and Scandinavian birth rates were only slightly higher than death rates, and population growth slowed in Germany, Italy, and elsewhere. This decline in demographic vitality was itself a reflection of the insecurity of the period; marriage rates remained high, but couples were simply not willing to take the economic risk of having many children. As a result, there was little expansion of the market due to population rise.

Opportunities for export sales were also limited. New levels of tariff protection were thrown up by all major countries; again, a defensive reaction to economic difficulties itself increased those difficulties. Competition from non-European powers continued to cut into markets. British trade, for example, attained only three quarters of its prewar level. Finally, in 1927–1928 a collapse in the price of raw materials reduced export possibilities still further, because countries producing these materials could afford fewer purchases from industrial Europe. With the decline of agricultural prices, much of eastern and southern Europe entered a slump as early as 1926.

For a variety of reasons, then, Europe's productive capacities exceeded the possibilities of sales. Production on the continent as a whole increased only 1 per cent a year after 1923, in contrast to a 3 per cent annual rise before 1913. In a few countries, such as Germany, speculative investment created a façade of prosperity, but it was highly vulnerable. With the collapse of export possibilities after 1928, and then with the financial crash in the United States and the withdrawal of American capital, Europe entered, inexorably, a period of unprecedented economic depression.

The depression, which began in 1928 in the most industrialized areas and spread gradually to France and Italy, touched every aspect of economic life. It represented a financial crisis. Many banks closed, and credit was restricted; coming on the heels of inflation, faith in money and in financial institutions was severely shaken. Sales fell off sharply even with massive reductions in prices. As a result, production tumbled; German production had fallen 39 per cent by 1932. Profits declined, wages fell, and unemployment increased tremendously.

All major social classes suffered. Members of the middle class were hit by declining profits and by loss of stock investments. Their morale was shaken by the mere fact of depression; confidence and optimism about the economic system were reduced. Many managers and recent university graduates suffered from unemployment or were forced to take jobs beneath their station. The lower middle class, similarly, lost many jobs. Peasants were able to sell fewer agricultural goods because of the decline in urban income, so their earnings were reduced still further. But it was the working class that bore the brunt of unemployment and loss of income. In Britain 22 per cent of the workers who had some social insurance were unemployed by 1932. Over six million people in Germany and 850,000 in France, not exclusively workers, were out of work. This massive unemployment made recovery from the depression difficult, because it proved hard to stimulate sufficient demand to set the economy in motion once more. And the fact or fear of unemployment greatly weakened public morale. The unemployed survived on some insurance payments and on charity, but they could do no more than survive. Consumption levels fell drastically. Prolonged joblessness reduced many to apathy and stirred others, including those with jobs who feared unemployment for themselves, to new anger.

European economies recovered only slowly and partially from the crisis. The depth of the depression was reached in 1932–1933, although France experienced her trough a bit later. Production after this low point rose; by 1938 the British economy was turning out more goods than ever before. Yet even then more than a million and a half were still unemployed. France did not manage to recover her previous levels of production or employment before World War II. Germany under Hitler did restore full employment and greatly increased production, largely through state programs of investment, military purchasing, and labor service. Wages, however, did not rise to their earlier levels.

In general, new economic policies involving increasing government action were called forth by the depression. The British government went off the gold standard, extended credit to industry and encouraged exports, retrained some workers, and tried to modernize agriculture. Scandinavian governments, and France after 1936, tried in various ways to stimulate the economy, and the fascist regimes in Germany and Italy acted with considerable vigor. Hitler's government exerted some control over prices and profits and allocated resources under a state economic plan. Massive public works programs and a year-long program of youth labor service built up Germany's military potential and stimulated employment.

Innovation did occur under widely different regimes, but only after at least four years of severe hardship; and in most cases it was only partially successful in relieving the depression as a whole. Coming after an earlier decade of shaky economic development, the 1930s brought real suffering to many groups. The interwar period as a whole was shaped by substantial and varied economic dislocation.

THE SOCIAL CLASSES

Aristocrats Outside Northwestern Europe

Economic and political changes in the postwar period put renewed pressure on the aristocracy, especially in eastern and southern Europe, where the class had maintained its greatest strength. The continued difficulties in agriculture, particularly the heavy competition in grains, posed grave economic problems for aristocratic landowners. Most, such as the Junkers in Germany, sought and obtained high tariff protection; the Junkers even received state subsidies late in the 1920s. Despite this support significant difficulties remained.

More important, and certainly more novel, were the alterations of political structure and their effects on landholding. In Russia the revolution seized aristocratic estates and eliminated the class as a formal element of society. Many aristocrats participated in counter-revolutionary efforts, and many more simply fled the country. The repercussions of the Russian revolution made aristocrats in other countries increasingly fearful. Political reforms in other states seemed to portend similar attacks on the position of the aristocracy. The rise of the political left, even among the peasantry in some areas, added to the menace. However, nowhere outside of Russia was the aristocracy eliminated, and rarely was it significantly attacked. An ominous situation resulted; sufficient changes were made to discontent the aristocrats and to make them fear further deterioration of their position, but their power base was not removed. Inevitably, the aristocrats and other large landholders used their power to effect favorable changes in the political structure of their country.

Political reforms after the war, particularly in the states of eastern Europe, radically altered the balance of power among the social classes. States such as Poland and Czechoslovakia were established as parliamentary democracies. This meant an increase in the importance of urban middle-class elements who were attracted to this political structure and relatively skilled in its operation. It also meant the possibility of peasant political activity independent of aristocratic guidance; in most countries peasant parties were formed, sometimes with urban leadership, and agitated for redistribution of land and other reforms. Older countries, such as Rumania, increased the power of national parliaments. Under the impact of the war, during which reforms had been promised to keep the peasants in line, and especially with the example of communist revolution next door and Bolshevik agitation among Rumanian peasants themselves, universal suffrage was granted for the lower parliamentary house. The upper house continued under aristocratic control, and the king retained a veto over all legislation. Germany adopted a democratic, parliamentary republic for the first time. In Spain the collapse of the monarchy in 1931 led to a democratic, parliamentary regime and therefore to the rise of urban and peasant political elements, including the large anarchist group, that were hostile to aristocratic interests. Those regimes not only altered political forms at the center but also attempted to reduce some of the local political rights and influence of the nobility.

All these changes offended the aristocratic sense of tradition. In Spain and Germany the class remained attached to the monarchy, and where kings remained, as in Yugoslavia and Rumania, the aristocrats clustered around them. More generally, aristocrats resented the political rise of new social elements and, of course, the reduction of their own influence.

Finally, aristocrats resented the efforts at land reforms that most of the new regimes introduced. Under middle-class leadership but backed by peasant political elements, the new states attempted some redistribution of land. A few estates were purchased and divided by the republican regimes in Germany and Spain. The Czechoslovakian regime seized about 11 per cent of the land, held by German owners, and divided it. Some redistribution took place also in Poland and Hungary, but in both countries large holdings still predominated. In Hungary .7 per cent of the population owned 48.3 per cent of the land; in Poland, .6 per cent owned 43 per cent. But in all these countries something was done, and the rise of peasant parties seemed to portend more changes in the future. In Rumania a major redistribution did take place. In 1907, 49 per cent of the land had been owned by .56 per cent of the population; by 1922 only 7 per cent of the land remained in large holdings. Rumanian landlords received monetary compensation and used it to enter commerce and industry. There was widespread discontent, however; and again, the process of change did not seem to be over, for a peasant party won control of the lower house in 1928. Everywhere, aristocratic hostility to political change was supplemented by fears for the land itself. It was small wonder that the class took action to protect itself.

Aristocratic action took the form, almost uniformly, of support for an authoritarian regime that would protect the large estates and discourage protest from below. In Rumania and Yugoslavia the aristocracy supported efforts by the monarchy to assume full control. Landowners were also instrumental in backing Franco during the Spanish Civil War; and from Franco they received protection for their land, their local political power, and even important positions in church, army, and the central government. Southern Italian landowners acquiesced in Mussolini's rise to power, preferring it to the threat of socialist gains in the parliamentary monarchy, and he repaid them by leaving the large estates untouched. In Germany the Junkers facilitated the Nazi takeover. They remained personally attached to more traditional conservatism, but their political representatives made crucial deals with the Nazis that enabled the latter to seize power; and the class preferred Nazi rule to the republican regime. Once more, the large estates were protected by the new government.

The aristocrats in eastern and southern Europe were not solely responsible for the development of authoritarian systems of government, but they played a major role. Everywhere they had been under new attack; their political traditions were affected and their landed bases threatened. The reaction had been swift and effective. Although the class in most instances had to accept new types of regimes, it managed to preserve some political power and succeeded, for the most part, in saving the large estates.

Peasants

The same economic and political forces that influenced the landed aristocracy affected the peasantry during the interwar period. In eastern and southern Europe many peasants found at least brief opportunity to express their continued hunger for land. These were areas still severely pressed by increases in population and limited further by the existence of large holdings. During the war peasants were forced to assume a disproportionate share of military service. They had been the traditional source of troops and seemed more dispensable than many of the workers in heavy industry. In all areas peasants were marked by the effects of fighting and many returned full of bitterness and frustration. In some instances this led to renewed agitation for land. Under the impact of revolution in the cities Russian peasants seized more land from the large estates, and some of the poorer peasants attacked the richer ones. Elsewhere in eastern Europe peasant agitation was far more limited, but together with changes in regime, it was enough to win some land reforms. Finally, when civil war broke out in Spain in 1936, peasants again attempted to seize some land directly. Although the interwar period was not marked by so frequent peasant rioting as before, eastern and southern European peasants remained clearly interested in capitalizing on any opportunity to express their land hunger. In some instances their wishes seemed partially fulfilled.

For the most part, peasants in the east and south actually gained little. Russian peasants kept the individual holdings they wanted only briefly. By 1918 the Soviet government attempted to press for greater collectivization of agriculture and particularly for new state controls over output and distribution. The peasants resisted, largely by restricting their production to their own needs. In 1921 the government, as part of Lenin's New Economic Policy, relaxed its pressures, and the peasants enjoyed a new period of private individual holdings. Earlier trends toward the concentration of land in the hands of a minority of wealthy kulaks continued, and agricultural production rose once again. At the end of the decade, however, renewed repression, including the extermination of the kulaks, attacked the peasant agricultural system, and collectivization was fully imposed. Again, some poorer peasants joined the attack on the kulaks but only in the interest of acquiring land themselves; the policy of collectivization thwarted them just as it did the more substantial farmers. Overt resistance to the new system was limited, but in the early 1930s many peasants destroyed their livestock and smashed equipment before entering the unwelcome collectives. Although the government imposed its will by military force, the peasants' traditional desire for individual holdings remained unquenched.

Elsewhere in eastern and southern Europe the peasants, although not subjected to radically new systems, remained severely limited by the continued existence of large estates. Their conditions were further affected by the decline of agricultural prices during the period. In all these regions, except Czechoslovakia, which had been the industrial center of the Hapsburg empire, there was little industrialization and urbanization, and so little relief from population pressure. The vast majority of the populations remained rural. Population increase had slowed in the east and south but continued at a far higher rate than in western Europe. The pressure on the land was therefore intense. The small amount of land reform that occurred was scarcely noticed.

Over 70 per cent of the peasants in eastern Europe possessed less than twelve and a half acres of land—enough for a bare subsistence at best. In Rumania, where land reform was extensive, 50 per cent of the peasantry held less than seven and a half acres. There was little new provision for credit or technical assistance for the peasantry. Upon acquiring small plots of land, Rumanian peasants actually reduced the average yield of the land. They were not yet attuned to market agriculture and produced only what they needed to subsist. They also switched from wheat, the only grain useful for export but expensive to plant, to the rougher grains they were accustomed to consume themselves. The small size of peasant holdings and the backwardness of methods inevitably produced extremely low material standards. Peasants in these areas, including those who worked on large estates for miserable wages or who served as sharecroppers, had only the meanest housing, clothing, and diet. Health standards were low, and in some regions 20 per cent of the population died before they reached one year of age. The continued decline of domestic industry and the imposition of some new taxes by governments dominated by the upper classes simply increased the misery of the peasant masses.

Peasants did not react with particular vigor to their misery. They did begin to gain some political experience as long as democratic forms endured. Peasant parties, usually led by urban reformers and advocating land reform and government aid to agriculture, won more and more of their votes; their programs seemed clearly in the peasant interest. There were also some signs of changes in personal behavior. Church attendance declined in certain regions, such as Rumania. Crime rates rose in many cases. The gradual spread of education, although it left many peasants illiterate still, did bring new ideas even to the more backward rural regions. On the whole, however, peasants continued to rely on traditional methods and village structures as the focus of their lives. They faced some increasing material difficulty, and they encountered certain new forms of government action, but they were not capable of making major adaptation to those changes.

In western and central Europe peasants also faced increasing economic hardship. There was a period of prosperity in the first years after the war before production was fully restored. Many peasants managed to pay off their debts and raise their personal consumption. French peasants borrowed to buy more land, Germans to buy new equipment. But by 1923 or 1924 pressure on agricultural prices returned, and the new debts became a great burden. The depression made matters worse by reducing agricultural prices up to 50 per cent. In France peasant buying power compared to 1913 was down 10 per cent by 1930, 28 per cent by 1933. Peasants continued to introduce some technical improvements in an effort to meet this pressure. There was also a steady exodus to the cities, and in France some land was abandoned. Still, material levels remained low—well below those of the cities. In France the average peasant's house was at least a hundred years old. Government programs allowed some improvements, particularly by extending electricity to most villages. But only a minority of peasants had indoor plumbing facilities.

During the 1920s there were few signs of increased peasant discontent. Political patterns remained largely traditional and conservative. French peasants often elected conservative estate owners, the traditional notables, to newly created agricultural bureaus. Some new farmers' lobbying groups were formed in both Germany and France, but there was little significant change.

With the advent of depression and the new political movements in the cities, peasant political patterns began to alter somewhat. Leaders of both left and right began to solicit peasant support more actively. And peasants themselves had a greater desire to express their material discontent and, often, their distrust of the growing power of urban workers. There was a growing feeling that the governments were hostile to agriculture and that special protection for factory labor was unfair.

In France communism made some headway among peasants and the C.G.T. had 180,000 peasant members by 1936; in 1937 many farm workers struck for collective bargaining. More important were the gains of agricultural parties and groupings on the right. A Peasant Front was formed in 1934 that stressed the need for a political system more attuned to the needs of agriculture. The Front was soon split, but important currents of activity in defense of specifically peasant movements remained. There were also some cases of direct action. Demonstrations occurred in several areas, and in 1934 a peasant group marched to Paris. A milk strike occurred in the same period, the first time that peasant owners, as opposed to agricultural workers, had banded together for protest action. Finally, cooperative movements continued to gain. Whereas before the war only a tenth of the French peasantry had belonged to cooperative groups, by the 1920s a full third of the class was enrolled. The cooperative movements continued to provide important assistance in matters of credit, purchasing, and processing; they also represented the new willingness and ability of peasants to join together in matters of mutual concern. The various efforts by peasants to better their lot had only limited success. Material conditions remained poor. Governments offered some new technical assistance, and in 1936 the Popular Front ministry established a Wheat Office to support wheat prices and improve peasant incomes. Various other subsidies were extended. For the most part, these measures relieved but did not remove the major economic difficulties. Increasing peasant activity was not yet sufficient to win substantial material improvements.

German peasants also developed some distinctive political expressions during this period, particularly after the depression brought new and widespread hardship. As in France, the basic grievances concerned falling prices and lack of capital. There was also some general resentment over the declining status of the peasantry in society as a whole, the growing dominance of big business, and the rise of communist and socialist movements that threatened private property and seemed to give the workers undue influence. As a result of these various sources of discontent, many peasants proved vulnerable to Nazi propaganda. The first areas to offer majorities to the Nazis were regions such as Thuringia, which lacked a substantial industrial population and were dominated by peasant smallholding. Traditional, tightly organized villages were particularly liable to turn to the Nazis.

To many peasants the Nazis offered protection against change. They promised to support peasant tenure. They praised the peasantry as the true bearer of German tradition and promised to promote peasant traditions of dress and behavior in an effort to return to the essence of German culture. To be sure, peasants did not win what they wanted; the Nazi regime, once in office, continued to pay lip service to a peasant ideal, but in the interests of efficiency it busily furthered consolidation of agricultural holdings and the displacement of the smaller peasants.

Quite generally, even in eastern Europe, peasants exhibited certain new forms of action during the period, particularly in the political sphere. The specific political patterns varied widely, in some cases approaching both extremes of the political spectrum, although there was a tendency to favor rightist movements, which promised support for peasant traditions as well as material aid. There was a certain underlying consistency in these diverse movements; peasants were gaining in political consciousness, although they controlled no major political movement, and they tried to express their desire for greater material well-being and greater security. In no case, however, did they achieve notable success. Even when they supported victorious political movements, they found that their voice was not sufficient to win major gains. A real solution for the difficulties of agriculture was yet to be found.

The Middle Classes: Economic Base

The conditions of the middle and lower middle classes changed notably in the interwar period. Their numbers grew as extension of state and private bureaucracies and of sales and service industries provided many new opportunities in the 1920s. Many workers rose to various levels of the middle class. By 1929 6.4 per cent of the British higher civil servants came from families of manual workers. In Germany up to 25 per cent of the white-collar group had blue-collar origins. Expansion of educational facilities in most countries also allowed new mobility.

The economic growth of the 1920s, moderate though it was, improved the position of some in the middle class. A few made huge profits; there were many newcomers to the ranks of the very wealthy. Many at least maintained their earlier standards.

Finally, the middle class retained most of the political power that it had possessed before the war. In eastern Europe its political opportunities often increased with the establishment of new parliamentary regimes. Except for the Soviet Union, no government in the period took measures fundamentally hostile to private industrial and commercial property and profit. The middle class was afflicted by a number of difficulties during the period, but it did not lose its basic social power.

The pressures on the middle classes came from a variety of sources. The basic difficulties were economic. Although certain entrepreneurs and speculators made substantial gains during the 1920s, inflation and relatively slow growth limited the earning power of many members of the class. And despite some new opportunities, mobility declined within the middle classes. The formation of small firms slowed notably under the pressure of large commercial and industrial combines and the low rate of economic growth. At the same time, advancement to managerial posts became more difficult than it had been before the war. A large number of managers came from established managerial families; and the decrease in industrial growth limited the number of new positions still further. In Britain the result was a decline of almost 50 per cent in the number of managers who had risen from the lower classes. In Germany the growth of large enterprises and the steady rationalization of management similarly reduced the opportunities for advance from the lower middle class. There were many complaints that the few posts available were given to outsiders, sometimes relatives of the owner, instead of being used as channels for promotion from within. Opportunity for mobility still existed but at an obviously lower level than before. At the same time, many lower-middle-class tasks were becoming more monotonous due to the introduction of office machinery and the growing specialization of clerical labor.

Most important, however, was the damage caused by inflation and subsequent depression. In Germany inflation destroyed over 50 per cent of the capital of the lower middle class by 1925. Pensions were reduced in value and many retired bureaucrats lived in near-misery and some actually starved. Even such an eminent professor as Ernst Troeltsch subsisted in retirement only on aid from friends. The government prohibited the raising of rents during inflation, so many property owners saw their incomes lag behind prices. Half a million members of the lower middle class were forced into factory work during the 1920s as a result of economic pressure. The lower-middle-class advantage in earnings over the working class was reduced although not totally eliminated. In Germany by 1929 four million members of the class earned no more than the average worker. And at the same time the incomes of the wealthy capitalists were visibly increasing. A hatred of big business and of labor, already evident before the war, inevitably increased in the lower ranks of the middle class.

Furthermore, these difficulties did not end with the termination of inflation. A great deal of unemployment remained. In 1926, 14,000 of 48,000 trained physicians in Germany were not able to practice medicine and were engaged in clerical or other lower-middle-class professions instead. The prewar phenomenon of excessive production of university graduates had increased. The wealth of society, as it was distributed at least, simply could not maintain a demand for the numbers of people, usually from the middle class, who obtained university education in the hope of gaining prestige and advancement. Small shopkeepers were hard-pressed by competition from large retail stores. Even those who survived found their profits increasingly limited and their prices and sales conditions dictated by big manufacturing cartels. In Germany, where the problems of the middle class were greatest, it was not uncommon by 1929 to see newspaper advertisements proclaiming personal misery: "30 years old, married, 3 children. Nothing earned for 3 years. Future? Poor house, madhouse, or the gas jet." In many European countries rising rates of suicide reflected the extremes of despair.

The depression heightened this distress. Many investors lost at least part of their holdings; big and small businessmen suffered from a drop in profits, and many were forced out of business. Shopkeepers suffered as their clients' purchasing power declined. Increased taxes on small business, as in Germany, added to the problem. Professional people had difficulty finding work. In Germany seven thousand engineers lost their jobs, and by 1930, 300,000 German university graduates were competing for 130,000 positions. European governments fired literally hundreds of thousands of bureaucrats and clerks as tax revenues declined during the crisis. Thousands of teachers were unemployed—forty thousand in Germany alone. Of four million salaried employes in Germany, 600,000 were out of work—almost as high a proportion of unemployment as in the working class. Furthermore, unemployed members of the middle class did not receive the social insurance benefits and union protection accorded to the workers, and their resentment of the working class increased as a result.

In general, important segments of the middle class met economic disaster during the period, particularly during the depression. Some were entirely out of work; others had to accept jobs beneath their levels of training and their social status. An even larger segment of the class suffered from the decline in economic growth during the period. For all but a few, the age of confidence and of high spending seemed to be over. A class that had based its position on earnings and property ownership now found both eroded by apparently uncontrollable trends in the economy. Recovery after the trough of the depression brought renewed profits to many elements of the class and restored employment for numerous clerks and professional people. Many businessmen adopted improved techniques to meet the crisis and emerged stronger than ever before. The class as a whole, however, had lost its economic impetus, and certain elements continued to receive incomes well below their expectations. The economic difficulties of the middle class were the key to changes in general social attitudes during the interwar period.

The Middle Classes: Morale and Politics

The morale of the middle class had been severely shaken by the world war. The new interest in pleasure and enjoyment reflected the confusion of middle-class values. The traditional family ethic and social attitudes loosened, but the class did not discover any clear substitutes.

New political challenges arose that disturbed the class increasingly. The political gains and growing hostility of the working class caused particular concern. The Russian revolution had proved the possibility of workers' uprising and the growth of communist movements, however small, in western and central Europe confirmed the threat. The expansion of socialist parties and their control of governments, as in early Weimar Germany, seemed almost as menacing.

In combination with the economic difficulties the working-class threat appeared intolerable to the middle class. An increasingly defensive attitude was adopted. The class felt that it had to defend its basic economic and political position. This determination was reflected in Germany by the unprecedented growth of employee unions; by 1929 such unions had 1.2 million members, a full quarter of the total number of white-collar workers. In France one result of middle-class defensiveness was a private resistance to governmental measures, particularly taxation, of which members of the class did not approve. A mood of *incivisme* arose, a lack of willingness to fulfill the duties of citizenship. Businessmen, from small shopkeepers to large industrialists, made it almost a matter of pride to avoid paying taxes. This reflected the economic difficulties of many, especially the small shopkeepers who faced increasing competition, and also the growing sense that the government itself had become an enemy. Heightened resistance to working-class demands also indicated the new defensiveness of the middle class. The rate of favorable or compromise strike settlements decreased in many countries, despite the improved organization of most unions; manufacturers saw no reason now to yield. In Britain the general strike of 1926 provided a clear illustration of middle-class hostility to the demands of labor, for it was marked by willingness of members of the middle class, including students at Oxford and Cambridge, to replace workers in loading jobs, in the running of trains, and in other functions. There was a clear desire to keep the economy operating sufficiently to defeat the strike; and the middle class won its victory. In the following year legislation was passed forbidding sympathetic strikes and weakening the general bargaining power of labor. Class interest was now predominant.

The active defensiveness of the middle class was clearest, of course, in the political field. From the early postwar period middle- and lower-middle-class voting patterns displayed greater conservatism than had been typical of the prewar period. Existing regimes were accepted for the most part, and in eastern Europe elements of the middle class helped sponsor the limited land reforms that were enacted. Generally, however, there was no desire for further change. Traditional middle-class political vehicles such as the British Liberal Party declined rapidly, as the class switched its votes to the Conservatives. The French Radical Party retained substantial middle-class support only because of its resistance to any real social reforms. In Germany as early as 1921 the middle class largely abandoned republican parties in favor of the conservative Nationalists. The interest in the vigorous conservatism continued to typify the middle classes in many areas, particularly Britain, throughout the interwar period.

Under stress, however, major segments of the class turned to other political movements. The stress was created by economic collapse and by the rise of working-class radicalism, in the form of vigorous socialism or of communism, which accompanied such collapse.

In Italy after 1919 certain middle-class elements joined with other groups in support of the fascist party. To the middle class fascism offered an acceptable defense against working-class revolution, in the name of national unity; the Italian middle class was interested in nationalist causes anyway and had been disappointed by the lack of gains from the peace settlement. Fascism also proclaimed a need to protect small business against large stores and industries. It promised an end to antagonistic labor unions and parties and a solution to economic difficulties. Italy was wracked by the postwar depression, the rise of a militant socialist party, and a wave of strikes. These developments induced some members of the middle class to support fascism directly and others to acquiesce in the fascist takeover. Crucial to the fascist government was an arrangement with businessmen whereby the control and profits of industry remained in the hands of the upper middle class, despite the earlier anticapitalist talk of the party.

In Germany the Nazi party was formed in the years following the war and was led by a man from the Austrian lower middle class. It attracted little initial support. Only in 1924, at the peak of resentment over the inflation, did a coalition of which the Nazis were a part poll nearly two million votes. With the onset of depression, however, Nazi power rose rapidly, and the party achieved far more massive direct support than the Italian fascists ever knew. The party polled 37.3 per cent of the vote in 1932, largely at the expense of traditional middle-class parties. It attracted many members of the lower middle class by its promises of full employment and welfare aid and its attacks on communism and big business alike. Like Italian fascism, the movement appealed to the older middle-class desire to protect the small firm against modern capitalism as well as against the power of organized labor. It was particularly popular, therefore, in the smaller towns. At the same time, as in Italy, the party depended for its final seizure of power on an agreement with business leaders in which protection for business was promised in exchange for financial support. The upper middle class was not committed to Nazism, but it saw in the movement a chance to defeat the rising threat of communism. Thus, for various reasons, by 1933 many elements of the German middle class had turned to Nazism.

Elsewhere in Europe, of course, middle-class support for fascist movements was more limited; conservatism remained more powerful. And a minority of the class turned left to protest; by 1936 some of the most ardent supporters of the French socialist party were clerks and teachers. On balance, however, the rightist impulse predominated. In France violent rightist groups such as the *Jeunesses patriotes* attracted some middle-class support even before the depression. As the economic crisis deepened and as socialist and communist parties grew in strength, semifascist groups like the *Croix de feu* and, after 1936, the *Parti populaire français,* obtained the backing of hundreds of thousands of members of the middle classes. These groups appealed to the new desire for economic protection against both depression and the leftist threat to private property and cited the need for attention to the nation instead of to the divisive elements of class warfare.

These various movements represented a radical departure from middle-class political tradition. They denied the virtues of liberty and of parliamentary regimes; they denied the very rationality of man, stressing the need for physical activity, violence, and war. Yet, in many countries, they did attract substantial middle-class support. They clearly reflected the defensive posture of the middle class in this period. The radical rightist movements drew widespread support only in intense economic crises. They achieved great importance only in a few countries and never attracted all the elements of the middle class. Along with more orthodox but stubborn conservatism, however, they did represent the new political position of the class.

Middle Class and Upper Class in Western Europe

The upper class in western Europe was increasingly separated from the middle classes in this period. There were some new entrants to the group, largely from the middle classes, but its position was distinctive.

The basis for the class was its great wealth; in Britain 5 per cent of the population earned at least four times more per capita than the upper limit of middle-class income. The economic superiority of the upper class was not subtly marked off; its spending and investment power vastly exceeded that of the middle class, and it gained social prestige as well by its continued intermingling with the aristocracy and by lavish spending patterns. Furthermore, most members of this upper group were able to rise above the economic perils of the middle classes. The inflation was an opportunity rather than a threat. This was a class with enough capital and foresight to borrow during inflation rather than allow its savings to dwindle. For many, then, the inflation brought real gains and elevated the upper class still further above smaller business groups. The depression caused some damage, to be sure, but it was largely temporary.

The political stance of the upper class was also distinctive. The class had great influence in governments. In Germany it tried to solidify this influence by subsidies to a variety of political movements, even those of the left. And with very few exceptions the interests of the upper class were not attacked by any government, no matter what its form. Hence the upper class was not directly attracted to protest movements; although it hoped to use fascism in both Germany and Italy as protection against radical socialism or communism, it was not won over.

The existence of a distinctive upper class was clearly recognized by other elements of society. Middle-class fascism was in some senses a protest against upper-class power. Working-class movements increasingly turned their attention to the upper class. The nationalization of the Bank of France by the Popular Front government was a definite effort to break the hold of a very few families over French economic life. But even there the upper class maintained its power. Related to the middle class and many middle-class values, the upper class had risen well above the middle class. It was a vital element in the social structure of the industrial nations.

The Workers: Postwar Agitation

The working class did not lag behind other elements in developing new forms of expression during the period. During the war most governments officially recognized and dealt with socialist parties and union organizations. They had consulted unions on labor policies in return for which the unions had restrained strike activity. They had even encouraged union recruiting, which broke down many barriers to extension of membership. Union activity seemed easier and more respectable than ever before. Socialist leaders, having been involved in coalition governments, seemed less fearsome now to timid elements of the working class and other groups. In Germany the party became the principal supporter of the new democratic, parliamentary regime and controlled the government with great moderation during the first years of Weimar. Much of the massive new backing and membership that socialist and union movements received immediately after the war was due to the prestige and position that had been won in association with the government. The French unions more than doubled their membership by 1920, and the central organization, the C.G.T., quadrupled its numbers, rising past the two million mark. In Britain the Labour Party rose for the first time to a position of major importance, displacing the Liberals as one of the two principal parties in the country. Everywhere, unions grew and socialist parties received more support.

Although some were undoubtedly attracted to the labor movement by its increased respectability, there was a widespread desire to use the movement to effect real improvements in working conditions. Many had a vague hope of instituting a new and better general social order. Workers were greatly impressed by the fact of the Russian revolution and the proof that a proletarian society was possible. Syndicalist and socialist movements grew rapidly in Spain, where government repression incited workers to attack the established order. In some of the more disordered countries, particularly in central Europe, the idea of spreading the communist revolution attracted a significant segment of the working class. Even where the class was not won to the notion of revolution, there was some expectation of major change, an expectation encouraged by wartime promises of a better society. Beyond this, the desire for definite material improvements was intense. Many veterans came back to their factory jobs with a combination of hope and bitterness. In the early part of the war workers generally had known higher wages and so higher hopes than ever before, but after 1916 conditions deteriorated steadily. There was an intense desire to reverse these trends after the war was over. This desire was expressed both during the boom of 1919 and to a more limited degree during the two-year depression that followed. Much of the new participation in union and socialist activities resulted from the high expectations of the working class, and the massive strike efforts in many areas showed the same feeling of impatient grievance.

The new burst of worker activity was conditioned, finally, by changes in the leadership of working-class movements. The wartime stress on compromises with the established order alienated many socialist and union leaders from the main body of labor, and the Russian revolution convinced many of them of the possibility of a more purely revolutionary movement. By the early 1920s, in fact, separate, communist union and party organizations had been founded by those who had abandoned the socialists. Even before this, however, many leaders believed that the time had come to seize control of society. Russian revolutionaries encouraged this belief, and the waves of discontent that rippled through the working masses seemed to promise success. This radical trend among some labor leaders did not touch all areas; Britain and Scandinavia were largely unaffected. Where the revolutionary sentiment did spread, however, it gave a distinctive tone to the most vigorous forms of worker action. There were direct efforts to stimulate revolutionary strikes and riots. The general strike in France on May 1, 1920, was called by syndicalist leaders who hoped to topple the social order. There was in these efforts some correspondence to what the workers themselves wanted. Workers in Italy in 1920, for example, clearly expressed a real desire to change the social order and the patterns of ownership and control.

In general, however, the most specifically revolutionary efforts did not win wide support; and what support they did receive was based more on specific grievances than on hopes for social upheaval. The French general strike, for example, attracted mainly railroad workers and not all of them; the railroad workers had a definite complaint against one company over disciplinary questions; an earlier strike over this issue had given the syndicalist leaders the idea for the more general effort. The desire for revolution was not, then, total or even common. There was a hope for major change and a willingness to accept some leadership by professed revolutionaries. The revolutionary leaders were only one element in the vigorous outburst of the working class in the years immediately after the war.

The heightened consciousness of the working class was expressed in many ways. An increase in union membership and socialist voting were the most widespread indications of the desire to promote class interest. In Italy the socialist party, expressing vague revolutionary aspirations, became the largest political grouping. Beyond this, strikes and other agitation drew a significant minority of workers into more direct protest. A wave of major strikes swept across France and Britain in 1919 and 1920. In Germany numerous strikes were coupled with revolutionary demonstrations led by communists. The first of these occurred in January, 1919, only two months after the war's end; it consisted of a large march in Berlin. A mood of some agitation persisted in Germany until 1923. There was even a short-lived communist regime in Bavaria. The inflationary pressure of 1923 and the French occupation of the Ruhr brought strikes and agitation in the Ruhr. A few final communist efforts at risings, all abortive, closed the period of major leftist disorder. The later communist efforts had become increasingly contrived in any event and lacked significant support from the working class. In Italy the excitement and disturbance of the war led to the major strike movement of 1920. This consisted not only of walking off the job with a set of demands but also of actually occupying factories in many industrial centers in the north. There the hope for general change, in addition to specific material improvements, was clearly expressed. A strike by Austrian workers in 1918 won the creation of workers councils, which participated in the enforcement of government economic decrees. Some German workers had urged in 1919 the establishment of worker councils to set industrial policy. The prewar desire for greater control in industry was finding new and heightened expression. On the whole, the general movement of agitation reflected some discontent about the position of workers in society; it went beyond purely material demands. Even the increasing trend of socialist voting showed a new sense of identity on the part of the working class, a new desire to act as a class.

The Workers: Conditions in the 1920s

The wave of discontent passed rather quickly; its peak was reached in 1920. In Italy strikes and support for the socialists continued after that but at a lower rate. French union membership fell off drastically; by the middle of the decade it was only half what it had been in 1920. Communist parties in France and Germany survived and could still create disorder, but they received only a minority of working-class votes.

There were a number of reasons for the general decline of agitation. The intense excitement of the war and the subsequent agitation could not be maintained. And the major strike efforts had failed. The depression at the end of 1920 made it more necessary to stick to the job and earn what one could; and it made demands on employers almost certainly hopeless, for in conditions of unemployment and sagging production there would be no reason for employers to yield.

Important divisions in the labor movement further reduced the power of organized labor and the zeal of many workers. The split between socialists and communists, particularly in France and Germany, weakened unions and parties alike. In France 600,000 workers remained in the socialist C.G.T., but 450,000 entered the new *Confédération générale du travail unitaire*. Socialist leaders themselves became less dynamic. They were depressed by their failure to win major changes in the postwar period. Deprived of the prod of revolutionaries, who were now in a separate, hostile movement, they yielded more easily to their impulses of moderation. The weakness of union treasuries, depleted by the inflation, added to the leaders' difficulties. Efforts to win improvements also encountered greater resistance from the middle class. Socialist parties were unable to win from middle-class groups the sorts of welfare improvements that had been current before the war. Unions found bargaining more difficult; strikes encountered a notably higher rate of failure. These developments reflected not only the new defensiveness of the middle class but also changes in industry itself. The continued growth of average firm size increased the numbers of workers in factories. New rationalization procedures, borrowed from the United States, subjected workers to assembly-line pace and discipline. Managerial control became more intense, and the power of the average firm was obviously greater.

Finally, special factors operated in several countries to reduce the opportunities for labor action. The fascist government in Italy simply banned existing leaders and organizations and substituted groups controlled by state and party. Action by British workers was hampered throughout the period by high levels of unemployment and inept leadership of the Labour Party. In France the large number of immigrants in the labor force made extensive organization and action difficult, for the new arrivals did not speak French and were confused by their new setting. For a variety of reasons, then, labor agitation declined markedly during the greater part of the 1920s.

Furthermore, there was considerable reason for contentment on the part of workers after the postwar difficulties ended. Real wages rose between 1924 and 1929, particularly for some of the lowest-paid, unskilled groups. A few new welfare measures were introduced, though more slowly than before the war. An unemployment insurance act was passed in Germany in 1927. British unemployment insurance was extended to cover most categories of workers, including agricultural labor, right after the war. The German regime tried to open greater educational opportunities for the working class through a new type of secondary school, which stressed contemporary and technical subjects. Generally, the atmosphere of enjoyment and pleasure reached well into the working classes. The workers' desire for recreation was being increasingly fulfilled by the new media of entertainment. For most, there was more leisure time than before. After the war the French government limited hours of work to eight, and many workers had half a day off on Saturday as well. Clearly, some important gains were being made, particularly on the continent.

But the labor movement did not fade into unimportance. Union membership remained higher than before the war. British workers, particularly miners and others who were afflicted by massive unemployment, launched the largest strike movement in British history in 1926, when two and a half million workers reacted to the grievances of the miners and the intransigence of mine owners. The movement failed, but the power of labor could not be doubted.

Most important, the political expressions of working-class sentiment remained solid. Union membership fell in France, but the numbers of votes for socialist and communist parties steadily rose. Increasingly, the focus of working-class action shifted from unions and strikes to the political sphere. The major strikes themselves commonly aimed to impel the government to introduce changes in industry. The British general strike was primarily intended to induce government investigation of mining conditions. Major strikes in the 1930s, most notably those in France of 1936, similarly tended to be coupled with political efforts. Workers were clearly learning that political action could win more general and more solid gains than collective bargaining alone. Purely economic strikes were not abandoned; they increased in number, though not in size and duration, in some countries, notably Britain. But generally the growing difficulty of winning strikes and of enrolling certain types of workers in unions increased the importance of political action. Finally, the leaders of the labor movement stressed political power and were themselves primarily politicians. Socialists had long maintained a political emphasis, and now the most revolutionary wing of the labor movement, the communists, did the same.

Not all workers, of course, were attracted to labor parties. A high level of apathy persisted in many cases, although in towns where active parties provided organizational experience and a variety of social services the participation could be intense. In Berlin and Vienna, for example, over 90 per cent of the working class regularly voted. There were divisions in the political orientation of the class. Skilled workers tended to be more conservative than others. Workers in large factories were usually more radical than those in smaller units. Certainly, the split between socialism and communism continued to split the whole labor effort.

Nowhere were labor parties able to win undisputed government control in the 1920s. They might win worker votes, but those did not give absolute majorities. Nevertheless labor leaders continued to cherish the hope of ultimate political power. And in factory towns socialists and even communists often won control of the local governments. Such new city governments furnished important assistance to the working class by providing housing programs and improvements in public facilities. Much of the direct power of the labor parties was rooted in their local action and its benefits. At all levels the political arena was drawing increasing attention from the labor force.

The Workers: Impact of Depression

The tendency of the workers to turn to political action became abundantly clear during the depression. As wages plummeted and massive unemployment developed, the working class sought new expression for the obvious grievances. It wanted greater security and the elimination of unemployment; it wanted, at least vaguely, some new regime that would prevent such disasters in the future.

Union membership rose as one expression of the new and vigorous sense of grievance. By 1935 French unions had risen from 785,000 to four million members. In 1936 an important series of strikes was conducted for improvements in wages and hours. Factories were occupied, often for several weeks; and the workers won their point. The action had been spurred by the election of a Popular Front government controlled by the socialists, for workers wanted to make sure that the government would take the corrective action they wished.

The principal focus of working-class protest against the depression had to be political. Union action, particularly strikes, was of little avail in this depression, as in any other; what was needed was government action. Furthermore, government programs themselves were proving patently inadequate to alleviate worker misery. The British unemployment-insurance program, for example, ran out of funds under the impact of depression. Middle-class politicians had accepted the insurance scheme when it was solvent, a solvency depending largely on the contributions of workers themselves; but a new system was clearly necessary, and yet the government refused to countenance a significant increase in unemployment assistance. Not until 1934 were tax funds committed to the program, and even then the duration of assistance remained limited. Quite generally, earlier welfare programs did not meet the needs of workers during the depression. The unemployed, particularly the majority that suffered from long-term unemployment, received only a small and somewhat uncertain dole. Again, it seemed clear that action had to focus on governments if any real solutions were to be found.

The result was a major increase in support for socialist and, in some areas, communist parties. Elements of the middle class and peasantry, themselves suffering intense economic hardship, also gave some support to these parties, but the major impetus came from the working class. In Britain the Labour Party vote fell off in the elections of 1932 because of the party's ineptitude during the first stages of the depression, but in subsequent elections its support steadily grew. The victory of the Labour Party in 1945 was in part a continuation of this movement. Scandinavian socialist parties received clear majorities and took control of the governments. Votes for the French socialists increased, but even more notable was the steady rise in communist political power; in the 1936 election the number of communists in the Chamber of Deputies rose from ten to seventy-three; and they had become a major political force for the first time.

Spanish socialist parties in the industrial areas of the north steadily increased in strength, and a small communist movement was founded. In Germany the communist party provided a particularly vigorous expression of working-class grievance. German workers had long supported the socialists; to express their new discontent, some of them naturally turned to a more radical movement. By late 1932 the communists had almost 17 per cent of the total vote.

The new political efforts of the working class had varying results. In Scandinavia the socialist parties were able to introduce a variety of social-insurance schemes and increased governmental control of the economy. Political backing was given to cooperatives and to unions; collective bargaining became general in Scandinavian industry. Public housing was developed and greater assistance given to large families, to the aged, and to the sick. Under this administration the effects of the depression on the working class were soon eliminated; production rose and relatively full employment was restored. The working class was more protected and more prosperous than ever before, and the attachment to socialist parties was solidified.

In Germany the more radical political efforts of the labor force proved futile in the face of the Nazi victory. The new regime did not abandon the working class; it even won some contentment if not active support. But the benefits the workers received were conferred from above, not achieved by a dynamic labor movement.

The French labor movement won only limited results. Only in 1936, after the depression had already made major inroads, did the socialists gain control of the government, and that control was extremely shaky. The socialists depended on the cooperation of the middle-class Radical Party, and this was soon withdrawn in opposition to the various economic measures that the socialists took. The perpetual division between socialists and communists further weakened the government. Communists supported the government at first but refused to participate in it; and gradually their support became undependable. The Popular Front government was doomed to failure, and many of its measures were subsequently rescinded. It did attempt, however, to counter the effects of depression and to provide an economic structure more favorable to the working class. There was some effort to guide the economy, particularly by government operation of the Bank of France. Most important, the government tried to meet the demands of the workers, expressed in the strikes of 1936, for significant improvements in working conditions. It sponsored a series of compulsory collective bargaining arrangements, the Matignon agreements, between employers and unions. The possibility of providing the workers a greater voice in industry, with government assistance, was a notable feature of the settlement. The agreements set higher wages, established a minimum wage and a forty-hour week, and guaranteed two weeks paid vacation a year. These gains were not well administered, and some, such as the limitation on hours of work, were soon abandoned. The discontent and material hardship of the workers were not eliminated, and they were reflected in the steady increase in communist power. Nevertheless, the Popular Front had introduced some new principles into French industrial life. It represented the sort of approach workers clearly sought and supported.

The impact of the depression on workers and on their political habits proved enduring. The new voting patterns were maintained well after the peak of the depression and even after World War II, except in countries such as Germany, where the leftist political movements were disbanded by government action. Workers and their leaders continued to seek economic devices, centering around greater government action, that would guarantee full employment.

The depression had been a great shock. Many workers were without jobs for years. They received enough aid to survive, but prolonged unemployment was demoralizing and confusing. Many of those who suffered lengthy unemployment lost their sense of purpose. There was very little to do, particularly since there were few resources, with weeks and months of leisure. Problems of unemployment were particularly agonizing for some highly traditional groups of workers, such as miners, whose functions were simply not needed by economies even after recovery began. Retraining programs, few in number anyway, had only limited success among these people. And the workers proved reluctant to leave traditional centers to seek employment in more prosperous regions. Clear psychological as well as material hardship was involved in the depression. Even workers who were not themselves unemployed saw the results of the disaster and often lived in fear of the loss of their own jobs. This was why the labor force clustered increasingly around parties that promised to work for a solution to the problems of labor and expressed worker resentment against the social order. This was why some workers supported parties that professed to attack the existing social order as a whole. Even before this period workers had been suspicious of established political and economic forms. The depression convinced most of the class that radical changes, though not necessarily revolution, were essential in political and economic relationships.

CLASS CONFLICT

The conflicting attitudes and economic positions of the major social classes led to virtual class warfare in the interwar period. In eastern Europe outside of Russia the major opponents were peasants and landowners, with the middle class coming to side with the latter. The landowners, with the aid of authoritarian government, had little difficulty in imposing their will.

In western and central Europe the principal opponents were clearly the middle class and labor. Aristocrats supported the middle class, as did most peasants. Workers had as allies only minority segments of other groups, which translated their own discontent into support for socialist causes. The working class was outnumbered, and it certainly lacked the wealth, established position, and experience of the upper classes. It had, on the other hand, greater social unity than the other classes, whose traditions and interests were more diverse.

Both sides became increasingly rigid and tended toward more extreme positions. The impact of the depression played a major role in this process by attacking the economic well-being and security of most groups. (In Italy the depression of 1920–1922 had served somewhat the same function.) In addition, action on one side led to increasing counteraction on the other. Communist demonstrations and strongarm tactics in France in the 1920s led to paramilitary organizations with fascist overtones, on the right. More generally, the rise of the extreme left directly stimulated the rise of the extreme right. In Italy this occurred soon after the war, with the rise of the maximalist socialists. In Germany and France the depression brought the advent of substantial communist power and the corresponding rise of fascist groups. Fascist groups in turn stimulated more activity on the left; the French Popular Front was a direct response to rightist agitation in 1934–1935. The circle was clearly vicious.

Class warfare involved a certain amount of violence. Communists and even socialist groups occasionally broke up political meetings. In Spain the perpetuation of the anarchist tradition among many workers and peasants led to even greater violence, including murders, during the republican period.

On the whole, the methods of the left were not so violent as those of the right. Worker parties and unions relied on their increasing strength of organization and growth in numbers to win their purposes. Major strikes, such as the British general strike or the French sit-ins in 1936, involved almost no violence at all. Workers and their leaders were also afraid of the repressive power of the troops and the police, whose officials were usually conservative in inclination and notoriously more ready to repress workers than to attack conservative demonstrations. Working-class protest, therefore, was limited primarily to the polls, to strikes, and to many gigantic but calm street demonstrations.

The right was more unruly, particularly in Spain, Italy, Germany, and France, where significant fascist movements arose. Fascist rioting, beatings, and murders were common during the period of greatest social tension. Fascists themselves praised violence as a true expression of the human spirit, and they tried to attract attention to themselves by its use. They hoped to create sufficient chaos to provide an opportunity for the seizure of power and recruited large, uniformed forces to stimulate such chaos. Brownshirts in Germany, blackshirts in Italy, and several different colors in France did create a situation of considerable disorder. The fascist shock troops were drawn from young unemployed professional people, unemployed workers, clerks, and the like. One vicious French group, led by the perfume maker Coty, simply paid unemployed North Africans to do the fighting. In Spain, of course, massive participation of the military in the conservative cause brought about a bloody civil war, the extreme expression of the class conflict that had developed. In Germany and Italy considerable fascist rioting and demonstrations preceded the actual takeover. France saw large demonstrations and some rioting early in 1934, which culminated on February 6, when thousands of Parisians rioted against the parliamentary regime, attacked policemen and deputies, and stormed government buildings.

Labor groups responded with counterdemonstrations, and France came close to civil war. This was the worst outburst in France during the decade, but demonstrations and beatings continued even later.

It was in the political arena proper that the principal manifestations of class conflict took place. Only a minority was involved in violence on either side. Fascist leaders themselves recognized, except in Spain, that they could not take power by force alone. In many countries leading elements on both left and right refused to accept the existing regime and took all possible measures to bring about its downfall. The Spanish republican regime was subjected to attacks from the anarchists and even some socialists on the left and the fascist Falange and other conservative groups on the right. Long before civil war broke out, the regime had been rendered virtually powerless by this conflict. In Germany massive communist and fascist parties in the early 1930s created the same sort of government impotence. Similar chaos existed in Italy in the early 1920s and in France during much of the 1930s. Everywhere, a dynamic political center was missing. The middle class and its allies largely withdrew allegiance from parties that were interested in bridging the social gap between them and the workers. Workers, for their part, supported either socialist parties, which were reluctant to become too involved with the existing regime, or communist parties, which rejected the regime altogether. Even in England, where political extremes were less marked, there was a tendency toward polarization of parties on a class basis. In the major continental countries the polarization threatened to become total. The only link between left and right was a common hostility to the existing situation.

In most countries extreme social chaos lasted for only a few years. The Scandinavian nations, which, like Britain, were not afflicted by the most radical political hostilities and in which, furthermore, the depression was not severe, resolved many of the tensions by their welfare policies. These policies were sufficiently effective to alleviate workers' grievances and to prevent their recourse to more vigorous action. At the same time, the measures were mild enough not to provoke the hostility of the middle class. Conservative elements were displeased by most of the new programs, but their resistance was expressed only through the normal channels of parliamentary action. The welfare policies did not destroy fundamental middle-class ownership and wealth; they only modified both in the interests of general well-being.

In other European countries, however, social tensions were relieved most clearly by the total victory of the extreme right. This was the pattern in Italy, Germany, Austria, Spain, and to an extent in the authoritarian states of eastern Europe. The new fascist or semifascist regimes obviously protected the interests of large landowners and the leaders of industry. Despite the anticapitalist elements of fascist doctrine, little was done to control industry or profits; landed estates were left untouched. Only in Germany were certain limitations placed on private industry, in the interest of increasing the economic power of the state; but even there private ownership and substantial profits were not affected. For the lower classes, even those that had opposed fascism, the new regimes offered numerous benefits. Full employment was restored in Germany, and public works in Italy improved the economic position of many workers, although the depression did cause some unemployment. The governments of both countries offered subsidies to large families in the interest of promoting population growth and in Germany an increase in population growth rate resulted. Organizations such as the "Strength through Joy" movement in Germany fulfilled the workers' desire for leisure and recreation by promoting hikes and outings. New state unions gave some workers a sense of participation in decisions about labor conditions, although in fact the interests of management remained dominant.

Beyond this, the fascist state organized an elaborate propaganda and police apparatus that actively promoted public satisfaction with and loyalty to the regime. Educational systems were altered to stress fascist principles. A state of national tension was maintained through the many news media under government control, which induced even greater attachment to fascist leaders. Finally, organizations with a potential for protest were quickly and completely eliminated. This affected the working class particularly, for workers represented the class most hostile to fascism before the takeover. They were also dependent on established leaders, doctrines, and institutions to voice their views. These were now eradicated. Communist and socialist parties were outlawed, and many labor leaders were arrested. In Spain the execution and exile of thousands of leftists removed the possibility of worker protest in a similar if bloodier manner. Unions were disbanded and replaced by the state organizations.

Thus, the new regimes stifled protest by a combination of benefits and repression. Almost no resistance to the fascists developed. Class warfare had been ended by an alliance of the upper classes and dynamic lower-class leaders. The resulting regimes proved impossible to dislodge except by war.

In Britain and especially in France hardly any solution to social conflict was discovered during the interwar period. The British government, under Conservative party control, did take steps to alleviate social and economic distress. Increased government economic activity was developed to retrain workers, to channel investments, and to promote exports. The extension of earlier social insurance programs, notably unemployment insurance, did allow some redistribution of income. Before World War I workers had paid more in dues and taxes than they had received in government aid. By 1935 the working class paid in only about 80 per cent of the money it received in benefits. The continued high rate of unemployment, however, nullified this redistribution. Although some workers profited from the rising levels of production, the class as a whole remained economically weak. Certainly, the considerable social tension that existed between the middle class and labor was not alleviated, although its expression was more moderate than that on the continent.

In France the government was far more completely paralyzed by a network of political and social divisions. The promising measures of the Popular Front did not relieve working-class grievances, for economic conditions continued to deteriorate. Communist strength mounted steadily. At the same time, larger elements of the middle class were attracted to radical conservative movements; by 1938 the *Croix de feu* claimed two million members, and several other groups had formed on the extreme right. Economic difficulty and the perpetual conflict between right and left made it impossible to undertake any significant action or reform after the failure of the Popular Front.

Furthermore, internal social conflicts affected diplomatic policies as well. Social divisions in Britain and France paralyzed both countries internationally during the 1930s. The rise of Nazi Germany was recognized as an international threat, but the western nations lacked the will to act. The political right, although not for the most part favorable to the Nazi regime, feared communist Russia as the primary enemy. The political left was willing to take action against fascism but was not strong enough to impose its will. Divisions over foreign policy first became clear during the Spanish Civil War, when the French Popular Front was forced to remain idle while its Spanish counterpart was gradually crushed. Powerful conservative movements opposed action in coordination with Russia and against the advocates of private property and religion, and they could not be overcome. From that point onward, the governments of France and Britain worked for peace at almost any price, for they lacked the internal strength to do otherwise. The results of their efforts, the Munich agreements of 1938, were hailed by large elements of the citizenry. The desire for peace was not confined to politicians. Yet the threat of war loomed over western Europe and created new uncertainties and fears.

When war did come, it caught Europeans in a far different mood from that of 1914. There was no confidence, no belief that the war would be easy or pleasant. At best, there was a grim determination to see it through; at worst, the alienation of important groups from the established order hampered the war effort itself. In contrast to 1914, important segments of the labor movement resisted participation in the war, for the communists regarded Germany, however temporarily, as an ally because of the Nazi-Soviet pact. The social conflicts of the period were carried over into the war itself in France. And yet, curiously, the developments during and after the war solved or alleviated many of the social and economic problems of the preceding period. The mood of hopelessness so clearly apparent in western Europe before the war receded, and a new period of social development began.

6

CONTEMPORARY
EUROPEAN SOCIETY

INTRODUCTION

By the twentieth century most social groups were dependent for their sense of well-being on steady advances in material prosperity. Many urban elements also relied on extensive opportunities for social mobility. During the interwar period the essential weakness of the economy had inhibited both prosperity and mobility. Along with the shock of war itself, economic hardships produced a widespread unease; general behavior patterns and new political trends both reflected this. Many groups, both in the peasantry and in the middle classes, attacked the very idea of modernization.

The tone of society since World War II has been quite different. The basic change seems to have been twofold: a new orientation of government to the economy and to general welfare and the development of a mass consumption economy. These innovations, though prepared before the war, have marked a new stage in European industrialization. They have brought increased prosperity to every major group and unprecedented opportunities for mobility. Class lines are blurring. In western Europe almost a third of the urban population has moved either from middle class to worker or, more commonly, from worker to middle class. Clearly, the postwar period has been a dynamic one for European society. Not all the implications of change can be fully determined, but some outlines can be indicated.

WORLD WAR II

Dislocations

World War II, like World War I, gave ample cause for discouragement and dislocation in European society. It came as less of a shock to a people whose confidence was already shaken. Nevertheless, the rapid victories of the German troops were profoundly demoralizing. The many restraints and the constant threat of police oppression brought home to whole populations the magnitude of defeat during the Nazi occupation. Economic conditions rapidly deteriorated in the occupied countries as the Germans drained men, money, and materiel into the war effort. Even Italy, officially an ally, was compelled to pay its tribute in forced labor.

Later in the war the continent began to face the pressure of bombing and then of allied invasion. Bombing raids, which affected Britain from the beginning, provided new and more extensive involvement of civilians in the danger and strain of war. Invasion, resistance, and liberation involved a far wider geographical area than had been the case in World War I. Again, the results on civilian morale were significant.

The bombings and the invasions subjected Europe to far more extensive economic damage than it had suffered in the earlier conflict. Together with the economic dislocation caused by German occupation this damage brought truly massive material disorder. One tenth of Germany's productive capacity was destroyed by the war. Vast sections of Germany, France, and eastern Europe were left without railroad lines, bridges, or transportation equipment of any sort. A substantial, if temporary, return to local subsistence economies was the inevitable result of this situation.

Finally, population losses in the war were again substantial. Germany lost more people than before, and the mortality rate in eastern Europe was far higher then it had been in the previous war. In addition, thirty million people had been driven from their homes by the war, either under orders from the Germans or simply in flight from the various invasions.

The immediate results of the war added to those hardships. Eastern Europe was faced with a series of revolutions imposed in part by the Russians. Germany was afflicted by the incalculable confusion of defeat after years of being assured of German superiority and invincibility. The allied powers made no immediate attempt to rebuild the German economy, and Russia was concerned primarily with appropriating as much German equipment as possible. Britain was anxious to avoid any resurgence of German industrial power and competition, while some Americans thought of returning Germany to a pastoral, agricultural economy. Food supplies were deficient and ordinary transporation links were broken. The monetary system itself seemed to have been destroyed. Tremendous inflation once more reduced the value of money to almost nothing, and nonmonetary units of exchange, such as cigarettes, replaced currency.

Furthermore, Germany and the rest of Europe were faced with a vast population movement. Many of the people made homeless by the war wanted to return to their own regions, while others fled the territorial changes of the peace. More than a million persons from eastern Europe refused to return to their homes, which lay now under Soviet domination. Millions of Germans fled from East Prussia, now part of Poland, and later from the East German government itself. All these refugees had lost property and homes, many were bitter and confused, and most were ill and weak from the deprivations they had suffered during the war. Their psychological and economic integration into the countries to which they flowed was extremely difficult.

The larger diplomatic situation after the war further damaged the morale of Europe. It soon became apparent that the old power structure in Europe had been destroyed, perhaps forever. In its place two superpowers, both partially non-European in territory and ideology, dominated the diplomatic scene. Eastern Europe seemed totally embraced by Soviet Russia, while western Europe was only a little more loosely gripped by the United States. There was widespread fear of a new war, a war in which Europeans would be pawns of the superpowers and one that would be fought with weapons more terrible than any the world had ever seen.

Europe's feeling of power was further reduced by the wave of attacks on imperial holdings. Within fifteen years after the war most of the major European empires had been liquidated. Britain surrendered her colonies without great resistance, but nationalist elements were shocked by the loss of Britain's traditional place in the world. The French relinquished their empire more reluctantly; the French military long hoped to compensate for its defeat in the war by forcibly resisting the currents of colonial unrest. The long struggle to retain Indo-China and Algeria strained the economy and morale of France and left a legacy of bitterness and disillusionment.

New Opportunities

On the whole, however, the war did not disorient European society so greatly as the earlier conflict had done. Dislocation seemed dominant, perhaps insuperable, in the first three or four years after the war; but it was not allowed to persist. Some problems of morale remained. Patterns of dishonesty developed in wartime resistance and in the chaotic postwar years continued to be reflected in relatively high rates of crime. A certain sense of constriction, due to the weakened diplomatic posture of Europe and the fear of renewed war, continued to afflict many people. Yet a new willingness to rebuild Europe and to experiment with different and constructive economic and diplomatic forms came to dominate European society. Certainly, the contrast with the interwar period was marked. Twenty years after World War I Europe had undergone disastrous inflation and depression. New and warlike regimes had been installed in two major European powers. Class tension, reflected in politics, seemed to paralyze the principal western countries. In the twenty years after World War II, on the other hand, Europe underwent an unprecedented economic rise. Class tensions were reduced and some of the most bitter opposition to reform was eliminated. European diplomacy was marked by a willingness to create new and almost revolutionary structures in an effort to eliminate longstanding and paralyzing continental conflicts. New cultural movements arose that carried on earlier developments but with greater optimism. Serious weaknesses and difficulties remained, but the change of tone and outlook could not be denied.

The ability of European society to take effective action despite the dislocations of the war was in part conditioned by the war itself. Many of the difficulties of the postwar period were more temporary than fundamental; they proved surmountable in the long run.

In the diplomatic sphere the two superpowers came to balance each other to a certain degree, thus gradually reducing the tension between them and allowing increased freedom of action within Europe. By 1952 the period of greatest strain had passed. Furthermore, both powers took constructive action within their own spheres of influence. Russian dominance allowed unprecedented social and economic change in eastern Europe, while in western Europe, American economic assistance and guidance were of primary importance in compelling both economic and diplomatic recovery.

The loss of colonies also had beneficial effects. It stopped an economic drain on European countries, for most colonies had cost more than they had returned. Jobs and resources were lost by some small groups, particularly the upper classes, but for society as a whole the disappointment at the loss of national prestige was not keenly felt. Moreover, European countries continued to exercise important economic and cultural influence in their former colonies. It was a sign of the renewed strength of European society that the new situation was quickly accepted and in many ways turned into an opportunity for development.

More important, the internal structure of Europe was not totally devasted by the war. Material destruction was great but not insuperable. The greatest damage was to buildings, housing, and to transportation facilities, but much machinery remained intact. For example, more than three quarters of the German industrial plant was still usable; it could be effective only after bridges and rails were restored and the currency was made stable, but it was there, and it proved essential to the rapid economic growth of Germany after 1948.

The population of Europe, similarly, was in many cases more dislocated than profoundly damaged. Only in the East had the level of absolute loss been notably higher than in World War I. Germany lost more people, but not many more, than it had during the first war. France lost far fewer and benefited from a small but surprising rise in birth rate during the war itself. Britain lost only half as many people as it had during World War I and saw an increase in birth rate during the war. Furthermore, in Europe generally a notable population rise began after the war and continued, with only slightly decreased intensity, into the 1960s.

In Italy and much of eastern Europe, where population growth had been substantial during the interwar period, the postwar years saw a drop in the growth rate. East Germany actually declined in absolute numbers because of the flight of millions to the west. On the other hand, Poland developed the highest birth rate in Europe by 1960. More generally, and notably in Italy, the peripheral regions of Europe were affected by the same sort of reduction of growth rates that had developed in the west after 1870. Increasing industrialization and urbanization in these areas took many people out of the orbit of peasant tradition and exposed them to a new knowledge of the possibility of limiting births in the interest of material well-being. New social security programs reduced the need for large families to support the aged. At the same time, birth rates did not fall to a level of stagnancy, and medical improvements continued to reduce mortality figures. Populations continued to grow.

In western Europe the earlier trends of near-stability were clearly reversed in this period. The British population rose from 45 to 47 million during the war itself and later passed 52 million. France's population grew by more than 5 million after the war, an increase of over 12 per cent; this in turn represented a more rapid rate of expansion than France had experienced since before the nineteenth century. Scandinavian population rates increased at similar rates, and the pace of German growth exceeded that of the interwar period. Population growth was a significant inducement to the further economic development of Europe. It also reflected the real gains in economic prosperity and security that characterized postwar Europe. Most directly, population growth followed from a new relationship between government and people, a relationship that included direct encouragement to larger families. In economy and demography, then, the war not only failed to paralyze development but also helped set in motion a real advance.

THE WELFARE STATE

Toward Social Reform: Great Britain

Most basically, the war created a new social spirit in Europe that affected relationships among the major classes as well as the political structure of society. The sense of purpose developed during the war united many groups, and this in turn resulted in positive action for social reform. There was a common revulsion against fascism, often due to direct knowledge of its atrocities. The political threat of communist Russia helped induce the upper and middle classes to compromise with the workers.

The process was clearest and most immediate in Great Britain, a country untouched by direct invasion and one in which social tensions had been relatively moderate before. The war immediately reduced party frictions in Britain, and all major political elements were represented in the wartime cabinet. The inclusion of the Labour Party promoted a belief in its respectability among many elements of society. At the same time, the war provided greater opportunities for contacts among members of different social classes. There was a sense of unity against the enemy, forged through the realization of the tremendous danger Britain faced. Military service and war work offered common experiences that reduced, although they did not eliminate, class barriers.

The war modified the privileges of the upper class. Heavy taxation and control of profits prevented much of the profiteering characteristic of World War I and actually reduced the income of many landowners and business men. Rationing of essential consumer goods allocated scarce products on a basis of per capita need, not per capita income, so that the gap in standard of living between rich and poor was narrowed. The wealthy accepted these measures in the interest of national defense. Many people realized that new policies were needed to cure the unhealthy social situation of the interwar period; British manufacturers, for example, were willing to grant labor a greater voice in industry by 1949. The wartime loyalty of the working classes stimulated the conviction that the poor should be rewarded in some way for their sacrifices.

Concrete measures during the war itself were intended to aid the lower classes. Rationing procedures assured supplies of milk and meat for all; for many of the poor this meant better diets than ever before. The war also provided full employment for the first time since the previous conflict, and wages rose in most essential industries. Finally, the government began to plan for further social gains after the war. The Beveridge plan, drawn essentially in the spirit of middle-class humanitarianism, suggested the expansion of social-insurance measures to prevent unemployment and even to redistribute income. Other plans urged extension of education facilities for the poor. These programs reflected new social concern on the part of governing groups. They also stimulated the expectations of the lower classes.

The altered social attitudes were expressed most clearly in the first postwar election in 1945. The principal issues in the election were economic, with the problem of housing heading the list. Not only the working class but also large sections of the middle class felt that government action was essential. The result was a clear majority for the Labour Party for the first time in British history. The party received the vast majority of the working-class vote but also, crucially, a full third of the middle-class vote. This partial transfer of middle-class support was not permanent for by 1951 only a quarter of the class voted Labour; but the vote in 1945 was a vital sign of the new needs of the class itself and the new realization of general social problems.

The Labour government's attention between 1945 and 1951 was primarily devoted to providing greater material protection for all citizens. Existing social-insurance schemes were elaborated, and the unemployment-insurance program was extended; for the first time in British history no unemployed person would have to rely on a dole. In addition, a national system of health care was instituted, giving virtually free medical attention to all citizens, with the bulk of the funds coming from tax sources. This measure obviously increased the medical facilities of the poorer classes. It was also, in its reliance on tax support, a major means of redistributing income.

Other programs were adopted that combined direct aid to the lower classes with a certain reallocation of income through taxation. Housing programs were greatly expanded. They were designed partly to compensate for wartime damage and neglect; but they resulted in the provision of better housing than ever before for many citizens. By 1960 more than a quarter of the entire population resided in government-built housing. Direct financial aid to large families was also established by the government.

Finally, two of the principal programs of the Labour government were intended to raise economic levels and to alter the existing system of class relationships. First, educational facilities were greatly expanded. Particular attention was given to the secondary schools; the school-leaving age was raised to fifteen years, then to sixteen. At the same time, university scholarships were greatly increased, and many new university facilities were created. Only a small minority of the population could go to the universities even now, and university students were still drawn primarily from the upper classes, but the earlier stratification of education was considerably modified. Working-class youths, a rarity at universities before the war, now passed unnoticed. Even larger segments of the working class were given new opportunities in some of the major industries. The Labour government brought mining, the railroads, and the steel industry under state ownership, and worker groups were given a voice in the direction of those industries. It was hoped that such basic industries could be more efficiently run, in the interests of the economy as a whole.

In a variety of ways, then, British society was altered by the Labour government. A new minimum material standard was set for all by the various insurance and public-aid schemes. New opportunities were created in education, and greater government control over the economy was established. Most of these programs proved irreversible. Later Conservative governments denationalized steel and raised the fees for the national health program, but they did not tamper with the basic aspects of the welfare state. Quite clearly, the political attitudes and expectations born during the war had forged a new social outlook for the postwar period.

Toward Social Reform: The Continent

On the continent, under the heel of Nazi occupation, wartime conditions were obviously far different from those in Britain. Living standards fell to near-subsistence levels. Nevertheless, attitudes and programs were being shaped that were not very different from the British. They resulted in the years immediately after the war in the elaboration of welfare systems quite similar to the one being created in Britain at the same time.

Continental wartime governments themselves introduced certain measures that were to endure as part of a more general welfare program. The Nazi government had already developed a commitment to full employment. In France the wartime Vichy regime attempted to encourage consultation between workers and industrial managers, and it extended a system of financial aid to families that was to become a major element of the French postwar welfare program. Family aid had already been developed in Germany and Italy as part of the fascist encouragement to population growth.

However, it was not from the fascist governments but rather in resistance to them that the impulse to postwar welfare measures really arose. In every occupied area significant resistance movements developed at some point during the war; those movements dominated the national governments in the three years immediately after the war. In all cases, they used their period of dominance to elaborate a series of major reforms. For the resistance movements, despite considerable diversity in social composition, were not simply hostile to fascism; they also wanted to create a new Europe free from the national and social conflicts of the past. They hoped to develop some new comity among nations, perhaps even a real unity within Europe. Internally, they intended to modify the capitalist system in the interest of social justice; they wanted to use the government to introduce greater economic equality and security. Much of the idealism of the movement was to be disappointed; but it provided a stimulus to change that could not be totally denied.

The resistance movements, though small in size at least until victory was in sight, were supported by elements of several social classes.

Working-class movements were well represented in the resistance through socialist and particularly communist participation. After Hitler's attack on Russia communists provided the major force for resistance in many areas. They had the organization and the experience in subversive activity required for resistance work. And from the resistance the communists derived new support, funds, and even respectability, that were to prove invaluable after the war. In Yugoslavia they were able to seize power directly. In the remainder of eastern Europe they seized power with Russian support.

In France and Italy they took over the principal union movements and became the primary political representatives of the working class. And in all these cases communists participated in postwar governments and in the development of programs to aid the lower classes.

Workers and their representatives were not alone in the resistance. In eastern Europe elements of the middle class developed a new interest in reform. Men like Stanislaw Mikolajczk in Poland helped establish peasant parties, which drew substantial support after the war and which actively sought changes in the social structure, although they were soon superseded by the communists.

In western Europe elements of the peasantry and the middle class participated in the resistance movement. For some young peasants activity in the resistance encouraged a desire for reform, which was reflected in higher levels of voting for communists after the war in France and Italy and in new efforts at technical change and a general pressure on governments for greater attention to the problems of agriculture.

The involvement of a minority of the middle class in the resistance was to have even greater political effects. The most important middle-class resistance groups were formed under the banners of Christian democracy. This was not a totally new movement; it had been suggested in France before the war and had arisen briefly in Italy prior to the fascist takeover. The Christian democrats tried to allay middle-class hostility to sweeping change by a definite recognition of social problems and by advocacy of greater social justice. After the war the new Christian democratic parties of France and Italy actively participated in the elaboration of new welfare programs. As in Britain, then, an element of the middle class was now willing to join with the working class in developing significant social reform.

On the continent this movement was facilitated by the eclipse of many former conservative leaders and by the virtual disappearance of fascist elements. The defeat of the fascists in war and the trials and executions of many collaborators temporarily eliminated the possibility of unduly conservative resistance to the postwar reforms. In eastern Europe resistance was further reduced by the elimination of the aristocracy as a class and the destruction of its control over land. Communist repression prevented any overt resurgence of conservatism in these areas. In western Europe conservatism did rise once more, either in separate parties, as in France, or within the Christian democratic movement, as in Italy and Germany. Nevertheless, this resurgence occurred only after important reforms had been enacted and accepted. A significant minority of the middle class continued to support the principle of further reform.

The political pendulum had swung to the left all over Europe. This change involved the expansion of working-class parties and the reorientation of middle-class groups. Political divisions along class lines were not eliminated, but there was new agreement on certain principles of reform. The basis for the development of welfare states had been established.

Welfare Policies in Eastern Europe

Governments in eastern Europe, both before and after the communist takeover, were active in creating welfare programs. Social insurance for workers protected them in illness, accidents, old age, and unemployment. Only Czechoslovakia had developed such programs before the war. A variety of state-sponsored vacation schemes supplemented the benefits to workers. Government housing programs gradually repaired wartime damage in the cities, although the growth of cities continued to limit the housing opportunities for most workers.

Generally, the workers were not allowed much independent participation in welfare plans and in industry; this was a major distinction of the east European systems. Unions were under state control. In Yugoslavia, however, a program of factory councils was developed in the 1950s and provided a real voice for the workers in the determination of work conditions and even in investment and production plans.

Eastern European governments were active also in the spread of educational reforms. Many peasants received education for the first time, and opportunities for able people from the lower classes to advance to secondary and university training were greatly increased.

Immediately after the war peasants also received a large number of individual land holdings, as large estates were conclusively eliminated in all eastern countries. In Poland and Yugoslavia peasants were allowed to retain the bulk of these small holdings. Elsewhere a program of collectivization began late in 1948 that was over 80 per cent complete by 1960. This program was designed to carry out communist principles of collective ownership and to promote agricultural efficiency by destroying small units and allowing a higher level of agricultural technology. The program proved to have grave drawbacks. There was little direct resistance, but many peasants lost their motivation for vigorous production. The old peasant yearning for private holdings clearly remained: it was this that had dictated a general renunciation of collectivization in Poland and Yugoslavia. Nevertheless, the collectives did provide peasants with certain facilities for education, medical care, and the like, which they had not previously possessed. And peasants benefited from many of the same social insurance plans that protected the workers.

Finally, government programs of industrial investment tried, with some success, to alleviate the pressure of people on the land. Factory industry grew everywhere, and a major movement to the cities naturally resulted. Eastern Europe remained preponderantly rural. In the late 1950s Yugoslavia was still 70 per cent rural, Rumania 65 per cent, Hungary 60 per cent, and Poland 54 per cent. The industrial levels of the west had not been attained. Nevertheless, change was clearly underway. Population pressure was relieved in the countryside, but at the same time peasants were faced with new requirements for market production and better agricultural technology. All of this, in general outline, resembled earlier developments in western Europe, but the movement in eastern Europe was conditioned by a combination of state control, imposed even on peasants through the collectives, and of state protection, which differed substantially from earlier patterns. Some of the earlier dislocation and hardship were avoided by the protective measures; and certainly much of the possibility for active discontent was repressed.

The Welfare State: Western Europe

In western Europe the welfare programs established after the war were obviously less novel than those of eastern Europe, and they involved far less complete government control. The Italian government, for example, divided some of the large estates in the South, but not all. It encouraged industrialization in the South by state investment and tax privileges to private entrepreneurs, but progress was not so rapid as in eastern Europe. Nevertheless, there and elsewhere the reforms induced by governments had extensive social effects.

Government control of industry increased. In Italy and Germany the government already owned facilities such as the railroads; the postwar period saw some extension of government ownership, as in the Italian takeover of electric utilities in the 1960s. Everywhere, government aid to housing grew. This was made vital by wartime destruction—40 per cent of German housing had been ruined—and by the growth in population; only gradually did building programs begin to catch up with need. Everywhere there was a vast extension of social insurance programs. Unemployment insurance and medical programs received the greatest attention. In Sweden, for example, a program of ninety days of free medical care was established after the war. Greater material security, new educational opportunity, and more extensive government economic encouragement and control were provided quite generally in western Europe.

The most complete new welfare program was developed in France, particularly in the years 1945–1946. France had long lagged in such programs; in a sense, it was now catching up with leaders such as Germany and the Scandinavian countries. And it was in France that the political effects of resistance movements were most keenly felt. The French government in the immediate postwar years was directed by a coalition of communists, socialists, and Christian democrats, all of which were interested in social reform.

A real social-security program was established for the first time. Hospital costs were insured, and coverage was provided for old age and unemployment. Workers, both in industry and agriculture, were compelled to participate in the programs. They paid a part of the costs, but employers paid 30 to 40 per cent of the cost and the state also contributed. Supplementing these measures was a large program of family aid; families received annual payments from the state for each child, the aid increasing with the size of the family. These payments were given to any family, regardless of income. Drawn from tax funds, these payments allowed substantial redistribution of income in favor of the poor. (And because it remained true that poorer families had more children, their benefits increased on this basis as well.) A laborer with low earnings and a large family could increase his income by as much as 40 per cent by the family aid he received. The program provided a minimum of material well-being for most families and promoted population growth as well. All in all, about 16 per cent of the French national income was being devoted to the various social-security programs.

In addition, the French state participated actively in educational reform. The school-leaving age was raised from fourteen to sixteen, and the curriculum of secondary schools was altered to meet the needs of a larger segment of society. Classical subjects, though still important, gave ground to science, modern languages, and social studies. Attendance at the most advanced secondary schools, the *lycées,* increased markedly. In the 1930s only 15 per cent of French children had attended these schools. By the 1950s this had grown to 20 per cent, and the *lycées* included all strata of the middle class and some children from the lower classes as well.

Finally, the French government introduced several measures to alter the control of industry. Experiments were made with a system of *comités d'entreprise,* joint labor-management councils, that would rule on working conditions and on general industrial policy. These experiments were not fully successful, partly because the unions resisted involvement with management, preferring to remain independent and free to protest. At the same time, the French government attempted to encourage worker participation in more traditional ways. Collective bargaining was facilitated, and the government extended direct aid to unions for training programs, including training in union management. Most important, of course, was the government's increasing direct role in the economy. Several industries were nationalized. Railroads were taken over entirely; in Europe generally it was felt that transportation links were too vital to the economy to be left in private hands. Coal mines were nationalized because of their economic importance and the hardships of mine labor. The government also developed a general agency, the *Office du plan,* to set basic standards for economic development. By a combination of direct government allocation of funds and tax benefits and a program of persuasion, this office tried to encourage the economy and maintain full employment. This general economic encouragement provided the final element of the French welfare program.

Characteristics of the Welfare State

The welfare systems that had been developed in western and central Europe varied considerably in details. Britain possessed the most complete medical program, France the most extensive program of family aid. One of the keynotes of the welfare state was a certain pragmatism and flexibility, but certain common ideals did operate in the various programs.

There was a belief in the responsibility of society to banish poverty. A clear effort was made to set minimal conditions in factory work, in the incomes of the lower classes in both industry and agriculture, and for the whole society in such matters as medical care. There was a desire to limit, though not to eliminate, inequalities of wealth by funding the welfare programs by graduated taxes. The state was to serve as a redistributive agent.

The material goals were the most obvious and, in many ways, the most fully successful aspects of the welfare state. Beyond them, however, was an interest in eliminating class barriers to opportunity by extending educational facilities. There was a hope, finally, of giving the lower classes, particularly the workers, greater participation in their own governance. Nationalization was undertaken in part to allow workers more voice in crucial industries previously dominated by large firms. The nationalized industries tried to involve their own workers in decisions by creating mixed governing boards within the industry. The French *comités d'entreprise* represented a similar attempt in private industry to allow worker participation. In 1951 Germany set up supervisory boards in the iron, steel, and coal industries; heavy worker representation on these boards was designed to provide greater social control of vital industries. State encouragement of collective bargaining and of recognition of unions obviously promoted a bilateral determination of conditions of work. In Scandinavia particularly, but elsewhere to a great degree, collective bargaining represented an important part of the welfare state. It helped raise wages, improve material conditions, and moderate class hostility and the sense of isolation of workers in industry.

The welfare programs obviously represented a great extension of the power of the state to compel for the public good. The size of government bureaucracies increased substantially. Regulatory action was extended from traditional fields to cover minimum wages and even the conditions under which workers could be dismissed. Direct government action in matters such as housing and industrial ownership was vastly increased. Compulsion was extended not only to participation in the new insurance programs but also to such fields as doctors' fees, in the British health scheme, and to requirements that certain people reside in old age homes, as in Sweden. Social compulsion most notably affected the size of incomes through the state's power to tax substantially. Taxes were raised everywhere, particularly on the highest incomes and on inheritance. The British financed 50 per cent of the war through taxation, especially by a surtax on the rich. And in many areas wartime taxes were continued or extended to pay for the new welfare programs. At the same time, compulsion was not total in the welfare states; there was still great stress on persuasion and substantial reliance on private initiative. The new attention to worker participation in decisions extended some initiative to wider groups than ever before. The old middle-class ideal of a severely limited state was clearly dead; new controls affected the lives of all people. But the welfare state did not involve rigid or complete domination. After setting certain minimum standards of material conditions and some guidelines for general economic development, the welfare state intended to leave society with more opportunities for effective initiative than ever before.

The benefits as well as the controls of the welfare state penetrated the whole society, for welfare principles were extended to groups beyond factory labor. Insurance programs were fully applied to clerical and agricultural workers and even to many of the self-employed. Medical plans and new educational facilities affected society generally. Protective legislation covering matters of hours, vacations, and wages applied to almost all categories of employes. The intensification of welfare measures brought the results more clearly into the normal lives of most people than ever before. Earlier programs, aside from general regulation of working conditions, had tended to concentrate on disasters—unemployment, illness, old age. These programs were increased after the war; there was un-precedented security from risk. Even farmers received greater protection from the hazards of weather and blight by systems of income support. Beyond this, however, welfare programs extended assistance to daily life. Measures such as family aid and medical care were of far more constant benefit than many of the earlier insurance schemes.

The extension of benefits to all groups in society and their application to more aspects of material life were leading characteristics of the new welfare states.

The success of the welfare measures introduced after the war was not immediately apparent. The programs were undoubtedly satisfactory to many elements of society, particularly the working class, but they could be fully effective only in a prosperous economy; they were not sufficient to bring real prosperity and security in the postwar economic chaos. The leading planners of the welfare state recognized this fact; and it was apparent to all in the strikes and agitation of the working class during the period. Specific programs of insurance and assistance were therefore to be completed by a general encouragement to economic growth and full employment. Only then could real well-being and some social harmony be achieved. A major aspect of the new activities of government therefore included economic development. Government funds were poured into industrial investment. France had the most elaborate planning of the western countries, but Scandinavian states were active in the field, and all governments exerted some control. Italian and French governments tried to bring industry to backward regions such as southern Italy and western France by subsidies and tax credits; these programs gradually reduced some of the economic gaps within the countries. States quite generally attempted to encourage private development by keeping corporate taxes relatively low. Thus the political intention to increase economic prosperity was quite clear; gradually, the intention was translated into fact.

ECONOMIC DEVELOPMENT

Postwar Dislocation

Until 1948 confusion seemed dominant in the European economy. People in many areas were near starvation. French miners, for example, were unable to work regularly because of their low nutritional levels. Much agricultural land and animal stock had been destroyed. Loss of transportation facilities and equipment made it difficult to distribute what food was produced. France, for example, had lost three quarters of her railroad rolling stock. Loss of workers due to death and dislocation added to production difficulties, as did interruption of the regular supply of raw materials.

In every area the lag in production was reflected in massive inflation as people tried to buy goods that simply were not available. Excessive demand was magnified in many cases by the inflationary measures introduced by governments seeking to increase investment, often at the expense of balanced budgets. Germany suffered from rampant inflation until 1948, when the government stabilized the mark. Italy stabilized her currency only in 1952 on the basis of a devaluation of the lira to one fiftieth of its previous value. French inflation persisted until the latter part of the 1950s, although successive devaluations reduced the franc to less than one twenty-fifth of its earlier worth. British inflation continued until about 1950, and it too was cured only by substantial devaluation.

The inflationary problem did not prevent all economic advance. In France production levels began to rise well before the currency was stabilized. Generally, however, inflation prevented major economic gains. Savings were lost, and the faith of entrepreneurs in the economy was severely limited. Workers were disgruntled as prices rose more rapidly than wages. To many groups there seemed to be little incentive for productive work.

Inflation also weakened the ability of the European countries to sell, and so to buy, abroad. It meant that European goods were in effect overpriced on the world market. This was really a reflection of the fact that European production was below its traditional levels; it could not meet demand at home, much less produce for export. But precisely because of the lag in production, exports were vitally necessary. To rebuild, Europe needed equipment from abroad, particularly from the United States. But in this early period it was unable to earn the dollars for these purchases. Real progress seemed impossible.

In this situation American aid after 1947 was of vital significance. The United States had assisted Europe before this but primarily in the form of relief rather than in aid for reconstruction. But the increasing tension between the United States and Russia led to an American desire to rebuild Europe. This desire was furthered by the growth of communist movements in France and Italy. Accordingly, the Marshall Plan was devised to provide American funds to close the dollar gap and allow European purchases of equipment and to encourage government and intergovernmental economic planning. Nations that received aid first, notably Germany, rebuilt most rapidly. All western countries were ultimately aided, however, and all began to advance with extraordinary rapidity.

Economic Growth

Beginning in 1948 in Germany and in the early 1950s in France and Italy, an economic advance of vast proportions arose and continued into the 1960s. Even recessions in the United States did not halt the advance; they resulted in a slower pace of growth but not in a cessation. For the time being, at least, Europe seemed to have eliminated the pattern of recurrent crisis that had plagued the continent since the industrial revolution began. State guidance helped channel resources to points of real need and prevent speculative overdevelopment. The provision of minimal standards for all classes and the maintenance of full employment opened a mass market of unprecedented size for all goods. The result was more rapid economic growth than had occurred since the early stages of industrialization. Wartime damage was quickly made good, and production rapidly soared to new heights.

The German economy expanded at an annual rate of 6 per cent for much of the 1950s. France attained 8 per cent annual growth in the latter part of the decade, and by 1959 Italy was expanding at the rate of 11 per cent per year. Many eastern European countries achieved roughly comparable growth rates. The British economy expanded at a somewhat lower level, about 4 per cent a year. On the whole, however, the economic advance involved both new and mature industrial countries. Italy became highly industrialized for the first time. Eastern Europe and, later, Spain developed new industry.

In the areas of industrial maturity the expansion of production involved stress on relatively new industries and increasing use of rational, mechanical methods. Agricultural output rose under the impact of better equipment. France, always a substantial gain producer, developed a surplus for export in the postwar years. West Germany, cut off from the agricultural east, raised her agricultural productivity rapidly: by 1952 her wheat yield per acre was 1.2 tons, compared to .7 tons in France and .4 in the United States. And this new level of production was achieved with a smaller number of agricultural workers than ever before.

In industry earlier weaknesses in some branches of production continued. Textiles and particularly mining did not attain their prewar levels of employment. Some mines were completely closed, unable to compete with petroleum fuels. On the whole, however, this decline of certain traditional industries was balanced by the new stress on petrochemicals, electronics, and heavy consumer goods such as automobiles and appliances. The factory labor force did not grow substantially, but opportunities for industrial employment remained high. And the continued expansion of clerical and service jobs brought work to a large number of people.

Changes in industry altered the geographical balance of national economies. In Italy, industrialized relatively recently, the traditional concentration of manufacturing in the north continued despite the location of a few important firms in the south. In France and Britain, however, the earlier industrial focus on coal regions was obviously no longer necessary. Many of the newer industries preferred to locate in regions free from the grime of the mining centers. Service industries, such as insurance, and many company bureaucracies tended to settle in the capital cities. The result was the rapid expansion of these cities and the regions around them. Southern England, long eclipsed by the industrial North, was now reversing the process. A few traditional factory areas in Britain and in the coal regions of Belgium were afflicted with noticeable levels of unemployment. More commonly, as in northern France, a certain stagnancy settled in, a rate of growth lower than that of the country as a whole. Generally, the expansion of the economy was more than sufficient to compensate for areas and industries that lagged a bit. There was a need for some mobility. Movement to new types of work and sometimes to new areas was essential. But this movement was more to take advantage of new opportunities than to flee desperate conditions at home. The general and tremendous economic expansion of postwar Europe neglected no major segment of the population.

Incomes and Consumption

Economic growth naturally brought high rates of profit and salary to the European middle class. The effects of the war and of the new taxation had hit elements of the upper middle class quite hard. Some of the higher levels of established wealth had been clearly lowered. After this transitional point, however, renewed economic growth allowed new opportunities for profit. For the most part, traditional inequalities of income were not restored. In Germany during the early 1950s the growth of profits exceeded that of wages because the government encouraged the development of investment funds and labor proved surprisingly content with modest earnings. In France in 1958–1959 government programs of wage restraint allowed profits to rise more rapidly than working-class income; the latter, in fact, remained stagnant during those two years. With some exceptions, the expansion of profits did not erase earlier redistribution of income, but it allowed a satisfying improvement in material standards for most members of the middle class.

More novel was the rapid increase of earnings by the lower classes, both clerks and factory workers. These groups benefited greatly from the combined effects of welfare programs and economic expansion. Unemployment was virtually eliminated after the economic boom began, although there were more than two million unemployed in Germany as late as February, 1954. After the midfifties rates of no more than 2 per cent unemployment were maintained in France and Germany. For the most part, the unemployed were workers in transition from one job to the next; in many cases, demand for workers exceeded supply.

Both countries, and other industrial nations to an extent, relied extensively on immigration to fill the tremendous demand for workers created by economic growth. Large numbers of Italians, Spaniards, and Turks were brought in to work in Germany. Several hundred thousand Algerians found employment in France. This new immigration brought problems, from the misery and political tension among Algerians to the question of what sort of family welfare arrangements Germany should adopt for a Moslem worker who had more than one wife. Generally, however, the rapid growth of employment opportunities allowed a smooth integration of new workers into the economy.

The trend toward full employment was quite widespread. Britain maintained a slightly higher rate of unemployment than the rest of Europe, but it was still below that of the interwar period. Italy, which for centuries had suffered from underemployment, particularly in the south, saw the rate of joblessness reduced to 5 per cent or less by 1960. Continued emigration helped, but internal migration to the industrial north was far more important. Eastern Europe also reduced underemployment by expanding industrialization. Finally, growing numbers of women found employment, which provided a real boost to family income. In Britain the number of working-class women with jobs rose six times over the level of the 1930s. Without major interruption or exception, economic growth brought jobs to all who sought them.

Full employment and a steadily rising demand for workers naturally induced a rise in wages. Demands by individuals and unions for new raises met little resistance. Throughout most of the economic boom, and particularly by the end of the 1950s, wage rates were rising fast. By this time, in fact, the increase in purchasing power among the masses had generated so much demand that there was renewed threat of inflation in many countries. Even with steadily growing mechanization, production was not rising so rapidly as wages. The spread of installment buying increased mass purchasing power in many instances. By the early 1960s there were noticeable price rises in France and Italy and some inflationary pressure elsewhere. Economic stability seemed threatened, and governments began to urge that wage rises be kept in line with gains in productivity. Even with price rises and some stabilization efforts, the real incomes of most workers continued to mount.

During the period as a whole most of western and central Europe entered, as a result of wage rises, a period of high mass consumption. This was not a mass consumption of the type developed before World War I. It involved not only improvements in diet and clothing but also mass purchase of large and expensive consumer goods. By 1900 the masses in industrial countries had risen out of poverty; by 1960 they had risen to affluence. Ownership of items such as television sets and refrigerators spread to the majority for the first time. The average family in the industrial countries now possessed a motor vehicle, either a scooter or, increasingly, an automobile. Relatively elaborate vacations also reflected the new economic position of the lower classes. Most workers were legally guaranteed at least two weeks of paid vacation, and in France they received three. Not all were able to travel extensively during their holidays, but increasing numbers could and did. Trips by workers and clerks to foreign countries, particularly to southern countries, became common. Virtually all aspects of mass standards of living improved greatly. There was great desire for new acquisition and enjoyment and the means to achieve them.

Economic hardship remained in Europe. In the east and south recent and incomplete industrialization brought some relief from misery but no improvements in living standards comparable to those of the West. Even in industrial nations, pockets of poverty remained among old people, the unskilled, and many agricultural workers. For the masses generally, improvements in standards often seemed insufficient. There were still some needs that could not be filled. Nevertheless, the gains were great. The new levels of material well-being were, surely, the most important social result of economic expansion and welfare protection.

THE SOCIAL CLASSES

The Aristocracy

For the aristocracy postwar developments marked a further stage in the long decline of the class. In eastern Europe, where the nobility had preserved its greatest power, the class was officially eliminated and its great estates seized. This reduction of the aristocracy was a truly revolutionary development in Germany and in the east.

In western Europe the changes were not so drastic. Land reforms in southern Italy reduced the large estates but did not eliminate them. In the Iberian peninsula the large estates remained untouched. Elsewhere, the aristocracy had long been separated from primary landed power. New levels of property taxes, such as those in Britain, hurt the remaining estates severely.

The aristocracy retained some social prestige, particularly in alliance with the upper middle class. The class still played an important role in cultural patronage and in the setting of fashions. Aristocrats also continued to serve in government, both in elected office, as leading members of conservative parties, and in appointive positions.

Except in the communist countries, then, the aristocracy was left with some special economic power, through landed holdings or participation in business. It retained some political position, though only by abandoning its traditional conservatism and serving the interests of the welfare state. And it preserved a sense of social distinction, although that too was much reduced as the class developed increasing contacts with other groups. The political and economic trends of the previous century had almost completely undermined the traditional position of the aristocracy. By accepting those trends aristocrats in the west had maintained a social role, albeit greatly diminished, and an identity as a group.

The Peasantry

The position of the peasantry was significantly altered by political and economic changes after the war. The greatest change, of course, occurred in eastern Europe. The seizure of large estates freed the peasantry from the dominance of landlords. Industrialization drew some of the excess population away from the countryside. Governments gave increasing attention to peasant education and tried to draw peasants away from traditional loyalties, including the church. Technical development was encouraged by education and by investment in machinery. Agricultural productivity improved somewhat through these changes, although it remained far lower than that of western Europe. And peasant consumption standards remained low, partly because of the inferior productivity and partly because the state limited consumption gains in order to increase industrial investment. Nevertheless, important improvements in living standards were effected. Electrification spread; some new housing was built. East European peasants remained a depressed group, and traditions were still strong. Peasant life was being changed, but as before the change was largely imposed. Peasants were being pulled into market agriculture and into the communist system, but the effects of this change on basic attitudes and behavior were not yet entirely clear.

In western Europe peasants continued their adaptation to the industrial economy. Only in the Iberian peninsula and, to a lesser degree, in southern Italy did traditionalism and misery remain dominant. In Spain economic conditions actually deteriorated for much of the peasantry as a result of the devastation of the civil war and the reassertion of the power of the landlords. With this exception, peasant conditions clearly improved in western Europe after the war. Southern Italian peasants were aided by some land reform and other government aid and by the emigration of much excess population to the industrial areas in the north. They continued to be largely conservative in politics and in religion, but their contacts with urban culture steadily increased. In western Europe generally, the development of welfare programs brought new protection and income to many peasants. Family aid and medical care improved standards for a large number. Special efforts were made to protect agricultural workers, and most states developed extensive programs of minimum agricultural prices and established tariffs on agricultural commodities in an effort to maintain peasant income. At the same time, new systems of technical education and credit speeded the modernization of agricultural methods.

The peasants themselves showed an increasing interest in economic change, both in production and in consumption. Observers noted a real revolution in the attitudes of younger French peasants. Interest in technical development seemed overriding; tractors became a more important symbol of status than land itself, and some were purchased by peasants whose plots were too small to allow their use but who wanted the prestige of ownership. In general, however, the interest in technical development was rooted in a desire for economic improvement. The cooperative movement continued to spread, aided by government subsidies. Through cooperatives peasants were able to purchase equipment more cheaply and to process and sell their products with increasing efficiency. The incomes of peasants, however, remained inferior to those of urban workers. There were important gains through state aid and improved productivity. Peasants were increasingly able to adopt urban styles of clothing and to develop more varied diets. Their trips to cities and their enjoyment of urban recreational facilities became more frequent. These changes simply whetted the appetites of many peasants for further improvements and increased their awareness of the gap between rural and urban standards.

Peasant political interests, though still often focused on conservative parties, grew keener and more demanding. In France and northern Italy peasant discontent was expressed in significant minority support for communist parties. In France a peasant protest movement developed by the early 1960s. Led by precisely those peasants who had adopted the most advanced technical improvements, the movement spread to conservative as well as radical areas of the countryside. It found expression in massive and repeated demonstrations designed to call the attention of the government and the public to the economic hardships of the peasants. Some producer strikes were also attempted.

For the most part, the protests remained unheeded. In France and elsewhere governments occasionally raised agricultural support prices, but they offered no great improvement in peasant income. The problem of integrating peasant producers into an industrial economy had not been fully solved. Nevertheless, new government policies, and particularly new efforts by the peasants themselves, had led to important gains. Many peasants, even in France, were largely satisfied with these gains, and combined new forms of recreation and consumption with their attachment to traditions of religion, land, and village. Peasants who were most discontent simply left the land and took advantage of the abundant opportunities for work in the cities. Signs of stress remained, however, and in France threatened to become crucial. Peasant expectations seemed to be changing more rapidly than their economic conditions.

The Middle Class

The situation of the middle class changed dramatically in the postwar period. The earlier defensiveness of the class was largely replaced by a willingness to accept changes in government functions and in the position of the lower classes, which it had vigorously opposed in the interwar period. Hostility to socialist groups was reduced. The majority of the middle class voted against socialist parties, but there was no major resistance to socialist gains; and even the threat of communism seemed less menacing. In France polls taken in the 1960s indicated that the majority of the middle class accepted the communist party as a normal part of the political scene.

The new confidence of the middle class was also reflected in its willingness to accept new international economic arrangements. Tariffs were reduced, particularly within the Common Market, for the first time since the midnineteenth century. Businessmen were willing to adopt new methods of production and distribution to meet the challenge of foreign competition. This attitude was particularly striking on the part of businessmen in France and Italy, where a desire for protection of routine methods had long prevailed. The economic advance of these and other nations depended in considerable measure on the new spirit of the middle class.

Finally, there were no notable movements of middle-class reaction such as had developed during the interwar period. Small neofascist groups in Italy appealed only to a few, particularly in small towns in the south. A Poujadist party arose in France in the 1950s; its hostility to taxes appealed to some small shopkeepers, but the party had only brief success. The middle class and the lower middle class seemed largely content and confident.

There were several reasons for this new attitude. The disasters of depression and war had taught many the futility of previous defensive policies. Specifically, parties of the far right had been discredited by military defeat. More important, the economic boom that developed soon after the war obviously expanded the opportunities of the middle class. Savings and much property had been lost in the war and in postwar nationalizations, inflation continued to hurt many property owners; but the new increase of profits and employe salaries benefited the leading elements in the middle class.

New chances for advancement were created with the expansion of company and governmental bureaucracies. A significant number of workers rose to the middle class through the bureaucracies. In 1929 only 6.4 per cent of the higher civil servants in Britain had blue-collar worker origins; by 1950 this figure had risen to 16.8 per cent. Opportunities for mobility and renewal were an important element in the confidence of the middle class. The total size of the class increased after the war. There was new need for clerical and sales personnel, and the growth of industrial and governmental research created a vast number of new technical jobs.

In general, the most dynamic elements of the middle class were increasingly managerial, professional, and technical employes. The older criterion of property ownership became steadily less important. This trend had, of course, been developing for several decades, but it seemed to reach a peak after the war. The growth of governmental planning staffs and the steady expansion of managerial bureaucracies gave new importance to this segment of the middle class. Property ownership continued, to be sure, but the day of the giant entrepreneur seemed to be over. In Germany several leading industrial dynasties were destroyed by the war, and others abandoned the administration of their interests to professional managers. The great Krupp concern continued, for example, but it was actually directed by a new manager, Beithold Beitz. The old industrial upper middle class was declining in importance. At the lower level, too, the shopkeeping element steadily gave way to clerical employes as the main constituent of the lower middle class, for larger retail outlets displaced many shops as clerical jobs expanded. Again, this meant a reduction in the stress on property ownership.

The managerial elements, some of them newly risen to their positions on the basis of education rather than extensive capital, expected substantial earnings, but they were not preoccupied with the need to accumulate personal savings and property. The high levels of earnings resulting from economic expansion gave many the consumption standards they expected. Because they were less concerned with the defense of property, the managerial elements were less offended by such measures as taxation, collective bargaining, and even state planning than older owners had been. They were often interested in improving their relations with labor and with the state for the sake of smooth and rational economic operation. There was no total change here; the middle class did not renounce its interest in property or in a separate and superior economic status, but it did develop a new flexibility and a certain acceptance of the new economic arrangements.

The realism and the impatience with older ideologies that had arisen in the middle class were encouraged by the development of the welfare state itself. The new opportunities for employment in government were, of course, largely the result of the extension of welfare and planning services.

Professional elements were greatly aided by welfare programs. The expansion of education gave jobs to many new teachers at all levels, a vivid contrast with the unemployment of teachers in the interwar period. Expanded medical programs and the general increase in prosperity gave new jobs to doctors. Many doctors resented government control, and some collective agitation occurred from time to time over the levels of pay they received. But job opportunities increased in the medical profession, and average incomes rose. Intellectuals and artists were benefited by the new activism of the state. State patronage of theater, films, and music gave material support to many artists and performers, including some of the leading stylistic innovators. Housing programs attracted and supported many architects, and again modern styles received the preponderant attention. Much of the earlier gap, both in earnings and in taste, between artists and the general public, including the state, was narrowed. In many ways, then, elements of the professional classes were assisted by the policies of the welfare state.

More generally, the middle class benefited by aspects of welfare programs such as family aid and new medical care. This assistance was of special importance for the lower middle class. The expansion of educational facilities and scholarships benefited the entire middle class. Only a small fraction of the lower middle class had previously been able to go beyond secondary training; now a large number entered the universities. The attainment of higher educational levels by the middle class obviously promoted managerial and professional advancement, which depended on technical training. Modernization of curricula encouraged new attitudes in the class generally. Improved training in economics, for example, helped modify much of the earlier rigidity of the class in matters of policy and planning.

Finally, the welfare state did not totally contradict even the traditional values of the middle class. It depended on parliamentary government; it did not modify civil liberties. Property ownership and private initiative remained crucial in most areas of the economy; in fact, much state assistance and guidance were devoted to making private industry more profitable than ever before.

As a result, then, of changes in the middle class, of economic prosperity, and of welfare policies themselves, the middle class accepted the society that developed after the war. Middle-class political parties abandoned their traditional conservatism. Christian democratic movements and, in France, the Gaullist party adopted important programs of social reform with middle-class backing. The Conservative party in Britain underwent much the same evolution. In many ways, the changes in middle-class attitude constituted the most important new social factor in postwar Europe.

In Eastern Europe the position of the middle class seemed vastly different. State ownership of industrial and commercial concerns was almost total. Many members of the older middle class were expropriated and sank into the ranks of workers; some were executed or imprisoned in the wake of the communist takeover. With time, however, it became apparent that a new managerial class had arisen in the east; its members, drawn from various social groups, had risen on the basis of new educational opportunities. Without doubt, some members of the older middle class found a place in the new managerial elite. The new middle class, like its counterpart in western Europe, was primarily professional and managerial. Its members received relatively high incomes, though not comparable to those of the west. Dependent on substantial education, they tried to assure educational opportunities for their children. The traditional middle-class desire to preserve status was apparent here. Because of this interest and the desire for high material standards the new middle class limited birth rates severely. Women in the class often had jobs of their own and did not want the distraction of too many children. As in the west, the class dominated the economy, exerted significant pressure on the government, and constituted a major element in the structure of industrial society.

The Workers

The years of hardship during and after the war saw renewed discontent within the working class. In many cases, particularly in France and Italy, where the communists benefited from wartime prestige, the discontent reached a higher pitch than it had during the depression. In both Latin countries membership in communist unions expanded, partly because the communists simply took over the leading union organizations; even many noncommunist workers stayed in these unions out of an overriding sense of class solidarity. The majority of the working class now supported the communist parties, and other elements of society contributed many votes. By 1948 communists in France were drawing a full quarter of the popular vote, while in Italy they attracted almost a third. Socialist parties remained, but they depended increasingly on some middle-class support. Christian democratic unions and parties, despite intensive efforts, won only a small minority of the working class.

Until 1947 workers expressed their discontent mainly in political terms. Communist leaders disciplined their followers and prevented strikes in the interest of economic recovery, for the communists participated in the postwar governments of France and Italy and saw the pressing need for stable reconstruction. After their expulsion from both governments, however, communist leaders unleashed a massive wave of strikes, demonstrations, and near-insurrections. Barricades were actually set up by workers in Milan for two days in 1948. More generally, large industrial strikes testified to the discontent of the labor force and their attachment to communism.

In other western European nations communism was not a major factor. In Britain and Germany, for example, there had been no wartime resistance movements the communists could exploit. And Britain lacked any previous communist tradition. There was, however, definite working-class discontent in all countries. It was expressed in the rising level of support for the Labour Party in Britain and by substantial strike movements everywhere. Of the industrial countries, only western Germany, stunned by the war and the need to rebuild, avoided substantial agitation; and even there the workers quickly returned to socialist voting patterns and to a large, well disciplined union movement. Until economic recovery began, then, discontent was high among the working class; and in France and Italy it seemed truly revolutionary.

After full employment was restored and wages began to rise, the manifestations of worker protest and grievance subsided. Workers clearly enjoyed the new opportunities for consumption and leisure. Hours of work fell once more to about forty-four a week after having risen in response to the needs of the war effort and postwar reconstruction. High levels of employment allowed women to find work without difficulty, and a substantial percentage helped augment the family income. As economic conditions improved, most workers lost their feelings of discontent. The development of welfare programs reduced the hostility many had felt against the state. The interest in some traditional worker organizations began to decline. Attendance at union meetings and participation in union elections dropped severely in Britain and elsewhere, and union leaders in many areas noted a waning of interest among younger workers. Communist parties in France and Italy lost some votes after reaching their peak in 1948, although the loss was not great. Equally serious, at least until 1964, was a decline in party membership and the aging of party leaders. In both countries most workers still support the parties at election time, but rising prosperity has clearly reduced the intensity of interest.

Workers were increasingly attracted by goals of personal consumption and were willing to work quite hard to fulfill them; a minority even took on extra work for this purpose. Polls taken in Britain showed many workers actively devoted to a variety of personal hobbies. Interest in family life rose as television brought entertainment to the home, and families began to have more children than before. Divorce rates were stabilized, in this class as in others, for the first time since the late nineteenth century. There were a number of signs of an important reorientation of interests.

Many of the prewar gaps between workers and other classes declined. A significant number of workers began to take advantage of opportunities for higher education, particularly at the secondary school level. Many of the ablest workers now advanced into industry or government service. Far more remained workers but broadened their interests significantly, developing new satisfaction in their families and in the ownership of personal property.

For the most part, however, the working class remained distinct in attitudes and political behavior. The economic levels of the class were still below those of the middle class. Educational opportunities were not so widely exploited by the labor force as by the middle class. In most countries examinations were administered at about age eleven to determine the eligibility for entrance into those secondary schools designed to prepare students for the university. Working-class children were at a disadvantage in these examinations, for previous cultural background played a large role in scholastic abilities and worker families could not offer the same backgrounds as those of the middle class. And worker interest in education remained lower than that of the middle class. It seemed more important to obtain jobs as early as possible. Generally, then, workers remained workers; there was even some feeling that efforts to rise out of the class were treasonable.

Similarly, workers continued to be attached to specifically labor parties and unions. Voting for socialist and, in France and Italy, communist parties remained high; union membership, as opposed to union participation, did not decline. However, a change in the orientation of the labor movement, corresponding in large measure to the new contentment of the working class, did occur. The parties also realized that working-class support was not sufficient to win elections; part of the middle class had to be won as well. For both these reasons socialist parties began to modify their traditional programs. In Britain and Germany particularly, traditional stress on class hostility and on rigid plans for nationalization was replaced by emphasis on the extension and more efficient administration of welfare programs and economic planning. On this basis the British Labour Party gained a new electoral victory in 1964, although only by the slimmest margin, and won decisively in 1966. By the late 1950s socialist leaders in France had begun to adopt a similarly flexible tone. Even communist parties, most notably in Italy, began to change their orientation somewhat. They recognized, publicly, the gains that postwar capitalism had brought and the benefits of welfare programs. They still hoped for a revolutionary change in society, but they talked less of insurrection and more of political advance. And they took an increasingly independent stance toward Russian communism. The changes in political orientation on the part of the various worker parties were extremely important, for they reduced middle-class fear of worker hostility and represented a clear diminution of discontent within the labor force. The traditional attachment of workers to labor parties remained strong, but those parties were no longer primarily seen as weapons of class war.

Strike movements also reflected these changes in the position of the labor force. After the early 1950s most strikes lost their political tone. Strike movements among Spanish miners and other workers, which developed extensively around 1960, did have some political implications, for those workers were interested not only in better wages but also in effective freedom of unions from state control. Otherwise, specific issues such as wages dominated the strike movements. This was in marked contrast to the postwar wave of strikes and demonstrations, particularly in France and Italy, which was launched for directly political purposes. Until the early 1950s it had been possible to rouse significant agitation in both countries over electoral issues or even diplomatic matters such as the establishment of NATO. After that time, however, efforts at stirring agitation of this sort encountered widespread indifference.

Major strike movements were roused by economic grievances alone. Economic expansion and full employment created obvious opportunities for successful strikes for wage increases and these became more frequent after the mid-1950s. Strikes in private industry were generally brief, for employers, who were enjoying expanding profits and sales, had every reason to yield; often, indeed, the mere threat of a strike was enough to win concessions.

The most bitter conflicts occurred in public industries such as mines, utilities, and railroads, for the governments, concerned with their budgetary position and with the inflationary effect of wage increases, proved more resistant to labor demands than did private employers. Often, too, the state industries suffered from stagnant rates of growth and productivity; this was notably the case in mining, where the problem was not new. For various reasons, then, many countries saw significant wage agitation in public enterprises. Often several union movements cooperated in the strikes, a cooperation that both reflected and promoted the deep feelings involved. The strikes ranged from a day-long interruption of services, either in the nation as a whole or in a leading city, to prolonged walkouts. Discipline in both cases was usually quite high, and there was little violence. The demands issued were usually quite precise and limited, reflecting commonly a feeling that state employes were not receiving their fair share of rising prosperity. There was no claim that the strikers were in misery. Instead, there was both recognition that improvements had occurred and specific expectation of more of the same. The desires bred by prosperity itself and a certain disparity in gains among different categories of workers caused demands that even expanding economies found hard to fulfill. Still, there was no widespread agitation for structural change, and most strike movements were neither bitter nor prolonged.

The continued focus of the working class on material advance was clear in the postwar period. Serious discontent occurred only in the years of hardship immediately after the war. The general increase of prosperity determined the relative mildness of the labor movements. Workers expected, however, not prosperity alone but also expanding prosperity. This was reflected in most of the strike movements. It was reflected in personal buying habits, particularly the growing use of installment credit. Even in eastern Europe, where strike movements were rare and heavily repressed, workers put pressure on the governments for improvements in material standards. By 1960 those pressures resulted in increased attention to consumer goods, in both quantity and quality.

The growing material interests were reflected also in the continued decline of religious concern in many areas. The governments of eastern Europe met little resistance from the working class in their efforts to diminish the role of religion and the churches, although Poland was an exception. Increasing attention by the Roman Catholic Church to social problems resulted in no real gain of working-class support. Some workers remained Catholic in France and Italy and eagerly joined newly vigorous Catholic unions. Far more were unaffected. A worker-priest movement in France in which priests were sent in to mingle with workers on the job seemed to result in more conversions of priests to communism than of workers to Catholicism. With the exception of Germany, where over 90 per cent of the population was at least affiliated with a church, religious practice was very low in the most industrial nations. Regular church attendance in Britain, for example, involved only about 12 per cent of the population. Again, the focus of life for workers, and for most other groups, was the job and its earnings. In the prosperity of the period, this focus seemed to bring contentment to many.

SOME GENERAL CHARACTERISTICS OF SOCIETY

Certain indications of stress arose in postwar society generally. By the late 1950s some intellectuals, writers and film makers particularly, had begun to point to a sense of boredom and frustration at many levels of society. Novelists such as Alan Sillitoe in Britain concentrated on the working class, claiming that greater prosperity had not brought it a sense of purpose and that the variety of new welfare regulations simply increased its confinement. Federico Fellini and others on the continent dealt with boredom even among the middle classes. In part these approaches reflected renewed disillusionment with the materialism of contemporary society. Many intellectuals, perhaps unrealistically, had expected more from the working classes than an aping of middle-class acquisitiveness.

There were, however, certain signs of correspondence between the comment of some critics and wider social patterns. Higher rates of gambling, in state lotteries and football pools, reflected new affluence; they might also reflect some desire to escape the limitations of daily life. In certain areas, particularly those most subject to cold-war tension, such as Berlin and Austria, rising rates of suicide and mental disorder were recorded. Prostitution rose rapidly in many German cities until the mid-fifties, reflecting both poverty and postwar disillusionment. Most important, there was a general increase in juvenile crime. New terms—Teddy boys, *blousons noirs, Halbstarke*—designated the teenage gangs that formed after the war and included many delinquent elements. The phenomenon of delinquency was quite general, although a few areas, notably Britain, were most affected. In Britain, 1,663 male offenders per 100,000 in the fourteen-to-seventeen age group were recorded in 1953; by 1960 this figure had risen to 2,436. A significant number of young people had turned against all authority, parental and governmental alike. Most were from the working class, products often of broken homes. Although they represented only a small minority of the youth— less than 30,000 people belonged to the Teddy boy gangs—their discontent was so total and so vigorous that it inevitably called into question the society that had produced them.

From the vantage point of the mid-1960s, however, forces of radical discontent did not seem dominant in European society. A sense of futility was not pervasive. In eastern Europe Communist systems were increasingly flexible and increasingly accepted on the basis of greater prosperity and lack of realistic alternatives. In the west prosperity brought new opportunities for many groups, both in work and in leisure. Older social conflicts had declined, even though they had not disappeared. International conflicts had also decreased. International exchanges of goods and entertainment rose steadily and more and more workers and tourists poured across state boundaries. Many of the new planners and technicians in the middle class were attracted by the possibilities of international European institutions. They devised and staffed organizations such as the Common Market and seemed disposed to extend this sort of integration if possible. More generally, large numbers of people were finding purpose and opportunity in their new resources. They had more time and greater means to seek enjoyment than ever before. The revival of family life and the rise of birth rates reflected the growth of social confidence. Problems remained, to be sure. Juvenile crime, peasant agitation, and pressure by many workers challenged governments and economies. European society was by no means stable; further change was bound to occur.

In fact, most major social groups now depended on change. They expected continued economic and technical advance. Few elements of European society, even in rural areas, clung to static traditions. New class traditions had arisen in many cases, but they assumed continued change. There was, of course, a hope that change could be controlled and developed. Governments, private enterprises, and unions had increasingly developed their ability to control the factors of change. How well the controls would work in the future remained uncertain. During most of the postwar era they had operated to the satisfaction of the major elements of society. Europe had reached a new level of adjustment to the continuing process of industrialization.

7
CONCLUSION

European society underwent a great transformation during the century and a half that followed the beginnings of industrialization. This transformation was exceedingly complex, and it is important to understand its principal dimensions.

The amount of total wealth vastly increased. All social classes ultimately gained some share in this wealth and raised their levels of consumption. Class lines themselves were increasingly shaped by amounts of earnings and patterns of consumption and an interest in material acquisition rose in every major group. In 1800 an active desire to improve earning and consumption power was relatively uncommon. Many in the middle classes had such a desire; this was to be a leading motive for social change. And there were some aristocrats, landed peasants, and master artisans who shared such an interest. For the bulk of society, however, stability of conditions, rather than improvement, was the primary concern. Gradually, this situation changed. Experience of new wealth or the realization that new wealth was possible stimulated many groups to seek steady improvements in their material standards. Traditional concerns such as religion, which focused on nonmaterial goals, declined in importance. Materialism had spread; even more important, a conscious desire for change, for economic growth, affected most social groups.

Major geographic relocation accompanied the development of industrial society. Improvements in transportation facilitated this. Economic hardships and new economic opportunities both impelled the movement of masses of people. The steady urbanization of Europe was the most significant result of this relocation. But peasants travelled too—to schools, to markets, to military service; many even moved to different regions to practice their agriculture. And by the midtwentieth century mass recreational patterns often involved extensive travel. These various movements of people provided new contacts, new horizons; they virtually eliminated the local loyalties that had predominated in 1800.

The class structure of Europe changed with industrialization. All older social classes faded in importance; all had to alter their manner of life in order to maintain any position at all. The aristocracy, the peasants, the artisans, the older elements of the middle class—all were reduced in relative size and wealth, all had to abandon vital traditional structures and values. The aristocracy was almost destroyed as a distinguishable social grouping after many efforts at resistance and adjustment. Artisans, though still visible, increasingly became an element of either the middle or the working classes.

The largest and most dynamic classes in the period as a whole were associated directly with industry and were therefore essentially new. A middle class with new functions of ownership and management arose and grew rapidly in size and wealth. From the middle class came a new upper class, which grew increasingly distinct but which maintained many middle-class values, including a persistent interest in commerce and manufacturing. The upper class was not closed, and it certainly preached the virtues of mobility; most of the continuing accessions to its ranks came from the middle class, thus preserving the links between the two groups. Upper class and middle class together came to dominate society, at least in western Europe; and even in the east the spread of industry during the twentieth century created a recognizable managerial class. Not only industry but also much of agriculture came to be owned or managed by the upper and middle classes. These groups demanded and maintained control of government. The official values of society—the stress on education, on economic and material expansion, on efficient arrangement of men and things, on the desirability of ambition—were shaped by the new ruling group. Important segments of the lower classes were partially converted to these middle-class interests. Finally, the class least converted by the middle class, the class most capable of mounting important opposition, was itself a new one. Older elements of society tried in various ways to resist the rise of the middle class, but all failed and accommodated themselves as best they could. The urban working class, on the other hand, proved to be a more dangerous rival precisely because it too was based on the new economic structure. But outright class war was not constant; both groups proved capable of making accommodations. The fact remained that industrialization had created a new ruling class and new governing social values; and the class least completely integrated into this new structure was itself a direct product of industrialization.

The great changes in social structure involved unprecedented social mobility. In the early industrial period the middle class actively tried to rise, and many of its members came from other social groups. At the same time, population growth forced mobility on masses of peasants. Market agriculture promoted mobility even within the village. After a few generations mobility was actively sought by many people outside the business groups. The lower middle class, most notably, was defined in large part by its desire to rise. But significant minorities of workers and peasants sought and achieved advancement also. The development of new economic and governmental forms and the spread of educational facilities both encouraged a growing interest in mobility. Obviously, not everyone was converted to a desire for advancement; many workers and peasants avoided the impulse. Equally important, opportunities for mobility did not always coincide with expectations. But the interest clearly spread. Along with the desire to improve material standards, it provided a leading motive for social change and social conflict.

Industrialization radically altered the institutional framework of society, introducing new forms of organizations of unprecedented extent. In 1800 the leading organizations were the village, the feudal estate, the guild, and the family firm. And behind all of these was the family itself, an economic and educational unit of primary importance. These organizations provided the framework of life for most people. Governments existed, of course, and their actions shaped general conditions; but for most people their direct influence remained rather remote.

Industrialization and associated changes began to reduce the older structures rather quickly. New forms of transportation and communications facilitated new and larger organizational structures. People and goods were concentrated in unprecedented numbers. New organizations were required in this situation. Factories grouped workers, capital, and materials on an unprecedented scale. Almost immediately they reduced the importance of the family for the working class. Concomitant legal and economic changes attacked the guild and the village. Soon even the family firm was threatened as business units developed radically new methods of finance and management. Governments also developed new functions; city governments often took the first step. They engaged in new economic activities and regulated many others. They assumed the main educational functions. Finally, even matters such as culture and recreation were increasingly influenced by large organizations, both public and private.

The traditional institutions did not give way easily. Much of the history of the industrial period can be understood in terms of resistance to new organizations in the name of old. Elements of the aristocracy, the peasantry, the artisans, and the middle class all protested at various times. Peasants often sought a return to some idealized village structure; artisans demanded the restoration of guilds or the substitution of some comparable local and cooperative economic unit. By the end of the nineteenth century many small businessmen sought some guarantee for the family firm. Elements of these protests continued into the twentieth century. Fascism appealed to many people who wanted to preserve older forms, including the family. However, despite its promises, fascism really offered greater and more novel organization than ever before. In essence, the many protests in the name of smaller, more traditional units failed completely.

The development of large and novel organizations was a general trend intimately associated with industrialization. The extent and form of organization obviously varied greatly. At the extreme, industrialization provided the technical basis for totalitarian systems. More commonly, massive organizations arose in both the public and private spheres, without seeking total control. A combination of giants—unions, cooperatives, corporations, and government itself—developed in western Europe.

Whatever the form, the new organizations were more massive than any developed before. They relied less on tradition than on detailed instruction and supervision. They dominated or destroyed most earlier organizations; they even brought some control over such forces as competitive supply and demand. And they involved new loyalties. Attachment to older forms obviously waned; even the family unit declined in significance. At the same time, loyalties to nation or to union or to party grew increasingly strong, as these units actively sought mass support. The new loyalties were essentially political, whereas the old had been largely apolitical. The rise of political interests was itself a major change. The development of large-scale units for regulation and participation was one of the most important social products of industrialization.

The evolution of industrial society can be seen in two distinct phases after 1800. Each phase had important effects on the various social classes, both new and old, and on the new forms of organization. In the first phase primary attention was given to marketable, productive work. Work itself had always dominated most elements of society, and most groups had produced to some extent for the market. But in rural society marketable production had been a secondary concern; now it became primary. Work itself became more intensive, less leisurely, in the nineteenth century. The result was a change in position and attitude for every major social class.

Aristocrats declined largely because they were oriented toward consumption, not production and because they were incapable of devoting extensive attention to new productive needs and possibilities; as a result, even their consumption levels declined and became less exclusive. Peasants were forced to alter their methods and structures in the hope of developing better market potential, impelled by legal changes and population pressure. The result was a steady evolution of new agricultural techniques and new patterns of land tenure and use. In western Europe peasants relied primarily on individual holdings in their adaptation, but they came to supplement them with cooperative efforts. In eastern Europe adjustment began only late in the nineteenth century and seemed to follow western patterns at first; certainly the interests of peasants themselves resembled those of the peasants in west. Communist regimes, however, attempted to impose a new form of adjustment to market production through the system of collectives. To date, these forms have proved less successful economically than those of the west. Clearly, a process of basic adaptation both to market agriculture and to the collectives is still going on in eastern Europe.

The phase of stress on production affected urban classes significantly. Artisans had long produced for a local market; they lacked a sense of maximization of production, and their guild institutions existed above all to limit production. Artisans therefore had to make a considerable adaptation to the new conditions of economic life. This adaptation was imposed in part by law, in part by efforts of artisans, particularly masters, to develop new productive forms.

The new urban working class existed primarily to provide productive labor. The long working hours left little time for anything else. For most workers hard labor was a matter of necessity, not of conscious choice; but it dominated their lives nevertheless.

For the middle class productive work was an ideal as well as a necessity. This was the class that led in creating new forms of production, in the factories and to some extent in agriculture on newly purchased estates. This was the class that created the basic tone and ethic of early industrial society. Members of the class expected to work hard and expected others to do the same. Family life, cultural interests, and political concern centered around the pre-eminent virtue of work. The rigid morality and self-restraint the class imposed on itself and others reflected the high value placed on productive labor.

In the twentieth century, eastern Europe, despite a different political system and the absence of a preindustrial middle class, adopted the stress on work that the early stage of the industrial revolution imposed. Communism and communist leaders preached the virtue of work in Russia and elsewhere. Long hours of labor for workers and managers alike were essential for the industrial efforts of the regimes. A severe moral code reflected and reinforced the emphasis on work. Culture was bent to the glorification of labor. The gap between eastern and western Europe in the twentieth century was in part still a gap in the phase of industrialization and of resultant moral tone. Communist leaders often expressed genuine shock at the looseness and relaxation of western Europe—much as the industrial leaders of the west would have done in the early nineteenth century.

Propelled by the new work ethic, European society began to rise above the subsistence levels that had prevailed since the beginnings of human history. Habits of production for the market became increasingly natural to peasants; the pace of factory labor was now normal for the workers. Previous accumulation of capital made further investment easier; managerial and technical staffs in industry made the organization and even the increase of production increasingly a matter of routine. And the growing sophistication of machines themselves reduced the efforts necessary to produce tremendous amounts of goods in the cities and countryside alike. At the same time, precisely because of this new ability to produce greater attention had to be given to the distribution and consumption of goods. For a variety of reasons, then, the stress on production lessened in favor of new attention to consumption. This new phase of industrial society was reached in western and central Euorpe by the end of the nineteenth century. In eastern Europe there were signs of a similar change by the midtwentieth century.

The new orientation toward consumption caused a crisis in values and structure in western and central Europe, most notably during the interwar period. Workers benefited from rising incomes and increasing leisure time, both major products of the new phase of industrialization. But their expectations increased more rapidly than their means. Peasants, who had adopted the measures needed to raise their market production, found their power to consume limited by the ironic fact that they now produced too much, in combination with the output of the rest of the world. At the same time, peasant values gradually came to include a greater desire to consume.

In many ways, the shock of transition was greatest for the middle class. The valuation of individual ownership was increasingly challenged by the new forms of industrial and commercial organization. Middle-class assumptions of superiority and control were threatened by the rising agitation among the lower classes. And the middle-class productive ethic was increasingly eroded as leisure increased and the interest in consumption rose. The cultural interests of the class were broadened as the willingness and ability to spend increased. Yet old values of family life, of saving, and of independent work were not fully abandoned, even as they seemed largely displaced. Important elements of the class were profoundly upset by the passage to a new phase of economic attitudes.

Partly because of resistance to the new phase, partly because of the dislocations of World War I, the European economy itself did not make a smooth transition from the first to the second phase of industrialization. From 1900 until World War II the power to produce consistently exceeded the power to consume. Periods of prosperity were few, limited in area, and temporary. Levels of income for peasants, workers, and even many elements of the middle class were too low to permit the consumption the economy required and which the classes themselves expected. The result was economic crisis and rising social tension.

Beginning in the late 1930s new economic forms and massive state action facilitated the full transition to the mass consumption phase of industrialization. The income of workers and peasants rose. The middle class increasingly abandoned its traditional ethic, including the emphasis on private property, for the sake of the effective management of the economy and the growing attraction of high levels of leisure and consumption. Difficulties and doubts remained. Some questioned the soundness of the economy, although there was little evidence of structural weakness. Many peasants and workers continued to demand a greater share in prosperity. Some intellectuals questioned the validity of the general focus on material consumption. Whatever the value of these criticisms, whatever their future, it was clear that European society had entered a new phase, a phase that recognized and utilized the tremendous increase in wealth that industrialization had created. National and even social differences were declining in the common adjustment to the stress on consumption. European society successfully passed through the second of the transitions that industrialization demanded.

BIBLIOGRAPHY

The following bibliography is intended to fulfill a dual purpose. It provides a basis for further reading in the major topics of modern European social history, where such reading is available. In this category preference has been given to studies of broad geographical or chronological scope and, where possible, to work in English. At the same time, there is some indication of the most important monographic material. These studies can offer insight into subjects and methods far beyond the limits of the topic itself; they provide important guidelines for further efforts. Certainly, much exciting work has recently been done in a variety of aspects of modern European society.

The bibliography is divided into sections, the first dealing with general works, demography, and economic history. After this come bibliographies for the major social classes, primarily in the nineteenth century. Sections on religion and culture, on the interwar period, and on postwar developments complete the list. Obviously, a large number of works transcend the individual headings; in some important cases, cross listing is provided.

Many of the major topics of modern European social history remain almost untouched. In a few cases an excellent study can be cited for one small area and time period, but no general work has been done. In other instances, central problems have scarcely been treated at all. Only a few subjects, such as labor organization, can offer a really full bibliography. Leading categories, such as the peasantry and the artisan class, have received only scattered treatment. Even the middle class, so often cited, has rarely been studied. The bibliography offered here is not, of course, an exhaustive list. A large number of works relate to the field in some tangential way; others deal with central issues, but repetitiously or badly. Still, the field is open to much further study. It is hoped that the foregoing essay and the reading suggestions here will indicate the topics of greatest importance and promise. If they provide also some guidance and stimulus for the work still to be done, the purpose of the book will be fulfilled.

I. GENERAL WORKS

Allem, Maurice. *La Vie quotidienne sous le Second Empire.* Paris, 1944.

Ariès, Philippe. *Centuries of childhood; a social history of family life.* New York, 1962.

Barbagallo, Corrado. *Cento anni di vita italiana. 1848–1948.* Milan, 1948–9.

Bertaux, Pierre Félix. *La Vie quotidienne en Allemagne au temps de Guillaume II en 1900.* Paris, 1962.

Blanquis, G. *La Vie quotidienne en Allemagne à l'époque romantique (1795–1830).* Paris, 1958.

Bruck, Werner F. *Social and economic history of Germany from William II to Hitler, 1888–1938.* Cardiff, 1938.

Burnand, Robert. *La Vie quotidienne en France de 1870 à 1900.* Paris, 1947.

La Vie quotidienne en France en 1830. Paris, 1943.

Dodds, John W. *The Age of paradox: a biography of England, 1841–1851.* New York, 1952.

Dupeux, Georges. *La Société française, 1789–1960.* Paris, 1964.

Gregg, Pauline. *A Social and economic history of Britain, 1760–1960.* London, 1962.

Hobsbawm, Eric J. *The Age of revolution, 1789–1848.* Cleveland, 1962.

Lefebvre, Georges. *The Coming of the French revolution.* Princeton, 1947.

Lémonon, Ernest. *L'Italie économique et sociale, 1861–1912.* Paris, 1913.

Lipset, Seymour Martin and Reinhard Bendix. *Social mobility in industrial society.* London, 1959.

Macartney, Carlile. *The Social revolution in Austria.* Cambridge, Eng., 1926.

Marsh, David Charles. *The Changing social structure of England and Wales, 1871–1951.* London, 1958.

II. POPULATION CHANGE AND URBANIZATION

Briggs, Asa. *Victorian Cities.* London, 1953.

Chevalier, Louis. *La Formation de la population parisienne au XIXe siècle.* Paris, 1950.

Dickinson, Robert E. *The West European city: a geographical interpretation.* London, 1951.

Köllmann, Wolfgang. *Sozialgeschichte der Stadt Barmen im 19. Jahrhundert.* Tübingen, 1960.

Moller, Herbert. *Population movements in modern European history.* New York, 1964.

Morazé, Charles. *La France bourgeoise.* Paris, 1952.

Reinhard, Marcel R. *Histoire de la population mondiale, 1700–1948.* Paris, 1949.

Weber, Adna. *The Growth of cities in the nineteenth century.* Ithaca, 1963.

Wrigley, E. A. *Industrial growth and population change, a regional study in North-West Europe in the later nineteenth century.* Cambridge, Eng., 1961.

III. ECONOMIC HISTORY

Alpert, Paul. *Twentieth century economic history of Europe.* New York, 1951.

Ashton, Thomas S. *The Industrial revolution, 1760–1830.* London, 1948.

Bechtel, Heinrich. *Wirtschaftsgeschichte Deutschlands.* v.3. Munich, 1956.

Bowden, Witt, Michael Karpovitch, and Abbott P. Usher, *An Economic history of Europe since 1750.* New York, 1937.

Cameron, Rondo. *France and the economic development of Europe, 1800–1914.* Princeton, 1961.

Cipolla, Carlo M. *The Economic history of world population.* Baltimore, 1962.

Clapham, Sir John H. *The Economic development of France and Germany, 1815–1914.* Cambridge, Eng., 1936.

An Economic history of modern Britain, 1820–1929. 3v. Cambridge, Eng., 1930–38.

Clough, Shepherd B. *Economic history of modern Italy.* New York, 1963.

Dunham, Arthur L. *The Industrial revolution in France, 1815–1848.* New York, 1955.

Heckscher, Eli. *An Economic history of Sweden.* G. Ohlin, tr. Cambridge, Mass., 1954.

Henderson, William O. *Britain and industrial Europe, 1750–1870.* Liverpool, 1954.

The Industrial revolution on the continent. London, 1961.

The State and the industrial revolution in Prussia. Liverpool, 1958.

Lewinski, Jan. *L'Evolution industrielle de la Belgique.* Brussels, 1911.

Miller, Margaret Stevenson. *The Economic development of Russia, 1905–1914.* London, 1926.

Rostow, Walt. *The Process of economic growth.* Oxford, 1960.

Usher, Abbott P. *A History of mechanical inventions.* Cambridge, Mass., 1954.

IV. THE ARISTOCRACY

Blum, Jerome. *Lord and peasant in Russia, from the ninth to the nineteenth century.* Princeton, 1961.

Noble landowners and agriculture in Austria, 1818–1848.

Bovill, Edward. *English country life, 1780–1830.* London, 1962.

Gerschenkron, Alexander. *Bread and democracy in Germany.* Berkeley, 1943.

Kelsall, Roger. *Higher civil servants in Britain from 1870 to the present day.* London, 1955.

Kohn-Bramstedt, Ernst. *Aristocracy and the middle classes in Germany.* London, 1937.

Mazour, Anatole G. *The first Russian revolution, 1825: the Decembrist movement, its origins, development, and significance.* Berkeley, 1937.

Muncy, Lysbeth. *The Junkers in the Prussian administration under William II, 1888–1914.* New York, 1944.

Ponsonby, Arthur. *The Decline of the aristocracy*. London, 1912.

Rémond, René. *The Right wing in France from 1815 to de Gaulle*. J. M. Laux, tr. Philadelphia, 1966.

Rosenberg, Hans. *Bureaucracy, aristocracy and autocracy: the Prussian experience, 1660–1815*. Cambridge, Mass., 1958.

Schlingensiepen, Georg H. *Der Strukturwandel des baltischen Adels vor dem ersten Weltkrieg*. Marburg, 1959.

Thompson, F. M. L. *English landed society in the nineteenth century*. London, 1963.

V. AGRICULTURE AND THE PEASANTRY

Augé-Laribé, Michel. *L'Evolution de la France agricole*. Paris, 1912. *La Révolution agricole*. Paris, 1955.

Braun, Rudolf. *Industrielisierung und Volksleben*. Winterthur, 1960.

Brenan, Gerald. *The Spanish labyrinth: an account of the social and political background of the civil war*. Cambridge, Eng., 1950.

Conze, Werner, ed. *Quellen zur Geschichte der deutschen Bauernbefreiung*. Gottingen, 1957.

Diaz del Moral, Juan. *Historia de las agitaciones compesinas andaluzas Córdoba (antecendentes para una reforma agraria)*. Madrid, 1929.

Evans, Emyr Estyn. *Irish folk ways*. London, 1957.

Fel, André. *Les Hautes terres du Massif central: tradition paysanne et économie agricole*. Paris, 1962.

Freeman, Thomas Walter. *Pre-famine Ireland; a study in historical geography*. Manchester, 1957.

Halpern, J. M. *A Serbian Village*. New York, 1958.

Hamerow, Theodore. *Restoration, revolution, reaction: economics and politics in Germany, 1815–1871*. Princeton, 1958.

Hammond, John L. and Barbara Hammond. *The Village laborer, 1760–1832*. London, 1911.

Haushofer, Heinz. *Die deutsche Landwirtschaft im technischen Zeitalter*. Stuttgart, 1963.

Hobsbawn, Eric. *Primitive rebels, studies in archaic forms of social movement in the nineteenth and twentieth centuries*. New York, 1957.

Hoskins, William G. *The Midland peasant; the economic and social history of a Leicestershire village*. London, 1957.

Knapp, G. F. *Bauernbefreiung und der Ursprung der Landarbeiter in den älteren Theilen Preussens*. 2 v. Munich, 1927.

Lefebvre, Georges. *Les Paysans du Nord pendant la révolution française*. 2v. Paris, 1924.

Lucarelli, Antonio. *Il Brigantaggio politico del mezzogiorno d'Italia dopo la seconda restaurazione borbonica* (1815–1818). Bari, 1942.
Il Brigantaggio politico delle Puglie dopo il 1860: il sergente romano. Bari, 1946.
Makal, Mahmut. *Village in Anatolia.* London, 1954.
Pitt-Rivers, Julian. *The People of the Sierra.* Chicago, 1961.
Prothero, Lord (Ernle, Rowland). *English farming, past and present.* G. E. Russell and O. McGregor, eds., London, 1961.
Robinson, Geroid T. *Rural Russia under the old regime.* New York, 1932.
Rossi, Adolfo. *L'Agitazione in Sicilia.* Milan, 1894.
Sanders, J. T., *Balkan Village.* Lexington, 1949.
Rainbow in the rocks: the people of rural Greece. Cambridge, Mass. 1962.
Slicher von Bath, Bernard H. *The Agrarian history of western Europe, 500–1840.* Olive Ordish, tr. London, 1963.
Tracy, Michael. *Agriculture in western Europe, crisis and adaptation since 1880.* London, 1964.
Vakar, Nicholas. *The Taproot of Soviet society,* New York, 1961.
Walter, Gerard. *Histoire des paysans de France.* Paris, 1963.
Williams, David. *The Rebecca riots: a study in agrarian discontent.* Cardiff, 1955.
Woodham-Smith, Cecil. *The Great Hunger.* New York, 1963.
Wylie, Lawrence. *Village in the Vaucluse.* New York, 1957.

VI. THE MIDDLE CLASSES, AND RELATED TOPICS

Anderson, Eugene. *The Social and Political Conflict in Prussia, 1858–1864.* Lincoln, 1954.
Bendix, Reinhard. *Work and authority in industry; ideologies of management in the course of industrialization.* New York, 1956.
Bruce, Maurice. *The Coming of the welfare state.* London, 1961.
Byrnes, Robert F. *Anti-Semitism in modern France.* New Brunswick, 1950.
Daumard, Adéline. *La Bourgeoisie parisienne de 1815 à 1848.* Paris, 1963.
Fohlen, Claude. *L'Industrie textile au temps du Second Empire.* Paris, 1956.
Kaplow, Jeffry. *Elbeuf during the revolutionary period.* Baltimore, 1964.
Kelsall—see section IV.
Klass, Gert von. *Krupps, the story of an industrial empire.* London, 1954.
Kohn-Bramstedt—see Section IV.

Lambert-Dansette, Jean. *Quelques familles du patronat textile de Lille-Armentières (1789–1914).* Lille, 1954.

Laufenburger, Henri, and P. Pflimlin. *Cours d'économie alsacienne.* 2v. Paris, 1930–32.

Lewis, Roy and Angus Maude. *The English middle classes.* London, 1950.

Lhomme, Jean. *La Grande bourgeoisie au pouvoir, 1830–1870.* Paris, 1960.

Lockwood, David. *The Blackcoated worker; a study in class consciousness.* London, 1958.

Morazé—see section II.
Les Bourgeois conquérants. Paris, 1957.

Perrot, Marguerite, *Le Mode de vie des familles bourgeoises, 1873–1953.* Paris, 1961.

Pulzer, P. G. J. *Rise of political anti-semitism in Germany and Austria.* New York, 1964.

Rohr, Donald G. *The Origins of social liberalism in Germany.* Chicago, 1963.

Sombart, Werner. *The Quintessence of capitalism.* London, 1915.

Tolédano, André. *La Vie de famille sous la restauration et la monarchie de juillet.* Paris, 1943.

Young, George M., ed. *Early Victorian England.* 2v. Oxford, 1934.

VII. NINETEENTH-CENTURY PROTEST MOVEMENTS IN WHICH MIDDLE-CLASS INVOLVEMENT WAS EXTENSIVE

Demarco, Domenico. *Una Rivoluzione sociale, la reppublica romana del 1849.* Naples, 1944.

Demoulin, Robert. *La Révolution de 1830.* Brussels, 1950.

Droz, Jacques. *Les Révolutions allemandes de 1848.* Paris, 1957.

Fischer, George. *Russian liberalism from gentry to intelligentsia.* Cambridge, Mass., 1958.

Griewach, K. *Deutsche studenten und universitäten in der Revolution von 1848.* Weimar, 1949.

Quentin-Bauchart, Pierre. *La Crise sociale de 1848.* Paris, 1920.

Rath, R. John. *The Viennese revolution of 1848.* Austin, 1957.

Robertson, Priscilla S. *The Revolutions of 1848.* Princeton, 1952.

Romani, George T. *The Neapolitan revolution of 1820–1821.* Evanston, Ill., 1950.

Stadelmann, Rudolf. *Soziale und politische Geschichte der Revolution von 1848.* Munich, 1948.

Weill, Georges J. *Histoire du parti républicain en France de 1814 à 1870.* Paris, 1900.

VIII. THE ARTISANS

Babeau, Albert. *Les Artisans et les domestiques d'autrefois.* Paris, 1886.

Braun—see section V.

Chevalier, Louis. *Classes laborieuses et classes dangereuses à Paris pendant la première moitié du XIXe siècle.* Paris, 1958.

Hamerow—see section V.

Hammond, John L. and Barbara Hammond. *The Skilled labourer, 1760–1832.* London, 1919.

The Town labourer, 1760–1832. London, 1917.

The Village labourer—see section V.

IX. THE WORKING CLASS

Booth, Charles. *Life and labour of the people in London.* London, 1891.

Bruce—see section VI.

Chadwick, Edwin. *Report on the sanitary condition of the labouring population.* London, 1842.

Cole, G. D. H. and Raymond Postgate. *The British common people, 1744–1946.* London, 1961.

Dawson, William H. *The German Workman.* London, 1906.

Duveau, Georges. *La Vie ouvrière en France sous le Second Empire.* Paris, 1946.

Engels, Friedrich. *The Condition of the working class in England.* Henderson and Chaloner, eds. London, 1958.

Fay, Charles R. *Life and labour in the 19th century.* Cambridge, Eng., 1947.

Gordon, Manya. *Workers before and after Lenin.* New York, 1941.

Halbwachs, Maurice. *L'Evolution des besoins dans les classes ouvrières.* Paris, 1933.

Lasserre, André. *La Situation des ouvriers de l'industrie textile dans la région lilloise sous la monarchie de juillet.* Lausanne, 1952.

Redford, Arthur. *Labour migration in England, 1800–1850.* London, 1926.

Smelser, Neil J. *Social change in the industrial revolution: an application of theory to the Lancashire cotton industry, 1770–1840.* London, 1960.

Thompson, Edward P. *The Making of the English working class.* New York, 1964.

Villermé, Rene. *Tableau de l'état moral et physique des ouvriers employés dans les manufactures de coton, de laine, et de la soie.* 2v. Paris, 1840.

X. LABOR MOVEMENTS

The first portion of this list concerns activities prior to 1872, and therefore deals primarily with artisans. The second portion, on activities after 1872, stresses factory workers. For contemporary literature of the labor movements in several countries, see: Edouard Dolléans and Michel Crozier, eds. *Mouvements ouvriers et socialistes; chronologie et bibliographie.* Paris, 1950.

A. Before 1872.

Aguet, Jean Pierre, *Les Grèves sous la monachie de juillet.* Geneva, 1954.

Briggs, Asa, ed. *Chartist Portraits.* London, 1959.

Cole, G. D. H. *Attempts at general union; a study in British trade union history, 1818–1834.* London, 1953.

Darvall, Frank O. *Popular disturbances and public order in Regency England.* London, 1934.

Dolléans, Edouard. *Histoire du movement ouvrier.* v. I. Paris, 1953.

Droz—see section VII.

Gammage, Robert G. *History of the Chartist movement, 1837–1854.* Newcastle-on-Tyne, 1894.

Köllman, Wolfgang. *Wuppertaler Färbergesellen-Innung und Färbergesellen-Streiks, 1848–1857.* Wiesbaden, 1962.

McKay, Donald. *The National Workshops.* Cambridge, Mass., 1933.

Mason, Edward S. *The Paris Commune.* New York, 1930.

Obermann, Karl. *Die deutschen Arbeiter in der ersten bürgerlichen Revolution.* Berlin, 1950.

Quentin-Bauchart—see section VII.

Rudé, Fernand. *Le Mouvement ouvrier à Lyon de 1827 à 1832.* Paris, 1944.

Rudé, George. *The Crowd in history, 1730–1848.* New York, 1964.

Schmidt, Charles. *Les Journées de juin 1848.* Paris, 1926.

Thrupp, Sylvia, ed. *Millennial dream in action.* The Hague, 1962.

West, Julius. *History of the Chartist movement.* London, 1920.

B. After 1872.

Champion, Henry H. *The Great Dockers' Strike.* London, 1890.

Clegg, Hugh A., et al. *A History of British trade unions since 1889.* v. I. New York, 1964.

Cole, G. D. H. *Short History of the English working class movement.* 3v. London, 1927.

Comín Colomer, Eduardo. *Historia del anarquismo español.* Barcelona, 1956.

Deutsch, Julius. *Geschichte der österreichischen Gewerkschaftsbewegung.* Vienna, 1908.

Dolléans, Edouard. *Histoire du mouvement ouvrier.* v. II, III. Paris, 1953.

Gualtieri, Humbert L. *The Labor movement in Italy.* New York, 1946.

Hall, Frederick S. *Sympathetic strikes and sympathetic lockouts.* New York, 1898.

Hiller, Ernst T. *The Strike; a study in collective action.* Chicago, 1928.

Hobsbawm, Eric. *Labouring men.* London, 1964.

Knowles, K. G. J. C. *Strikes—a study in industrial conflict.* Oxford, 1952.

Lamberet, Renée. *Mouvements ouvriers et socialistes: l'Espagne (1750–1836).* Paris, 1953.

Lorwin, Louis. *Syndicalism in France.* New York, 1914.

McConagha, William A. *Development of the labor movement in Great Britain, France, and Germany.* Chapel Hill, 1942.

Manacorda, Gastone. *Il Movimento operaio italiano.* Milan, 1963.

Martí, Casimiro. *Orígenes del anarquismo en Barcelona.* Barcelona, 1959.

Pelling, Henry. *History of British trade unionism.* London, 1963.

Ritter, Gerhard. *Die Arbeiterbewegung in wilhelminischen Reich.* Berlin, 1959.

Roth, Guenther. *The Social Democrats in imperial Germany; a study in working class isolation and national integration.* Totowa, N.J., 1963.

Tillett, Benjamin. *History of the London transport workers' strike, 1911.* London, 1912.

Umbreit, Paul. *25 Jahre deutscher Gewerkschaftsbewegung.* Berlin, 1915.

Welbourne, Edward. *The Miners' unions of Northumberland and Durham.* Cambridge, Eng., 1923.

XI. RELIGION AND CULTURE IN THE 19TH CENTURY

Altick, Richard D. *The English common reader; a social history of the mass reading public, 1800–1900.* Chicago, 1957.

Barnard, Howard. *A History of English education from 1760.* London, 1947.

Brinton, Crane. *A History of western morals.* New York, 1959.

Carr, Clarence F. and Frederick Stevens. *Modern Journalism*. London, 1931.

Dansette, Adrien. *Religious history of modern France*. London, 1961.

Duroselle, Jean B. *Les Débuts du catholicisme social en France, 1822–1870*. Paris, 1951.

Engelmann, Susanne C. *German education and re-education*. New York, 1945.

James, Louis. *Fiction for the workingman, 1830–1850*. New York, 1963.

Ledré, Charles. *Histoire de la presse*. Paris, 1958.

McGregor, Oliver R. *Divorce in England; a centenary study*. London, 1947.

Monroe, Paul. *Textbook in the history of education*. New York, 1932.

Moody, Joseph N., ed. *Church and society; Catholic social and political thought and movements, 1789–1950*. New York, 1953.

Reisner, Edward H. *Nationalism and education since 1789*. New York, 1923.

Schmidt-Volkmar, Erich. *Der Kulturkampf in Deutschland, 1871–1890*. Gottingen, 1962.

Stern, Fitz. *The Politics of cultural despair; a study in the rise of the Germanic Ideology*. Berkeley, 1961.

Wearmouth, Robert F. *Methodism and the struggle of the working classes. 1850–1900*. Leicester, 1954.

Methodism and the working class movements of England, 1800–1850. London, 1937.

XII. INTERWAR PERIOD

Alpert—see section III.

Bracher, Karl D. *Die Auflösung der Weimarer Republik*. Stuttgart, 1957.

Earle, Edward M., ed. *Modern France; problems of the Third and Fourth Republics*. Princeton, 1951.

Ferré, Louise M. *Les Classes sociales dans la France contemporaine*. Paris, 1934.

Geiger, Theodor. *Soziale Schichtung des deutschen Volkes*. Stuttgart, 1932.

Graves, Robert and Alan Hodge. *The Long weekend; a British social history, 1918–1939*. New York, 1941.

Guillebaud, Claude W. *The Social policy of Nazi Germany*. Cambridge, Eng., 1941.

Hunter, Neil. *Peasantry and Crisis in France*. London, 1938.

Kracauer, S. *Die Angestellten*. Frankfurt-am-Main, 1930.

Kulischer, Eugene. *Europe on the move; war and population changes, 1917–1947.* New York, 1948.

Mitrany, David. *The Land and the Peasant in Rumania.* London, 1950.

Mowat, Charles L. *Britain between the wars, 1918–1940.* Chicago, 1955.

Rosenstock-Franck, Louis. *L'Economie corporative fasciste en doctrine et en fait.* Paris, 1934.

Shotwell, James T., ed. *Economic and social history of the World War.* New Haven, 1936.

Sturmthal, Adolf. *Die grosse Krise.* Zurich, 1937.
Tragedy of European labor, 1918–1939. New York, 1943.

Tomasević, Jozo. *Peasants, politics, and economic change in Yugoslavia.* Stanford, 1955.

Wright, Gordon. *Rural revolution in France; the peasantry in the twentieth century.* Stanford, 1964.

Zweig, Ferdynand. *Poland between two wars.* London, 1944.

XIII. POSTWAR EUROPE

Bouvier-Ajam, Maurice. *Les Classes sociales en France.* Paris, 1963.

Clements, Roger V. *Managers, a study of their careers in industry.* London, 1958.

Collinet, Michel. *L'Ouvrier français; essai sur la condition ouvrière, 1900 –1950.* Paris, 1951.

Djilas, Milovan. *Land without justice,* New York, 1958.
The New Class. New York, 1957.

Fleisher, Wilfred. *Sweden, the welfare state.* New York, 1956.

Friedl, E. *Vasilika; a village in modern Greece.* New York, 1962.

Frumkin, Gregory. *Population changes in Europe since 1939.* New York, 1951.

Grindrod, Muriel. *The Rebuilding of Italy, 1945–1955.* London, 1955.

Grosser, Alfred. *Colossus again; Western Germany from defeat to rearmament.* New York, 1955.

Gubbels, Robert. *La grève, phénomène de civilisation.* Brussels, 1962.

Hendin, Herbert. *Suicide and Scandinavia.* New York, 1964.

Hoffman, Stanley, ed., *In Search of France.* Cambridge, Mass., 1963.

Korbonski, Andrzei. *Politics of Social Agriculture in Poland.* New York, 1965.

Lorwin, Val R. *The French Labor movement.* Cambridge, Mass., 1954.

Martarelli, Joseph. *Economic Developments in Southern Italy, 1950–1960.* Washington, 1966.

Mayne, Richard. *The Community of Europe.* New York, 1963.

Meynaud, Jean. *La Révolte paysanne.* Paris, 1963.

Park, Julian. *The Culture of France in our time.* Ithaca, 1954.

Schorr, Alvin L. *Social Security and social services in France.* Washington, 1955.

Shonfield, A. *British economic policy since the war.* London, 1958.

Titmuss, Richard M. *Essays on "the welfare state."* London, 1958.

Wylie—see section V.

Zweig, Ferdynand. *The British worker.* Harmondsworth, 1952.
   The Worker in an affluent society; family life and industry. New York, 1962.

INDEX

[419]

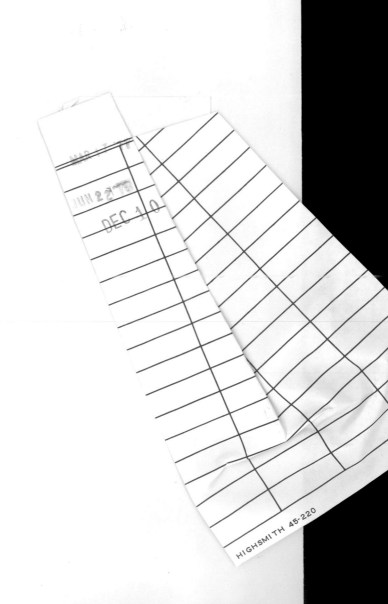